CONTENTS

PR
6064
.I2
A6
1987
vi

Peter Nichols

A Chronology of First Performances

Music by Monty Norman. Revised version opened at
Adelphi Theatre, London, 1983. Society of West End
Theatre Award, Best British Musical. Pub: Methuen

Feeling You're Behind (autobiography). Pub: Weidenfeld
and Nicolson, 1984. Penguin, 1985

Film work, apart from screenplays of own plays – *Joe Egg,
The National Health, Privates on Parade* – has included
Catch Us If You Can, 1965, and *Georgy Girl*, 1966.
Another dozen or so scripts of various kinds remain
unproduced, including two films, a sequence of five for
television (*See Me*) and a stage anthology of the works of
Orwell.

CASTING THE AUDIENCE

The only thing old Phoebe liked was when Hamlet patted his dog on the head. She thought that was funny and nice and it was. What I'll have to do is, I'll have to read that play. The trouble with me is, I always have to read that stuff by myself. If an actor acts it out, I hardly listen. I keep worrying about whether he's going to do something phoney every minute.

J.D. Salinger, *The Catcher in the Rye*

Who, apart from Holden Caulfield, reads plays? Actors, looking for parts or audition speeches. Credit-hungry American students. Critics charting a trend. Plays on the stage are plans for action. Apart from Shakespeare, they're not for reading – and how far would Holden have got with *Hamlet*? Actors often do bring something phoney, but without them – and a director and various designers – scripts are skeletal, mere propositions for an event, interesting but spare. Performers give them flesh and a sort of animation, but the real life of a play doesn't start until the public is let in: in other words, when the play becomes interplay. But who are these watchers? Why have they come? More to the point, why have they stopped coming? We can hardly blame them for not wanting to gather in discomfort with a lot of strangers to catch snatches of dialogue through a clamour of coughing, hawking, yawning, seat-creaking, paper crackling and demands of 'What did he say?' when they could have stayed home and watched something far better on the video. Even the first performance of deathless lines was probably punctuated by all this irrelevant din:—

Absent thee from felicity awhile
And in this harsh hrrm draw thy tschoo in what-did-he-say?

Yet without this bronchial congregation, drama is a ritual conducted in an empty church. Nabokov damned theatre for this very quality – 'stone-age rites and communal nonsense' – but in his youth (and mine) responses weren't encouraged. The audience was supposed to be as silent and anonymous as at a Soho strip-club. The ultimate show of this kind would be, I suppose, the exhibition where any sound from the voyeurs out front would break the trance-like concentration of the fornicators. It would be interesting to know whether these performers convince themselves that they're alone or only demand silence to stimulate the viewers by implying a sort-of two-way mirror. A less rigid form of this was called naturalism, a purgative reform that became an inflexible genre. A direct appeal, an aside, any breach of the two-way mirror was seen as a sign that the playwright didn't know his job. Yet, of course, there was always interplay: actors responded to the audience, spoke in loud clear voices, waited for laughs, were arranged in pictures that told the story. At its best, this fashion made possible the irony and fatalism of Chekhov and Ibsen. We felt powerless to help these poor fools, mirror-images of ourselves, blundering to their doom. The interplay here was odd, tense, as between mortals and impotent gods. We felt for them but could do nothing. At the end, the actors came out smiling to remind us it had all been a game and we applauded that as much as their skill. No-one pointed out the absurdity of a style that otherwise ignored the audience. It would be some time before Joe Orton could make one character confide in another 'Just between these three walls'. It was a form ripe for television and that's what – in the 1950s – it became. The box in the corner is Strindberg's chamber drama, and we can advise and abuse the actors out loud as we never can in the theatre – or cinema. Films are shown to an audience but no-one must acknowledge that or they will risk the event I witnessed when, in the film version of the play *Alfie*, Michael Caine turned to the camera after learning that a girl-friend was pregnant.

'What shall I do now?' he asked.

'Get out the knitting-needles,' advised someone from the circle – but Michael Caine didn't bat an eye and went on with his next line.

At the time I was earning a living writing plays for television, keyhole naturalism in monochrome. I'd already thrown out a basketful of stage plays in other men's styles but never found my own. In the course of wondering what was left for theatre to do, I defined a rough approach to playwriting. I would try to find a role for the spectators. Straightforward in its early drafts, my first real stage play *A Day in the Death of Joe Egg* broke the mirror more and more as I revised it. The audience was shouted at, appealed to, confided in; some of the actors broke up or seemed to be improvising and at such moments it wasn't at all clear whom to trust. Either the actors or the characters or the author – probably all – were betraying the implicit licence the audience had granted them: to play the game of illusion by understood rules. But many works of fiction are also critical demonstrations and, if *Joe Egg* is a problem play, the problem is not only how to live with a handicapped child but how to describe that life (as the Husband puts it) 'in a way that will prevent a sudden stampede to the exit-doors'. Its final draft became a criticism of its first. It's a play about a play.

In the ten or so stage plays I've written since, some thought has always been given to casting the audience, a method that works best when they're not allowed to settle comfortably into any one role. It's one way of accepting, while at the same time exploiting, the limitations of the form. The means are certainly spare, compared to films for instance, but capable of great variation, like those of any good game. Henry James, about to embark on his brief, disastrous playwriting career, wrote that 'one may use them, command them, squeeze them, lift them up and better them. As for the form itself, its honour and inspiration are in its difficulty.' There came a point when I began to feel this difficulty to be too attractive in itself. Trying to manage what James later called 'the hard meagreness of the theatrical form' can become an end, virtuosity for its own sake. I tired of the restrictions and wondered if perhaps my real bent was towards fiction, where scene and costume changes were so easy, weather so convincing and where you never missed a line because another reader coughed. In so many ways, too, my plays had been misplaced novels. But when I tried, I found the old problem of address had to be tackled again, though without the hard meagreness to help. Now that I could do anything, I could do nothing. Institutionalised, I ran back to my familiar cell. *Born in the Gardens* is a defence of life in a cage, and it occurs to me that all my plays have been about captivity and all the characters captives. The latest too. It shows a playwright who tries to write a novel, fails and falls back instead on writing a play about a playwright who tries to write a novel . . . the audience in this case being cast as a flock of sheep. This has come to be thought of as My Line. Inasmuch as I'm thought to have a style at all, it's the use of bits and pieces from the kind of theatre I enjoyed before seeing plays – Variety, revue, magic shows and pantomimes. In fact, most of them haven't been like this and, of the six plays in this collection, only two – *Forget-me-not Lane* and *Privates on Parade* – break the two-way mirror. Of course, two others – *Hearts and Flowers* and *The Common* – are for television, which hasn't developed a dramatic form of its own and probably never will. When I wrote my first play for the box, I hadn't even seen one. It wasn't hard to guess that it could only do small-scale films, mostly for talking heads. Television's been called tapwater, but in fact it's only the conduit through which the water flows.

For many years theatre was the best part of my life. These days I seldom go, not wanting to find myself at some play that pretends to ignore me. 'Communal nonsense' appeals to me more. I enjoy those parts of the event that more fastidious writers find tiresome – the audience assembling, intervals, curtain calls, even the accidents that aren't to do with art or entertainment. I wish I'd seen the performance of *The National Health* when someone in the stalls had a cardiac arrest and, from a stage full of actors robed and masked for a surgical operation, one had to ask, 'Is there a doctor in the house?'. The writing of scripts might well go on, even if all the theatres closed, because it is a spare, enjoyable and demanding form of composition, what Charles Wood calls 'our side of it'. Revivals and musicals are what the public wants; new plays are risky. Already they have more or less gone from The Great Dark Way. All that can make up for the bother and discomfort and high prices are the rare, small miracles and they will only happen when an event is caused that can't happen anywhere else. When our side of it meets theirs.

Note

The reader of the introductions that precede each play will need to know that Thelma is my wife; Louise, Daniel and Catherine our children. The eldest daughter Abigail stayed in permanent hospital care near Bristol when we moved to London in 1968. Charles Wood, the playwright, and his wife Valerie had been close friends in Bristol. Thelma and Valerie had been at school together as girls. They met again and realised they'd both – separately – married dramatists. They deserved better.

Michael Blakemore was also married and had directed both my stage plays so far – *A Day in the Death of Joe Egg* and *The National Health*. My father had died in 1965. My mother stayed on in her new flat in Bristol, not far from my brother and sister-in-law.

PETER NICHOLS
June 1986

FORGET-ME-NOT LANE

Forget-me-not Lane

With the royalties from Albert Finney's short run in *Joe Egg* on Broadway, we bought a detached Victorian house beside Blackheath in South East London and named it The Albert Hall. A short walk across the common and through the ancient park brought us to the new Greenwich Theatre. When Ewan Hooper, the founder and director, invited me to join the board and contribute a play to his 1971 season, I jumped at both chances. They were what I'd never been given in my own city of Bristol: to have a real say in how my local theatre was run and to come up with an example of the sort of play they ought to be doing. The open nothing-up-my-sleeve stage and the egalitarian bank of seats suggested the form. The characters and situations were to be taken from a few of my recent scripts for tv; the music was borrowed from old swing and from popular songs of the forties; from Meyerhold's *Government Inspector* I cribbed the notion of a semi-circle of doors in a blank wall. Michael Blakemore directed (as he already had my first two plays) and, with Roger Butlin the designer, refined the scenic idea to being three walls which, echoing the three-sided projecting stage, formed a hexagonal acting area occupied only by a sofa of uncut moquette. Like an image from Magritte, this dull but redolent object stood against the dun screen of doors. Only when they opened was any colour allowed to warm the drab uniformity of this unlikely 'room'. Then conjurors, comedians, a girl dancing on roller-skates, a half-naked slave (from *White Cargo*), all the hero's festering fantasies, burst on to tempt and taunt him and to remind the audience that they too were in thrall to their past. The room where Frank packed a case was the dingy present; behind the doors were his garish memories.

John Russell Taylor, reviewing the West End transfer, wrote that he could think of few plays where the dramatic syntax was so functional. Certainly none of mine before or since came up with so neat a trick. Though the theme was gloomy and pessimistic, the play kept smiling through. Nothing in it was exactly new, yet it worked better on the stage than anything of mine before or since. *Forget-me-not Lane* is still my favourite, the most personal and satisfying, though it has had only moderate success since the first magical performances at Greenwich. Probably no other stage has suited it as well as the one it was written for.

For the programme, I collected some bits from Diary to describe how it had come to be produced. Here they are again, with a few later entries that bring the story to its happy ending.

April 1st, 1970. Dreamt last night I was examining one of my father's shirts, striped blue and white with no collar but white cuffs to be fastened with links. I thought it a splendid garment and decided to buy some collars and wear it at once – with his suit, which in my dream was of an expensive worsted. I felt, as I rarely do when awake, a warm and comforting sadness. Awoke, mystified by the intensity of the image, to hear Daniel and Louise pounding up the stairs and into the bedroom shouting 'Someone's left the tap on and the bathroom's flooded.'

'Who?' I groaned. 'What? Why?'

'Don't know but it's all wet,' and they were giggling with excitement.

'Then it's nothing to laugh at. Turn the tap off.'

'April Fool!' they shouted.

As they tumbled downstairs again to report success to Thelma, I realised it was Dad's birthday. Five years now since he died. If he'd lived, he'd be eighty-two today. He's been in my mind a good deal lately, as I'm struggling with a play about my adolescence and his part in it. He comes alive – pathetic, pompous, likeable, nagging, meaningless. Real people don't, as a rule, 'mean' anything. Our lives make no sense. His didn't – but I'm trying and perhaps it will in time.

April 25th. My new stage play nearly finished now and, of course, it's disappointing. Well, it's a sort of paper-chain and later I may be able to hang some lanterns on it.

July 31st, 1970. Yesterday was occupied with being forty-three and dealing with a recurrence of prostatitis.

August 21st. I have a hi-fi now and have bought a batch of pre-stereo L.P.s – Ellington, Armstrong, Basie, Condon, Crosby, Goodman & Waller. Philip Larkin's *All What Jazz* has been a help in putting me back on target for my new play and his anti-modernist bias is stimulating and consoling to someone of my conservative taste in music. His introduction pins my heroes down – or at any rate, their Home Counties counterparts:

> Sometimes I imagine my readers, sullen fleshy inarticulate men, stockbrokers, sellers of goods, living in thirty-year-old detached houses among the golf courses of outer London, husbands of ageing and bitter wives they first seduced to Artie Shaw's 'Begin the Beguine' and the Squadronaires' 'The Nearness of You'; men in whom a pile of scratched coverless 78s in the attic can awaken memories of vomiting blindly from small Tudor windows to Muggsy Spanier's 'Sister Kate' . . .

September 23rd. My aching teeth announce the approach of winter. A cool morning starts the steely tingling that bars me from ice-cream and mousse. Took Catherine to school and, at the door of her class, a small black girl looked at me with astonishment.

'Is that your Daddy? Your Mum looks young but your Dad looks real old.'

Came home to revise the play.

November 15th. Still on *Forget-me-not*. Diminishing enthusiasm. Vowed not to write more plays about my poor family. Or at least to write something else as well that doesn't entail accuracy and checking in this diary and all those finicky habits of the naturalistic drama. Because, no matter how they try to break it down, my plays remain bound by naturalism, inasmuch as the people behave somewhat as they did in life and the events are never far-fetched. Vowed to write a far-fetched play before long.

November 25th. Michael Blakemore likes it and will direct. Michael Medwin may come in with Albert as co-producer. Ewan Hooper wishes he'd seen it earlier, as then he could have presented it in tandem with John Mortimer's as contrasting memory plays with dominating fathers. Michael and I began casting.

January 16th, 1971. A press conference at Greenwich to announce the season, which includes mine. Found myself sitting next to Elsie and Doris Waters, stars of radio in the days my play describes.

January 21st, 1971. Now we've cast the four principals, we have the treat of auditioning young women for the parts of Young Ursula and Miss 1940. Today this was on the stage of The Prince of Wales. Mike and I discussed our preferences – old versus new theatre buildings. As in most other life-styles, he favours baroque. I said it was all very well, as long as you could afford to sit in the stalls.

January 25th. Saw more Miss 1940s. Mike explained they might be asked to remove their bras and most said they wouldn't. They also went straight back to their agents and complained. Permissive society a sell!

January 26th. Two dancers sent by Lionel Blair – a burst of delicious sunshine, lovely busty leggy girls without the inhibiting braininess of actresses. Both said they'd happily have their bras ripped off. Chose the first: Stephanie Lawrence.

February 3rd. Charles Wood came from Bristol to stay the night. When I told him three of the actresses had complained when asked to make clean breast, he said, 'Oh, you haven't got bare tits, Peter? We're not doing that any more, love, not in the avant-garde. Everyone's fully clothed and nobody touches and it's all true love.'

February 21st. Michael Bates is playing Charles. He and his family came to tea. I had been Sebastian to his wife's Viola in rep in the 1950s. Michael's a deeply conventional man with little trilby and neat moustache. Father was in the Indian Civil Service.
'Is it true Greenwich Theatre hasn't got a curtain? I love a curtain down when I go to a play. I like the lights to dim and the curtain

to rise and there you are, a nice lounge.'

But he's a natural comedian too and, as with Dad, you can't be sure how much he's playing games. He was very amused by my tales of Dad but concerned that old snapshots make him look distinguished and imperious. He's worried too about how to grow old.

'Shall I wear two hair-pieces, I wonder?'

March 1st. First reading in church hall near the theatre. I'd taken Joan Hickson to look at the stage.

'Oh, my God!' she exclaimed as we walked in.

Bates was very funny. I cried with laughter to hear my own jokes read aloud at last. Embarrassing and impossible to explain away. Joan seems unhappy, as though she can see no way of adding to her performance as the mother in *Joe Egg*.

March 7th. With Michael Blakemore, discussed the question of dialect. Should Anton Rodgers as Frank have a Bristolian accent at all? Should Ian Gelder as Young Frank lose his accent by the time he comes home from National Service?

'The point is, Mike, a lot of people keep their accents all through their lives.'

'Yes, but when you're living in Bristol among Bristolians, you're not very much aware of their accents. It's only after you leave that you really notice. Now if we emphasise Frank's local accent, we'd be in danger of taking a metropolitan attitude towards the characters, making it into a regional comedy, which it shouldn't be.'

I agreed. He does think well as a director, despite his flaws.

8th March. Started going to rehearsals regularly – and uninvited. At a party, Mike told Thelma he had to have some time on his own to do *his* creative bit. I quite understand but it's also true that an author who's spent most of a year on a play has too much at stake to stay away for long. They finished blocking yesterday and I think my being there was helpful, as I corrected a few awkward or unhelpfully ambiguous lines and cut some superfluous words. Better now than after the actors have learnt them, when they are more resistant to change. That's one reason for an author's presence. Another is to find out where the director hasn't grasped the author's meaning. Like I.A. Richards and Practical Criticism. How many pianos did Lawrence have in mind? Turned out yesterday that Mike thought 'Old Butterfingers up there' meant God, not the deceased Dad. Should it perhaps be 'Our Father that art in Heaven'?

9th March. A morose day with Michael. I asked him when we were done whether there was anything wrong, but he said no. Had he asked me not to turn up, I'd have had to argue and insist on my right to be there.

The last moments of the play are sad and funny at once, even erotic in a wistful way. The slave-girl images are comic but exciting too. Wanted sex afterwards but Thelma read her French grammar.

10th March. Stayed away from rehearsal till after lunch. Even so Michael led me aside to ask if I would not sit by him as it upset the actors.

'You were pissing yourself at Michael Bates but did you see what it did to the other actors?'

'Nothing, that I could see.'

'They started laughing at him too to show that they didn't mind.'

'I don't think so. You exaggerate my importance.'

'No, I don't. You're the ultimate authority. It inhibits me to have you there, I feel I may be wrong and have to look at you to know if I am.'

'I'll certainly sit to the side if you think that'll help.'

'You shouldn't feel unwelcome but you've already done your creative bit writing the thing. Now it's my turn.'

Not a fair analogy. If directors want to do a 'creative bit', they should try a fresh version of a classic. Their job with a new work is accurate interpretation, the definitive performance by which all others will be judged, and in the interests of accuracy they should welcome, not dread, the author's advice. He knows what he meant, after all, and any sensible playwright will change it when he sees it's not working, but it must be tried the way he intended.

28th March. The ups and downs have levelled out to a steady satisfaction at the way things look. Anton greatly improved, now that he knows his lines. Bates has started getting jumpy, questioning every direction, fussing about the choice of a bowler hat, the exact handling of a bag of eggs. Additions have been stimulating – the pianist coming to run the songs, the costume parade with Stephanie in union-jack knickers. How I love her!

29th March. We struggled through a technical run of Act One. I sat beside Sandra Payne and Stephanie whenever I could as they waited in gym-slip or slave-girl sarong to represent my dream-girls. Tried to chat them up but how did they regard me – as a dirty old man, a shy professor? Gave it up, crippled by shyness.

31st March. Public preview to a full house. Friends galore and a good local crowd received the play as you hardly dare to hope. Obvious enjoyment, applause on individual lines and exits, and a heart-stopping moment right at the end as the actors turned to go upstage for the last few lines of the song and everyone suddenly burst out clapping. An evening of sheer happiness. Actors euphoric at supper afterwards with Priscilla Morgan and husband Clive Dunn. Michael Blakemore, cool as ever, said it was bound to go down tomorrow night and of course he was probably right. Rex Harrison's Rolls was in the way when we left the restaurant at midnight.

1st April, 1971. Telegrams included one from John Osborne signed 'All Those at Frinton'. Not a bad show either, though my first act *was* down after the marvellous preview. I wandered on my own in the picture gallery during half-time but met a neighbour who told me young people might like being reminded of the war but she didn't.

Second act far better. Albert Finney kissed me on both cheeks, tears in his eyes, all the locals watching. I can't say why the end's so affecting. Michael says it's due to the potency of Tony Martin singing 'You Stepped Out of a Dream' as Sandra shows Anton her naked body beneath the school mac. Certainly a popular image.

Diary made no mention of the play opening on my father's birthday. I had been given the odd privilege of giving him a second life, a very special case of the child being father of the man.

Forget-me-not Lane.

First: 1st April, 1971, Greenwich Theatre.
Same production with same cast opened at the Apollo Theatre on 28th April, produced by Memorial Enterprises.

FRANK	Anton Rodgers
CHARLES	Michael Bates
YOUNG FRANK	Ian Gelder
AMY	Joan Hickson
IVOR	Malcolm McFee
MR MAGIC	Eddie Molloy
MISS NINETEEN-FORTY	Stephanie Lawrence
URSULA	Priscilla Morgan
YOUNG URSULA	Sandra Payne

Directed by Michael Blakemore
Designed by Roger Butlin

In a translation by Claude Roy, it was presented as *Ne M'oubliez Pas* at the Théâtre de la Renaissance in Paris in June 1972 with Daniel Gélin as Frank and Guy Tréjan as Charles.

In America, Arvin Brown directed it at the Long Wharf, New Haven, Connecticut and later at the Mark Taper Forum, Los Angeles, California. This was later transmitted by WNET TV.

In 1975, a BBC TV production by Alan Bridges featured Albert Finney as Frank, Bill Fraser as Charles and Gemma Jones as Ursula.

The London critics in *Variety* voted it Best British Play of the season.

ACT ONE

A semicircular screen contains perhaps six, perhaps eight doors. Closed, they are hardly noticeable. They open inwards on to the acting area, and only two have knobs or handles. With front lights on, the impression is of a plain wall enclosing a space. On the forestage this space breaks into a number of levels. A four seater sofa centre. The screen need not be more than ten feet high and the theatre wall can be seen beyond. One of the doors is open at the beginning and in the opening is a tape recorder on a cabinet. We are to assume that it is from here the music comes.

Before the action starts, there is a record recital for about twenty minutes. Throughout this, FRANK *comes on and goes off several times. He is forty. First, he brings on a cheap suitcase, open and half-full. He leaves it and goes. On his next appearances, he brings on personal articles and puts them in the case. He pays more attention to the music than the case and often stops to mime to the records, which he knows by heart. At the end of one, he bows to an imaginary audience.*

FRANK [*softly*]: Thank you very much. Thank you. [*Sometimes he looks into the case and rejects an article.*] No, no . . . [*And after returning several times, he says:*] What exactly are you doing, man? [*And takes the case off with him. Returning in time to listen to a good deal of the last record, he mimes Bechet's soprano sax. He takes a cheque-book, cigarettes and money from drawers under the player and puts them into his pocket, brings out a handkerchief, holds it up and looks at it, shrugs, returns it to his pocket. He turns off the tape and closes the door.*] Why don't you leave off packing now? [*He keeps moving.*] Not as though you show any improvement as a packer. The same feeble indecision – same refusal to believe the weather might change – shivering through a frost in light-weight suit and pack-a-mac. [*Now he addresses the audience directly.*] And when you consider how large packing has loomed in my family. Both my families. The one I was issued with and the one I escaped to. [*He takes his cigarettes out and lights one. He coughs.*] Christ. [*He recovers.*] When my wife is packing, our bedroom looks as though we've had the burglars in. Before our first second honeymoon, I said, 'Wellington boots *and* tennis rackets?' And she said, 'If

11

you're going to stand there carping, you can do the packing yourself!' 'All right,' I said, 'then let me.' 'You can't,' she said, 'you're a hopeless packer.' My parents went over the same ground more times than I care to remember. Setting out from Bristol to Minehead at last in the Wolseley, my mother would say, 'I hope you packed my laxatives.' And Dad, 'If your laxatives were listed, they were packed. The old man's not exactly a novice at packing suitcases.' Not exactly, no. And yet – in thirty-five years commercial travelling, he never once got ready on time. Every Monday morning he'd start at dawn with the best intentions but hours later he'd still be ransacking the house for indelible pencils, spectacle cases, samples of cake decorations such as nodding robins on sugar logs – or silver horseshoes for wedding-cakes with real bells that tinkled . . .

[*Bow windows are projected on the screen with checks of paper strips.* CHARLES *comes on, aged fifty. He wears a bowler hat, raincoat, grey spats, blue suit underneath, and carries a small leather case.*]

CHARLES: Frank!

FRANK [*remembering*]: Hallo?

[*Pause.* CHARLES *takes no notice but looks off stage.*]

CHARLES [*louder*]: Frank!

YOUNG FRANK [*off*]: Hallo?

CHARLES: Hallo who?

YOUNG FRANK [*off*]: Hallo, Dad.

CHARLES: Come in here.

FRANK: Trying to get him off was like some primitive attempt at man-powered flight. The great flapping steel wings, the sudden loss of energy . . .

[YOUNG FRANK *comes on, aged fourteen now, and wearing shirt and trousers, carrying a newspaper.*]

YOUNG FRANK: What?

CHARLES: What? What's 'what'?

[YOUNG FRANK *shrugs, reads.*]

And straighten your shoulders when I'm talking to you, stand up straight.

YOUNG FRANK [*groans*]: I'm trying to finish breakfast.

CHARLES: At ten o'clock! Most people have been out, done a day's

work by now. Your mother pampers you, gives in to you, she's
not got the least idea . . .

YOUNG FRANK: I'm on holiday. What's the matter with having
breakfast . . .

CHARLES: Wossermarrer? What's wossermarrer?

[YOUNG FRANK *groans, goes on reading.* CHARLES *grabs the
lobe of his son's ear and peers into it.*]

Have you washed the wax from your ears?

[YOUNG FRANK *groans, moves away.*]

FRANK: He was like an upset beetle.

CHARLES [*moving about*]: I was up this morning at quarter to seven.
All this time trying to get away from this house but nobody ever
puts anything back where they found it. You been smoking my
cigarettes?

YOUNG FRANK: No.

FRANK: But a chill of fear.

CHARLES: No who?

YOUNG FRANK: No, Dad.

CHARLES: Well, it's beyond my comprehension. I've never let
smoke, strong drink or vile language pass my lips since I signed
the pledge at fourteen. Your mother only has the odd cork-
tipped.

[CHARLES *stands not looking at* YOUNG FRANK *but seems to be
expecting a confession. He has the air of a prosecutor with an
irrefutable case.*]

YOUNG FRANK: I haven't touched them. Honestly!

[*Pause.* YOUNG FRANK *looks at* CHARLES. CHARLES *looks at
him.*]

CHARLES [*in a softer tone*]: If you tell me honestly, boy, I believe
you.

FRANK: Oh, yes. That sudden Band-of-Hope piety. [*He looks at his
paper.*] Even if I was telling the truth, I'd blush with shame.

CHARLES: And look at me when I'm talking, you great pudden.

[YOUNG FRANK *groans.* AMY *enters from a different door,
wearing spring clothes with apron and turban. She is forty.*]

AMY: Here. [*She gives* CHARLES *two packets of cigarettes.*]

CHARLES: Where were they?

AMY: Pocket of the winter suit you've just left off.

13

FRANK: She was trying to turn him over and point him in the right direction.

CHARLES [*hopelessly*]: Could have sworn I looked in there.

YOUNG FRANK: Told you.

CHARLES: I believed you, Son. I know you're a truthful boy.

FRANK: Still can't tell a lie, even today.

CHARLES: Now that smokes are in short supply, branch managers appreciate a packet on the firm.

AMY: I should think they did . . .

CHARLES: Mister Steel, the manager of Yeovil branch . . .

AMY: With queues at every shop.

CHARLES [*after pausing*]: Friend Steel of . . .

AMY: And they say it's going to get worse.

[CHARLES *looks at her.*]

CHARLES: Friend Steel of . . .

AMY: I said, I don't see how it *can* get worse.

CHARLES [*quick and loud*]: Friend Steel of Yeovil branch chain-smokes from morn till night and coughs his heart up and turns a lurid purple. I said to him, 'Friend, if I speak quite frankly, you're a noodle, coating your lungs with nicotine instead of God's good air.'

YOUNG FRANK: Then you passed him another packet?

CHARLES: You've got it boy, and licked my indelible pencil and said, 'Now, friend, how you off for custard powder?' A very good line. 'Another gross of tins?'

FRANK: Early lessons in commercial duplicity.

AMY: If you don't get a move on, Friend Steel will be gone to dinner.

CHARLES: Lunch, Amy.

AMY: Lunch, then. [*He takes off his bowler hat, kisses her, puts it on.*]

CHARLES: See you Friday afternoon.

AMY: Be careful. Got your gas-mask?

CHARLES: In the car.

AMY: And your torch in case there's a power cut?

CHARLES [*looks at a list*]: Yes. [*To* YOUNG FRANK.] During the air-raids, do as your mother tells you.

YOUNG FRANK [*reading his paper*]: Okay.

CHARLES: Okay? What's okay?

AMY: Don't go on at him.

CHARLES: You spoil him, Amy, you side with him. How long since you had your hair cut? Buzfuz? I'm talking to you.

YOUNG FRANK: Fortnight.

AMY: It does want cutting badly, Frank.

CHARLES: No, Amy, it doesn't want cutting badly, it badly wants cutting. But we want it cut well, not badly. [*He moves about, staring over the audience.*]

FRANK: Of course he was trying to find a reason not to go.

CHARLES: Just look at the car! Standing there since eight this morning. The only car in the avenue, it looks like showing off. I detest showing off almost as much as I detest foul language or dirty fingernails.

AMY: Now's your chance to move it.

CHARLES: They can't wait to get rid of the old man. Good-bye, Frank.

YOUNG FRANK: 'Bye.

CHARLES: Good-bye who?

[YOUNG FRANK *groans.*]

AMY: Come on.

[CHARLES *is driven to the door by* AMY, *then turns.*]

CHARLES: I think I'll go down the avenue, save turning the car round, along Appian Terrace and up Tuscan Vale to the main road . . .

AMY: I should.

[AMY *pushes* CHARLES *off.* YOUNG FRANK *follows their progress into the wings, down stage and across the front.* FRANK *watches with him.*]

YOUNG FRANK: Go, go, go.

FRANK: Into the lobby where sunlight through Edwardian stained-glass colours the morning's loaf and milk-bottles —

YOUNG FRANK: Don't let him talk any more, Mum —

FRANK: — where open umbrellas stand drying out on rainy days —

YOUNG FRANK: Shut the gate behind him, one last wave . . .

FRANK: — and the only car in the avenue won't be seen again until Friday afternoon.

YOUNG FRANK: Another five days of freedom!

[*The first quarter of a tinkling Westminster chime is heard.* AMY *enters, carrying a loaf and bottles of milk.*]

AMY: Quarter past ten on washing day. Before I know where I am

15

it's going to be dinner-time and I shan't know where I am. [*She puts down the bread and milk, takes a cigarette and matches from her apron.*]

YOUNG FRANK: Well, anyway old Hitler's gone.

AMY: You shouldn't talk like that about your father. [*She goes to the window and looks into the street.*]

YOUNG FRANK: He's *worse* than Hitler. Bet you anything Hitler wouldn't stop me using his wind-up gramophone if he already had a great big radiogram! [*He sees her.*] What you looking after him for?

AMY: Make sure he's gone.

YOUNG FRANK: He knows you smoke.

AMY: He doesn't like it. [*She comes down and lights up.*]

YOUNG FRANK: He doesn't like anything. Smoking, drinking, being with your friends and wearing the kind of clothes you like.

AMY: He's got his funny ways.

YOUNG FRANK: He's a cruel tyrant. [*He pronounces it 'tirrant'.*]

AMY: Cruel what?

YOUNG FRANK: Tyrant! This is a tyranny. He tries to crush the spirit of freedom.

FRANK: I can't have said that. Tirrant?

AMY: He's done his best for you, Frank. Put you through a good school . . .

YOUNG FRANK [*incredulous*]: Good school?

FRANK: With a Latin song and motto.

YOUNG FRANK [*to* FRANK]: But no girls.

AMY: Saved up all that money in cerstificates that you can draw when you're twenty-one.

YOUNG FRANK [*correcting*]: Certificates.

AMY: Yes. Cerstificates.

YOUNG FRANK: I don't want money. I want liberty. I think everyone should be allowed to do as they like all the time.

AMY: Don't talk silly.

YOUNG FRANK: I think everybody should be happy and go out in the fields and have picnics and – you know – take all their clothes off even, if they want to –

AMY: That *would* be nice, I must say.

YOUNG FRANK: – and sing and dance and just be friends and no-one would have too much to eat while other people haven't got enough –

FRANK: Oh, no! [*Embarrassed, he hides his face with his hand.*]

YOUNG FRANK: – and people would stop hating each other.

FRANK: It sounds like a Pop Festival.

AMY: Have you finished your breakfast?

YOUNG FRANK: And all the people who don't agree with freedom will be put in special places to be educated. And if they still don't want to be free, they'll be put on desert islands. People like Goering and Mussolini and Dad.

AMY: I see, as the blind man said. [*Suddenly worried.*] If everyone's just enjoying themselves, who's going to clear up all the mess?

YOUNG FRANK: Mess?

AMY: After the picnics.

YOUNG FRANK: Machines. Some huge great vacuum cleaner. Machines will do all the work.

AMY: That'll be nice. Meantime I'd better get the copper going. Or before I know where I am, it'll be dinner-time and I shan't know where I am. [*She starts to leave.*]

[YOUNG FRANK *reads his paper.*]

FRANK: I know!

[*The air-raid siren sounds the alert.*]

AMY: Oh, not those devils again! [*She goes to the window to look out.*]

YOUNG FRANK: Mum! You say I shouldn't call him Hitler but think how he stopped you singing.

AMY [*turning back*]: I had a lovely singing voice. Mister Dunn the adjudicator said I was a natural mezzo with perfect pitch and a wide range and all I needed was experience.

FRANK: The self-pity!

YOUNG FRANK: But he was jealous. He wouldn't let you follow your career because it would have meant you singing for other people, not just him.

[*Gunfire. They take no notice.*]

AMY: He is a miserable devil in some ways. I sometimes wish I'd never bumped into him at that dance. He was acting the goat and like a fool I laughed. Well, before I knew it we were out there doing the fox-trot and the whole floor stopped to watch us. He was like a gazelle with his patent pumps and his hair smarmed down.

[AMY *blows her nose with her handkerchief, then makes for the door.* YOUNG FRANK *returns to his paper.*]

Did you wet the bed last night?

YOUNG FRANK: Yep.

FRANK: As usual.

AMY: Do try not to.

YOUNG FRANK: I *do*.

[*Loud gunfire.*]

AMY: Poor Mother, all alone! She hates the gunfire. Twice in my lifetime those German devils have started a war with us. When my brothers came home from the trenches, Mother made them take off their uniforms in the yard, they were so infested with lice.

YOUNG FRANK: She ought to come and live here.

AMY: She and Dad are at each other's throats, she says she'd rather be independent.

FRANK: He couldn't stand the sight of Grandma drinking stout.

[*The front door slams.*]

AMY: What's that? [*She looks out of the window.*] Oh, no, the car's outside.

[CHARLES *enters, as before, but carrying one shoe in front of him, at arm's length.*]

YOUNG FRANK: What are you back for?

CHARLES: For what are you back?

AMY: I thought we'd got rid of you.

CHARLES: The usual sunny welcome. Mister Dick was filling Leonora with petrol when the sirens went. I said, 'There's not the slightest use rushing off to Yeovil now. Friend Steel makes straight for the convenience the moment a raid begins and for some time afterwards he's quite unable to bring his mind to bear on cake decorations and desiccated coconut.'

AMY: What you holding out your shoe for?

CHARLES and YOUNG FRANK: For what are you holding out your shoe?

CHARLES: Hold your tongue, Buzfuz. I'm talking to Woodbine Winnie here. 'In fact,' I added, 'I think there's very little point in leaving now till after lunch.'

[YOUNG FRANK *and* AMY *groan. Gunfire.*]

AMY: The larder's empty.

CHARLES: And Mister Dick said, 'They won't cheer to see you back.' I said, 'I don't care tuppence.'

AMY: But what's the shoe for?

CHARLES: Crossing the pavement from the car, I'm dashed if I didn't inadvertently step where a dog had used the convenience!

AMY: Fancy bringing it in the dining-room!

CHARLES: I'm on my way to wipe it clean with a copy of *Reynolds News*. But it's beyond my comprehension – after I'd put a up a notice: Dogs not to foul the public footway.

YOUNG FRANK: Lot of dogs round here can't read.

CHARLES: Don't try to score me off, Sonny Jim. You're not half bright enough! [*He moves towards the other door.*] And you can help me open the garage doors, we'll put the car away, it might get struck by shrapnel out there.

[CHARLES *goes.* AMY *picks up the bread and milk.*]

AMY: Don't make a mess in my clean scullery.

[AMY *goes.*]

YOUNG FRANK [*appealing to the ceiling*]: Oh, God, please help us to be free of him. Please make a bomb fall on him, God.

[YOUNG FRANK *goes off another way with the newspaper. The bow windows fade.*]

FRANK: How could I possibly understand them at fourteen? Their complicated middle-age game of regret and recrimination? My own experience was confined to chasing high-schoolgirls through the city museum at lunchtime. Oh, those stuffed kangaroos! Those tableaux of British wildlife! That scent of gravy! I took a party of students last week and I'm glad to say it's resisted all attempts at modernisation. The hippopotamus still yawns beside the fire buckets. [*He screws his eyes tight shut and claps his hands.*] Stick to the point, man! The point was that I couldn't understand the sophisticated war my parents were conducting – either the issues or the strategy. But I *was* in the line of fire. So instead of understanding I took sides. Dad was a monster, Mum was a martyr. What does my own boy make of it when at thirteen he watches Ursula and me growling and roaring at each other? Yes, that's one of the reasons I left her. Having seen my parents like cat-and-dog year after year, I wanted to save my son that spectacle. [*He ponders, shrugs, and does a Churchill imitation.*] We shall fight on the landing-grounds, we shall fight in the living-rooms, we shall fight in the only car in the avenue. Everyone was exhorted to take sides at the time and Dad became my personal Hitler. [*He glances at the door* CHARLES *came from, and goes on quietly.*] No wonder I wet the bed three times a week at fourteen. Poor man. Thirty years too late I can see what he must have been suffering, separated from his beloved wife five days a week, packed off gladly Monday mornings to share commercial hotels with heavy drinking, dirty-joke telling travellers. And on Fridays welcomed back as warmly as Messerschmitt.

> [YOUNG FRANK *comes on, opens the door to the gramophone and puts on a record – scratched 1941 'Woodchoppers Ball' by Joe Loss, or Woody Herman. He wears a suit and polished shoes. He conducts the band, miming the tenor sax.*]

Especially by me and my close friend Ivor.

> [IVOR *comes on from the same door that* FRANK *used, arriving just in time to mime the clarinet solo.* YOUNG FRANK *signals him in and keeps the band quieter so he can be heard.* IVOR *is fourteen as well and also wears a suit.*]

FRANK [*after listening for a while*]: This was just before we moved from swing to jazz.

> [CHARLES *enters from another door, behind the boys. He is dressed as before but carries a case in one hand, a bunch of flowers in the other. He puts down the case, frowns at the oblivious boys and takes off the record.*]
>
> [YOUNG FRANK *and* IVOR *see* CHARLES *and groan.*]

CHARLES: I can hear that blessed racket on the far side of the street.

YOUNG FRANK: You home again?

CHARLES: The usual sunny welcome.

> [YOUNG FRANK *makes a face at* IVOR. IVOR *facially imitates* CHARLES. CHARLES *looks closely at the record-player.*]

And still using steel needles, tearing your records to shreds. Why don't you take a bone one?

YOUNG FRANK: Cause they sound terrible. You can hardly . . .

CHARLES: Hullo, Ivor, are you quite well?

IVOR: Hullo.

CHARLES: Hullo, who?

IVOR: Hullo, Mister Bisley, I suppose.

CHARLES: And stand up straight when you speak to me. Stooping over like that, how can you expect to fill your lungs with God's good air?

IVOR [giggles]: Good old God.

CHARLES: What d'you say? Taking the Lord's name in vain?

[A piano is played off – Sinding's 'Rustle of Spring'.]

Listen to that – your mother playing. Always been one of my greatest pleasures, Frank, hearing your mother play.

YOUNG FRANK: As a matter of fact . . .

CHARLES: Hold your tongue, boy, give yourself a chance to hear some decent music for a change. I shall go to her, throw open the door, and drop on one knee before her, saying, 'You, my dear, are playing "Rustle of Spring" and I've brought you a spring bouquet.' What do you think she'll say to that, boy? 'You home again?'

YOUNG FRANK: No, she'll probably say, 'That's not me playing, it's my pupil.' She's giving a lesson.

[There is a mistake in the music, which has otherwise been adequate. Pause. The pianist begins again from a few bars back.]

CHARLES [without conviction]: Fancy playing records when your mother's teaching! [He puts the flowers on the table.]

[IVOR moves to YOUNG FRANK and whispers.]

YOUNG FRANK: Going up the back room.

CHARLES: Why are you both in your best?

IVOR: We're entertaining tonight.

YOUNG FRANK: An anti-aircraft station.

FRANK: Or fighter base or military hospital or isolated wireless unit.

CHARLES: Your mother, too?

YOUNG FRANK: We're all in the same concert party, you know that.

[CHARLES glares, betrayed, towards the piano music.]

CHARLES: And I've been away since Monday! She promised she wouldn't go entertaining Friday night.

YOUNG FRANK: We've all got to pull our weight.

FRANK [to YOUNG FRANK]: Show a bit of understanding.

IVOR: If the troops want us, we've got to go.

CHARLES: What makes you think they want you? [*He imitates a sergeant.*] 'Fifty volunteers to watch some crackpots do a concert, the others will peel the spuds.' That's how it's done.

YOUNG FRANK: How d'you know? You've never been in the army. Dodged both wars.

CHARLES: I was medically unfit in the first due to the deafness caused by my father clouting me across the ear.

YOUNG FRANK: Any case, our show's much better than you and your corny old recitations.

CHARLES [*quietly*]: Not so much of the jolly old buck. You don't know about what you're talking. Haven't you ever read my notices? Ivor, you?

IVOR: Yeah.

CHARLES: 'If laughing ensures growing fat, each one of the audience must bulk considerably as a result of Charles Bisley's sketches of London low-life.' 'One cannot too highly praise Mr Bisley's characterisation of Ikey Cohen.'

IVOR: Well, anyway, I reckon we all ought to do our bit.

YOUNG FRANK: Remember what old Winnie said, 'I have nothing to offer but blood, toil, tears and sweat.'

CHARLES: Acting the goat in a concert party is not exactly what Mister Churchill strove to convey by those beautiful words.
[*They groan.* IVOR *imitates* CHARLES *facially.*]
It's a pity you don't put some of your blood, toil, tears and sweat into your school work. Pass your exams and get a job in the Civil Service.

FRANK: Which is what I did in the end. Some years later.

CHARLES: Have you done your prep for tomorrow?

YOUNG FRANK: I can do it in the break.

CHARLES: You sprawl about in your best clothes, listening to rubbish and tell me you can do your prep in the break?

YOUNG FRANK: It's only revision and I'm nearly top in French, anyway.

CHARLES: *Nearly* top's not good enough. One day, when the war's over and France is liberated, you may go as your mother and I did and how glad I was to know a little of the language. No-one could claim your mother had the gift of tongues and like a piecan she said to a lady in the hotel, 'Can you tell us the way to Marshal

Joffre street?' I said, 'Amy, for goodness' sake, stand aside, let the old man. '*Ou est le Rue de Marshal Joffre, s'il vous plaît, Madame?*' She said as quick as a flash, '*A le droit, Monsieur, à le droit.*'

[*They wince at his accent.*]

IVOR: Lucky she was a Cockney, too.

[YOUNG FRANK *laughs.*]

CHARLES: You give me cheek in my house, you won't come here again, Sonny Jim.

FRANK: The strongest threat he could use. Ivor was my life.

YOUNG FRANK: I've only got to revise the subjunctive of irregular verbs from *devoir* to *ouvrir* and I know them already, Dad. Honestly.

CHARLES [*quietly*]: You tell me honestly, boy, I believe you.

[YOUNG FRANK *looks at the floor. The rustle of spring has passed by and the pupil is playing scales.* CHARLES *looks towards the sound then back again.*]

Right, Ivor, in this bag are one or two presents from branch managers.

FRANK: The few he hadn't estranged by his Puritanism.

CHARLES: A pound of bacon from Wiltshire, a Battenburg cake from Cardiff and a tin of salmon from Glastonbury.

IVOR: Black market.

CHARLES: Not at all. I'm in the distributive trades and fragments are bound to fall off here and there in the process of conveying the goods from hither to yon.

IVOR: Okay.

CHARLES: I haven't noticed your father averse to the odd hand-out.

FRANK: All the same it was wicked at a time when most people welcomed rationing as a first step towards some degree of fair shares.

CHARLES: Come here, Son.

FRANK: A step not even the ruling class could postpone any longer.

[CHARLES *gives* IVOR *the case.*]

CHARLES: Take it to the scullery and as you pass through the music-room . . .

YOUNG FRANK: The music-room?

CHARLES: Hold your tongue! As you pass through, look

23

unconcerned, don't draw the pupil's attention to the suitcase in any way.

IVOR: She's only eleven.

CHARLES: If you paid more attention to what's going on in the world, you'd know children have been betraying their own parents in Germany.

FRANK: We had this pantomime every Friday because he was really excited by the thought of wickedness.

CHARLES: And take those flowers . . .

FRANK: Afraid of every kind of pleasure he had put behind him when he rose from the Edwardian poor.

CHARLES: Fill with water the vawse, vayse or vahse you will find on the window-sill and place them therein. Who said that, the old man? I'll give him a kick in the pants. [*He kicks himself and laughs.*]

IVOR: Okay.

[IVOR *takes the case and flowers and goes.*]

CHARLES: Got one or two more cases you can help bring in from the car, Frank. The longer I leave it standing there, the more it looks like showing off.

[YOUNG FRANK *goes and* CHARLES *follows. Bow windows fade and piano practice finishes.*]

FRANK: Having stowed the plunder, my mother and Ivor and I would catch the bus to meet the cars that took us into the country where we did Our Bit. Sometimes we'd have to shout through gunfire and – once I remember at a fighter station, the audience were gradually called into the air one by one and those that stayed shouted, 'Carry on!' Perhaps Dad was right and it was a choice between watching us and cookhouse fatigues. But we never believed it . . .

[*A Union Jack unfurls at the back. A concert party piano plays an elaborate introduction.* AMY *enters in a velvet evening gown with a pearl necklace.*]

AMY [*singing*]:   There'll always be an England
                    While there's a country lane,
                    Wherever there's a cottage small
                    Beside a field of grain.

[*A middle-aged man enters in the costume and make-up of a*

Chinese magician. While AMY *continues, he shows a number of separate silk squares: red, white and blue.* FRANK *comes on with a Chinese kimono and shows an empty cylinder,* MISTER MAGIC *puts the squares into the cylinder.*]

> There'll always be an England
> Where there's a crowded street,
> Wherever there's a chimney tall,
> A million marching feet.

[IVOR, *as before, comes on and opens a door behind which is a large sketch-pad. He begins drawing while* MISTER MAGIC *and* FRANK *continue packing squares into the cylinder.*]

> Red, white and blue –
> What does it means to you?
> Surely you're proud,
> Shout it aloud,
> Britons, Awake!

[*A* YOUNG BLONDE *enters, wearing Union Jack satin briefs, with roller-skates on and begins tap-dancing.*]

> The Empire, too,
> We can depend on you.
> Freedom remains.
> These are the chains
> Nothing can break

FULL CHORUS: There'll always be an England

[FRANK *holds the cylinder and* MISTER MAGIC *takes from it the first square, now a Union Jack. He walks across the stage and pulls out a long tape strung with flags.*]

> And England shall be free –

[*They point to* IVOR's *drawing, which is now seen to be a caricature of Churchill.*]

> If England means as much to you –

[*They form a line down stage and the* DANCER *finishes by doing the splits, her hands held by* YOUNG FRANK *and* IVOR.]

> As England means to me.

[*Coda and arpeggios from the pianist. All except* FRANK *wave, bow, then go, shutting the door. The flags disappear.*]

FRANK: We never gave a thought to the old man at home, listening to Beethoven, sharpening his bone needles, imagining our wickedness. My only thought was for the peroxide blonde.

[MISS NINETEEN-FORTY *enters without roller-skates*.]

At eighteen, only four years older, she was already a different generation. Soldiers roared at her satin drawers, her legs browned with liquid make-up. I roared, too, but silently, inside my head. Please God let her sit alongside me in the car home. Not that I ever *did* anything – but I could smell the powder, feel the warmth, the beat of her heart, the rise and fall of her breasts . . . [*He shuts his eyes to expel the thought*.] One night she sat on my hand –

[MISS NINETEEN-FORTY *sits on* FRANK's *right hand*.]

– I couldn't think how to tell her. An hour, the journey took, and when we dropped her, my fingers were paralysed. Nobody noticed. Nobody ever noticed us much. It was a time for grown-up people. And as we approached the city, the sky was orange, searchlight beams were trying to find the bombers, a balloon burned over the house, the ack-ack pounded away – and my hand was crushed beneath a dancer's thighs.

[MISS NINETEEN-FORTY *rises and goes*.]

Next day I was expected to be fourteen again and decline irregular verbs – from *devoir* to *ouvrir* . . . [*He moves excitedly*.] But at lunch-time down to the City Museum. British Wildlife had been hit by incendiaries but we chased the high school girls through Transport Down The Ages and struggled with them behind the horse-drawn fire-engines.

[URSULA *comes on, aged thirty-eight, attractive and well-dressed*.] [*To her*.] You were about thirteen.

URSULA: Thinking about me again. You said you wouldn't. You should be packing while I'm at the evening class. Not dreaming.

FRANK: I find those years exciting to remember.

URSULA: I expect the peroxide blonde does, too.

FRANK: She must be among those middle-aged women who flock the local palais on Glenn Miller night. But at least she'll have some memories worth having. Whereas mine! God!

URSULA: Whose fault's that?

FRANK: Mine, I know.

URSULA: I tried hard enough. From the first moment I saw you.

FRANK: You didn't make it very obvious.

URSULA: You were too busy being scathing and sophisticated to notice.

FRANK: Pride.

URSULA: Yes. But a deep disapproval of pleasure, too. An urge to spoil people's fun.

FRANK: Only because I was afraid.

URSULA: You still are. Still spend most of your spare time dwelling on your lost opportunities. Remembering the war.

[*They are standing at some distance from each other.*]

FRANK: Well, the war was the last time, it seems to me, that pleasure and duty coincided. When they weren't chasing U-boats and incendiary bombs, the men and women of that time seemed to be chasing each other.

URSULA: Especially after the Yanks arrived.

FRANK: Yes, skidding about the semis in their sexy jeeps with tight-arsed trousers and Hollywood names. And the good-time girls used to . . .

URSULA: Good-time girls! [*She laughs.*]

FRANK: They used to sit in rows on our front wall waiting for their lovers to pour from the evacuated orphanage. My grandma called them brazen hussies. To me, they were at least as exotic as the camel that came by once with a circus and started nibbling our privet.

URSULA: I was arrested for loitering once.

FRANK: Did you really pick up Yanks?

URSULA: No. Mum lost her temper and told the policeman I was only fourteen and still at school, but that meant nothing.

FRANK: Most of the tarts weren't that much older.

URSULA: The nearest thing I got was spending so much time with Denise Carter.

FRANK: Denise Carter!

URSULA: I suppose she must have been flat-chested and putty-coloured, but by the time she'd got on her painted face with the huge crimson lips and plucked and pencilled her eyebrows and Vaselined her lashes – curled her hair with sugar and water – pushed her breasts up into the padded brassière – and climbed into a low-neck magenta sweater in brushed angora, she seemed to me like a film-star. And when you consider some of the oddities we tried to look like then . . .

FRANK [*nodding*]: She probably did, yes. [*He smiles appreciatively.*]

URSULA: While the Americans were here, she promoted herself through the ranks from Private to Major.

FRANK: Hands across the sea.

URSULA: Yes.

FRANK [*imitating Churchill*]: Give us the tools and we will finish the job.

[*She laughs.*]

While you were being initiated in the ways of women, Ivor and I were playing puberty games in the back room.

URSULA: That back room!

[*IVOR enters, opening a screen of pin-up pictures up to nineteen-forty-three.*]

FRANK: You didn't come there till you were fourteen.

URSULA: Will there ever be a sexier room?

FRANK: One afternoon, if you'd been five minutes earlier, you'd have caught us at our games.

[*IVOR, now sixteen and in sports clothes, takes a cigarette from a tin and lights up.*]

URSULA: What games?

FRANK: I suppose there's no harm telling you now.

IVOR: Frank. [*He leans by the door.*]

URSULA: What harm could there be?

FRANK: Losing face.

URSULA: What does it matter now?

[*IVOR and YOUNG FRANK laugh.*]

FRANK: All right.

[*YOUNG FRANK follows IVOR on. Now sixteen years, he wears mother's headscarf, skirt, shoes, blouse, padded brassière; also lipstick, pencilled eyebrows, rouged cheeks, etc. He carries his own clothes in a case and puts them on the sofa.*]

URSULA: Oh, no!

FRANK: Yes.

URSULA: It's Denise Carter to the life.

YOUNG FRANK: Give us a cigarette.

[*IVOR offers his tin. YOUNG FRANK lights up.*]

URSULA [*laughing*]: Why didn't you ever tell me?

[FRANK *shrugs, watching her watch* YOUNG FRANK.]

And now you stand here wishing you had. Wondering what I'd have said.

FRANK: Yes.

IVOR: That was terrific, man!

YOUNG FRANK: What about the Yank sentry? [*He takes off his make-up.*] What did you do when he whistled after me?

IVOR: Nothing.

YOUNG FRANK: I felt all funny. Bit scared.

URSULA [*sympathetically*]: Aaah! [*She goes to Frank and kisses him, maternally.*]

IVOR: Hey, be great if your mum wears these clothes next time she goes past the orphanage and that Yank whistles at her thinking it's you again!

YOUNG FRANK: They whistle at Amy anyway.

IVOR: My old man said, 'Those Yanks go for anything in skirts between eight and eighty.'

YOUNG FRANK: Old Philip would say that, wallowing about and dreaming of terrific sexual orgies. [*Hard 'g'.*] The English are all jealous 'cause the Yanks get all the girls – but I'd go with a Yank if I was a girl.

URSULA: Does that mean, if Ivor hadn't been with you, you'd have spoken to the sentry?

FRANK: I'd never even have gone outside alone. Now I think of it, people must have known I was a boy. They *must* have.

IVOR: Hey, man, you know when you toss off –

YOUNG FRANK: Yeah.

IVOR: – d'you pretend you're a man or a woman?

YOUNG FRANK: I keep changing about. Sometimes I'm a slave girl like Hedy Lamarr and my master whips me a lot and I cringe and beg for mercy. Then I come in and the brave bloke . . .

IVOR: Alan Ladd?

YOUNG FRANK: Yeah – keep changing round.

IVOR: I pretend I'm the bloke all the time.

[*They smoke for a while.* IVOR *coughs.* YOUNG FRANK *begins changing into his own clothes.*]

YOUNG FRANK: Hey, you know Jacobs in Four A.

IVOR: Terrific swot, yeah.

YOUNG FRANK: I saw his tool when we changed for gym. You seen it?

IVOR: No.

YOUNG FRANK: It's different to everyone else's.

IVOR: More like a knob.

YOUNG FRANK: Yeah.

IVOR: I've seen some like that.

FRANK: We knew so little about the Jews.

URSULA: They were in the Bible and Shakespeare.

FRANK: But that was nothing to do with Jacobs of Four A.

URSULA: And my uncle sometimes made a veiled remark about band-leaders.

FRANK: When you think what was happening a few hundred miles away!

URSULA: And our history lessons were still about Clive and Wolfe and Arkwright's Spinning Jenny.

YOUNG FRANK: Another thing about old Jacobs – he never does Divinity.

IVOR: Wish I didn't. Divinity's a dead loss.

YOUNG FRANK: Know what old Muller told me?

IVOR: What?

YOUNG FRANK: If a bod and a woman are shagging and she gets frightened by a mouse or something, her minge can tighten up and the bod can't get it out.

IVOR: Togger White told me that. He said they come from the hospital and throw buckets of water over them and –

YOUNG FRANK: Cri-kee!

IVOR: – if that doesn't loosen it, they have to put them on a stretcher and carry them out to the ambulance.

YOUNG FRANK: With all the neighbours looking!

IVOR: And sometimes they have to operate.

YOUNG FRANK: Cut it off?

IVOR: He didn't say. He said it used to happen a lot during the Blitz. A bomb used to frighten the woman and . . . [*He makes a strangled face and sounds.*]

YOUNG FRANK: Terrific agony, man.

IVOR: Terrific embarrassment. Would you like to have been a woman?

YOUNG FRANK: No.

IVOR: Wish you had been. Be wizard to be terrific friends with a woman.

YOUNG FRANK: Wouldn't have minded having tits.

[*By this time* YOUNG FRANK *has changed into his boy's shoes, trousers, etc., but still wears the bra. He pushes out his chest.* IVOR *touches the padded bra.*]

FRANK: That's enough!

[*The doorbell rings,* IVOR *and* YOUNG FRANK *jump up.*]

IVOR: Your mum?

YOUNG FRANK: She's at the aircraft factory. And Hitler's in Newton Abbot till Friday. You go and see.

[YOUNG FRANK *fans away smoke, then puts on a record of Chicago jazz.* IVOR *goes.*]

URSULA: I always passed your house on the way home and when I saw Ivor's bike outside I knew you must be in. Of course it was safe if there were two of you.

FRANK: You'd have been even safer alone. I used to kiss you sometimes in front of Ivor just to prove myself.

URSULA: But I didn't know that. I thought you were experienced.

FRANK: The lost opportunities!

[YOUNG FRANK, *his change finished, puts his mother's clothes away in the case.* IVOR *enters with* YOUNG URSULA, *fourteen, wearing school uniform and carrying a satchel.* YOUNG FRANK *is jazzing. He sees* YOUNG URSULA *and groans.*]

YOUNG URSULA: Terrific pong.

YOUNG FRANK: We been smoking.

YOUNG URSULA: Pong of lipstick.

[*Pause.*]

IVOR: Been making up. We're going to do a Marx Brothers sketch at the end-of-term show.

YOUNG URSULA [*approaching* YOUNG FRANK]: Still got some on your face. Smells nice. Sexy.

[*She touches his face, smells her hand.* IVOR *and* YOUNG FRANK *groan.* IVOR *lies on the sofa.* YOUNG URSULA *goes to look at the pin-ups.*]

This Harry James?

[*The boys croak and groan with laughter.*]

31

YOUNG FRANK: No. Mantovani.

YOUNG URSULA: No, it's not. Is it?

YOUNG FRANK: No. It's Eddie Condon.

URSULA: You weren't the easiest boys to make advances to.

YOUNG FRANK: How's life among the common folk?

IVOR: The salt of the earth?

YOUNG URSULA: How d'you know what it's like where I live? You never come.

YOUNG FRANK: Don't want to.

FRANK: I was too frightened. Alone with you on your home ground! You might have found out how little I knew.

YOUNG FRANK: Some of the common folk might breathe on me and give me a disease.

IVOR: They're the sort of people when they go to the pictures think it's all acted on the roof of the cinema and reflected down on to the screen by mirrors.

YOUNG URSULA: They don't!

IVOR: I argued with one of them.

YOUNG URSULA: What did he say?

IVOR: Hit me in the belly-button.

YOUNG FRANK: That's how they finish every discussion, the plebs.

IVOR: I shouted 'Brawn versus Brain', but he was half-way back to his slum by then.

[IVOR and YOUNG FRANK laugh and jeer.]

YOUNG URSULA: Got any maths homework?

YOUNG FRANK: Got some simultaneous equations for Thursday.

YOUNG URSULA: Easy. Do yours if you do my composition. This week it's 'My Ideal Birthday Party'.

[The record finishes. YOUNG FRANK takes off the arm. Shuts the door.]

Shall I tell you what I'd like and you can say it in wizard English?

IVOR: Hellish boring.

[YOUNG URSULA sits on YOUNG FRANK's lap.]

YOUNG URSULA [ignoring him]: I should like all the best-looking boys to come to it and each of them to have a girl except you. And we should play sardines and I'd be hiding in the Anderson shelter and you'd find me straight away.

FRANK [admiring]: You were so rude!

YOUNG URSULA: And all the others would give up looking and I'd be your prisoner.

YOUNG FRANK: Better not put that.

YOUNG URSULA: Why not?

YOUNG FRANK: Get kicked out.

[YOUNG URSULA *smiles and takes his hand*.]

YOUNG URSULA: How you getting on with School Certificate?

YOUNG FRANK: Okay in French, English and History.

IVOR: That'll be enough to get you into the Civil Service. Make your old man happy.

YOUNG URSULA: Mummy says I've got to matriculate as a present for Daddy when he comes home.

IVOR: We're not bothering.

YOUNG URSULA: You're no good at school, anyway. Only art.

IVOR: What good's School Certificate to a Film Director?

FRANK [*scornfully*]: Film Director!

IVOR: Frank and I are going into films.

FRANK: Ten years later I had to slog away for A levels in the evenings. As a first step to getting my external degree.

YOUNG URSULA: Frank's father thinks you bring him down.

YOUNG FRANK: We know that. 'You want to drop that crackpot Ivor, boy . . .'

IVOR [*imitating*]: 'He's beyond my comprehension.'

YOUNG FRANK: Show her your drawing of your parents, Ive.

[IVOR *takes a drawing from his pocket and shows* YOUNG URSULA.]

IVOR: My parents and Fran's at one of their hellish boring bridge parties. There's your mum puffing a Craven A and your dad with a great load of black market sweets for my mum. My mum's false teeth have got stuck on a toffee. And there's my old man pretending to read the rules of bridge but really it's a picture of a wore.

[*Pause.* YOUNG URSULA *looks at the picture.*]

YOUNG URSULA: A what?

IVOR: A wore. That pin-up girl in bra and panties.

YOUNG URSULA: Whore, isn't it, Fran?

YOUNG FRANK [*thinking*]: Dunno.

IVOR: *Wore* it is.

YOUNG FRANK: No, hang on. I remember the blackmailed wreck reading it aloud . . .

YOUNG URSULA: Who's the blackmailed wreck?

YOUNG FRANK: Our English master. Now I think of it, you must be right, Urse.

   'Thou rascal beadle, hold thy bloody hand,

   Why dost thou lash that whore? Strip thine own back . . .'

YOUNG URSULA: *King Lear* – terrific!

YOUNG FRANK: 'Thou hotly lusts to use her in that sport . . .'

YOUNG URSULA: Kind. 'That kind for which thou whipst her.'

YOUNG FRANK: Yeah.

   [*Pause.* IVOR *moves away, folding up his picture.*]

IVOR: I might do a whole great series of these.

YOUNG URSULA: Hey, half past four! I've got to get my mother's tea by the time she's home from the factory. [*She prepares to go.*]

URSULA: Making bombers and getting a decent wage for the first time.

FRANK: And your father was in North Africa.

URSULA: Yes. The government had found him a job at last. After keeping him out of work for most of the thirties.

YOUNG URSULA: You'll do my composition?

YOUNG FRANK: I'll give you my algebra downstairs.

FRANK: Whatever did he think he was defending? The right to be on the dole?

URSULA: Oh, the poor are always more patriotic in every country. Only the rich are international. Our rich had made friends with Hitler before and they'd have done it again if we'd lost. But the poor would have been in labour camps.

FRANK: They didn't *know* that at the time. Not till we saw the newsreels of Buchenwald. During the war all we had was Churchill's word for it.

URSULA: Surely he didn't say much about that. A lot about Going Forward Together.

FRANK: That's funny, too, from a man who knew so little about us he'd never even travelled on a bus. [*To the audience*]. *Never once!*

URSULA: 'We shall fight on the fields,' he said, and a lot of people who'd hardly *seen* a field suddenly felt they were the yeomen of

England. Can you imagine him in my mother's lounge?

FRANK [*imitating Churchill*]: As I look around me at this humble hearth – the chair of uncut moquette – the wireless shaped like an Aztec temple – the Polyfoto of the absent father in uniform . . . the years fall away. I see another Agincourt, another Waterloo.

URSULA: We all thought he was lovely, though.

FRANK: I remember hating him when he came to inspect our officer material in the Training Corps at school and the rest of us had to stand and cheer and I didn't get home in time to hear the Radio Rhythm Club. And as for understanding what he represented . . .

URSULA: Nobody in our circles understood anything. That was left to the Brains Trust.

FRANK: None the less there were pleasures, never to be equalled! Listening to jazz. Imitating our elders. Oh Christ, those years we lost before the flesh of your thighs collapsed and the whites of my eyes turned red! No wonder you've lost interest *now!*

[YOUNG URSULA *folds her arms impatiently as she sees an old argument coming.*]

No wonder it's 'I don't mind as long as we have the light out' or 'Quick then before I drop off . . .'

URSULA: I sometimes want it just as much as you.

FRANK: Too much too young, that's your trouble.

URSULA: Too little too late. Why dwell on it?

FRANK: Because I can't help it. Still emotionally in that back room, my mind a collage of pin-ups, craving the promiscuity you had and I missed.

URSULA: I wasn't promiscuous in fact —

FRANK: Come on —

URSULA: – not for long, anyway —

FRANK: – ah!

URSULA [*to the audience*]: Only long enough to discover I don't like being treated as just a body.

[FRANK *approaches behind and embraces her. She wearily removes his arms.*]

FRANK: And I'm always afraid women are only after my mind. Wish someone would treat me as a body.

URSULA: You've got your chance. You're free. With three dependent kids, no man's going to bother, I'll *have* to make do with memories. [*She goes towards the door.*]

FRANK: Easy for you —

[URSULA *goes, closing the door.*]

[*Shouting after her.*] – with memories stretching back to the Year One! [*To the audience.*] Memories of meadows – sand-dunes – innumerable divans – the upper decks of buses – once, even she told me, a wing of the Bodleian Library. [*He moves distractedly.*] But mine! Please!

[*The* CHINESE ILLUSIONIST *from the concert party enters without make-up but wearing a cheap silk Chinese kimono. He is smoking a cigarette.*]

MR MAGIC: I think it's so important to wear the proper clothes for anything, don't you, Frank? Even in our early lessons, before we go to the Baths, it's best to get the feel.

[YOUNG FRANK *comes in in swimming trunks, with a vest.*]

And so few boys do what you tell them, d'you know that?

[MR MAGIC *makes the cigarette disappear, then reappear.* YOUNG FRANK *stares.*]

I've had boys working for me. Some of my assistants. Neither use nor ornament, really. I'm not saying I'm not fond of them, they're sweet boys at heart, but you're all the same, aren't you, full of mischief. [*He takes a cigarette from* FRANK'*s ear.*]

YOUNG FRANK: That's terrific, that. I'm just learning but it's hellish hard.

MR MAGIC: You stay and work with me, Frank, I'll teach you all the tricks you've ever seen. And quite a few you haven't. [*He throws the cigarette in the air and it disappears.*]

FRANK: A sad old queen.

MR MAGIC: You lack technique, that's all.

FRANK: Well, old? I suppose he was a bit older than I am now.

MR MAGIC: Next time you're in London, you mention my name to any of the impresarios in Cambridge Circus. They'll say, 'There's no finer artiste in the business than Li Chang.'

FRANK: Alias, Mister Magic, alias Walter Chambers —

MR MAGIC: Never anything cheap and nasty —

FRANK: – described as a magician, of no fixed abode —

MR MAGIC: – never anything artistically degrading, like some you see, with their half-naked tarty girls, their great chests bulging out.

FRANK: – sentenced to six months . . .

MR MAGIC: Nothing to turn your stomach. [*He sits.*] We'll have to think of a name for you. Wun Hung Down. How's that?

> [YOUNG FRANK *looks cold.*]

Uncle's only joking. What about this breast stroke?

FRANK: No.

MR MAGIC: Come and sit here.

> [MR MAGIC *holds out his hand towards him.* YOUNG FRANK *approaches and* MR MAGIC *sits him on his knee. He looks awkward.*]

Can you swim at all?

FRANK: No.

MR MAGIC: Float?

> [YOUNG FRANK *shakes his head.*]

Let's start with floating. Your mother knows where you are, I suppose.

YOUNG FRANK: She knows we're rehearsing, yes. She's gone to my gran's this evening.

MR MAGIC: Now imagine yourself on the surface of the water. Completely relaxed.

FRANK [*moving quickly, dismissing them*]: No more!

> [YOUNG FRANK *looks at him, then jumps from* MR MAGIC's *lap and runs off by the door he came from.*]

MR MAGIC [*calling after him*]: Frank! Whatever's the matter? What a strange boy you are! Honestly!

FRANK [*shutting his eyes as though to dismiss the thought*]: Get off, get out!

MR MAGIC [*to him*]: Don't you shout at me. You can't push people out as easily as that!

FRANK: Can't I! [*He moves swiftly towards* MR MAGIC.]

> [MR MAGIC *goes, leaving the door open.* FRANK *slams the door and holds it shut.* MR MAGIC *opens another door nearby.*]

MR MAGIC: All your life you'll be wincing at the memory.

> [FRANK *leaves the door, runs to shut him out again. The sound of footsteps continues behind the wall and* FRANK *follows the sound until it stops on the opposite side of the stage. He waits for the door*

to open. It does not. He opens it wide. Nobody there. MR MAGIC
opens the door by which he first went out.]

I'm part of your mental landscape for ever, duckie, whether you
like it or . . .

[FRANK *runs to the door and slams* MR MAGIC *out.* MR MAGIC
laughs behind the door.]

FRANK [*to the audience*]: I ran home in the summer evening,
frightened and mystified. I thought only boys did that and then
only until they could find a girl. But why men? And old heavy-
breathing men with brown teeth. Some of the girls I passed had
great chests bulging out which far from turned my stomach.
Ursula was waiting with the rest of our crowd in the local park
but first I had to collect some cigarettes I'd stolen from Dad and
hidden up my bedroom chimney. But I was not to be let off so
easily, there was more bewildering unpleasantness to come. He
appeared in a cloud of steam from the bathroom as I climbed the
stairs and insisted I take over his water. 'I've used rather more
than the regulation five inches, boy, and we should help the war
effort any way we can.' The bathroom was exhausted, the walls
sweating, the soap melting in the high humidity. And while I lay
in this warm soup, he pottered about from room to room,
gradually dressing.

[CHARLES *comes on, wearing an open shirt without collar and
trousers, but with bare feet. Around his neck is a towel and he is
reading a book. He carries one slipper and one shoe. He speaks to*
YOUNG FRANK *off.*]

CHARLES: Cleanliness is next to godliness. I shall always remember
my mother saying that.

FRANK: As soon as possible, I rubbed down and pulled on my
trousers.

CHARLES: And we had no bathroom in those days, boy, only a hip-
bath before the fire and a clothes-horse round with towels hung
over it. I recall one night my brother saying to Sister Emma,
'Don't come in when one of us boys is in the bath, Sis. You never
know what we may be a-doing-of.' [*He laughs at the thought,
consults the book and rolls up his left trouser-leg, sitting on a chair level
to do so. He hears a movement off, and goes to look.*] You out? Bring
the *Reynolds News* from the attic stairway, will you, Son?

FRANK: Later on Ivor taught me swimming in the public baths with an inflatable belt.

[CHARLES *opens a door to reveal shelves full of patent medicines and toilet preparations in jars, bottles, tubes and tins.*]

Ten years of samples. Friar's Balsam, Cascara, Vapour Rub, Golden Eye Ointment. It was among his boasts that he never recommended any line he hadn't personally tested.

[CHARLES *takes down a bottle, a wad of cotton wool and nail-scissors.* YOUNG FRANK *comes on, wearing trousers, shirt and tie, no shoes or socks. He carries a newspaper.*]

CHARLES [*taking the paper*]: It's Brother Edwin about whom I'm talking. Used to frighten the life out of Sister Emma. [*He places the medicines and other articles on a raised surface and spreads the paper on the floor by his seat.*]

[YOUNG FRANK *continues tying his tie.*]

D'you know his term for the convenience, Frank?

YOUNG FRANK: The Gold Mine.

CHARLES: He used to call it The Gold Mine. [*He laughs.*]

[YOUNG FRANK *looks at his eccentric clothes, shrugs and starts to go as* CHARLES *turns to him.*]

Buzfuz!

YOUNG FRANK: What?

CHARLES: What's 'what'?

YOUNG FRANK: What is it?

CHARLES: 'What is it, *Dad?*'

YOUNG FRANK: I'm just off out.

CHARLES: Where are you going, Son?

YOUNG FRANK: Meeting Ivor in the park.

CHARLES: And what's that round your neck?

YOUNG FRANK: A dragon tie. Ivor painted it. The dragon's luminous.

CHARLES: What a way to dress!

YOUNG FRANK: What about *you!* What's your trouser rolled up for?

CHARLES: For what is your trouser rolled up? [*He pauses. He realises this is not quite right yet.*]

YOUNG FRANK [*smiles*]: Up for what is your trouser rolled?

CHARLES: Don't talk big, you make yourself look small.

YOUNG FRANK: Why one slipper and one shoe?

CHARLES: If I'm doing it, Son, you can bet there's a jolly proper reason. I wouldn't walk through the streets like it, any more than I'd wear a luminous dragon tie and chase young Ursula and her friends in and out of the air-raid shelters.

YOUNG FRANK: Who said we do?

CHARLES: Mister Lewthwaite lives beside the park overlooking the static water tank. He can see you from his bedroom window.

YOUNG FRANK: I'll bet he's up there every night with b-b-b-binoculars.

CHARLES: I hear you making fun of anyone's afflictions, you'll feel the back of my hand.

YOUNG FRANK: *You* do it!

CHARLES: Don't answer back.

YOUNG FRANK: You're always doing it. You always call him tah-tah-Tiny Lewthwaite.

CHARLES: Mister Lewthwaite's an influential man these days. Chief Buyer in Fancy Goods. And what's more, a Master Mason. He's sponsoring me for admission to his lodge. And that's why I'm dressed like this, you great coon. [*He approaches* YOUNG FRANK *and seizes his ear.*] How long since you cleaned your ears out?

[YOUNG FRANK *groans.* CHARLES *peers in.*]

By Jove! [*Takes a handkerchief from his pocket, folds and twists it into a flexible spike.*]

[YOUNG FRANK *finishes his tie and makes to go.*]

Stand still when I tell you. [*He holds* FRANK's *head, plunges the spike into one ear.*]

YOUNG FRANK: Ow!

CHARLES: Don't jerk away.

YOUNG FRANK: You'll break my eardrum. Uv'you got a matchstick in that hankie?

CHARLES: Don't be absurd.

YOUNG FRANK: You had last time. Nearly deafened me for life.

CHARLES: I wonder you're not deaf already. Enough wax here to furnish Madame Tussauds.

YOUNG FRANK [*breaking away*]: Hey, shurrup!

CHARLES: Shurrup? What's shurrup? If I'd spoken like that to my father, I'd have felt the back of his hand.

YOUNG FRANK [*moving away*]: You're not going to hold him up as an example, are you? A drunkard.

[CHARLES *sits down, cutting his toenails into the newspaper.*]

CHARLES: Yes, and when he was drunk, he couldn't move very fast, he couldn't see to hit us. We boys got pretty nimble dodging his fists. He used to shout: 'Come here, you little b-u-double-g-a-r!'

YOUNG FRANK: *E*-r.

CHARLES: Pardon?

YOUNG FRANK: B-u-double-g-*e*-r.

CHARLES: How d'you know?

YOUNG FRANK: I've seen it written on walls.

FRANK: In conveniences.

CHARLES: You shouldn't *read* it! You must develop the habit of turning away from smut in any size, shape or form. D'you think as a grocery traveller I haven't had to wrestle with temptation on the road? D'you think my colleagues in commercial hotels don't hang about the lounge-bars swapping smut? They sometimes say, 'Come along, Charles, be social, have a lemonade shandy with us,' and I look into the bar and smell the booze and see the landlord drawing ale and d'you know what always comes to me, Son?

YOUNG FRANK: The words of . . .

CHARLES: The words of Shakespeare, 'How like a fawning publican he looks!' [*He continues cutting his toenails into the paper.*]

[YOUNG FRANK *waits.*]

[*Standing.*] Get a bottle of wintergreen, I'll rub some into your legs.

YOUNG FRANK: I don't want that terrific pongy stuff wherever I go.

CHARLES: I'll empty these clippings out of the window. Do the garden good. [*He shakes the newspaper over the audience, folds it and puts it on the seat.*] And women, too, on the road. Normally decent but after a few gins, they make their loins available. These are bad times, Frank, you've been going round entertaining, you've met girls whose conduct isn't quite what it should be, I dare say. [*He fetches a bandage from the cupboard and begins binding his ankle.*]

FRANK: Had he heard about my hand beneath the dancer's thighs? Say something!

YOUNG FRANK: Why d'you put that bandage round your leg?

CHARLES: You surely know already. My varicose veins?

YOUNG FRANK [*innocently*]: No.

CHARLES: During the First World War, as I was due for military service. Months in hospital, a hundred stitches. That – together with the deafness caused by that clout across the ear – saved me from the trenches, so I'm not sorry. If the war's still on when you're eighteen, you may get out with bed-wetting.

YOUNG FRANK: I'd rather go to war than wet the bed.

CHARLES: That shows a very decent spirit. But use your savvy, there are always plenty of piecans prepared to fight.

YOUNG FRANK: Your veins must be all right now. Why d'you still wear the bandage?

CHARLES: Nobody's ever told me to stop. Besides, it keeps my ankles cosy.

[YOUNG FRANK *grins.*]

FRANK [*praying*]: Ursula, please wait for me, I'm coming as soon as I can get away.

CHARLES: Well, while you're so busy reading smut on the walls of conveniences, perhaps you could spare a glance for the Ministry of Health's announcement about g-o-n-o-r-h, no, double r-h-e-a, no . . .

YOUNG FRANK: Double-r-h-o-e-a.

FRANK: I could spell anything.

CHARLES: Your mother and I have never interfered, only tried to set an example of clean living. You follow me?

YOUNG FRANK: Okay. Going to see Ivor now.

CHARLES: Wait a jiffy. Before you go out fondling young Ursula, you can help . . .

YOUNG FRANK: I'm seeing Ivor!

CHARLES: Don't tell me fibs, Son. I called at Ivor's on the way home with a pound of bacon for his father. They're all going to his aunt's for the evening. Now tell me honestly, Son, where are you going?

YOUNG FRANK: The park.

CHARLES: To fondle young Ursula?

YOUNG FRANK: No.

FRANK: If her mother got to hear of it, she'd keep her in.

YOUNG FRANK: Honestly.

CHARLES: You tell me honestly, boy, I believe you. [*He stands and faces him.*]

    [YOUNG FRANK *looks at his feet.*]

    Do your finger-nails need cutting?

YOUNG FRANK: No. [*He turns to go.*]

CHARLES: Your toenails?

YOUNG FRANK: No. [*He turns to go again.*]

CHARLES: What's the hurry? Here, take this book. I'm trying to learn the ceremonial. [*He gives him the book.*]

YOUNG FRANK: What for?

CHARLES: My initiation. Once all the applications have gone through and no-one rules me out, I get the call, you see.

YOUNG FRANK [*reading the book*]: It says you've got to surrender all your money.

CHARLES: I've left it on the chest of drawers, all five and eightpence-half-penny. It's so that when in future I meet a Mason needing help, I call to mind the day I was received, poor and penniless.

YOUNG FRANK: You get the money back afterwards?

CHARLES: Well, what d'you think, you great pudden?

YOUNG FRANK: It's all a fake then.

CHARLES: The entire movement of Freemasonry a fake? You're going to set yourself up in opposition to all the great men who've believed in it, are you?

YOUNG FRANK: What great men? Tiny Lewthwaite?

CHARLES: Mozart, Sir Christopher Wren, George Washington, Frederick the Great, Garibaldi, our present King. Percy Tombs.

YOUNG FRANK: Who?

CHARLES: Mister Tombs, Grocery Manager for the whole South-West division. He's the Worshipful Master of the Lodge.

YOUNG FRANK: You're supposed to be blindfold.

CHARLES: Hoodwinked, yes. [*He has his handkerchief ready, and blindfolds himself.*]

YOUNG FRANK: And wear a noose round your neck.

CHARLES: You haven't a handy length of rope?

YOUNG FRANK: No.

CHARLES: We'll take it as read. Now. The Tyler escorts me to the threshold and the Inner Guard, his dagger to my bare breast, leads me before the Worshipful Master. He asks certain ritual questions, the answers to which I mean to commit to memory.

FRANK: But his memory was as cluttered as mine is now.

CHARLES: With my gift of the gab, I should find no difficulty responding in a loud clear voice like a sergeant-major. Then – with my right foot formed in a square – I kneel before the Worshipful Master.

YOUNG FRANK: Percy Tombs.

CHARLES [kneeling]: Mister Tombs. And swear not to reveal – um – what is it, Sonny Jim?

YOUNG FRANK: Write, indite, carve, mark, engrave or otherwise delineate . . .

[CHARLES repeats these words quietly after him.]

CHARLES: The secret of Masonry, yes. These are the bits I must get off pat.

YOUNG FRANK: On pain of having your throat cut across, your tongue torn out by the root and buried in the sand of the sea at low water mark – or a cable's length from the shore. Can't wait to tell old Ivor this.

CHARLES [sitting back on his heels]: You what? You dare, boy!

YOUNG FRANK: To think of old Tiny Lewthwaite doing this terrific Bela Lugosi act . . .

CHARLES: Not so much of the jolly old buck! The disrespect.

YOUNG FRANK: Well, it's so hellish corny.

CHARLES: It's dashed easy for you to sneer, boy, you're not away from home Monday to Friday wondering how to fill the time in draughty commercial hotels. You're not standing around in God-forsaken grocery departments awaiting the pleasure of foul-mouthed branch managers, swallowing their insults, laughing at their smut. D'you think I like that?

YOUNG FRANK: Dunno.

CHARLES: Dunno? What's dunno? No's the answer. Any more than Mister Lewthwaite liked it. And how did he get a job at H.Q.? When did he move from traveller to buyer? Six months after joining the Masonic Lodge.

YOUNG FRANK: Okay, I'm going out . . .

CHARLES [*taking* YOUNG FRANK's *arm*.] Listen till I've finished. How else am I to get promotion, bring myself to the attention of the powers-to-be?

FRANK: I felt he was leading somewhere. But where?

CHARLES: Mister Tombs is one of those powers, boy. A very big cheese in the grocery trade. And a Worshipful Master.

YOUNG FRANK: Be getting dark soon . . .

CHARLES [*suddenly seizing his hands*]: Where you off to, eh?

YOUNG FRANK: The park, I told you.

[YOUNG FRANK *moves slightly, pulling* CHARLES *so that he has to move on his knees.* CHARLES *strengthens his grip on* YOUNG FRANK.]

CHARLES: Going to your mother, Son?

YOUNG FRANK: Eh?

CHARLES: Have you said you'd meet your mother?

YOUNG FRANK: No. She's at Gran's place.

CHARLES: That's where she *says* she is. But you know more than I do, you're here all week. She *says* she's spending all this time at her mother's but – do you think she is, Son?

YOUNG FRANK: Why not?

CHARLES: You know.

FRANK: I didn't *know*. It was the first I'd heard of it.

[YOUNG FRANK *tries to go.*]

CHARLES: Frank, don't go to her!

YOUNG FRANK: I'm not.

CHARLES: You're not seeing Ivor, you're not seeing Ursula, then where *are* you going if not to her? Listen, Son, if your mother left me, would you go with her? Please, Frank, if she goes – she might ask you to choose between us, you see what I mean, boy – well, look, stay with me, there's a good boy. Remember all I've done for you.

[FRANK *turns away, wincing at the memory.*]

YOUNG FRANK [*frightened*]: Going to the park . . .

CHARLES: Given you an education, put you by a nest-egg —

[YOUNG FRANK *stands, looking away.*]

– there's more in my will, if I don't change my mind.

FRANK [*wincing*]: I'm not sure he said that.

CHARLES: Frank!

FRANK: But he might have, which is all that matters.

CHARLES: I've had to be strict, coming home as I do at week-ends – and sometimes perhaps I seemed too strict – but it's all very well for your mother to spoil you – I don't seem able to talk to you.

YOUNG FRANK: All right. [*He stands for a long time.*]

CHARLES: Don't be late.

YOUNG FRANK: No.

[YOUNG FRANK *goes quickly.* CHARLES *unrolls his trouser leg, still kneeling.*]

FRANK: More than anything, I've inherited his sexual nature. Inasmuch as I understand it. A lack of mastery. Dependence.

[CHARLES *blows his nose in his handkerchief, wipes his face.*]

[*He turns to look at* CHARLES. *To him.*] I didn't mention it to her. Never mentioned those two encounters to anyone. Not even Ivor.

[CHARLES *does not seem to hear. He stands, puts away the slipper and shoe.*]

That should give you some satisfaction.

[CHARLES *shuts the door.* FRANK *turns to the audience.*]

Conveniently deaf. But it's true.

[CHARLES *goes off, taking the newspaper.*]

I was so keen to find Ursula that I at once forgot those manifestations of the male menopause. Didn't remember them again till years later. The church clock showed half past eight as I free-wheeled past the water-tank and glimpsed our crowd lounging by the shelters. For twenty minutes we jeered at each other and groaned with derision at the girls' stupidity. Now and then there was a chase in and out of the shelters and Ursula could always find me inside by my quietly glowing dragon. Then a sudden sound, a shouting of orders, some cheers and the beautiful silver barrage balloon lurched up behind the bandstand. It had broken moorings and was now carried away over the rooftops – and giggling Waafs in battledress pursued it through the streets to mark where it fell. More than enough to make you forget your family – that great shining whale racing on the evening breeze! [*He shuts his eyes, pulls himself back to the present, looks about, then at his wrist-watch.*] Time to go for a bite.

[*He goes to the door, opens it, pauses in the opening. Then goes on to the audience as an actor.*] If you'd like a drink, there are several bars you can go to.

[*Another door opens and* YOUNG FRANK *appears.*]

YOUNG FRANK [*imitating* CHARLES]: What's 'you can go to', you great coon?

[IVOR *appears at another door.*]

IVOR [*also imitating* CHARLES]: To which you can go, boy . . .

YOUNG FRANK: ⎱
IVOR: ⎰ To which you can go.

[CHARLES *appears at another door.*]

CHARLES: Don't talk so big, you make yourself look small.

[AMY *appears at another door.*]

AMY: Oh, do stop going on at the boy.

[MR MAGIC *appears at another door.*]

MR MAGIC: Boy! That was a long time ago and through a gauze!

FRANK: Can't you leave me alone for ten minutes!

[*They all slam the doors together.*]

ACT TWO

During the interval there is another record recital
'The Day War Broke Out' by Robb Wilton
'Don't Get Around Much Any More' by Duke Ellington
'Room 504' by Hutch
'Milkman, keep those bottles quiet' by the Andrews Sisters
'High Society' by Bing Crosby
Towards the end of the records, FRANK *comes in finishing a newspaper of fish and chips. He stands listening to the music, then eats the last chip, screws up the paper and discards it in the bin below the record-player. He wipes his hands on his handkerchief. He alerts the source of the speakers from records to tapes, sets one playing, and steps back. The tape continues with a recording of* FRANK, URSULA *and the younger children singing 'A Song of Sixpence'.* FRANK *leaves it playing, goes off, and returns at the end with a glass of milk. He stares again at the recorder. After the songs,* FRANK *and* URSULA *tell the children how well they sang.*

FRANK [*on tape*]: Now shall we listen to that?
> [*Recording ends.* FRANK *switches the tape off, closes the door, and comes down, drinking.*]
FRANK: Is the family inevitable? Even our religion is based on a family – and with *two* fathers. I always identify with Joseph, the best-known victim of *droit de seigneur* – sawing away out the back while angels are streaming in and out of the bedroom window. When we're kids we don't really question the adult world, just blunder about in a jungle of meaningless rules. But at twelve or so, confused by erections and periods, armed with the pure logic of puberty, we start fighting in earnest. Which scares our parents and sets up conflict. French verbs and wanker's doom. Then at last – escape, freedom ! – lovely to start with but eventually we need a regular cuddle at night and there's no other way but a family of our own choice. One without rules. Paradise. But before we know it, most of our time's spent dabbing snot, healing greedy screams with ice-lollies – saying do this, don't do that – law-and-order becomes first a necessity, then, if you're not very careful,

attractive for its own sake. Our wives, who were sex-pots a minute ago, are nagging shrews from a seaside postcard. Our girl Jenny, at three, already took profound pleasure in organisation, bullying her dolls, lining them up, smacking her teddies and being motherly. When Matthew was born, of course, and began to grow, she set him down amongst the teddies and nagged him, for all the world as though they were married. I used to watch him dreaming through it all and in the end he'd crawl away and she'd come howling that he'd spoilt the game. Our lives are an extrapolation of infancy – termagant girls and dreamy boys. Then of course, infants are imitating adults. So how do you break the circle? [*He pauses and moves away.*] Well, I'm trying.

[URSULA *comes in quietly and stands listening.*]

I'm going to take on the loneliness of bachelor life again. But with the loneliness a freedom, too – from family car-trips, children's telly, Wellington boots – fish-fingers . . .

URSULA: If you loved your children, you'd accept all that.

[*He turns to her.*]

FRANK: I love them.

URSULA: Not enough.

FRANK: What is 'enough'? There were times when I thought them the whole reason for living.

URSULA: On the Kibbutzim, they tried to break up families. Most of them have voted to have the children back.

FRANK: The women. I wonder what the men had to say. And the children for that matter. It'll take a couple of generations to form a proper opinion.

URSULA: And the opinion will be the same: the family's inevitable.

FRANK: Then God help us.

URSULA: And while working out this crappy theory did you ever consider me? My life afterwards? A woman of – [*She pauses.*] – past her best . . .

FRANK [*to the audience*]: Thirty-eight . . .

URSULA [*glancing at the audience, then smiling icily at* FRANK]: Thank you. With three children.

FRANK: Of course and it kept me with you for years. But you're tough, Ursula, you're a survivor. Other people tend to say, 'Wait till Ursula comes, she'll know what to do.' I knew you could manage without me far more easily than I . . .

URSULA: And do you think I *want* to be like that?

FRANK: You *are* like that.

URSULA: Because I have to be. With four people depending on me.

FRANK: That's my point. Without the family, you wouldn't. You and I could chase each other from room to room. But you spend more time buying potted geraniums than making love to me.

URSULA: Are we back to this? Who mentioned this? I'm talking about my life and what I should like to be.

FRANK: Well?

URSULA: I'd like to do what you do. Sit about all day with a lot of students and set the world to rights.

FRANK: Before we had kids you were so exciting.

URSULA: You're jealous of them.

FRANK: I think I had cause.

URSULA: It's your age. You remember it as better than it was.

FRANK: I remember. [*He opens the pin-up door.*]

    [YOUNG FRANK *comes on wearing nineteen-forty-five utility casuals, with* YOUNG URSULA *in school uniform, carrying a satchel.*]

YOUNG FRANK: How d'you get off hockey?

YOUNG URSULA: Forged an excuse-note.

URSULA: I was a clever counterfeiter. I used to forge everyone's notes.

    [YOUNG URSULA *drops her satchel and takes off her raincoat.*]

FRANK: Excited, breathless, gratified, but wishing I'd never asked you.

    [YOUNG FRANK *yawns.*]

URSULA: Scared as a rabbit with a snake, wondering when you'd start.

YOUNG URSULA: Your mum's out?

YOUNG FRANK: Pictures. And Dad's in Worcester. [*She sits.*]

YOUNG URSULA: Your holiday's nearly over.

YOUNG FRANK [*nodding*]: Go next week.

YOUNG URSULA: You frightened?

YOUNG FRANK: Glad to be getting away from this dump. With Ivor gone and everything . . .

FRANK: He'd been called up a few months before.

YOUNG URSULA: Have you heard from him again?

YOUNG FRANK: Nearly finished square-bashing. Sent some traffic drawings of the plebs. He says quite a few of them can't even read the comics. Blokes of eighteen and twenty can't even read!

YOUNG URSULA: Hellish dim.

[*He stands by her, yawns again. She stretches her legs out in front of her, looks at them. Then she takes his hand.*]

YOUNG URSULA: Hullo, Handsome.

YOUNG FRANK: Oh, Christ!

YOUNG URSULA: What d'you want me to say?

YOUNG FRANK: Hullo, Skinny.

YOUNG URSULA: You're not skinny, you're slim.

FRANK [*like someone watching a prizefight*]: Get on with it, man!

YOUNG URSULA [*kissing his hand*]: I like thin boys.

YOUNG FRANK: Then why've you been going round with that brawny crowd from near the Baths?

YOUNG URSULA: They were hellish boring.

URSULA: Because you seemed to prefer Ivor. But when he went I came running back.

YOUNG URSULA: All they talked about was getting in the air and shooting down Germans and Japs. They never saw it as a film like you and Ivor.

YOUNG FRANK: 'I can't stand any more, I tell you, let me go.'

FRANK: 'Pull yourself together, for Pete's sake, Jerry's watching.'

YOUNG URSULA: I like boys who make me laugh.

[*She stands, puts her arms round him, and kisses him on the mouth. He embraces her.*]

URSULA: I deserved a good hiding.

FRANK: You were marvellous, but look at me!

URSULA: When Dad was released, he took me in hand.

[YOUNG URSULA *pulls out* YOUNG FRANK's *shirt. He yawns.*]

YOUNG URSULA: You tired?

[*He shrugs.*]

YOUNG URSULA: Let's lie down. Shall we? [*She sits again.*] I'm hot. Aren't you? Hellish hot today.

[*He goes on his knees and takes off her shoes.*]

URSULA: This isn't nice at all.

FRANK: It's improving.

[YOUNG FRANK *kisses* YOUNG URSULA's *knee, then sits by her.*]

YOUNG URSULA: You're terrifically attractive, Frank.

FRANK: Tell her! Tell her she's attractive! Tell her about your dreams!

[YOUNG FRANK *plays with* YOUNG URSULA's *school tie. She waits. She unties it. He opens a shirt button. She opens one of his.*]

YOUNG URSULA: Quite a few hairs since last I looked.

YOUNG FRANK: Four.

FRANK: Mostly grey now.

YOUNG URSULA: I cried the other night in bed because I thought you might not come back.

YOUNG FRANK: Why not?

YOUNG URSULA: Might get killed.

YOUNG FRANK: The war's nearly over.

YOUNG URSULA: Not in the Far East.

FRANK: The Bomb was coming.

YOUNG FRANK: That's mostly the Yanks. They won't send me.

URSULA: But they did.

YOUNG URSULA: Shall I wait for you? While you're away.

YOUNG FRANK: If you like.

FRANK: What eloquence!

YOUNG URSULA: I'm fagged out. Shall we lie down?

[*She lies down and he leans over her.*]

URSULA: Why d'you have to dwell on this?

FRANK: You were wonderful.

[YOUNG FRANK *kisses her, then takes something from her cheek with his finger.*]

YOUNG URSULA: What is it?

FRANK: A piece of amalgam.

YOUNG URSULA: Silver stuff.

YOUNG FRANK: I had a tooth filled this morning.

FRANK: Remember that?

URSULA: Yes. I kept it in my souvenir box till you came home.

[CHARLES *comes in, wearing a suit and carrying a case. He shuts the door behind him.*]

YOUNG FRANK [*jumping up*]: That's the front door.

[YOUNG URSULA *gets up.*]

YOUNG URSULA: Are you sure?

YOUNG FRANK: Mum must have come home early.

CHARLES [*calling*]: Anyone home?

[YOUNG FRANK *and* URSULA *start dressing rapidly.*]

YOUNG FRANK: Hullo?

FRANK: I knew I had to answer.

URSULA: Why?

FRANK: If he'd thought I was out, he'd have gone to my room to read my diary.

URSULA: Would he, really?

FRANK: Yes. And found us –

CHARLES: You up there, boy?

YOUNG FRANK [*dressing*]: Coming down.

URSULA: Why?

FRANK: To see what I'd written about him.

URSULA: How d'you know he read it?

[CHARLES *puts his case on the sofa and opens it, pushing through the papers to find a paper bag. From this he takes a half-pound of butter and a packet of tea.*]

FRANK: He couldn't resist correcting what I'd put.

URSULA: 'Preposition at end of sentence'?

CHARLES [*shouting*]: Come on, noodle!

FRANK: Yes, or once, I remember, I had written: 'In a vase on the mantelpiece there is a Remembrance Poppy. Is the old man keeping it till next November to save a shilling?'

[YOUNG FRANK *and* YOUNG URSULA *go out by the same door.* CHARLES *unpacks half a pound of cheese and some biscuits. The pin-up screens close.*]

And he added in the margin, 'Do not tell untruths or show ingratitude to a father who has shown you every generosity.'

[YOUNG FRANK *and* YOUNG URSULA *enter by the same door as* CHARLES.]

YOUNG FRANK: Thought you were in Worcester.

CHARLES: The usual sunny welcome home. Hullo, young woman, are you quite well?

YOUNG URSULA: Hullo, Mister Bisley.

CHARLES: What are you a-doing of upstairs with Sonny Jim? My brother Edwin used to frighten the life out of Sister Emma, you know. He used to say, 'Don't come in when the old man is in the bath, Sis. You never know what he might be a-doing-of.'

YOUNG FRANK: I been helping her with her schoolwork.

CHARLES: Judging by the showing you made in your exams, she'd be better off without your help.

[YOUNG FRANK *groans*.]

You warm, Ursula? You look warm, your face is flushed. So's yours, boy. Open the window if you're warm. It was sweltering in Tewkesbury.

YOUNG FRANK: Why d'you come back then?

CHARLES: I'd completed all my calls in double-quick time and here I am, in person, the one and only, Charles the First and Foremost. And you can give me a hand unloading one or two samples from the car.

YOUNG FRANK [*taking a paper bag from the case*]: Some samples of fresh eggs here.

CHARLES: Leave them alone. They're a gift. Would your mother like a couple of eggs, Ursula? Naturally. Mister Lewthwaite of Fancy Goods, a real coon if ever there was one, said to me, 'There's massive supplies on the way from America.' I looked up at the ceiling, then at the window, then I looked him in the eye and I said, 'Oh?' very slowly, you know, boy, that frightens the life out of them.

YOUNG FRANK: Makes them curl up laughing.

CHARLES: I said, 'Then am I to assume that you are privy to Mister Attlee's innermost thoughts? Or have you received a p.c. from Mister Truman this a.m.? Good morning', and I walked off and left him gasping.

YOUNG FRANK: Left him thinking you were hellish corny.

CHARLES: Not so much of the jolly old buck, thank you, from a boy who can't even do up his shirt on the right buttons.

[CHARLES *begins unbuttoning* YOUNG FRANK's *shirt at the neck*.]

YOUNG FRANK [*embarrassed*]: I can do it.

CHARLES [*continuing to do it*]: Hold your tongue.

[YOUNG FRANK *suffers it*.]

URSULA: Touching you again, you see. He always struck me as a very tactile person, always trying to touch you and Mother, but you both avoided him.

CHARLES [*to* YOUNG URSULA]: Your buttons all right, young woman?

[YOUNG URSULA *giggles*.]

URSULA: I've always been ashamed of the way we must have appeared to him that day. And me only sixteen!

FRANK: I'll bet his puritan imagination ran riot.

CHARLES: You shouldn't go up to that back room amongst those photographs of uncovered girls. Might give you the wrong ideas, eh, boy? Might start uncovering herself. And if Buzfuz here starts making free with you, send him packing. Take a leaf from my mother's book. If the old man came sniffing round her in his cups, she'd say, 'Hands off, private property!' I've heard her.

YOUNG FRANK: No wonder he drank.

CHARLES: Your hair badly wants cutting.

[CHARLES *touches* YOUNG FRANK's *hair. He backs away*.]

URSULA: Touching again.

CHARLES: All curly in your neck. However. Look at that car standing out there. The only car in the avenue, it looks like showing off. Take these things to the kitchen, boy, pending your mother's return from the flicks. And both of you come and help unload.

[YOUNG FRANK *takes the packages*, CHARLES *closes the suitcase and holds it*. YOUNG URSULA *laughs*.]

D'you know this great coon has requested, nay demanded that the back room shall remain unaltered till he comes home from the army? Just fancy, His Majesty's Government, in their wisdom, have decided he's A1, in the pink and fit to defend our far-flung empire. Especially now he's stopped wetting the bed.

[CHARLES *laughs and goes off, followed by* YOUNG URSULA, *shyly*. YOUNG FRANK *goes by the other door*.]

FRANK [*shouting at the door by which* CHARLES *left*]: Insensitive, pre-Freudian clown!

[*The door opens and* CHARLES *looks in*.]

CHARLES: Don't raise your voice at me, Son.

[FRANK *slams the door on him*.]

URSULA: Did he keep the room as it was?

FRANK: Yes.

URSULA: I didn't go there again for years and the pin-up girls had gone by then.

FRANK: You were busy elsewhere.

URSULA: At school and then at college. My dad came home, with all the other men who'd voted Churchill out. He got a well-paid factory job and my brother and I went to college. Life was certainly better for us than before the war. I studied dressmaking.

FRANK: Funny name for it.

URSULA: What else would you call it?

FRANK: Dress removing?

URSULA [*understanding, and deciding*]: Right. [*She goes to the door.*]

FRANK: No, love, wait . . .

> [*But* URSULA *goes, shutting the door.*]

Ivor and I never met again till I was released. What my mother would have called a blessing in disguise. We vowed to write to each other every week and more or less kept the promise, but it was like a stale marriage. The crazy gags and caricatures of our adolescence weren't an adequate response to what I was seeing now: the end of British India, the cruelty of Calcutta, Ghandi's death. I knew that sooner or later I should have to tell him it was finished but sufficient unto the day, as my mother would have said.

> [AMY *enters from a door, aged forty-seven, dressed for nineteen-forty-eight.*]

AMY: You got home about – what? – half past two. Dad was in Cardiff so I'd had a spot of dinner on my own, after finishing the spring cleaning in the morning, because I wanted it looking nice. So I thought, 'I'll just sit down for ten minutes with a cork-tipped,' when this knock came and there you were. [*To the audience.*] Very sun-tanned but thin as a rake, I thought to myself, I'll soon fatten him up. You'd had dinner on the train, so I said, 'How about some tea?' and you said, 'Coffee,' you said you'd acquired the taste, and luckily there was just enough essence in the bottle.

FRANK: Before I'd drunk it, Ivor came on a second-hand motorbike and I had to struggle to remember our mutual vocabulary.

> [*The pin-up screens open. The bow window fades.* IVOR *comes on, a twenty-one-year-old civilian.* YOUNG FRANK *follows, tropical*

tan and uniform of R.A.S.C. private.]

YOUNG FRANK: It's so small.

IVOR: The houses look terrific small. I found that when I came home.

YOUNG FRANK: But otherwise unchanged.

IVOR: *You've* changed. You've got a posh voice.

AMY: How scruffy he looked.

[IVOR *and* YOUNG FRANK *are embarrassed.* YOUNG FRANK *studies the collage.*]

He still looks scruffy.

[AMY *goes.*]

IVOR: Like a record? One of the old ones. [*He opens the door revealing the player.*]

YOUNG FRANK: The acoustic gramophone!

IVOR: Acoustic? Bloody hell. Used to be 'wind-up'.

YOUNG FRANK [*with a shrug*]: 'Acoustic' is the proper word.

IVOR: Bloody hell. 'Maple Leaf Rag' – or Beiderbeck's 'Royal Garden'?

YOUNG FRANK: Tell the truth, Ivor, I find the insistent syncopation and predictable harmonies of jazz pretty boring these days.

IVOR [*in imitation posh*]: Oh, well, jolly good, what?

YOUNG FRANK: I've been listening a lot to Debussy and Ravel.

IVOR: Well, they were interested in jazz.

YOUNG FRANK: They transformed and elevated it.

FRANK: Poor prig.

[IVOR *shuts the door to the gramophone.*]

YOUNG FRANK: What's it like here?

IVOR: England? Bloody awful. Over in Germany you could get all the booze and fags you wanted, dead cheap. When I went first, you could get a Leica for a couple of bars of soap. Get a fraulein for a pound of coffee. And later on I had this bint, her parents were killed at Dresden. Couldn't half shag.

FRANK: The old familiar fear. Was I the only twenty-one-year-old virgin left?

IVOR: Worse than during the war here. Nothing in the shops, queues everywhere. Nobody cares that you've been doing your bit.

[AMY *comes in, wearing a hat and coat.*]

AMY: Frank, I must just run up to Montpelier's the bakers. Mrs Stock says they've got some cream horns in. You still like cream horns?

YOUNG FRANK: Expect so. Can't remember.

AMY: If I hurry, there might be one or two left. What a business, queueing still! Ivor says there's plenty of everything in Germany. Well, it makes you wonder who won the war. [*She pauses.*] I blame the Labour Government.

YOUNG FRANK: Where I've spent the last three years, they aren't very upset about the shortage of cream horns.

AMY: Well, I don't suppose the Indians eat many cream horns. Even if they can get them. Mostly rice, isn't it? [*She pauses, and looks to* IVOR *for help.*] I mean, they're not used to decent standards.

YOUNG FRANK: That's true, yes. I've sat in a Calcutta restaurant spending most of my pay on a tasty meal, with the faces of boys pressed against the window. Then the waiter sent them off and I saw them shoo the kitehawks from the dustbins and rummage through for anything the birds had left.

AMY: You must be glad to be home.

IVOR: Not our fault, though, is it?

AMY: Not our concern. We didn't send you out there, did we? And you didn't want to go. I said to Mrs Bentley, well, it's silly, taking boys away from nice homes and sticking them down among a lot of natives.

FRANK: Thank Christ they did!

AMY: Exposing them to nasty diseases.

YOUNG FRANK: But – it *is* our concern. Your nice cup of tea comes from India, Mum. And your cotton dresses. The petrol for Dad's car and the tyres it runs on from the Middle East and Malaya. Most of the food he sells is grown in countries where people are starving: coffee, chocolate, cinnamon, pineapple, coconut, sugar, pepper – we rely on Asia and Africa for all that just as the posh people in London rely on Crewe for their Rolls-Royces.

IVOR: Hey, you sound like one of those blokes used to spout politics on the Downs.

AMY: Oh, them. Mother always pushed us children past. 'Never mind them,' she used to say, 'we don't want our houses burnt down.'

YOUNG FRANK: What did she mean by that?

IVOR: That's what politics leads to, isn't it?

AMY: I think there was a man saying he'd send people to burn our houses if we didn't vote for him.

[YOUNG FRANK *laughs*.]

IVOR [*after a pause*]: Politics are boring. Only thing is have a good time, like I did in Germany. Wine, women and song.

[YOUNG FRANK *goes up to look his last at the pin-up collage. It fades as he watches.* AMY *listens to* IVOR.]

Get a guitar – decent woman – one or two mates you can have a drink with – a bit of money coming in but not too much – old car – paint some luminous dragons on it —

[YOUNG FRANK *looks at* IVOR *and goes off.*]

– few Sidney Bechet records . . . [*He takes out and lights a cigarette.*]

FRANK: Ivor tried to warm the embers for a few days but I went off to London to stay with one of my new service friends, discussing E.M. Forster and personal relationships. Listening to Debussy.

[IVOR *goes off, smoking. The others watch him go.*]

AMY [*coming down*]: He's never grown up, Ivor. Even now he's got six children, I call him Peter Pan.

FRANK: I wonder which of us retarded the other. He held back my understanding and I tried to spoil his good nature.

AMY: He was very good when Mother died, I've always had a soft spot for him because of that. Staying with her right to the end – banging the wardrobe to show there were no monkeys in it – telling her again and again there wouldn't be any more bombs. [*She takes her handkerchief from her sleeve and blows her nose.*] Whenever some ordinary plane went over, she used to say, 'Not those devils again?'

FRANK: I was watching a French film.

AMY: What?

FRANK: When she died.

AMY: Oh, you'd done a hard day's teaching, hadn't you, and in any case you were serious about films. What was it you wanted to be, when you were young?

FRANK: A director.

AMY: There you are. [*To the audience, as she goes.*] He's always ready to blame himself . . .

[AMY *goes.*]

FRANK [*moving and thinking*]: Who'd have thought I'd make a good teacher? But my newly-developed sense of duty prevailed and I began to think of myself as useful. Then at a party I met Ursula again, the same brazen hussy she'd always been but now twenty-three. She could spend days on end in bed, smiling to show the pleasure she took. [*He recovers from the dream.*] She never organised a thing in those days. But, of course, what women hide is not their dark inner sexual core but their urge to make arrangements. Still – laughing always comes to crying, as my mother would say, and all this joy led to a hasty scene at the registry office during which our great coon of an elder son gave Ursula such a kick in the stomach that one point she said 'ow'. And is that fifteen years ago? Nearly. The calendar pages fall away at silent film speed – the forties are my golden age, ten years of austerity. I know they were drab but austerity sounds so morally superior to affluence, with its suggestion of sewage and greed and waste. What there was then was shared – people gave you lifts in their cars – and Ursula's father voted Labour in the hope this might continue. Well, these days he's got an enormous Vauxhall, a motor-mower, a Japanese cine-camera and holidays in the Black Forest, so . . . [*He shrugs.*] Whereas mine declined in fortune, retiring on a pension the size of which showed that other people had profited by his thrift. An enormous confidence-trick. [*He moves up stage.*]

[*The bay-windows projection comes on: the living-room at home.*
It now lacks the strips of adhesive brown paper.]

My parents couldn't afford repairs and Corinthian Villa began looking the worse for wear. The radio with the lightning-flash motif only crackled now, despite the old man's desperate struggles with its insides. The cube-shaped Staffordshire teapots had lost their lids. The only car in the avenue had passed to me and finally gone for scrap. Whenever Ursula and I took the children to tea on Sunday, the house felt insufficient to contain my memories . . . [*He opens a door and pours himself a drink.*]

   [CHARLES *enters by another door, aged sixty-five, wearing cardigan, shirt, flannels and slippers.*]

CHARLES: Where are you, Buzfuz?

   [*They meet.*]

Look at this boy. Just the job. [*He holds out a pair of woollen underpants.*]

FRANK: Just the job for what?

CHARLES: I said to Mister Champness, the great manager of men's outfitting. 'These would be the very ticket for my son, whom you will remember as a mere boy but who has since become a huge ninny of nearly thirty, for ever complaining of the cold.' I said, 'Put me aside a dozen pairs.'

FRANK: Are you still buying wholesale?

CHARLES: Cheaper by the dozen, boy.

FRANK: Only if you *want* a dozen.

CHARLES [*sharply*]: D'you want them or not?

FRANK: Yes, thanks. If they're not too big.

CHARLES: Nothing worse than pants too small. Notice the gusset, boy. [*He handles it.*] No restriction on your scrotum. Ample room for your parts. Easy access. [*He sticks a forefinger through the fly.*]

FRANK [*taking the pants*]: Right. Thanks very much.

CHARLES [*moves about, sniffing*]: Smells like a four-ale bar in here.

FRANK: Mum told me to help myself to a drink.

CHARLES: Where *is* Old Mother Hubbard?

FRANK: Helping Ursula put Jenny to bed. I did Bill.

CHARLES: He's a fine boy, they're both fine children.

   [FRANK *pours a drink.*]

If you'd seen the sights I saw as a youngster, you'd put strong liquor behind you. My old man – he was a master butcher – I've seen him so drunk he brought the cleaver down on his own hand. Standing there, his blood mingling with the blood of the lamb, swaying about shouting, 'Bee-you-double gee-aye-arr the arr-you-double d-wye thing! – and he wrapped a rag soaked in methylated spirits around his hand and finished hacking the joint – and when he lit a fag, boy, his fist was alight, enveloped in a bright blue flame. And he stood there laughing. Laughing boy! I hear anyone pine for the Good Olde Days, I say, 'For goodness' sake hold your tongue, you can't possibly know about what you're talking!' That frightens them to death, boy . . .

FRANK [*nodding*]: Never put a preposition at . . .

CHARLES: That gets them groggy. Then I proceed to lay them low with eloquent denunciation. Have you heard my epistle to the Old Codgers on this question?

FRANK: Yes.

CHARLES: You've missed a treat. [*He sits, takes out and opens a wallet, taking from it a fat wad of newspaper cuttings, many yellowed with age. He lays them out carefully, sorting and separating.*] And – as I happen to have a copy to hand . . .

[*FRANK looks at his watch, drinks again. From a door comes* MISS NINETEEN-FORTY, *now dressed as a Hollywood slave girl,* TONDELAYO, *all bangles, briefs and long hair. She implores* FRANK *to help her.* MR MAGIC *follows, now a slave-trader with a whip. He threatens the girl but* FRANK *with one kick sends him flying backwards through the door.*]

Yes. This was the letter which riled me, written by some piecan from Ipswich. 'Your article, the Dear Departed, stirred in us many happy memories of the days of yesteryear. In times like these, when the very air we breathe is full of germs and atoms . . .

[*The* SLAVE GIRL *embraces* FRANK'S *legs beseechingly. He stands with his whisky looking down as she begins drawing herself up his body, caressing him, circling him.*]

'When young layabouts wait at every corner, is it any wonder old-age pensioners fear to walk abroad? But we cherish fond thoughts of times when Children honoured their old folk, when a fair day's pay brought a fair day's work . . .' – you listening, crackpot?

[*FRANK is about to remove the* SLAVE GIRL'S *scanty clothing but now he turns to* CHARLES *and she runs off.*]

FRANK: Yes.

CHARLES: 'Cherish fond thoughts of sunny days when a farthing would buy untold dolly mixture.' Which provoked from the Codgers the reply: 'Not arf, Alfred. We reckon the likes of you and your missus can teach the rest of us a thing or two when it comes to the March of Time. Makes you wonder if we aren't all barmy!' [*He puts aside this cutting and takes a piece of notepaper, much folded and worn.*] And here is my reply. 'Oldster of Ipswich can hardly know about what he's talking. My memories are of a different ilk and may be summarised as the Three D's: dirt, drunkenness and disease. The twin stars of our tiny firmament were Big Jim, the fawning publican, and Ikey Stein the pawnbroker.

[AMY *and* URSULA *enter.* AMY *is now fifty-five or so, neat and particular, in a twin-set and skirt, smoking a cigarette.* URSULA *as at present, though she may dress differently.*]

On the streets women of ill-fame plied their unholy trade . . .'

AMY: Oh, not this again! The Good Olde Days! [*She laughs and goes to the drinks.*]

CHARLES: Hold your tongue, Woodbine Winnie!

FRANK [*to* URSULA]: She gone down all right?

URSULA: She's playing with her plastic baa-lambs.

CHARLES: 'Sitting here now before a cosy fire listening to the Eroica symphony of Beethoven, I am indeed . . .'

AMY: You like sherry, don't you, Ursula?

URSULA: Yes.

CHARLES: 'I am indeed . . .'

FRANK: I'll get it.

CHARLES: 'I am indeed . . . !'

AMY: I'll have a vodka.

CHARLES: 'I am indeed . . .'

AMY: Vodka and orange.

FRANK: All right.

CHARLES: Talking to myself here.

AMY: Nobody asked you to.

[*Pause.* CHARLES *waits long-sufferingly.*]

CHARLES: 'I am indeed happy to have heard the last of the Good Olde Days.'

AMY: I wish *we* had. [*She sits.*]

[URSULA *sits beside her.*]

CHARLES: 'Yours Charles Bisley, Corinthian Villa, etcetera.' Absolutely beyond my comprehension why they never printed it.

FRANK [*pouring drinks*]: Bit too *avant-garde* perhaps.

[CHARLES *packs up his cuttings.*]

CHARLES: Too what?

FRANK: I only mean it's a column *for* the simple-minded *by* the simple-minded. The most subversive they can get is oh, for the days when the poor knew their place and there was more sunshine. A pink map and a closed mind and believing what Lord Northcliffe's papers told you – and sitting there throughout the thirties being thankful you've got the only car in the avenue.

AMY: Look out, Frank, you'll . . .

[FRANK *pours too much orange into the vodka and spills it.*]

URSULA: Too late!

AMY: All over my clean carpet, oh dear.

URSULA: I'll get a cloth.

[URSULA *goes.*]

FRANK [*putting the orange on the cabinet*]: But God bless the Prince of Wales and shall we take the boy to Weymouth?

AMY: If you'd stop talking for a second, Frank, you'd see that sticky orange is all over the carpet I've just shampooed.

CHARLES: Give him enough rope he'll hang himself.

FRANK: I'm trying to talk to you.

CHARLES: Talk? You talk? I will content myself with repeating to you what I said to Mister Lewthwaite of Fancy Goods.

[URSULA *returns with a floorcloth.*]

AMY: Thanks, Ursula, I'll do it. [*She rubs the floor.*]

CHARLES: You remember him, Buzfuz? Little squirt of a fellow about so high, pronounced stammer. I kept trying to get a word in edgewise but he was bah-bah-bahing away, I said, 'Mister Lewthwaite, I haven't got all day to stand here listening to your speech impediment.' And I added, 'Leave the talking to those with a gift of the gab. And – at the risk of blowing my own trumpet – for, after all . . . [*Mock clerical.*] Verily, verily, I say unto you, blessed is he that bloweth his own trumpet, lest it be not blown at all.'

[URSULA *laughs and* CHARLES *plays up to her.* FRANK *swallows a drink and opens a door. The scantily clad* SLAVE GIRL *is there, bound by her wrists, struggling to free herself. As she sees* FRANK *she cowers back in terror.*]

You should have seen his face, Ursula, I said. 'When it comes to talking none is more able' – notice, Buzfuz, none *is* more able, not none *are* –

[FRANK *comes back, shutting the door, impatiently listening to* CHARLES.]

– 'none is more able than the weird, wise and wonderful Colossus, Charles the First and Foremost.' I said, 'Good day to you, friend,' and left him gasping, boy, thinking to himself . . .

AMY: Good riddance to bad rubbish . . .

CHARLES: 'Good riddance to b . . .' – what d'you mean, good riddance? Hold your tongue, Capstan Connie. No, I left him thinking, 'That man is a veritable marvel. How was he born so wonderful?'

AMY: Why was he born at all?

CHARLES: 'Why was he born . . .' [*He breaks off again.*]

[URSULA *laughs.* FRANK *stares with a stone face.* CHARLES *looks at him. Having finished the carpet,* AMY *sits again and drinks.*]

Never one to outstay my welcome, Ursula, I shall leave you to your own devices for a moment while I use the convenience.

[CHARLES *goes.*]

AMY: I believe he's worse the older he gets.

URSULA: No, he's lovely.

FRANK: All very well for you to come and find him amusing *now*, now he's become a comedian.

[FRANK *gives* URSULA *her sherry. The women sit drinking.* CHARLES *reappears at the same door.*]

CHARLES: Talking about the old man the moment his back's turned? [*He comes in.*] No, I meant to say apropos of the Good Olde Days –

AMY: You set my teeth on edge about the Good Olde Days.

CHARLES: – think of your own enviable position, the advantages you had. Look at your lovely house, central heating – not that I like it, dries your mouth, I find, but very nice if you're used to it. No central heating here, that's because I gave up so much to give you a good education.

FRANK: Good education!

CHARLES: Fed and clothed you, gave you everything a boy could want, threw my money about —

AMY: – like a Jew with no arms —

CHARLES: Like a Jew with no arms. Who said that? Goldflake Gertie again? I'll give you a kick in the pants.

AMY: Why don't you go on up to the toilet?

CHARLES: And look at you, with a university degree, a wonderful job, teaching grown-up people, imparting your knowledge. Superannuation scheme.

[FRANK *howls with derision.*]

Nothing to laugh at. I made sure of my pension.

AMY: Lot of good it's done us, too. Navvies earn more than us these days.

FRANK: Don't you think they should?

CHARLES: You should be grateful, boy.

URSULA: He is.

CHARLES: Just as I'm proud, Ursula. Proud to have helped my son up the ladder a few steps. If I've done that and it's appreciated, my life will not have been in vain. [*He takes out his handkerchief.*]

[URSULA *looks at* FRANK *as though demanding that he express some thanks. He doesn't.*]

Oh, I've made mistakes in my time, I admit it. In a life as full as the Old Man's, it would have been a miracle not to have made the odd mistake. Perhaps some I shall regret until the day I pass away.

[*Pause.* URSULA *looks at* CHARLES. AMY *drinks.*]

[*Suddenly.*] This shirt was a mistake! [*He pulls out his shirt-tail.*] I like a shirt I can wrap round my buttocks and keep me warm. I said to Mister Champness, Big Cheese in the Men's Wear Department, 'Next time give me a shirt big enough for Lockhart's.'

URSULA: Lockhart's?

AMY: What's he on about now?

URSULA: Private parts.

CHARLES: What?

URSULA: Rhyming slang!

CHARLES: No! Big enough for Lockhart's elephants. They were the great music-hall turn when I was a nipper. Nothing to do with private parts, young woman. What d'you think of her, Amy? Got a one-track mind, I should think.

AMY: Your endless chatter makes my head sing, I know that.

CHARLES: No wonder she's got two nippers already. I shouldn't let young crackpot make so free with you in the jolly old double-bed.

AMY: Very nice. Could we change the subject?

CHARLES: Not having another, are you?

URSULA: Not yet.

CHARLES: I only thought when I saw you this afternoon, by Jove, Ursula's breasts look larger than ever.

AMY: Take no notice, dear, I don't.

CHARLES: She never takes a scrap of notice of me, Old Mother Hubbard. Do you?

[CHARLES *goes down on one knee by* AMY *and tries to kiss her. She recoils.*]

AMY: Not a scrap. Why don't you go to the toilet?

CHARLES: No chance of a spot of the slap-and-tickle these days.

[URSULA *moves to* FRANK. *They stand watching.*]

URSULA: See what I mean about touching?

FRANK: I know all about that.

URSULA: Kiss him, you block of ice! More bothered with your shampooed carpet than your man.

[CHARLES *stands.*]

CHARLES: I sometimes think of the chances I missed, the girls I turned away. Vicky Edmunds, for instance, lived in Leytonstone. I wonder what Vicky's doing now.

AMY: Drawing the old age pension, I should think.

CHARLES: Drawing the old age . . . ? [*He goes to a door and turns.*] I shall boil a kettle to fill my hot-water bottle. Once in bed, I shall place it scalding between my thighs.

AMY: I don't think Ursula's interested in what you do in bed.

CHARLES: Nobody is these days. Which accounts for the water-bottle. A last resort, eh, Ursula?

[URSULA *stops* CHARLES *on his way out and kisses him.* FRANK *turns away.* CHARLES *goes.*]

AMY: D'you think he's gone for good? Are we going to enjoy a conversation for a change?

[URSULA *looks at* FRANK *but he is turned away. She goes to stand near* AMY.]

No, what I was saying upstairs was we could have the children for a day or two so you and Frank could go away.

URSULA: D'you think it's possible?

AMY: Frank could do with a break, he looks so drawn.

URSULA: Would Mister Bisley mind?

AMY: Him? No. He'll take Bill to the park, give him something to occupy his mind, instead of hanging about the house and getting in my way. He's under my feet the whole day long otherwise.

[*A door opens near* FRANK *and* MR MAGIC *throws the* SLAVE GIRL *to the ground at* FRANK's *feet.* MR MAGIC *now seems to be a eunuch and threatens the* SLAVE GIRL *with a whip. He bows to* FRANK. FRANK *raises her from the ground and stands her before him. There is no pause in* AMY's *speech.*]

Tell the truth, he hasn't known what to do since retirement.

URSULA: I thought he enjoyed it.

AMY: After his fashion, yes, pottering about, getting in my way.

URSULA: He's got so many interests. Music, rugby, cricket . . .

AMY: When he was on the road, at least he was out from under my feet from Monday to Friday.

[FRANK *reaches out and tears the brassière off the* SLAVE GIRL. *She flinches and turns her head away.* FRANK *stares at her.*]

But now he won't go anywhere, he sits listening to his blessed records. I give him something to do now and then, nothing difficult. Well, he's like a baby half the time, he knocked a pot of plastic emulsion down the stairs last May. And only yesterday he vacuumed an enormous leaf off the rubber plant in the greenhouse.

[FRANK *gestures to* MR MAGIC, *who turns the* SLAVE GIRL *so that she submits to* FRANK, *raising one leg. He takes her ankle in his hands and begins to remove her bangles.*]

And sometimes I think if I don't get out of the house, I shall go stark, staring mad.

URSULA: Perhaps after all those years travelling, he wants to settle down.

AMY: Settle down? Fossilise! I feel like a fossil in a glass case.

[AMY *seems on the edge of an emotional outburst but* URSULA *stares at her unsympathetically so* AMY *blows her nose in her handkerchief and turns to* FRANK.]

Frank!

[FRANK *goes on taking off the* SLAVE GIRL's *bangles.*]

Look at him, dreaming again. Always got his head in the clouds. Frank!

FRANK: Hullo? [*He turns from the* SLAVE GIRL.]

   [*The* SLAVE GIRL *and* MR MAGIC *go out through the nearest door.*
   FRANK *moves to* AMY *and* URSULA.]

AMY: I was telling Ursula, Dad vacuumed a leaf off the rubber plant
   yesterday.

FRANK [*absently*]: Oh, dear.

AMY: Yes. I found him trying to put it back with a tube of Evostick.
   You do look drawn, don't you think so, Ursula? Working too
   hard at college? Reading too much? I think you can overdo
   reading.

   [FRANK *leans over* URSULA *and kisses her. She recoils.* CHARLES
   reappears wearing one slipper, one shoe, one trouser rolled,
   blindfold, length of rope about neck and carrying a flat box of long
   playing records.]

CHARLES: He's back and to prove it he's here!

AMY: Thought that was too good to last.

CHARLES: Well, what d'you think? Do I look the part?

URSULA: Depends what the part is. If it's Camille, for instance, no,
   you don't.

CHARLES: What does it look like?

AMY: Looks as though you've escaped from Doctor Fox's.

CHARLES: Old Mother Hubbard's not far off. This, believe it or
   not, is the crackpot way a Mason has to dress for admission to
   a lodge. Almost beyond one's comprehension that all those
   creepers and crawlers are prepared to make themselves look small
   for the sake of advancement. High on my list of dislikes: creepers,
   what-I-call Masonic types. Those who climb by licking aye-ar-
   ess-ee-ess. Little Lofty Lewthwaite sucking up to Mister Tombs.
   Some years ago I learned the oaths of allegiance with the sole
   purpose of baiting my colleagues in the Lodge. Friend
   Lewthwaite said to me, 'Freemasonry is Bah-bah-Betty Martin.'
   Now among his disabilities is a pronounced cast in one eye and
   whenever he's getting flummoxed, this eye starts swivelling
   round, you know, as though he's looking for an avenue of escape.
   My Number One Anathema: Creepers. Have you heard my list
   of dislikes?

FRANK: }
         Yes.
AMY: }

CHARLES: I was asking your good lady here.

URSULA [*laughing*]: I don't know.

FRANK [*to* URSULA]: We had it last time we came here!

CHARLES [*to* URSULA]: You've missed a treat. [CHARLES *begins listing on his fingers.*] Creepers. Filth in all forms: filthy fingernails, filthy talk, dog's soil on the footpath. I put up a sign on the tree outside:

'Dog-owners:

Let it not be said unto your shame

That all was beauty here until you came.'

AMY: And I took it down again.

CHARLES: And cork-tipped Katey took it down again.

AMY: Don't want the neighbours reading that.

CHARLES: Where was I, Ursula?

AMY: Think we've escaped from Dr Fox's.

URSULA: Filth in all its forms.

[FRANK *moves away.*]

CHARLES [*listing again*]: Bartok. Unmelodious, I always say. Central heating. Dries the mouth. Booze. Masonic types.

[CHARLES *moves after* FRANK *and confers with him quietly, showing the flat box.*]

AMY: Mister Lewthwaite sponsored Charles for his lodge but nothing came of it. They none of them liked him.

[FRANK *looks at the contents of the box – long-playing records.* CHARLES *opens the door to reveal the forties gramophone. He moves away, with a leaflet, leaving* FRANK *to put on a record.*]

CHARLES: And then, of course, my list of likes.

AMY: Likes and dislikes, good old days, you'll have us all in Dr Fox's.

CHARLES [*listing again*]: Cleanliness of thought and body. Giving people a fair chance in life. The ideals of the Co-operative Movement. A roaring fire. [*He considers.*] On reflection, I'm not sure I wouldn't put a roaring fire *before* the ideals of the Co-operative Movement. [*Music begins: Grieg's 'Hall of the Mountain King'.* CHARLES *begins dancing and conducting.*]

URSULA: Oh, good. I was about to ask for music.

AMY: Bang-bang-bang-bang.

CHARLES: You're a music-lover, Ursula?

URSULA: There was never any in our house, only Vera Lynn, but I'm . . .

CHARLES: I never creep and crawl. I won't. [*He reads from the leaflet, conducting the record.*] 'Hearthstone Concert Hall. Sixty-five complete selections of light classical music by thirty-eight immortal composers. These are the tunes to set toes tapping, heads nodding, fingers drumming . . .' – or in Mister Lewthwaite's case, eyes swivelling, eh, boy?

[URSULA *laughs.*]

'For Father, the hard-pressed business man, a musical education without tears. For Mother, almost twelve hours of companionship to keep the blues at bay. To help you waltz through the dish-washing.'

AMY: I don't think. Bang-bang-bang-bang, all day long.

URSULA: I thought you liked music.

AMY: In its proper place.

[URSULA *appeals to* FRANK, *who comes down to join them.*]

CHARLES: And listen to this, Old Mother Hubbard, listen, here's the bit you'll like: 'At Almost Half the Price in the Shops. Music your family will bless you for.' [*He tut-tuts disapprovingly.*] Music for which your family will . . .

AMY: Just a minute.

CHARLES: 'Costs absolutely nothing.'

AMY: Is this something you've brought?

[AMY *goes to* CHARLES, *who moves away.*]

This music? Is it one of these records? Is it?

CHARLES [*laughing*]: No, wait a minute, Amy. 'Costs nothing to receive this astounding bargain . . .'

AMY: Oh, yes, I'll bet. But something to keep it.

CHARLES: No, wait a minute. Come and help me, boy.

[AMY *chases him about as he holds the leaflet out of her reach.*]

[*Reading.*] 'Handel's Largo, one of the all-time greats!'

[AMY *runs at him again, but he dodges her and moves away with the leaflet, laughing.*]

Butterfingers, butterfingers. You'll have to move more smartly than that to get the better of the old man.

[AMY *bursts into tears. Everyone is atsonished and upset.*]

FRANK: Give it to her.

[FRANK *takes the leaflet from* CHARLES *and gives it to* AMY, *who reads it, sobbing aloud.* FRANK *comes down.*]

[*To the audience.*] I'm trying to remember exactly how sad it was. But in retrospect it seems funny.

AMY: Fifteen pounds! It costs fifteen pounds. Then you can send it back.

CHARLES [*subdued*]: I can't do that, Amy.

AMY: You've had it on approval, you can say you don't like it.

CHARLES: I've sent the cheque off.

AMY: I don't believe it.

CHARLES: Wonderful bargain. Twenty-five pounds . . .

AMY: He does it to spite me. [*She cries even more.*]

[CHARLES *has not managed the moment as he planned and does not know what to do.* FRANK *takes off the record.* URSULA *stands near* CHARLES. AMY *recovers and speaks to the audience.*]

Only last week I asked for the money for a new spring outfit and he said we couldn't run to it. As though he hasn't got enough blasted records banging away all day and night.

FRANK: Why don't you take some interest in his music? Isn't that one of your common interests.

CHARLES: Hold your tongue, Sonny Jim.

FRANK: Sonny Jim? I'm nearly forty. A middle-aged man with three whopping kids.

URSULA: No, at this time you were nearly thirty and Matthew hadn't been born.

FRANK: Oh, Christ!

CHARLES: Don't take the Lord's name in vain.

FRANK: The Lord's name? You haven't been inside a church since my christening. The nearest you've come to godliness is cleanliness.

AMY: You've no idea what I have to go through with him, week in, week out.

FRANK: But you're to blame as well.

AMY [*frightened*]: Me? To blame?

FRANK: You make no effort to understand him.

AMY: I don't expect much. No car, we never go on holiday, the house is falling about our ears. I'm only saying I expect a certain standard. Don't you think at our age you deserve a certain standard? Ursula? Don't you?

URSULA: I've never taken any standard for granted. It has to be worked for. Marriage has to be worked *at*. Understanding has to be achieved by hard work.

FRANK: Let it go.

URSULA: No, why should we allow them to use us as shock-absorbers? Every time they postpone their fights until we visit them. It's easy to blame your father but she's worse.

CHARLES: Now don't you raise your voice against Mrs Bisley.

FRANK [*to* URSULA]: There!

AMY: He's getting round me now. Like when he buys another lot of junk. Twelve straw boaters he brought home last week.

CHARLES: A dozen for a half a sovereign, Amy. That's less than a shilling each.

AMY: Oh, wonderful, if you happen to know twelve people who want straw boaters.

CHARLES: Say young crackpot here wants to do a Nigger Minstrel turn at his college show . . .

FRANK [*to the audience*]: But with his late-Victorian, Edwardian background – 'Appy 'Ampstead, Derby Day, drunk for two-pence and women were either old maids or always pregnant —

AMY: Our family wasn't like that, thank you . . .

FRANK [*continuing*]: – his way out was to resist the indulgences that gave pleasure to the poor – the harmless sedatives that, taken in small doses, might have made branch managers and other travellers welcome him instead of turning away.

CHARLES [*to the audience*]: Nobody ever turned away from the old man . . .

FRANK: I went with you. I saw them dodging out through the back doors. You were an embarrassment, you were dreaded. [*To* AMY.] I'm trying to make the point that his nature demanded some addiction, some indulgence. And his occupation showed the way: bargains, something for nothing.

CHARLES: We're getting a lecture, now, Amy.

FRANK: I suppose this is *my* occupational hazard. Lecturing.

CHARLES: We're not your students.

URSULA: It might not hurt you to listen, though.

CHARLES: Oh, d'you hear that, fag-end Fanny? We can profit from piecan's education here.

AMY: If you call me that once again, I shall scream. An occasional cigarette's not much to ask. In our family we were poor but happy. Mother was widowed twice but she brought us up, my brother and I. She slaved in a factory.

CHARLES [conciliatory]: She was a dear old soul.

AMY: She enjoyed a drink, a laugh and a song. When I told her we were marrying, she said, 'Considering you could have had your pick, you chose a miserable devil.'

URSULA: Why did you marry him then?

AMY: I didn't know any better. I was only a girl.

CHARLES: Twenty-eight.

AMY: What about you? Middle-aged *you* were.

CHARLES: Yes.

AMY: And set in your ways, like a fossil.

CHARLES: And I was her Last Chance, Ursula. Last Chance Charlie, eh, boy? Saved her bacon.

AMY: I had plenty of chances, then and later on. I only didn't take them for the boy's sake.

FRANK: That's enough, Mum.

AMY: He knows very well.

[CHARLES *goes and packs up his box of records, hiding from this revelation*.]

Because, after a time, it's not just what you want to do, is it? No, after a time, only the children count. You have to sacrifice your own desires. And though Frank used to say sometimes, while he was away, 'Let's go off somewhere . . .'

FRANK: No.

AMY: Oh, yes – [*To the audience*.] – but I wanted him to finish his schooling and how could I have been sure with anyone else . . . ?

FRANK: Will you shut up!

[CHARLES *goes off, taking the records and broom, without turning back*.]

AMY: You did say that, Frank.

FRANK: I didn't understand him then.

AMY: Oh, I don't *understand* him even now.

FRANK: Well. Perhaps Ursula's helped me.

AMY [*to the audience*]: Easy for her. So late in the day.

[AMY *goes.*]

FRANK: We only seem to understand people when there's no longer any need. When that phase of our life is over.

URSULA: You mean we understand each other?

FRANK: What?

URSULA: You and I. You've left me. We're living apart, that phase is over.

FRANK [*after a pause*]: Yes.

URSULA: We carried the sleeping children down to the car and made subdued farewells at the gate.

FRANK: Dad told me for the billionth time how to point the car in the right direction. 'I should go down the avenue, along Appian Terrace and up Tuscan Vale to the main road . . .'

URSULA: As soon as we got home, I felt sorry for them both.

FRANK: And excited.

URSULA: What?

FRANK: We were excited. After we'd put the kids to bed, you went for a *bath* and I came in and had you, all warm and slippery, my belly slapping on the surface of the water.

[URSULA *makes for the door and goes out as soon as he starts on this subject. He runs to the slammed door, opens it and shouts after her.*]

– I made you groan, deep down in your throat! Your tongue was everywhere! Like before we were married. Control yourself, man. Have you finished packing? [*He looks into the case, dreams again.*] After retirement, the old man gave up packing. Hardly ever left Corinthian Villa. So, to save Mum from fossilising we took her to a film from time to time. Or she would baby-sit if we were invited out. I'd drive over to fetch her and, while she put her coat on, Dad would give me one of his comic turns. [*Imitating* CHARLES.] You've heard my list of likes, boy?

AMY [*coming on*]: Have I kept you waiting, Frank? [*She puts on her gloves.*]

FRANK [*as* CHARLES]: Have you got everything? Mintoes? Spectacles?

AMY: Yes.

FRANK [*as* CHARLES]: Laxatives.

AMY: We're only going to the theatre.

FRANK [*as himself*]: He led us out to the pavement, laughing and

75

excited, picked up a passing child and stood him on our front wall. Then turned on the child's father and told him to take his hands from his pockets and stand up straight.

AMY: Wasn't that awful? A man of thirty-five.

FRANK [*as* CHARLES]: Which way you going, Frank? Down the avenue, perhaps, along Appian Terrace and up Tuscan Vale to . . .

AMY: D'you think Frank doesn't know the way by this time?

FRANK [*as himself*]: I shot the car away from the kerb as he belatedly signalled that the way was clear. In the nearside wing-mirror, I saw him picking rubbish from the gutter.

AMY: That was one of his funny ways – picking rubbish from the gutter.

FRANK: When I brought you home afterwards, the *Eine Kleine Nachtmusik* was being played so loud we couldn't make him hear the doorbell.

AMY: I didn't want to get my key out but in the end I had to.

FRANK: He was lying dead on the kitchen floor, his milk boiling over.

AMY: He must have gone very suddenly. The best way.

FRANK: Oh yes.

AMY: Funny thing, a few days earlier he'd asked for a drop of Scotch, where before he wouldn't even eat a trifle if he detected sherry.

FRANK: I always seem to be in cinemas or theatres while my relatives are dying.

AMY: Not your fault, though, is it?

FRANK: D'you realise, while he was lying there with the milk and Mozart, we were in the same theatre where one night during the war – d'you remember, Mum?

AMY: What?

[*Music. The lights change.*]

[MR MAGIC *comes on as a comedian, wearing a mock-elegant outfit and removes his gloves in parody of a toff.* MISS NINETEEN-FORTY *comes on as a showgirl and takes them for him. He also removes his hat and overcoat and she takes these, grinning, swinging her hips. As she goes off, passing him, he pinches her and she gives a shocked squeak and smile. He looks after her, then turns to the audience.*]

MR MAGIC: No use you looking. That's under the counter, that is.
But I'll tell you this for nothing: she's got a beautiful little
chihuahua. She has. Very fond of it, too. She showed her friend
and her friend said, 'Yes, lovely, but those little short hairs aren't
right. You want to get rid of those.' So she went to the chemist,
she said, 'I want something to get rid of little short hairs.' He gave
her some ointment, he said, 'Rub it on your legs twice a day.' See?
She said, 'It's not for me legs.' He said, 'No?' She said, 'No, it's
for me little chihuahua.' He said, 'In that case don't ride your
bike for a fortnight.' No – listen . . . ! A little monologue:
There was an old cow from Huddersfield –

[*From the auditorium comes a single slow handclap.* MR MAGIC
pauses.]

CHARLES [*from the audience*]: Get off!

AMY: Yes, I remember this.

CHARLES: Women and children present. If you can't do better than
that, get off! [*He continues the slow clap.*]

MR MAGIC: Now don't you knock your pipe at me, Grandpa. You
don't know how lucky you are. This is all continental stuff I'm
giving you.

CHARLES: No more filth! Get off home!

FRANK: I sat there, hot under the collar of my utility shirt.

MR MAGIC: I tell you what. We'll put it to the vote.

CHARLES: Get off! No more smut.

[CHARLES *has come down the aisle and is standing by the stage,
still giving the handclap. From other parts of the audience come
boos and cries of 'Shut up' and 'Throw him out'.*]

[*To the audience.*] Don't talk so big, you make yourself look small.

MR MAGIC: No, give him a chance . . .

CHARLES [*coming on to the stage*]: Anyone who has to resort to the
private parts of women to get a laugh . . .

[*Cries of 'Shame'.*]

AMY: Come on home, Charles. Everyone's looking.

CHARLES: Many of us have our wives and children with us here
tonight.

FRANK: Yet I was proud of him.

MR MAGIC: Now, listen, Dad, I only mentioned a chihuahua.

CHARLES: Cleanliness is next to godliness.

MR MAGIC: All right, mate, I've nearly finished anyway. [*To the audience.*] I'll come back in the second half after he's gone.

[MR MAGIC *goes off, to cheers.* CHARLES *remains with* FRANK *and* AMY.]

CHARLES: Jokes about conveniences and bee-you-double-gee-ee-are-why.

[*Loud boos.* CHARLES *turns in their direction and bows, slowly, with dignity.*]

I bowed slowly, boy, you remember?

FRANK: Shall I ever forget?

CHARLES: Frightened the life out of them.

AMY: You don't care how much you embarrassed me, I could hear people saying, 'He's escaped from Doctor Fox's.'

CHARLES: For a moment I toyed with the idea of giving an excerpt from my most successful recitation 'Jeremiah in the Turkish bath'. [*He takes up a posture and recites in a cockney dialect.*] 'And now, Jerry, if you'll lie on the table here, I'll just finish you awf.'

FRANK: All right, Dad, thanks . . .

CHARLES [*after an extravagant horrified reaction*]: 'Finish me awf?'

FRANK: Yes, fine, that's enough now.

[FRANK *and* AMY *try to usher* CHARLES *towards a door. He escapes and returns down stage.*]

CHARLES: 'I'm darned near finished awf already.'

FRANK: Come on, you've had your turn.

[FRANK *and* CHARLES *argue in whispers.*]

AMY [*to the audience*]: The band struck up and the dancing girls came on and he ran down the aisle peering at them through his opera glasses, cheering.

CHARLES [*to* AMY]: Nothing smutty about the female form. Only lewd innuendo.

FRANK: Right. Thank you.

AMY [*persuading him through the door again*]: Soon after that I got him into the foyer and on to the bus. [*She shuts the door on* CHARLES.]

FRANK [*to the audience*]: Well, the day of the funeral . . .

[*The door reopens and* CHARLES *appears.*]

CHARLES [*continuing his recitation*]: 'I've been pushed and

78

pummelled, pummelled and pushed. I'm black and blue.'

[*The audience cheers.*]

FRANK: Will you let me tell the rest of the story!

CHARLES: You tell a story, boy? You couldn't make a pudden crawl!

FRANK: And you're dead! So go!

[CHARLES *looks at* FRANK, *then at the audience. He bows slowly three times to mounting derision, then goes, leaving the door open.* FRANK *runs to the door, slams it, waits, then returns down stage.*]

The day of the funeral a heat-wave started. So, where once had stood the only car in the avenue, there was now barely room to squeeze his hearse in.

AMY: Mister Lewthwaite turned up at the crematorium. And Mister Champness of men's outfitting who had supplied your father with long underpants at wholesale prices.

FRANK: 'Man that is born of woman hath but a short time to live and is full of misery. He cometh up and is cut down like a flower,' said the priest and pressed a button and the coffin slid into the wall. I half expected him to slide out again for the last word but no, this *was* his final exit.

AMY: He was a good man, a good husband. He never kept me short. He had his funny ways – who hasn't? I blame his mother – all in black with her hair strained back and her lips a thin white line. Real Victorian. No wonder his father drank. In our family we were poor but happy. Mother enjoyed a drink, a laugh and a song. [*Exit.*]

[FRANK *looks at his list, brings some outer clothes to pack in case.*]

FRANK: His death made me feel the likelihood, the certainty of my own. I was the oldest man in the family now. The greater part of my life was behind me and the rest didn't look too hot. Somewhere between the black-out and the marriage-bed I missed young love, ecstasy, surrender. I suddenly saw my own son claiming the benefits of the new state I'd helped bring about – the new freedom – and it was so unfair!

[*Rock music blares out.* FRANK *puts hands on ears as* YOUNG FRANK *comes on, now late teens, dressed modern casual, carrying loud boogie box. After him comes* MISS NINETEEN-FORTY, *modern too, wartime nostalgia style, 1940+. They embrace and kiss, not seeing* FRANK, *who turns down their music.*]

FRANK: Hullo, Bill.

YOUNG FRANK: Oh, you here again?

FRANK: Usual sunny welcome. Who's your friend?

YOUNG FRANK: Sammy.

FRANK: And was that you on that scooter, making such a filthy row all up the street?

YOUNG FRANK: Yeah, Sammy's Yamaha.

FRANK: Well, I'm sure I speak for the whole street when I say it was tremendously impressive.

[YOUNG FRANK *and* MISS NINETEEN-FORTY *begin dancing in a copulative way. During his speeches, they get on the sofa, undressing each other.*]

I'm sure even those of our neighbours who had managed to get to sleep before you arrived were tremendously impressed when you woke them up. Motor bikes. Electronic groups. Jet flights to Katmandu. Your rejection of capitalism is a piece of cant until you reject the muck it produces. And rejection's not enough. You've got to know what kind of world you want instead. I've a far more defined view of that than you have. You haven't heard my manifesto?

YOUNG FRANK: If I were king –

FRANK [*listing on his fingers, as* CHARLES *did*]: If I were king – or president or whatever – first: ban all heavy transport using residential streets to convey another load of sea-dredged aggregates. Next: ban motor bikes to anyone under forty and over fifty.

[*About now,* BILL *and* SAMMY *tire of the noise and go off, taking the radio. He doesn't notice, goes on lecturing. Soon after this* URSULA *comes on by another door.*]

Go for strictly limited aims, you see. Legislate against luxury. We did very well without luxury during the war, very well without petrol and prawn cocktails and all the grotesque inequality of the present day.

[URSULA *is 38, wearing an outdoor coat, etc., carrying a large bag and portfolio with patterns, samples of material, etc. Kicks door shut behind her.*]

URSULA: Hello.

FRANK: Hello. How did it go, darling?

URSULA: Great – can't think why I enjoy it so much. Even if the money wasn't so useful, I'd still go on taking these evening classes. I like schools when all the children have gone home.

[FRANK *follows her back and stands listening, nodding.*]

All the chairs up on their desks. I like the fact that these people of all ages and shapes and colours come along in their spare time to learn dress-making – have a chat – no-one's pushing you to get you past exams – it's real teaching – how have you been? The kids slept soundly?

FRANK: Yes.

URSULA [*seeing the suitcase open*]: You have finished our packing?

FRANK: Um – well, I was just . . .

URSULA: I told you all that had to go in. Our sweaters, your jeans, your woollen socks to go inside your boots. And you put the four pairs of wellies in the car?

FRANK: Ah – now . . .

URSULA: I stood here and told you every single thing that had to go in! I asked you if you wanted me to make a list but you said no, you could remember. What were you doing – dreaming again? Haven't you put the boots in then?

FRANK: Well, not yet. I was just . . .

URSULA: And what about the sick bags? The polythene bags in case Jenny's car-sick? She always is. D'you want it all over the safety-belts like last time?

FRANK: No.

URSULA: You haven't done that! I don't believe it. What *have* you done? Gone into another bloody dream? Oh, God, honestly! Been playing that old wartime tape again. We're supposed to be getting off before dawn to miss the traffic and have as long in the country as possible! Now we shall have to do all this bloody packing in the dark and . . .

FRANK: No, I'll do it now.

URSULA: You won't. I'm dropping on my feet and if you potter about now you'll only wake me up again when you come blundering into bed. We'll do it in the morning. And even as I say that I know I mean: *I'll* do it in the morning because nothing wakes you until the last possible moment.

FRANK: D'you know what this trip started as?

URSULA: What?

FRANK: A second honeymoon. Our parents were supposed to be having the children and you and I . . .

URSULA: Well, they couldn't, as it turned out, could they? So that was the end of . . . [*She looks round uneasily, sensing something.*] What's the smell? The casserole! Have you only just had it then? The oven switched itself off at nine, I told you that, I told you to take it out soon after that before it got dried up or cooled off. Was it all right?

FRANK: Christ – d'you know, love, it must have slipped my . . . I'll have it now . . .

URSULA: You mean you haven't eaten it? Haven't eaten at all?

FRANK: Would you believe it, I had some fish and chips from round the corner?

URSULA: It took me half an hour to prepare that casserole. I haven't stopped all day. I nearly fell asleep in class tonight – oh . . . [*She groans and shakes her head, then thinks again.*] Fish and chips? Did you go and buy them?

FRANK: Yes.

URSULA: Left the children alone in the house?

FRANK: It was only ten minutes.

URSULA: When are you going to think of someone but yourself? When are you going to consider something but your own precious comfort? The answer's never, isn't it? You never have and you never will. So not only did I manage all the housework and all the preparations for going away but most of the packing, too, and bathed the children and got their meal and washed that up and made you a casserole and took my class and what were you doing all that time?

FRANK [*quietly*]: I was trying to . . .

URSULA: Standing about doing nothing!

[URSULA *grabs her bags and goes out by another door, slamming it behind her.* FRANK *holds his head, then goes to the case and looks in it confusedly.*]

FRANK: Can I stand much more of this? [*He moves away, assessing the value of two pairs of socks.*] Oh, yes. Much more.

[*Music: 'You stepped out of a dream' (Tony Martin).* YOUNG

[URSULA *comes on from another door. She is wearing a school hat, blue raincoat, white socks and shoes, but nothing else.* FRANK *turns to her. She stands down stage of him, unbuttons her raincoat and opens it so that he can see her body. He stands where he is, devouring her with his eyes. She moves slowly towards him and embraces him. He caresses her beneath the coat. A door opens and* URSULA *looks in. Music pause.*]

URSULA: Don't bother with that at this time of night. I want to get to sleep.

[URSULA *goes, slamming the door. Music resumes. With a last kiss,* YOUNG URSULA *steps back, wraps her coat around her and goes off the way she came, making one final obscene gesture at the door.* FRANK *packs the socks again, closes the case, and goes after* URSULA *turning out the lights.*]

[*After their bows the actors line up and sing:*]
>   Rainy days don't worry me,
>   There's a rainbow that I can see
>   And it's waiting for me
>   Down Forget-me-not Lane.
>
>   Fortune never comes that way,
>   I'll keep singing a song each day,
>   Keeping troubles away
>   From Forget-me-not Lane.
>
>   It's just a heaven they've made
>   And if you're a stranger there
>   You'll find a table well-laid
>   And you're welcome to a chair.
>
>   There's no highbrow etiquette,
>   Just plain people and once you've met,
>   They will never forget
>   Down Forget-me-not Lane.

[*They go by various doors, all at once.*]

HEARTS AND FLOWERS

Hearts and Flowers

In November 1969, I was struggling to begin a new play that would finally appear on the stage as *Forget-me-not Lane*. At the start, I had a good deal of trouble and, says Diary, in looking through my old journals for clues, I came upon the long account of my father's funeral:

> It seemed almost complete as it stood and I pitched in at once, after the usual miserable hours thinking up names for the people. Why shouldn't they be called 'Peter', 'Dick', 'Vi', 'Thelma', etc? Because we're only the starting-points, of course, and false names allow the characters to grow away in directions the real people didn't.

This play, *Hearts and Flowers*, is a good example. Bob lives in Bristol and teaches in a secondary school. His elder brother Tony left home years ago and is a well-known television journalist and presenter. Bob suspects and derides Tony's facile sentiments, his ability to turn on the tears like tapwater. But he's envious at the same time – of Tony's success, the glamorous life that enables him to do a programme on air pollution then 'fly off to New York in a trail of diesel and supersonic bangs'. As the play goes on, we learn of his deeper reasons for resenting his brother – that Bob's wife Jean married him after being jilted by Tony and harbours an unsatisfied longing for the elder man.

At the time I wrote it, my brother was still a teacher in Bristol and I was a playwright in London. There is a superficial resemblance between Tony/Bob and Peter/Geoffrey, and relatives and friends may have thought that I was debunking my own pretensions as Tony and claiming that my brother envied me as Bob. The truth is that, at the time of my father's death, I too lived in Bristol and had only recently been teaching in the same school as Geoffrey. Tony and Bob are two aspects of myself. Like everyone I know – including my brother – I am a divided character, hoping for an exciting and passionate life but equally enjoying the claims of work and duty. The play is based on that tension and the father's funeral is the setting which brings it briefly to the surface. The title reflects Bob's suspicion of Tony's sentimentality but is also an elaborate pun. One heart stops (the father's), Tony's is worn on his sleeve, Jean's misses a beat; flowers come as tributes but various aunts discuss their worth, one male friend brings rhubarb instead and a rose from Tony is the last thing Jean sees as she lies in bed after making love to Bob.

This small play was the fifth to be directed by Christopher Morahan. *The Common* was yet to come. The production was brilliant and had a fine cast, headed by Anthony Hopkins as Bob, a natural Mark Antony playing Cassius, bringing the part a sort of prosaic passion. Even so, as usual, the Bristolian background – for various unconvincing reasons – was more or less ignored. The funeral was shot, not among the bizarre monuments of Arno's Vale but at Norwood. Among the cast, only Constance Chapman as Marie was able to speak with the right accent. What would they say of a Scouse play where everyone spoke Welsh or Posh? Only half a dozen actors can manage Bristol at all. One who didn't have to was Leon Cortez as Uncle Will from London. He used to appear in Variety with his Coster Pals. During a lull in the filming, he told us, apropos of cremations, that the cost of getting the boilers going means they burn several bodies at a time so that the bereaved aren't getting the ashes of their loved one but 'fourpenn'orth of mixed'. It was the kind of joke my father would have made.

We watched its transmission with our daughter Louise, who kept asking 'Is that you?', 'Is that Nana?' till I told her off. As the final credits began to roll, Thelma said 'Charles* is late ringing up'. Next morning we realised why he hadn't rung when *The Guardian* carried no notice for mine but one for a play of his on Harlech. He wrote later enclosing a notice in the Bristol paper saying his was ten years ahead of its time like *Citizen Kane* but mine was more entertaining. 'About sums it up really', he wrote.

More telephone calls came than for any previous tv play I'd had on. Harold Pinter rang to say it hit him North, South, East and West. He hoped we'd be associated at some time. A few days before we'd much admired his production of Joyce's *Exiles*, so I was able

*Charles Wood. See introduction.

to reciprocate the compliment.

One of those faceless functionaries at the National Theatre with a name like a town – Lancaster, Halifax, Lincoln? – rang full of praise for the play's ironies and, even as I was thanking him, suddenly switched to *The National Health* and told me it was having only six more performances then being taken off for good. I choked back the rest of my thanks and said it was hardly any wonder audiences had fallen off when the play had been programmed not to be in the repertoire whenever American tourists were about. But what a characteristic bit of N.T. behaviour to ring under cover of praising one play to tell you they're axeing another!

A few months later Alan Bennett, Michael Frayn, John Hopkins and Tom Stoppard, who had all missed it, assembled at the BBC for a private showing. After five minutes the tape broke so they had to contain their impatience until it was shown again a year or so later. On that occasion I had a letter from a man in Scotland:

> This was a sick play, starting in bed and ending there. Even the sex acts under the covers were limited to the sudden passion of the animal in man and a reflection of your inability to understand a woman's needs . . . .
>
> The river of Time runs forever to the Sea of Eternity . . . pleasing the faceless blabbering baboons who pervade and prevail . . . I challenge you to a fight with the pen which will take you into realms of intellect which you have never known.
>
> > It's not for me because I'm free
> > To castigate another
> > But listen please to what I say
> > As you would to your mother.

A year or two after this, the British Film Institute applied to the BBC to include this production in a season of television plays for the National Film Theatre. They were told that it had been wiped. I am glad to include the text in this collection as it is now all that remains of a memorable performance.*

*A week or two after writing this, I was sent a black and white copy, taken from the first transmission.

Hearts and Flowers

BBC TV, 1970, repeated a year later.

BOB	Anthony Hopkins
JEAN	Priscilla Morgan
MARIE	Constance Chapman
TONY	Donald Churchill
WILL	Leon Cortez
LIONEL	Eric Francis
ERIC	Clifford Parrish
PHYLLIS	Betty Bascombe
VERA	Freda Bamford
UNA	Sheila Keith
MR FOWLER	Martin Wyldeck
MRS FOWLER	Grace Arnold
WITTS	Jeffrey Segal
LINDA	Maryann Turner
VICAR	Bill Horsley
WOMAN AT STATION	April Wilding
MR BRITTAIN	Roy Hepworth

Directed by Christopher Morahan

1. Interior. Bob and Jean's Bedroom. Night.

Double bed lit by table lamp. BOB's *head on one pillow, reading newspaper. He is thirty-two. He is wearing pyjama jacket. Sound of door opening and closing. He goes on reading but soon looks up and continues looking off-screen. Music: 'Salut d'Amour' by Elgar. Slowly.*

Opening Captions

He is still watching as JEAN *joins him in bed, wearing a demure nightgown. Settles her head on the pillow and smiles at him briefly, but is overcome by a yawn. Under the bedclothes, he reaches out to touch her. She smiles again cursorily, and moves her feet against his. She closes her eyes. Then moves her feet again and opens her eyes.*

JEAN: No pyjama trousers.

BOB: No.

JEAN: You hot?

BOB: Sweltering.

JEAN: I'm not. Sitting on Bill's bed waiting for him to use the pot, my feet are like ice. [*Turns away from him and closes eyes.*]
 [*He looks at back of her head, puts away paper. He kisses the back of her neck.*]

JEAN: Mmmm. [*Turns head, slightly smiling, eyes closed.*]
 [*He kisses her lips gently. She yawns.*]

JEAN: Oh, dear . . .
 [*He props himself on one elbow and looks at her. She yawns again.*]
 Oh, dear . . .

BOB: Terrific.

JEAN [*opening eyes*]: What?

BOB: I kissed you and you yawned.

JEAN: Did I? Sorry, love, only I'm dead. Bill's been a monkey, tramping chocolate mousse right through the Spanish rope mat . . . and making monster noises during Susan's science programme . . . [*Tails off into yawn.*] Oh, dear . . . it's her school holiday in case you've forgotten.

BOB: It's not only during school holidays.

[*Pause. Her eyes have closed again.*]

I don't much like admitting something's gone wrong with our
sex-life . . . but what else d'you suggest? What about the way you
undress? In that dark corner. And you put on your nightdress
before you take your skirt off. And you won't let me *help* you
either. All day you walk about with attractive clothes on but when
we come up here you won't . . .

JEAN: It's no good, I find it very embarassing having someone take
my clothes off.

BOB: You used to like it.

JEAN: No.

BOB: You *did*.

JEAN: I used to *pretend* to.

[*Pause. He is sitting up, wide awake. Her eyes keep closing.*]

BOB: You used to be more – social – about it all. With a lot more
smiling and chasing about and – unusual rooms. During the day.
Why is it always in the dark nowadays? D'you hate the sight of
me?

JEAN: All that was before children.

BOB: But what about when my mother has them for the day? Or
when Dad takes them to the zoo? How do we spend those
valuable hours? In bed? [*Shakes his head.*] Shopping.

JEAN [*angry*]: D'you think I *like* shopping?

BOB: I think *all* women like shopping.

JEAN: The house doesn't run itself. I'm busy morning till night and
at bedtime tired to death and can't stand bright lights shining in
my eyes.

BOB [*gently, caressing her*]: But, love, d'you think the busy-ness is
to fill the time I might otherwise try to occupy taking your clothes
off?

JEAN [*eyes open, angry*]: How often do I deny you?

BOB: It's not a question –

JEAN: How often do I refuse when you come telling me how much
you –

BOB: It's not a question of how often –

JEAN: Isn't it?

BOB [*louder*]: – but of what it's *like*. Whether you seem to be
suffering some nasty necessity that crops up every so often.

JEAN: Think yourself lucky.

BOB [*imitation*]: 'My husband's very good, he only troubles me twice a week.'

JEAN: You talk as though you're some pathetic lurker in a mac, forced to pick up tarts in doorways. It's a joke – really!

BOB [*as though he finds the description fits*]: Well – [*Makes a little face.*]
    [*She turns away and makes to sleep.*]
    [*He speaks softly:*] Do understand, love, I'm not complaining, I'm apologising . . . for not knowing how to keep our marriage fresh, surprising. Because I'm – not widely experienced. So perhaps I should pick up tarts in doorways.
    [*Pause.*]

JEAN: [*seems not to have listened, then*]: D'you *want* to?

BOB: I don't *want* to. I think perhaps I *ought* to.

JEAN: What d'you expect to learn?

BOB: I don't know. They're doing it all day.

JEAN: How d'you know your sessions with the tart won't be enough? All you want?
    [*Pause*].

BOB: Would that worry you?
    [*She turns again, eyes open, decisively*].

JEAN: *I* don't want you going with tarts. I'm happy with my sex-life as it is. I don't happen to like electric lights in my eyes last thing and you *have* put on weight a bit this year –

BOB [*while she continues*]: Then let's try a different –

JEAN: I'm sorry if you want me to dress as a nurse or a nun, I'm afraid I couldn't keep a straight face.

BOB: When we first married, we didn't need any frills, we excited each other so much.

JEAN: We only had ourselves to think of. [*Yawns.*] Oh, dear.

BOB [*noting this*]: Before the boredom set in.

JEAN: I'm not bored, I'm dead! [*Yawns again.*] Oh, dear. D'you know, when I sing Bill a lullaby, it's me that falls asleep. And what if I'm pregnant? What if it's about to start all over again? You do remember, don't you, I'm going to the doctor tomorrow for the test result? You know I'm late?

BOB: You lost the pills, yes.

JEAN: Forgot them, then couldn't find them. Three days. It's sure to be alright.

BOB: Well, if you are, the damage is done. If you're not, we must continue to place our faith in the drug manufacturers. Still, as you wish.

[*Turns out bedside lamp. As it goes, she yawns. Pause.*]

JEAN [*cockney*]: Hallo, dearie.

BOB: What?

JEAN: Want a nice time?

BOB: What's this?

JEAN: I'm the tart in the doorway.

BOB: You wouldn't know where to start.

JEAN: Think so?

[*Sounds of movements. Giggles, a little scream. Telephone bell rings. Movements stop.*]

BOB: Who the hell –?

[*Bell rings.*]

This time of night?

[*He answers it and with other hand, puts on lights.* JEAN *flinches, hides head under sheets.*]

Hallo? . . . Mum!

[JEAN *makes long-suffering face.*]

Yes, we are, as a matter of fact . . . it's alright . . . [*Manner changes.*] Oh . . . where is he? . . . right, I'll bc over as soon as I can . . . you've called the doctor?

[JEAN *looks at him.*]

Good. Nothing else, no. Shan't be long . . . 'Bye . . . . [*He puts down telephone, swings legs round.*] Dad's collapsed.

[*He goes.* JEAN *left alone, stares at him, off-camera.*]

JEAN: Where was she phoning from?

BOB: A neighbour's.

JEAN: Oh, Bob. Let me know what happens.

BOB: Yep.

[JEAN *thinks, closes her eyes at her thought.*]

JEAN: Poor dear.

2. Interior. Marie's Living Room. Night.

Neither large nor small, trying to be cosy, but with too many pieces of pre-war furniture; overhead light. BOB's *father lying awkwardly on floor in foreground, eyes closed. See nothing else for some time, hear the dialogue.*

MARIE: Bob –

BOB: Hallo, Mum.

MARIE: I walked right through the house without seeing him.

BOB: Where is he?

MARIE: There.

> [BOB *and* MARIE *have come in behind, and* BOB *now approaches his father, crouches by him. Slightly lifts him, dislodging an arm that is awkwardly twisted.*]

I'd been to the whist drive with Mr and Mrs Fowler and they dropped me at the door and I asked them in for a cup of tea but they said they'd better get on home.

> [BOB *is trying to detect a pulse in his father's wrist.*]

Well, you know the way your father tries to pull Mr Fowler's leg and I don't believe he ever really likes it. So they wouldn't come in for a cup of tea and I could hear the gramophone playing so I knocked on the window as usual but he didn't come, so I thought he's probably off in some other room.

> [BOB *sits back, looks at her, nods, returns to father, puts his hand on father's chest to feel a beat.*]

Well, Linda next door dialled the number and I spoke to his wife. He was out on a call, but she expected him back any minute. That was – what? – twenty-five minutes ago.

> [BOB *sits up again.*]

BOB: I suppose we shouldn't move him, or anything.

MARIE: Not till doctor's seen him, I don't think. What do you think?

BOB: No.

MARIE: He's comfortable enough.

BOB: Oh, yes.

MARIE: Perhaps a cushion under his head – what d'you think?

BOB: No.

MARIE: No.

[BOB *sits back on armchair.*]

BOB: It can't have been long before –

[*Doorbell rings.*]

MARIE: There he is.

[*Goes and* BOB *stands. Moves to a twenty year old radiogram. He opens the lid, turns the tone arm back to its rest, takes a long-playing record from the turntable and returns it to its sleeve and the sleeve to its rack.* MARIE *comes in with* DOCTOR, *an elderly man.*]

DOCTOR: Hullo, Mister – um –

BOB: Hullo, Doctor.

DOCTOR: Goodliffe.

[*Smiles, goes down beside father, begins examination.*]

You found him like this, Mrs – um –

MARIE: The funny thing was I didn't see him right away. I couldn't make him hear by knocking on the window so I thought well, he must be out the back. So I went right through to the kitchen and found the milk boiled over he must have put on for his bedtime drink. Then when I came back here, I saw him lying there . . .

[MARIE *weeps.* BOB *takes her hand and holds it with both of his, giving her a be-brave look.*]

DOCTOR [*looking for a pulse*]: Mmm.

BOB: There was still a record playing. When did it stop?

MARIE: I don't know. I know it was playing when I came in.

BOB: It had switched itself off but the radiogram was still –

DOCTOR: Have you got a small hand-mirror?

[MARIE *goes to her handbag.*]

BOB: Well, he can't have collapsed long before. A record takes twenty minutes to play.

[MARIE *brings mirror to* DOCTOR, *who holds it by the mouth for a few seconds. He looks at the glass, then at* BOB, *who is now crouching beside him.*]

DOCTOR [*quietly*]: I'm afraid he's gone.

[BOB *nods.*]

MARIE: I thought he was.

DOCTOR: He can't have known much about it. Much the best way.

MARIE: It's the way he would have wanted himself. Oh dear . . .

DOCTOR: How old was he?

MARIE: Seventy-two.

DOCTOR: Well –

MARIE: Seventy-three in August.

DOCTOR: Not a bad innings, when you look at it. [*He stands.*] Now. He hadn't been in to see me for some weeks, so there'll have to be a coroner's post-mortem.

MARIE: Oh, no.

DOCTOR: A legal formality, nothing more, when somebody passes over unexpectedly.

MARIE: He had some pains over the weekend. In his chest.

DOCTOR [*nodding*]: Angina.

MARIE: And I said shall I ring the doctor, but he said no don't disturb him on a Sunday.

DOCTOR: Perhaps it's best. I might have prolonged his life for a time, but . . . .

MARIE: This is how he would have wanted to go. Sooner than drag on, a burden to everyone. [*She cries.*]

BOB: What shall I do now?

DOCTOR: I'll give you a certificate to send to the registrar. Then in the morning, I'll notify the coroner. They'll be along some time tomorrow to take him away. Meantime – have you ever made arrangements with an undertaker?

3. Interior. Marie's Hall. Night.

BOB *crosses and knocks on door of front room. The door is opened by* WITTS, *a neat middle-aged man in black suiting. Seeing* BOB, *he smiles, opens wider.*

BOB: My mother wanted to know if you'd like a cup of tea.

WITTS: I shan't say no, if a cup of tea's being made.

BOB: What about your – friend?

WITTS: Mister Morley won't say no, sir. And – sir? – would you step in for a moment?

    [BOB *goes in.*]

4. Interior. Front Room. Night.

Larger than living room, with better furnishings. A coffin stands on trestles. MORLEY, *the other man, is tidying up.* WITTS *shows* BOB *some articles on a table.*

WITTS: The contents of the pockets, sir. His wallet. A quantity of silver and copper coin. Sundry keys on ring. A handkerchief. [*Shows him chair.*] His outer clothes. We usually leave the underwear on, though you can have it returned later, should you wish. More often than not, of course, it's soiled, so you may give us permission to destroy it.

BOB: Yes, fine. We shan't be wanting it, I'm sure . . . . [*Smiles apologetically.*]

WITTS: That's all, thank you, sir. We'll take advantage of the lady's invitation as soon as we've finished up in here. [*Hands him contents of father's pockets.*]

   [BOB *goes.*]

5. Interior. Bob and Jean's Bedroom. Night.

JEAN *in double-bed, on* BOB's *side, using telephone.*

JEAN: Alright . . . I'll make the bed in the playroom . . . is she taking it well? . . . I'm so sorry, Bob . . . I meant sorry for you, too . . . no, it can't be helped but even so -- . . . yes, see you. [*She puts telephone down. Lies back on* BOB's *pillow, staring at ceiling, tears in eyes.*]

6. Interior. Living Room. Night.

MARIE, BOB *and the undertakers standing with cups of tea.*

WITTS: Beautiful cup of tea that.

MARIE: I should think you need it.

WITTS: I always say, at a time like this, that's all you can do, really and truly, drink tea.

[BOB *returns his to tray.*]

MARIE: Want another?

BOB: No, thanks.

MARIE: Dad never had a cup of tea at night, he always had a milky
drink. He said tea kept him awake.

[WITTS *nods. They drink.*]

WITTS: He was a well-built man.

MARIE: He always walked like a serjeant-major, with his shoulders
back.

WITTS: My words to Mister Morley: military bearing. I said he had
a military bearing. Late seventies, was he?

MARIE: Seventy-two.

WITTS: Very well preserved.

MARIE: He was always athletic, you see.

WITTS: Kept him young.

MARIE: Cycling, football, rowing.

WITTS: Preserved him.

[MORLEY *nods.* WITTS *finishes tea.*]

This won't get the work done. Thank you, madam. And you'll
be here, sir, nine o'clock or thereabouts to let in the coroner's
officers?

BOB: Yes.

WITTS: Goodnight, sir.

[BOB *goes with men.* MARIE *puts cups on tray.*]

7. Interior. Hall. Night.

BOB *returning from closing front door. He speaks into living room.*

BOB: You've packed your case?

MARIE: It's there.

[*She comes to door.*]

BOB: Might as well get home then. Back to my place.

MARIE: I'd better wash the tea things.

BOB: I'll clear them up in the morning.

[*She comes into hall, switching off light of living-room.* MARIE
nods, takes down overcoat.]

MARIE: Is it still warm out?

BOB: Sweltering.

MARIE: But it could turn. I'll wear my coat save carrying it.

> [*He helps her on with her coat.*]

I can ring Tony from your place.

BOB: Yes.

MARIE: He'll want to make arrangements to come to the funeral. He and Dad were very close.

> [*She begins to cry.* BOB *turns to door, opens it and waits.*]

8. Interior. Bob and Jean's Bedroom. Night.

Double bed, as at start. JEAN *and* BOB, *sitting back to back on the edges of the bed.*

JEAN [*quietly*]: She's not too bad.

> [*Pause.* JEAN *starts to get into bed.*]

She had a little cry in the kitchen.

> [BOB *gets in other side.*]

BOB: And another little one as we were leaving Forty-Two.

> [*He pulls feet into bed.* JEAN *looks at him. He examines toe nails.*]

And a big one on the phone to Tony.

> [*He pulls off sliver of nail, pulls up sheet. Sniffs hand.*]

JEAN: You surely don't begrudge her a few tears.

BOB: Shame she didn't shed them sooner. They're no use to the old man now.

> [*Pause. He stares at ceiling.* JEAN *half-turns away.*]

As soon as death was certified, the whitewashing started. 'He was always athletic, rowing, cycling, football.' Not for the last thirty years, to *my* knowledge. There won't be anything left of Dad by the time she and Tony have finished.

JEAN: It seems only right to me for people to cry a bit. Even crocodile tears are better than nothing.

BOB: D'you think so?

JEAN: Yes.

BOB: Why?

JEAN: He'd like to feel mourned.

BOB: He doesn't exist any more, he's out of the question. What I'd mourn would be his lack of achievement. Seventy years and nothing to show for it! He did no harm, I suppose, but no good either.

JEAN: You and Tony.

BOB: That's all. Family. His entire energy devoted to his wife and sons. I loathe family life. As an idea. Net curtains and privet hedges and the sound of slamming bedroom doors. If all the energy lost in domestic friction could be canalised, we'd solve the traffic problem in a week.

[*Pause. He turns to her, realising he has upset her and wanting to mollify her.*]

Love –

[JEAN *moves from his touch irritably.*]

JEAN: What if I die first, is that all you'll feel?

BOB: I shall want to die too. But it's different, we *chose* each other.

JEAN: She chose your father. Presumably. Then shouldn't she cry?

BOB [*thinks, then nods*]: I only meant we don't choose our parents. We can't feel the same for them.

JEAN: I shall cry when my mother dies.

BOB: You're very close. Perhaps because your father left her. You drew together.

JEAN: Don't you expect your children to cry at your death?

BOB: Why should I want them to? I shan't be here to see it. I shouldn't enjoy it, if I could. [*He turns and embraces her from behind.*] Eh, my love?

JEAN: No. [*Pushes him off.*] All you think about.

9. Interior. Marie's Front Room. Day

Bright morning sunlight filtered through drawn curtains. Coffin on trestles, as before. After a few moments BOB *comes in wearing lightweight office clothes, with no sign of mourning. Blows air out and goes to open one of the windows a few inches at the top.* BOB *turns back to room and approaches coffin. He pulls back sheet over Father's face. He looks at it for some seconds, then leaves the room.*]

10. Interior. Living Room. Day.

At rear of house, overlooking garden. Windows uncurtained and light coming in. BOB *enters, takes from mantelpiece the contents of father's clothes. He spreads out the handkerchief on a table and puts the wallet, money and keys into it, folding it over into a parcel. He leaves it there. Sound off from front door.* BOB *goes out.*

11. Interior. Marie's Hall. Day.

BOB *arrives at front door and find the morning's mail on the doormat, one or two circulars, and a picture postcard.*

12. Interior. Bob and Jean's Hall. Day.

JEAN *at mirror, checking her appearance. Hear* MARIE'*s voice off, speaking on telephone.*
MARIE: . . . well, Eric, if you give me a ring here at Robert's place, I can let you know for sure what time the funeral's starting . . . yes, alright, I know he'd have wanted you to be there . . .
JEAN [*speaking through doorway, hastily*]: I shan't be long. You'll keep an eye on the children, they're in the garden.
MARIE: Yes, bye-bye. No, Eric, I was saying bye-bye, Jean, she's just off out.
  [JEAN *goes.*]

13. Interior. Marie's Living Room. Day.

Mail now on table beside father's personal effects. BOB *at mantelpiece, lighting a cigarette. He has a small, official-looking booklet in his hand, open at a page. He sits in an armchair and puzzles over it.*
BOB: 'It is essential to inform the coroner if you want cremation

rather than burial, so that he may issue his certificate-for-cremation, which is free of charge and obviates the use of forms B and C. Form F is signed by the medical referee of the crematorium on the medical evidence of forms B and C, or H, or in the case of a post-mortem, after the issue of the certificate-for-cremation.'

[*He closes the book and puts it in his pocket, goes to table and opens picture newspaper. There is not a lot to read, but he glances with some relief at the girlie pictures and scans the sports page. At last he returns to the girlie pictures. Doorbell. He closes paper, stubs out cigarette in ashtray on table, hesitates, wondering why he did not finish his smoke, shrugs, goes on stubbing, then makes to answer the door.*]

14. Exterior. Marie's House. Day.

MARIE's *house from opposite side. Sixty-year-old semi with small front garden. Parked cars line both sides of street and Coroner's van has had to double-park. Two men come from the house carrying the body in its coffin, now closed. They put it into their plain van.* BOB *watches from the front door. A motor-cyclist roars through the narrow gap between the van and the further row of cars.*

15. Interior Bob and Jean's Bedroom. Night.

Double bed, as before. JEAN *awake, no book.* BOB *climbs in, full pyjamas.*

BOB: Why didn't you go to sleep? No need to wait for me.

JEAN: I'd only wake up when you climbed in.

BOB: We could always get twin beds. Eh, love? [*Touches her.*] Separate beds?

JEAN: Mmmm.

BOB: How's Mum been?

JEAN: Busy telephoning her relations with the news. Tony's coming

Thursday morning, he's got a programme Wednesday night.

BOB: I suppose London will somehow manage to survive without him for a few hours.

JEAN: So she's kept busy.

BOB: I saw the body off. Then went to the office to find a blazing row going on about who'd leaked the Ring Road Proposals to the local press. Well, I say a blazing row but it was more a puff of smoke. And I couldn't dodge this evening's Action Group because I'm the prime mover. The Civic Society bloke was there.

JEAN: She was very helpful at bath-time.

BOB: We think the Fine Arts Commission will be on our side. Getting in with some funny company.

JEAN: And looked after the kids while I was out.

BOB: Good. Gave her something to occupy her mind, too, I expect.
    [*She looks at him as though wondering what he's doing there.*]
    Where d'you go? Shopping?
    [*He is winding his wrist-watch.*]

JEAN: No. I went to the doctor.

BOB: Doctor? What ab – Christ! Oh, love, I'm sorry, what did he say?

JEAN: He said yes. Positive. I'm pregnant. [*She smiles coldly, ironically.*]

BOB: Oh, no.

JEAN: Oh, yes.
    [BOB *shakes his head.*]

BOB: What are we going to do?

JEAN: Apply to the milkman for our subsidised pintas. The dentist for free fillings. Start buying maternity wear again . . . .

BOB: No, I mean . . . .

JEAN: I gave Peggy my old clothes for her prison visiting or whatever it is . . . .

BOB: That's what you want, is it? I mean, the doctor thinks you'll be alright?

JEAN: I'm only thirty-three. Of course I'll be alright!

BOB: Just as Bill's about to start at the Montessori!

JEAN: I know.

BOB: All that again!

JEAN: The third child means a second family allowance.

BOB: So much for the pill.

JEAN: I missed three. I left them in that duffle bag in the back of the van.

BOB: Look – you know the money we've been saving for the car? Perhaps if you felt, you know, you couldn't face it, well perhaps we could use it for a – nursing home.

JEAN: I didn't want to be pregnant, but now that I am, I suddenly feel – coming at the same time as your father's death, I'm very excited about it. I nearly sang in the bus coming home. I think I must have a touch of the tar-brush. Why can't we let off fireworks or put on masks or dance in the streets? Cause some kind of public nuisance?

BOB: I don't feel like dancing.

JEAN: And you didn't feel like crying at your father's death. What about those women we heard in Killarney, howling all night?

BOB: Professional mourners.

JEAN: Alright. They helped the other . . . people find a voice for their grief.

[BOB *considers*. *Pause*.]

BOB: Yeah. The undertaker said: All you can do at a time like this is drink tea. And I remember thinking: couldn't we scream or curse the gods or rend our clothes . . . but no, we're a long way from that. It worries me sometimes, I don't feel a lot. I can't pretend an emotion I don't feel.

JEAN: Ever tried? Perhaps you never feel because you never try to feel.

BOB: I feel for you.

JEAN: That's greed. [*She turns away, tired of trying*.]

BOB: Tony will show us how to feel. He's an expert.

16. Exterior. Main Line Station. Booking Hall. Day.

TONY *and* WOMAN *come from platform with arriving passengers.* TONY *is 38, dressed in dark suit with black tie, carries suitcase and large brief-case. She is young, bold, impressive. They are chatting.* BOB, *also in a suit and black tie, sees them coming, frowns.*

TONY: . . . find my childhood closes in on me as soon as I reach this station . . . Hullo, Bob . . .

BOB: Hullo.

[TONY *offers his hand.* BOB *shakes it.*]

TONY: D'you want a porter?

WOMAN: No. I'm being met.

[*She takes her case.*]

TONY: Bye-bye, then.

WOMAN: I shall watch you on the screen with a new interest.

TONY: Bless you.

WOMAN: Goodbye.

[*She goes off.*]

BOB: I thought you'd brought a friend.

TONY: Christ no. I made the mistake of smiling at her, then it turned out she knew me from the telly and talked my head off all the way down. Serves me right.

BOB: Smashing piece.

TONY: One of the problems of being on the box. People won't leave you alone.

BOB [*looking after* WOMAN]: Must be awful.

[PORTER *crosses,* BOB *collides with him.*]

Sorry.

TONY: One day, on this station, I called a porter and d'you know who turned up?

BOB: Uncle Arthur.

TONY: Right. Talk about embarrassing.

BOB: He's retired now.

TONY: I stared at this dominating figure of my childhood and he stared at me and picked up my case and carried it and asked me about the family.

BOB: I don't suppose it worried him.

TONY: No.

BOB: It must have happened before.

TONY: To him, perhaps, but not to me.

17. Exterior. Station. Day.

They are now crossing road to parked cars.

TONY: How's Jean?

BOB: Fine.

TONY: The kids?

BOB: She's expecting another.

TONY: No! Terrific! I don't know. *Is* it terrific? You tell me.

BOB: Oh, yes, she'd got to the stage of drooling over other people's. It's come just at the right time.

[*They have reached a Minivan;* BOB *unlocks the driver's door.*]

TONY: Why didn't you let me know?

BOB: Didn't know ourselves till a couple of days ago.

TONY: Talk about: in the midst of life.

BOB: Yeah.

[*He gets into the van and opens the passenger door.*]

TONY: I can't take it in. Mum's message came when I was halfway through an in-depth interview and I'm afraid the rest was a total cock-up. [BOB *puts case into van.*] How's she taken it?

BOB [*emerging again*]: What?

TONY: How's Mum taken the old man's death?

BOB: The funeral arrangements have kept her busy.

TONY: One justification for a funeral – takes your mind off it.

[BOB *seated at the wheel.* TONY *gets in.*]

BOB: Don't see a lot wrong with funerals. It's a way of showing you're sorry someone's gone. I hope people show they're sorry when I die.

TONY: *I'm* sorry he's gone. I don't need to show it. After that interview was over, I sat in my dressing-room and cried my bloody eyes out.

BOB [*almost laughing*]: Aaah!

[BOB *starts the motor and* TONY *stares at him.*]

18. Interior. Marie's Front Room. Day.

Begin on a splendid bunch of cut flowers, mostly roses, and move to show the room full of similar but less impressive bouquets, sprays and wreaths. Front door bell rings.

19. Interior. Hall. Day.

JEAN *comes from kitchen, elegant in simple black dress.* MARIE *and her neighbour* LINDA *may be seen in kitchen preparing food.* JEAN *opens door.* MRS *and* MR FOWLER, *in their sixties, carrying flowers and other things.*

MRS FOWLER: Hullo, Jean.

JEAN: Good morning. I'm sorry. I know you're friends of Mrs Goodliffe but . . .

MRS FOWLER: Mr and Mrs Fowler.

MR FOWLER: We were at your wedding.

JEAN: Yes, of course!

MR FOWLER: We gave you the carpet sweeper.

JEAN: It's still going. Do come in.

[*They come in, laughing slightly,* MARIE *comes from living room at back letting out a murmur of subdued conversation from many voices.*]

MARIE: It is nice of you to come.

MRS FOWLER: Are we the last?

MARIE: There's the boys yet.

MR FOWLER: We'd have been sooner but I wanted to get these flowers fresh.

MRS FOWLER: He's just this moment picked them.

MARIE: Aren't they beautiful?

JEAN: Lovely.

MR FOWLER: And while I was down the garden, I thought to myself, perhaps she'd like a few sticks of rhubarb. [*Gives* MARIE *that, too, wrapped in newspaper.*]

MARIE: Harry loved your rhubarb.

MRS FOWLER: Well, I said, 'You can't take rhubarb to a funeral' and he said to me 'Harry liked my rhubarb' and he said 'I think Marie liked it too'.

MARIE: Oh, yes.

MR FOWLER: I said 'I know Harry liked it but I'm not sure whether Marie did, but anyway,' I said 'she might as well have it'.

MRS FOWLER: He said 'Life goes on regardless'.

MARIE: You better take that, Jean.

[JEAN *takes the rhubarb to kitchen.*]

Come and see the rest.

[*They move off to front room. Favouring them for a moment, hear them exclaiming.*]

MRS FOWLER: Aren't they glorious?

MR FOWLER: I was only saying 'There's one consolation, it's a beautiful time of the year for blooms.'

[JEAN *in kitchen doorway*, LINDA *working beyond.*]

LINDA: What's that you've got?

JEAN: Rhubarb.

LINDA: For the buffet?

JEAN: No, someone brought it.

LINDA: To the funeral?

JEAN: Yes, for Mrs Goodliffe. What can I do now?

[*Doorbell rings. She leaves rhubarb and crosses hall again to front door, opening it to* BOB *and* TONY.]

Hullo, Tone.

TONY: How are you, love?

JEAN: Fine.

[*They neither kiss nor shake hands.*]

I'm sorry about your father.

TONY: I know you are, you were fond of him.

JEAN: Your mother's in the front room.

MARIE [*emerging*]: It's the boys!

TONY: Mum!

[*They kiss.*]

MARIE: You got your train alright then. [*She begins to weep, then stops. She turns to* FOWLERS, *still in front room.*] Tony and Dad were very close. They wrote each other these great long letters.

TONY: His in Victorian copperplate, mine in portable Olivetti. He never stopped complaining how ill-mannered it was to type personal correspondence.

MARIE: He had some funny ways but he was a very good father.

TONY: I know he was.

[*She cries again.* TONY *holds her.*]

MARIE: You didn't always see eye to eye. [*To* MRS FOWLER.] I think because they were too much alike. Bob never used to quarrel, he just went his own way, but Tony and he were always at each other's throats. I think the eldest boy's bound to be closer . . . and the father's bound to feel closer to him, I think, because –

TONY: Mister Fowler, how are you?

[BOB *and* JEAN *have not looked at anyone during this scene.* TONY *cut it short on purpose.* BOB *takes out a list and begins checking it.* TONY'*s move takes him into the front room to greet* FOWLER.]

20. Interior. Front Room. Day.

MARIE: You remember Mister Fowler in confectionary?

MR FOWLER: I say, you're looking well.

MARIE: I thought he looked drawn.

TONY: Mrs Fowler –

JEAN: Drawn? With that expensive sun-tan?

MARIE: *Under* the sun-tan.

TONY: I've been doing a filmed report from Israel.

MR FOWLER: We like your films. I say to Mrs Fowler, 'Switch it on, might as well see young Tony pop his head round the screen.'

TONY: Bless you.

MRS FOWLER: I said, you sent a lovely bouquet.

TONY: Is it alright?

21. Interior. Hall. Day.

[BOB, *checking list,* JEAN *with him.*]

BOB: According to my figures, there are thirteen people between two cars.

[JEAN *looks at list.*]

JEAN: Linda's staying here to do the food.

[BOB *crosses off* LINDA.]

BOB: Even so, that leaves – say – six in the limousine, at the most, and six to squeeze into your mother's eleven hundred, which is really only big enough for four, five at a pinch.

[LIONEL *comes downstairs, winks at* BOB, *goes to look through hall windows. A kindly apologetic friend of the family.*]

JEAN: There's Mister Fowler's!

BOB: Mister Fowler's Humber, completely slipped my mind. I was thinking I'd have to take a couple of aunties crouching in the back of the Minivan.

LIONEL: Panic stations, Bob. The hearse is arriving.

FOWLER [*Also coming from the window*]: The hearse seems to be arriving.

BOB: Right, thanks. Now. I'd better get Uncle Will and Cousin Eric and few of the aunties on the move –

LIONEL: No, it's driven by.

BOB: Driven by?

LIONEL: Another funeral in the street this morning, is there?

BOB: I don't know. Had I better go and shout after them?

MR FOWLER: No room to turn here, see. They're going to the roundabout, then come back pointing in the right direction.

LIONEL: Better get the troops fell in, Bob.

BOB: Right, yes. Now the way I see it is: chief mourners in the limousine – that's Mum, Uncle Will, Cousin Eric, Tony and me. Then in your mother's car –

JEAN: Stop organising.

BOB: This morning you told me to keep on my toes and make sure everyone was happy. [*Turns to door of living room.*]

22. Interior. Living Room. Day.

WILL, ERIC, PHYLLIS, UNA *and* VERA *waiting.* ERIC *moving about looking at various objects.*

111

BOB: The cars have arrived.
[*They all seem relieved that something is happening at last and at once stand with sounds of assent.*]

23. Interior. Hall. Day.

They fill the hall and MARIE *and* MRS FOWLER *come from the front room.*

MARIE: Oh, Mrs Fowler, d'you know my cousin Una?
MRS FOWLER: How d'you do?
UNA: Pleased to meet you.
MARIE: Vera Lambert you know already.
VERA: Hullo, Mrs Fowler.
MRS FOWLER: How are you?
VERA: Not getting any younger.
MRS FOWLER: That's true –
MARIE: Have you met my nephew – Eric?
[*And so on, while* WILL *struggles through and climbs the stairs. When he is halfway up.*]
That's Harry's brother Will on the stairs. Will!
WILL: Hullo?
MARIE: This is Mrs Fowler.
BOB: Uncle Lionel, someone, will you open the front door, please?
[*Waving his list.*] Mister Fowler, could you open the door, d'you think, and let somebody out?

24. Interior. Front Room. Day.

TONY *alone, looking about.* MRS FOWLER *in doorway, trying to get out.* TONY *picks up and examines with undue interest a plaster figure of a boy and girl beneath a parasol.* JEAN *comes in.*

JEAN: I left my coat in here.
TONY: Yes. [*He helps her on with it. Quietly.*] How are you, Jean?
JEAN: Oh, fine.

TONY: Happy?

JEAN: Yes.

TONY: Good for you. Bob tells me you're –

PHYLLIS [*coming in.*]: Had to say hullo to my favourite teevee star.

TONY: You sending me up, Mrs Long? How are you?

JEAN: Where's your coat, Mother?

PHYLLIS: In the hall, dear, but I can't get to it.

25. Exterior. Marie's House. Day.

Two great black limousines tower above the family cars on either side. One is a hearse. Beside that, BOB's *Minivan. Behind the other funeral car, an 1100 and a Humber. The usual other parked cars. The undertakers,* WITTS *and* MORLEY, *approach the front door, as it is opened by* MR FOWLER. WITTS *stands aside.*

26. Interior. Front Room. Day.

UNA *and* VERA *have come in.*

PHYLLIS: I was saying that's a bouquet and a half you sent, Tony.

VERA: At my husband's death, we had no flowers. He had it in his will. You can.

UNA: I think a funeral's nothing without blooms.

VERA: They make such a nasty mess on the carpet.

JEAN: Ours is a terribly skimpy bunch, considering what we paid.

UNA: Still, there you are, you don't much like to complain, at a time like this.

PHYLLIS: That's what they rely on to make their exorbitant profits.

VERA: I never believe in bringing live things into the house. You never know.

WITTS [*pushing in*]: Thank you, ladies. Perhaps you'll pass on out to the cars.

[*The older women go.* WITTS *collects some bunches and wreaths and follows.* TONY *has broken off a rose from his bunch. Now he*

113

offers it to JEAN.]

JEAN: Thank you.

[*He adjusts it on her dress, using a brooch to fasten it. She smiles and follows the others.*]

27. Exterior. Marie's House. Day.

They all move through the front garden to the street. WITTS *organises them into the limousine, the Humber and the 1100.*

FOWLER [*on pavement*]: See the police put 'No Waiting' signs on the road here?

BOB: I suppose the undertakers fix that.

MR FOWLER: No, it was me. I rang the station last night. I said 'We can't have the hearse double parking, infra dig.'

28. Exterior. Front Door. Day.

MARIE *is on the path and* LINDA, *her neighbour, is inside.*

MARIE: I should pop the sausage rolls in the oven about half-past-eleven, Linda.

LINDA: Right you are.

MARIE: Just for a warm through.

LINDA: Yes.

MARIE [*doubtfully*]: You'll be alright now?

LINDA: You go on.

MARIE: You know where everything is?

LINDA: I can find it. You better go.

MARIE: Alright.

LINDA: And – have a good –

[*Breaks off and smiles awkwardly.* MARIE *goes up path to limousine.* LINDA *waves and closes door.*]

29. Exterior. Marie's House. Street. Day

The hearse moves out to occupy the centre of the road, between the two rows of parked cars. The second limousine is about to follow the hearse when a small yellow sports car suddenly accelerates with a roar and pulls up sharply behind the slowly moving hearse. The second limousine leads the other two cars in the procession to a position behind the sports car. The sports car is driven by a swinger in dark glasses and the passenger is a blonde optional extra, also hidden behind enormous black glasses. The DRIVER *realises his position too late and crawls along behind the hearse.* PHYLLIS's *car is next.*

30. Interior. Phyllis's Car. Day.

JNA *in front passenger seat,* PHYLLIS *driving,* LIONEL *and* JEAN *behind.*

JNA: If I hadn't seen that with my own eyes, I shouldn't have believed it.

PHYLLIS: Oh, it's absolutely typical.

LIONEL: Time and tide wait for no man.

PHYLLIS: Not these days they don't. [*Lights a cigarette from the lighter on the dashboard.*]

JNA: No respect.

PHYLLIS: It's a rat race. They wait for no-one. Kids today.

31. Exterior. Funeral Procession. Day.

Close on DRIVER *and* PASSENGER *of sportscar: middle aged beneath their misleading gear. Slowly the procession continues.*

32. Interior. Limousine. Day.

BOB *and* TONY *on one seat behind the* DRIVER. MARIE *near them. On another seat*, UNCLE WILL *and* COUSIN ERIC.

WILL: Funny thing, I never cared that much for funerals, but recent years I seem to go all the time.

33. Exterior. Funeral Procession. Day.

The procession reaches the main road. The hearse waits, then moves forward, turning left. The sports car roars away to the right. The limousine follows the hearse.

34. Interior. Limousine. Day.

WILL [*laughs*]: There he goes! Now perhaps we can get a bit of a move on.

MARIE: We may not have much money, but we do see life.

35. Interior. Phyllis's Car. Day.

UNA: The hearses never go slow these days. Not like they used to.

PHYLLIS: They'd hold up the traffic.

UNA: Mind you, with burial it's different. But cremation, they can't wait to get you out the way. When I buried my Jack out Fairview, the attendants walked the street, one to each pavement, silk toppers and crêpe bands, as much as to say; look here.

　　[PHYLLIS *coughs over her cigarette. In the back seat*, LIONEL winks at JEAN.]

36. Interior. Limousine. Day.

WILL: A funeral was a big thing then, I'm talking about the turn of the century. Only time our street saw carriages.

TONY: Well, things haven't changed that much. You don't get many Rollses in your street, do you, Mum?

MARIE: Only funerals and weddings.

TONY: There hasn't been that much of a social revolution.

37. Exterior. Funeral Procession. Day.

Funeral goes under some railway arches.

38. Interior. Limousine. Day.

WILL: Another thing in our street, Tony, when your Dad and I were boys, was the urine woman.

TONY: The what?

WILL: The urine woman. She used to come with a cart full of vessels collecting urine.

TONY [*curious but smiling*]: What for?

WILL: The local dye-works. Apparently it was cheaper than ammonia.
[*Laughs.* TONY *smiles, tries not to laugh.*]

MARIE: Will!
[WILL *takes out handkerchief to wipe his eyes, looks embarrassed, stares ahead.* TONY *and* BOB *catch each other's eyes and struggle not to laugh.*]

ERIC: I once did a pen-and-ink landscape study from this very spot, d'you remember, Auntie?

MARIE: Did you, Eric? No, I can't.

ERIC: Some time ago now. Coming back after all these years, I find this quite a sentimental journey.
[WILL *mops his sweating brow with the handkerchief. They all look warm.*]

39. Exterior. Funeral Procession. Day

The procession passes some houses with washing visible. A lot of West Indians about, staring at the cars.

40. Interior. Limousine. Day.

WILL: Bit slummy these houses, Marie.
ERIC: Late Regency, aren't they? That portico's typical.
MARIE: They call it The Jungle now.

41. Exterior. Funeral Procession. Day.

A thirties street. Half-timbered detached houses in a variety of pre-war styles.

42. Interior. Limousine. Day.

WILL: These are a bit smarter.
MARIE: That one there, see, Will? That's where I wanted to move when our neighbourhood started going down. I can't tell you the Sunday afternoons we spent standing in empty houses arguing the toss.
BOB: He couldn't bear the sight of funerals going past.
WILL: That what it was?
MARIE: That's what he said.
BOB: 'Your mother and I stood and watched them for an hour, going slowly, coming back fast'.
    [WILL *laughs at the imitation.*]
MARIE: That was an excuse. He was happy where he was, that was his trouble.

43. Exterior. Funeral Procession. Day.

Traffic lights. The cars wait for green: the DRIVER *of the limousine glances at his watch.*

44. Interior. Limousine. Day.

Close-up BOB *as he notices.*

BOB [*Voice-over*]: An important factor of the successful funeral is timing the arrival of the cortege at the place of interment or cremation. Many cemetries and crematoria penalise latecomers by increasing or doubling their charges.

45. Exterior. Cemetry. Day.

Solemnly the hearse and limousine turn into the cemetery, leaving the other cars to wait for a break in the traffic. Beyond the gates are monstrous monuments. The road follows a circular course to allow funerals to approach the chapel and on the central island formed by this curve are memorials of great seniority, mock-classic temples decorated with statuary or vast petrified boxes with iron railings round them.

46. Interior. Limousine. Day.

TONY: God!

47. Exterior. Crematorium. Day.

The hearse arrives at a more recent porch and the procession halts. The UNDERTAKERS *and* CHAUFFEURS *get out. A* MAN *in sports coat and trousers crosses in front of the limousine. He also wears a clerical collar and carries some vestments. He hurries into the Chapel.* THREE MEN *in dark suits are sitting in a car which has arrived earlier.*

48. Interior. Limousine. Day.

BOB *leans forward to open the door.*
WILL: Wait till they open it.
BOB: Oh. [*He leans back and waits.*]

49. Exterior. Crematorium. Day.

Silence for some time but for birdsong and quiet traffic. The UNDERTAKERS, *joined by two others, carry the coffin into the Chapel.*

50. Interior. Limousine. Day.

ERIC: I could spend a week among these monuments without losing interest.
MARIE: That's nice and cheerful.
ERIC: They represent a broad spectrum of the visual tastes of the eighteenth and nineteenth centuries.
BOB: That one there reminds me of the Elephant House.
TONY: Superb location for a film.
BOB: I'd bulldoze the lot and make it into a children's park.
TONY: Look at the class distinction – carried to the grave. These lavish memorials here and – up on the hill – the ordinary stones in serried ranks. Just as they were in life.

BOB: Oh, come on –
TONY: What?
BOB: Let's be practical, at least. I'm not going to feel guilty about what happened before I was born.

51. Exterior. Crematorium. Day.

PHYLLIS's *and* MR FOWLER's *cars pull up behind the limousine.* LIONEL *gets out of the 1100 on the driver's side and opens* PHYLLIS's *door, then moves round to open* UNA's.
UNA: Nobody move. Nobody move till the chief mourners move.
> [LIONEL *stands embarrassed, his gesture spoilt. He closes the door and stands by it awaiting orders.*
> *At the Austin,* MR FOWLER *opens his door.* VERA *speaks to him urgently. He pulls door to quietly.*]

52. Exterior. Crematorium. Chapel Porch. Day

Undertakers hear organ music from Chapel and now open the door of the limousine. TONY *gets out and turns to assist* MARIE. BOB *follows and the* UNDERTAKERS *lead the mother and two sons to the Chapel. At the 1100* LIONEL *pulls open the door again.* UNA *speaks. He closes it again.*

53. Interior. Chapel. Day.

An USHER *directs* MARIE *and sons into a front pew. In a modest pulpit, of the same style and material as the other furnishings, stands the* MAN *who ran across before the car, now wearing his cassock and surplice. The coffin is on a catafalque between him and the mourners.*
VICAR: I am the resurrection and the life, saith the Lord: he that believeth in me, though he were dead, yet shall he live.

54. Exterior. Crematorium. Day.

ERIC *and* WILL *have got out from limousine and are moving after* MARIE *to the Chapel. At the 1100 we see but don't hear* UNA *say: Right – now.* LIONEL *opens the door and* UNA *begins to get out.* PHYLLIS *and* JEAN *follow suit. At the Austin the* FOWLERS *get out too.*

55. Interior. Chapel. Day.

WILL *and* ERIC *are directed into second pew.* MARIE, BOB *and* TONY *are finding their place in the prayer book.*
VICAR: We brought nothing into this world and it is certain we can carry nothing out.

56. Exterior. Crematorium. Day.

Other mourners now standing by cars. PHYLLIS *and* LIONEL *are locking the doors of the 1100,* MR FOWLER *the Austin.* MR FOWLER *even locks the boot.*

57. Interior. Chapel. Day.

ERIC [*quietly*]: D'you want a Prayer Book, Uncle?
VICAR: Psalm Twenty-Three.
WILL: I know the words of the Twenty-Third Psalm.
ALL [*reading*]: The Lord is my Shepherd, therefore can I lack nothing –
WILL: I shall not want – what's this?
ALL: He shall feed me in a green pasture and lead me forth beside the waters of comfort.
WILL: These aren't the proper words.
ERIC: Sssh.

[*Hands him Prayer Book, open at Psalm.* WILL *tries to read.*]
ALL: He shall convert my soul.

58. Exterior. Crematorium. Day.

The women watch while MR FOWLER *locks the passenger doors.*
LIONEL *stands between; the* UNDERTAKERS *watch them.* UNA *nods*
at VERA *and they lead the women towards the Chapel.* LIONEL *waits*
for MR FOWLER. *The three* MEN *in dark suits get out of their car.*

59. Interior. Chapel. Day.

As UNA *and* VERA *appear and are shown to a pew.*
ALL: But thy loving-kindness and mercy shall follow me all the days
   of my life and I will dwell in the house of the Lord forever.
VICAR: Amen.
ALL: Amen.
   [JEAN *and* PHYLLIS *and* MRS FOWLER *follow.*]
VICAR: Please sit down.
   [*Everyone sits.*]
   The lesson is from Corinthians one fifteen.
   [LIONEL *and* MR FOWLER *enter and sit. They are followed by*
   the three MEN *in dark suits.*]
   We shall not all sleep but we shall all be changed. In a moment,
   in the twinkling of an eye, at the last trump: for the trumpet shall
   sound and the dead shall be raised incorruptible and we shall be
   changed.
   [WILL, *moved, blows his nose violently.* BOB *and* TONY *notice that*
   MARIE *is weeping.*]

60. Exterior. Chapel. Day.

WITTS *and* MORLEY *light cigarettes.*

WITTS: See that fellow? One of the sons? Image of the fellow on tv, what's his name? On tv.

[MORLEY *shakes head.* WITTS *checks list.*]

Cox, Holloway . . . Goodliffe . . . that's him. Tony Goodliffe. Told you I knew him.

61. Interior. Chapel. Day.

All are kneeling on hassocks.

VICAR: Forasmuch as it hath pleased Almighty God of his great mercy to take unto himself the soul of our dear brother here departed.

[JEAN *screws her eyes tight shut to control her tears.*]

We therefore commit his body to the flames.

[*The coffin begins to sink out of sight.* WILL *stares appalled at* HARRY's *disappearance.*]

In sure and certain hope of the Resurrection to eternal life through our Lord Jesus Christ, who shall change our body of low estate that it may be like unto his glorious body.

[*Close up:* BOB.]

BOB [*voice-over*]: Cremation begins with the coffin going to a committal room, the body remaining in the coffin. Each coffin is individually burnt in a cremator, the ashes being removed after about ninety minutes and reduced to a fine powder.

[*When the coffin has sunk far enough a blue cover slides across concealing it.*]

62. Exterior. Chapel. Day.

WITTS *and* MORLEY *are bringing bouquets from hearse to garden plot nearby.* WITTS *approaches the Chapel to listen.* MORLEY *glances at a folded newspaper.* WITTS *stubs out cigarette.*

63. Interior. Chapel. Day.

With a click, organ music begins. See the discreet loudspeaker. VICAR *leaves his pulpit,* MOURNERS *stand. Doors opened by* WITTS *and* VICAR *stands at doorway nodding politely as* MARIE *leads out.*

VICAR: Goodday.

MARIE: Goodday. Thank you.

[VICAR *puts out his hand and shakes* TONY's.]

TONY: Goodday.

VICAR: Like to say how much I enjoy your programmes.

TONY: Bless you.

[TONY *goes out.* BOB *follows him.*]

VICAR: Goodday.

BOB: Goodbye.

64. Exterior. Crematorium. Day.

The THREE MEN *in dark suits stand by porch.* MARIE *draws* BOB *and* TONY *towards them.*

MARIE: This is Mister Keys of Footwear.

[TONY *and* BOB *shake hands with him.*]

And Mister Britain of – uh –

BRITAIN: Soft furnishing.

MARIE: Oh, yes.

BRITAIN: And Mister Lang, of Electrical Goods, representing our staff association. Just paying our last respects.

MARIE: Thank you.

[MORLEY *waiting with open door at limousine. They go and climb in. Once the* MOURNERS *are all in limousine, it is driven off.*]

65. Interior. Limousine. Day.

MARIE *tearful.* TONY *holding her hand.*
WILL: Those weren't the proper words to the Psalm.
ERIC: That was the Prayer Book version, Uncle.
WILL: They're not the words most people know.
ERIC: No.

66. Exterior. Gates of Cemetery. Day.

Limousine turns into main road and is driven off very smartly.

67. Exterior. Crematorium. Day.

At 1100 and Austin other mourners getting into the cars, MR FOWLER *unlocking the passenger doors.*

68. Interior. Limousine. Day.

Travelling fast.
TONY: No, I'm sorry, but I think if the church agrees to recognise this man's death, there should at least be a decent ritual, not a lot of tatty machinery going on and off.
BOB: Why? He never went inside but to listen to recitals or see the stained glass.

TONY: Then play some music. Where's the organist?

BOB: The vicar only gets a pound. The whole thing only costs about ten. What d'you expect – King's College Choir?

TONY: A man dies after seventy years of –

[MARIE *is crying.* TONY *stops, takes her hand and holds it. They drive on.*]

69. Interior. Marie's Hall. Day.

JEAN *coming from kitchen with tray of teacups and saucers.* MARIE *coming from living room, meets her, stops her.*

MARIE: Linda –

LINDA [*coming from kitchen*]: What?

MARIE: Where d'you get these teaspoons?

LINDA: I couldn't find yours, so I had to run and borrow mine.

MARIE: Fancy making people think I haven't any teaspoons. In the sideboard. Jean, you'll find a set of apostle spoons. Mister Fowler's wedding present.

JEAN: In the sideboard –

[*She moves into little room as* ERIC *comes from front room.*]

ERIC: Auntie, I shall have to be phoning a taxi soon. To the station.

MARIE: You can phone from Linda's next door. Later on.

ERIC: Alright, after the eats.

[*Goes into living room as* WILL *comes down the stairs.* LINDA *has gone to kitchen and returns, with a tray of food for living room.*]

WILL: I was sitting on the toilet, Marie, –

MARIE: Were you?

WILL: Thinking it's a good job Harry didn't pass away up there. You'd have had to up-end the coffin to navigate this turn in the stairs.

70. Interior. Living Room. Day.

TONY, BOB, JEAN, PHYLLIS, LIONEL, UNA, ERIC *and* LINDA, *eating and drinking:* JEAN *and* LINDA *passing the food from a table laden with plates of sausage rolls, cake, meat and cheese, biscuits, etc.*

ERIC: No sign of the Fowlers' car yet.

PHYLLIS: It was all I could do to keep up with the limousine on the way back.

UNA: And that service. Talk about short-but-sweet.

LIONEL: Mr Fowler and I'd hardly got our knees on the hassock before old Sandy McPherson started up again on the theatre organ.

PHYLLIS: These days people are having too much fun to dwell on death. And old age. Don't blame them either. Give me the chance.

UNA [*firmly*]: Excuse me, but in my young days we didn't know that much about life but we respected the dead and who's to say we were the worse for it?

LINDA: Mrs Long, d'you want a Scotch egg?

PHYLLIS: I'm supposed to be on a diet.

UNA: My husband and I reserved our plot when we got married and never mentioned it again until the day he crossed over. But I know where he is and I know we shall meet again out Fairview.

PHYLLIS [*eating Scotch egg*]: God forbid I should ever meet my old man again. The day I left him at the divorce court, I said 'Good riddance' and I've never felt the lack of a husband since. Nor Jean of a father, have you, Jean?

[JEAN *smiles and goes out with tray as* MARIE *comes in with teapot.*]

MARIE: Why don't one of you boys open the window? It's stifling here.

71. Interior. Hall. Day.

JEAN *leaves tray in kitchen and goes up the stairs.*

72. Interior. Rear Bedroom. Day.

Twin-beds, walnut wardrobe, dressing table with stools and chest of drawers. Lloyd loom armchair. Door is open and top of stairs can be seen on landing outside. JEAN *comes up and into room, sits on bed.*

73. Interior. Hall. Day.

FOWLERS *and* VERA *being let in by* MARIE.
MARIE: Gracious me.
MRS FOWLER: All behind like the cow's tail.
MR FOWLER: Thought I'd take a short cut but the swing bridge was open.

74. Interior. Rear Bedroom. Day.

JEAN *is crying.*

75. Interior. Living Room. Day.

The company is joined by the FOWLERS *and* VERA LAMBERT. *The meal is nearly over and* PHYLLIS *is knitting.*
VERA: But this friend I was telling you of, her husband died on the beach at Portofino, in front of everyone. And you've no idea the fuss and expense she had transporting him home for burial.
PHYLLIS: Waste of money. I should want to be buried there.
UNA: I've never been abroad, I hope I never shall. But if it happened to me, I should want to be brought home to lie with Jack. Excuse me.
PHYLLIS: 'If I should die, think only this of me –'

VERA: Cremation for me. No dirt and decay.

PHYLLIS: 'That there's some corner of a foreign field that is forever England', eh, Tony? [*She winks at him.*]

TONY: I'll drink to that, Mrs Long.

PHYLLIS: You ought to do a programme – Auntie Una and I, Burial versus Burning.

TONY: Bit too controversial for me, dear. [*He stands and makes to go.*]

MARIE [*frowning*]: I see you brought your knitting, Phyllis.

PHYLLIS: One of the manifestations of my neurosis.

WILL: I shouldn't mind a slice of cake now, Marie.

   [BOB *lights a cigarette.*]

76. Interior. Rear Bedroom. Day.

JEAN *still face-down on the bed. Hears someone climbing stairs. She gets up and fetches handbag from chair, goes to sit at dressing-table and repairs her face.* TONY *appears at top of stairs, comes in.*

TONY: God, those people! The giants of our childhood. Towering uncles reeking of tobacco. Aunts and quasi-aunts all talcum powder and plump white arms. Auntie Una, grim and upright, always avid for a death. 'I shall lie with my Jack out Fairview.'

   [JEAN *listens, amused.* TONY *moves about.*]

Cousin Eric, Osterley's Huw Wheldon. Mr Fowler, sprouting rhubarb from his fingertips. A living reproach to Dad, who killed everything he touched.

   [*He examines the furniture. The pictures, the wallpaper, the knick-knacks.*]

Even nowadays when they've shrunk to nothing, I've only got to hear their voices and part of me becomes a child again. [*He has come close and looks at her in the glass.*] Been crying?

JEAN: The funeral upset me. And, after that, my mother. She said I'd never missed having a father and, of course she's got to pretend she doesn't feel the need of a man, though I know she does. Two women alone is all wrong. Which may be why I was always fond of your Dad.

TONY: I know. Well, he's gone now. And Vera Lambert's removing every trace.

JEAN: She could hardly wait to get her hands on his muddle. Tipping the dustman to cart it off. The clothes she's mostly given to Uncle Lionel.

TONY: I wish to God I had the time to go through it. I might have found some clue to the man – or some hint of my first five years, which are a total blank.

JEAN: I doubt there was anything but useless rubbish.

TONY: I might have caught a scent . . . I feel my answers are here if I could spare the time to look. My dreams take place here, still. But this will probably be the last time I see it.

[*She, having paused, goes on making up.*]

This is the room, where Bob and I grew up. That mirror, where I did my first acting. This bed where I used to lie as a virgin wondering what it was like. And where I found out. [*Turns to window. Lifts net curtain to look out.*] On a day very much like this. You were as bold as brass. 'Shall we go straight to bed?' you said and I followed you upstairs, shaking with fright. [*Goes to bed, lies on it.*] But there was nothing to be frightened of. It was so easy. You kept whimpering with pleasure.

JEAN: I can't remember.

TONY [*shaking head*]: Oh, Jean –

JEAN: I remember but not the details. It's a long time ago. Sixteen years?

TONY: I don't believe you. It was unforgettable.

JEAN: I was your first, that's all. You were a late starter. You can't bear to think it was ordinary.

77. Interior. Living Room. Day.

More convivial. A lot of tobacco smoke and teacups still being passed. BOB *is listening to* MR FOWLER. LINDA *offering cake.*

MR FOWLER: Half-inch quadrant. No more, thank you.

BOB: No, thanks.

MR FOWLER: Nail and glue the half-inch quadrant, say, two, two-and-a-half inches from the back of your shelf. Five-eighths panel pins at nine, twelve inch intervals.

[LINDA *moves on past* WILL.]

WILL: That chocolate cake? I shouldn't mind a piece of chocolate cake.

[*But she doesn't hear.*]

No, I was saying – what was I saying?

MRS FOWLER: About hyacinths.

WILL: That's right. Every nipper would receive a pot of hyacinths to put on a family grave . . . and we'd have to troop to the cemetery and put out all these blessed pots. And later on old Gran would hire a pony and trap and drive through the graveyard . . . is that chocolate cake, Marie? . . . and woe betide any boy who'd got tempted by the four-ale bar. I'd like a piece of that cake, yes.

LINDA: A piece of this? [*Cuts him a slice.*]

WILL: Ta. [*Bites cake, makes face.*] Ginger.

[ERIC *is prowling about the room, looking at gramophone records in albums.*]

78. Interior. Rear Bedroom. Day.

TONY *is still on the bed*, JEAN *putting on perfume. He watches her.*

TONY: I want it back.

JEAN: What?

TONY: Youth.

JEAN: You can't.

TONY: I don't know. Here we are. In this room.

JEAN: You didn't like me quite enough at the time. You left me for Tina Carpenter. Two hours I waited outside the Central Library and when it began to rain, I went to the pictures. You were a few rows in front with Tina Carpenter. So I left again.

TONY: I didn't know you'd seen me.

JEAN: No, well, I never told you because by the time you were after me again, I was going with Bob. And I suppose you only came back because you'd had no joy with Tina Carpenter.

TONY: If I could start again, it would all be very different.

JEAN: No, you were too ambitious and she lived in the Paragon. She went riding on the Downs, for God's sake!

TONY: Born into the class we were, are you going to blame me for ambition? When I see those people downstairs, I'm bloody glad to have been ambitious. But it meant I took wrong turnings and in the process of escaping, somehow missed my youth.

JEAN: You can keep youth, there was too much crying in the rain and hurting each other. Whatever life's like now, at least it's painless.

[*She stands and moves, tries to see herself in the dressing table mirrors, straightening her dress etc;* TONY *goes to wardrobe. Opens the door, showing her the mirror on the inside. She smiles.*]

TONY: That could be boring.

JEAN: Satisfying. No time for tears.

TONY: Doesn't sound like you.

[*She shrugs. He moves from wardrobe and stands beside her as she uses mirror.*]

You're a passionate woman, like your mother. Still are. You have to steal away up here to cry.

JEAN: Having children cools your passion.

TONY: I wouldn't know. But I believe we don't change our essential natures. We stifle them, thwart them, pervert them, but our natures survive. We were passionate lovers and we still are. Or would be.

[*He embraces her from behind. She goes on looking into the mirror. he moves his hands down to her hips, caressing her stomach and moving upwards to her breasts. He kisses the back of her neck and she raises her head, closing her eyes. She slightly turns her head and he kisses her ear. Suddenly he stiffens, looks at the door, steps away from her.*]

Among other things, I remember we used to play lifts going up and down in that wardrobe.

[BOB *appears in the open doorway,* JEAN *goes on titivating.* TONY *goes back to the wardrobe.* BOB *stays in doorway.*]

Ah, hullo. I was just saying we used to play lifts in here and one day we tipped it over, you were only four or five. Mum and Vera Lambert were downstairs and Vera lifted the whole thing bodily and stood it up.

BOB: Mum was worried in case the glass had broken.

　　[TONY *laughs*.]

JEAN: Anyone missed me?

BOB: Uncle Will. I'm on my way for a pee.

TONY [*imitating* WILL]: 'Where's young Jean? Well-developed young woman!'

JEAN: His voice is so like your father's.

TONY: I know, it keeps taking me unawares. Keep thinking, what's *he* doing here?

BOB: Oh, Tone, I thought, as you're going back to London any minute, we ought to –

TONY: Not till this evening.

BOB: No, well anyway, while Mum's not around, we ought to talk about her and the old man's debts and the house. I mean, Jean and I will be *doing* it all, so we'd better be sure you approve.

TONY: I'll pay his debts.

BOB: Okay.

TONY: Goes without saying.

BOB: I'll send on the outstanding bills. Your secretary will know what it's all about, will she?

TONY: I'll tell her.

BOB: Mum wants to sell the house –

TONY: I know –

BOB: So until we find her a flat, she can stay with us.

TONY: Is that okay?

BOB: What else d'you suggest?

　　[JEAN *has returned to dressing-table stool and is listening*.]

TONY: No, I'm sure that's what she wants. Are you happy, Jean?

JEAN [*shrugs*]: Least we can do.

BOB: What she doesn't take of the furniture we'll have auctioned. It won't fetch a lot.

TONY [*moving*]: All these redolent chairs and tables, the landscape of our childhood. They're like the aunts and uncles, I've measured out my life against them. And now it's a quantity of nineteen-thirties junk in the corner of a sale.

BOB: It was always a collection of thirties junk.

TONY: And dustmen cart the rest away for a small consideration. His samples of merchandise, his ludicrous letters to the local rag, his war-maps . . . .

BOB: He wasn't Tolstoy.

TONY: He was a good man who lacked our advantages. The advantages he gave us. A good man who's gone. And deserved better than a ten-quid cremation and a cut-price prayer.

[*Pause.* JEAN *raises her head to look at him.* TONY *finishes, moved, and turns to look out of the window.*]

BOB: You could do a super piece on him in your next programme.

[*Pause. He makes to go on to bathroom.*]

TONY: What's wrong with showing a bit of feeling?

JEAN: Now come on –

BOB [*shrugs*]: Nothing. For you it's a good living. I just think there are more pressing matters. Nostalgia is enervating . . . in Britain almost a disease.

TONY: What are the more pressing matters?

BOB: Oh – sewage disposal, noise abatement, traffic control, clean air, population . . . all good for a belly laugh on your tv show.

TONY: You haven't been watching. Half my programme last Saturday was given over to the problems of air pollution.

BOB: Yeah, then you fly off to New York in a trail of diesel and supersonic bangs.

TONY: How d'you expect me to go? By rowing boat?

BOB: It's all too easy to do your bit on pollution, like the politicians. No-one expects any action. Like your bit on Dad's funeral. I don't hear you asking Mum to share your London flat.

TONY: She doesn't want to.

BOB: Have you asked her?

TONY: She wants to be near your children. I haven't got any, if you remember.

BOB: You could have done. You've had two wives. You were too busy feeling all over the place to see that it's hard work, marriage, like sewage disposal.

[TONY *laughs.* JEAN *smiles slightly. Both men have been partly aiming their remarks at her and we have seen her reactions.*]

I told you it would get a belly-laugh.

TONY: Well, honestly! Jean, is that how you see your marriage – sewage disposal?

JEAN: With young children, sewage disposal certainly plays a part.

[BOB *laughs and she smiles at him. By this gesture she shows that she has decided to take* BOB's *side, as she must.*]

TONY: No, I mean the new person will depend on sewage disposal – liver, kidneys, bowels – just as a new university depends on plumbing. But you don't establish a university so as to have more loos.

BOB: As an architect who works more on council flats than colleges, perhaps I'm too preoccupied with plumbing. A lot of people living decently is better than a few witty undergraduates.

JEAN: Can't you have both?

TONY: Exactly, Jean!

BOB: I don't want both. I believe in the ordinary, the prosaic. People who see themselves as special and who can't stop their brains working, gurus and pundits and so on, they create élites and make the rest of us feel excluded. And they raise our expectations of life.

TONY: But you're a special person –

BOB: Most of us would be happier with our lot if it wasn't for public spokesmen with their clouds of abstractions and nostalgia. The Free World. East of Suez. The Classless Society. The Golden Age. Our Finest Hour. Every time there's a mains water burst, the local rag comes out in a sweat about the old wartime spirit. You'd think this was Dresden or Nagasaki. But how many actually died in all the raids on this city; twelve hundred. And every year of peace, seven thousand are killed on the roads. Four thousand died in the last London smog.

TONY: All these numbers! They're meaningless. I can't take in one man's death. [*Looks at his watch.*] By now he'll be a handful of ashes.

[ERIC *comes into doorway from stairs.*]

ERIC: Auntie says I must look in the attics and see if Uncle's left anything I might want. As a memento.

BOB: Yeah, fine, carry on.

[ERIC *goes up further stairs.*]

JEAN: I must go down. They'll be wondering where we are.
[*But* MARIE *and* LIONEL *follow* ERIC.]

MARIE: What are you doing up here, you boys? [*To* LIONEL.] This used to be their old bedroom.

LIONEL: Very nice.

MARIE: It's a nice room. Uncle Will's been asking for you, Jean.

JEAN: I know. I'll go and see him. [*She goes.*]

MARIE: Uncle Lionel's trying on some more of your father's shoes. We found half a dozen pairs in the kitchen cupboard. [*Takes shoes from wardrobe.*]

LIONEL: Shame to throw them out.

BOB: Absolutely.

MARIE: He took care of his boots and shoes, polishing them every day like a sergeant-major.

[BOB *goes to bathroom.* LIONEL *tries on shoes.*]

79. Interior. Living Room. Day.

JEAN *arriving to* WILL. *Also present:* UNA, VERA, LINDA, PHYLLIS.

WILL: Here she is! Old Harry used to call you 'The Girl with the Ample Thighs'.

VERA: Very pretty.

WILL: But I think you've lost weight lately.

JEAN: I shall soon be putting it on again.

WILL: How's that?

JEAN: I'm going to have another baby.

WILL [*roars*]: Hear that, Marie?

VERA: She's busy upstairs.

WILL: D'you hear this, Vera? Young Jean pregnant again.

VERA: I should think the street's heard the way you shout. [*She goes out.*]

WILL: Your daughter, Phyllis.

PHYLLIS: Another millstone round her neck, I know . . . .

WILL: How many will this be? Three.

JEAN: Yes.

137

WILL: I shall have to send you a manual on birth control. A word to the wise by Marie Stopes, eh? [*Laughs and wipes his eyes.*] Did brother Harry know?

JEAN: No.

WILL: He'd have been tickled.

JEAN: Yes.

WILL: Nothing made him happier than ordering nippers about. [*Suddenly sad. Blows his nose with handkerchief.*]

80. Interior. Rear Bedroom. Day.

TONY *watching* LIONEL *try on shoes.* MARIE *brings pair of plimsolls.*

MARIE: These white daps any good to you?

LIONEL: On the beach in summer, just the job, yes.

[VERA *comes up stairs carrying overcoat.*]

VERA: I thought Lionel might like this overcoat of Harry's we found under the stairs.

[LIONEL *is putting on the plimsolls as* VERA *holds up the coat for him to look at.*]

MARIE: He loved herringbone.

[ERIC *comes down attic stairs, carrying several golf-clubs, a golf-bag and a metal A.R.P. helmet.*]

Found something you want in the loft, Eric?

ERIC: Not really, Auntie, it's mostly rubbish, but I'll take these clubs as a souvenir and the warden's helmet for the children.

[TONY *watches them all.*]

VERA: Attics only collect dirty filth.

[*Lavatory flush off.*]

I used to tell Harry that.

[LIONEL *has the shoes on and now puts on the coat.*]

ERIC: Is Uncle still downstairs? The taxi's due any minute.

VERA: He was bellowing about Jean expecting another baby.

ERIC: He gets a bit excited.

MARIE: It's nothing to shout about. Poor Bob's hard-worked enough already without another mouth to feed.

ERIC: I'll look through the books in the front room, shall I?
　　[*Goes downstairs.* BOB *comes from bathroom.* LIONEL *looks at his reflection in glass, now wearing overcoat and white plimsoles.*]
LIONEL: Perfect.
BOB: What the cautious Englishmen is wearing on the beach this summer.
MARIE: You'll need something to carry them in.
BOB: This case. [*Pulls it down from on top wardrobe.*]
MARIE: Mind the dust! Oh, my Lord!
　　[BOB *bangs the sides of it.*]
VERA: Not on the carpet.
　　[*She stoops and picks pieces of fluff from carpet as* BOB *throws case on bed and opens it.*]
BOB: Taking all these, Uncle?
LIONEL: Yes.
　　[*He takes off coat and* MARIE *folds it.* BOB *packs shoes into case.* TONY *suddenly goes from the room and down the stairs.* BOB *smiles.* VERA *puts fluff into waste basket or out of window and claps her hands clean.* LIONEL *takes off plimsolls.*]

81. Exterior. Marie's House. Day.

Taxi waiting in space between BOB's *Minivan and the* FOWLERS' *Humber.* WILL, ERIC *and* LIONEL *saying goodbye to* MARIE, BOB, TONY *and* JEAN.
WILL: You had a nice day for it, Marie. You'll come and see me soon, I hope.
MARIE: I shall have to see.
WILL: There's only me left now. I'm the last.
MARIE: That's nice and cheerful. Bye-bye, Will.
　　[*Kisses him. He gets into cab.* ERIC *now carries golf-bag, helmet, book and album of old records.*]
　　You sure you can manage all that, Eric?
ERIC: I took this Silver Jubilee Book as a memento.
MARIE: Thank you for coming. Love to your family.

[*Kisses him. He gets in.* LIONEL *carries suitcase.*]

LIONEL: Now don't forget. As soon as you're straight, come down and stay. My sister and I have got a bathing-hut for the season.

MARIE: Out of the wind.

LIONEL: Got an electric kettle in it.

MARIE: I'll have to see.

[*They shake hands.* LIONEL *goes. The taxi moves off, all waving.*]

JEAN: We're late for the kids.

TONY: Who's got them?

JEAN: Patsy. She can't control her own three, let alone mine.

MARIE: She's always up in the clouds.

JEAN: See you at home then.

[*She and* BOB *turn towards the minivan.*]

MARIE: Mr Fowler will give us a lift.

[*She walks back to the house.* TONY *shuts the front gate and follows her. See the ordinary house from his point of view.*]

82. Interior. Inside Minivan. Travelling Daylit Streets. Day.

BOB, JEAN *and their children,* BILL *and* SUSAN. *The children are sitting or crouching on a mattress in the back.*

ALL [*singing*]: Lloyd George knows my father. Father knows Lloyd George. Etc. Etc.

83. Exterior. Bob's House. A Victorian Terrace. Day.

Minivan arrives. JEAN *gets out and lets out children by passenger door, while* BOB *opens rear doors and begins unloading the equipment of their day away: a pedal jeep, a large plastic lavatory seat, a rubber bouncer with horns, spare clothes in bunches, a toilet-bag, a school satchel. He half-carries, half-wheels this load to the house. On the pavement a toilet-roll falls off and rolls to the gutter.* JEAN *is looking for her key as she climbs front steps but the door is suddenly thrown open and* TONY *appears, half-hidden by door. He 'shoots' the children and they immediately return fire.* TONY *makes expert ricochet sounds and then is hit and staggers out, his face contorted in agony.* JEAN *smiles, goes into house.* BOB *comes up steps as* TONY *finally collapses, dying. Makes one last effort to shoot his killers but fails.* BOB *struggles by with gear. Children delighted.*

84. Interior. Nursery. Day.

We see only JEAN's *head against a door, in half light through drawn curtains.*

JEAN [*singing*]: Where is the boy who looks after the sheep?
   He's under a haystack fast asleep.
   Will you wake him? No, not I,
   For if I do, he'll surely cry.
     [*Stifles a yawn.*]
   Night-night, Bill. Sleep well. [*Opens door and goes.*]

85. Interior. Bob and Jean's Hall. Day.

TONY, BOB, MARIE *and* JEAN.

TONY: Now promise me, when you've had enough of these two, you'll come and stay with me in Town.
MARIE: When they've had enough of *me*.
TONY: Promise now.
MARIE: I'll write to you.
TONY: Ring up, then we can fix the date.
MARIE: All that expense on a phone.
TONY: Reverse the charges.
MARIE: But then you pay.
TONY: It all comes off the income tax, love.
MARIE: Alright. But mind – until I come look after yourself, put

a bit of colour back in your cheeks. Make sure you get plenty of fresh air and exercise and a cooked meal at the proper time.

TONY: Right, Mum.

MARIE [*partly to others*]: Because it's all very well, as I said to Vera, to think of him meeting all these famous people but I think of the face the public don't see. At the end of his programmes, I think 'Yes, and now he's going back to a lonely flat with no-one to talk to, no-one to share his troubles.'

[JEAN *sings 'Hearts and Flowers'*. BOB *laughs*. TONY *joins in the song*. MARIE *smiles*.]

TONY: You're right, Mum, it's hell out there. [*Kisses her.*]

MARIE: Take care.

TONY: Bless you. Bye, Jean.

JEAN: Bye, Tone.

[*Offers her hand. He shakes.* BOB *opens front door and they go.*]

86. Exterior. Bob's House. Day.

BOB *and* TONY *getting into the Minivan.* MARIE *and* JEAN *wave from the front door. Van drives off.*

87. Interior. Bob and Jean's hall. Day.

JEAN *closes door.*

MARIE: But all the same I do feel sorry for him. The second child's lucky in many ways. We like to spoil the firstborn and make him think he's Lord Muck. For six years there was only Tony to fuss over. He had everything. But look at the way it's turned out – two rotten marriages, no family. Nearly forty and nothing to show for it. Bob even got *you* in the end.

JEAN: Bob doesn't see it quite like that. He thinks I'm one of Tony's cast-offs.

88. Interior. Bob and Jean's Bedroom. Night.

Lower part of BOB *and* JEAN's *bed. On the untidy counterpane,* JEAN's *black dress has been carelessly thrown. We stay on it, hearing dialogue.*
BOB [*ecstatically*]: Jean, love!
JEAN: Ssssh . . .
BOB: You bitch, I love you –
JEAN: Darling, ssssh, . . .

89. Interior. Children's Playroom. Night.

A single bed, bedside light on. MARIE *sitting up, going through an envelope bulky with old snapshots. She looks aside for a moment as though she'd heard something, then turns back to the photos. See one or two: her own married life with* TONY *and* BOB *as boys, herself in twenties and thirties fashions. One stilted portrait of her husband. One as a young man in athletic costume.*

90. Interior. Bob and Jean's Bedroom. Night.

BOB *and* JEAN's *bed again, lit as at beginning by table light.* BOB *and* JEAN *lying apart. He is buttoning up his pyjama jacket. Takes off wrist watch, looks at it, winds it. She is doing exactly the same.*
BOB: Would you like to read?
JEAN: Little read, I think. Settle my mind.
　　[*She turns her back to him, takes book. He takes a book too. Before turning from her, he speaks to her back.*]
BOB: Why was it so important to be quiet?
JEAN: Embarrassing for your mother.
BOB: Oh, hell. This is our house. I'm not giving *that* up. [*Then turns back to her, finds page in book.*]
　　Was it alright, Jean?
JEAN: What?

BOB: Treats. Just now.

JEAN: Smashing.

BOB: It's so hard to tell. You're so undemonstrative.

JEAN: Isn't that what you want?

BOB [*brief pause*]: Hardly make a sound.

JEAN: I never have made sounds. [*Rubs her foot against his. Yawns.*] Oh dear.

BOB: As long as you enjoy yourself.

JEAN: Mmmm. Oh, dear.

> [*Yawns again. They apparently read. But we see that he stares beyond his book and looks frightened. She stares beyond her book at the rose from* TONY's *bouquet, which is in a glass of water on her bedside table. Stay on the rose. 'Salut d'Amour' by Elgar. Fade out.*]

NEITHER UP NOR DOWN

Neither Up Nor Down

From my diary of 15th March 1970.

Tynan has been persuading me to write a turn for *Oh, Calcutta!*, an erotic review he's putting together. I finally sent for a book that had been advertised by a circular letter under plain cover. There's been some pious moaning in Parliament about this very sales campaign,, a harmless and very decent way, I'd have thought, of distributing dirty books to those who want them. *Variations on a Sexual Theme* turns out to be an octavo hardback of forty or so photographs posed by a nude man and woman in various coital positions and with an explanatory text, in which the partners are scrupulously described as 'the husband' and 'the wife'. 'We next come to three positions in which the wife sits or lies on a table at hip level to her husband'. It seems an informative and inoffensive enough thing, with not a genital in sight and the models' faces turned from the camera like drug-addicts on a tv talk show. At first I thought it would be no use for my purposes but finally found some humour in the situation of a husband trying to bring back the magic to his marriage with the aid of the book and some household objects.

Spent a day writing what seemed to Thelma and me a funny five minutes and gave it to Ken next morning. He later rang to say he found it funny but would have to show it to Clifford Williams, the show's director, when he came back from New York. This morning, weeks later, receive a nasty little note from Williams saying the sketch is too much like another in the show, which I know to be untrue because Tynan told me there was nothing remotely like it by anyone else.

And from 15th January, nearly two years later.

To Kentish Town to see Ed Berman's group who are

doing the sketch rejected by *Oh, Calcutta!* which I have now called *Neither Up Nor Down*. Tramped through muddy building sites from Inter-Action's H.Q. (room beside shops in mean terrace) to a private house with minimal furniture. The actress was in court for a speeding offence and the actor had some sort of gastric 'flu. However we read through the sketch and talked it over, then reported back to H.Q. and to the C.O. Berman is an ageing maverick with a beard and a soothing American voice, a fifties figure with an elaborate sense of fun. There was a half-seen staff of gentle-seeming people, and a dog slept on a bed. Downstairs in the squalid kitchen I'd had to time to glance at a printed table of dietary instructions: 'Penny – no meat or fish; Jim – plenty of dates but nuts and dried fruit come top, etc.'. Ed took several phone-calls, instructed one of his lootenants to deal gently with one of their sponsors – 'don't pull her leg too much, huh?' – and asked me to write a play for the double-decker bus he has brought from London Transport.

January 29th. Played squash with Michael Frayn and he showed me the only review so far of the sketch, the *Guardian's* second string saying I was a reactionary taste and it was an unspeakable play and 'What a triumph of technique to get three titters in thirteen minutes'. Enjoyed his choice of the word 'titters'.

The sketch is included here as a footnote to the plays. In *Chez Nous*, Dick and Liz actually discuss the manual, how he sent for it and how she laughed. For a more thorough comic treatment of the subject, I recommend Thurber and White's *Is Sex Necessary?*. In the chapter 'What Should Children Tell Their Parents?', they mention the method of leaving sex-books lying around, 'opened at the pertinent pages. Even this failed to work in most cases. The mothers usually just picked up the book, dusted it, closed it, and fitted it neatly in some nearby shelf. They thought it was dusty.'

It was humour like that, I imagine, that Tynan wanted to rid us of with *Oh Calcutta!*, in which case he was also right to reject my little sketch. I never saw the show but I believe it must share the credit – or the blame – for changing the way we think and talk about sex. In 1986 it can still be seen in New York, where for some years it has been the first choice of visiting Japanese businessmen.

Neither Up Nor Down

Presented by Ed Berman at Almost Free Theatre, Soho.

Low divan bed. Bedside table with telephone. Door. Man's voice singing offstage.

HE: Bobby Shaftoe's fat and fair
       Combing down his yellow hair
       He's my ain for evermair
       Bonnie Bobby Shaftoe.

[Pause. He enters, wearing glasses, pyjamas and dressing-gown, carrying slim volume. Shuts door, looks about room critically. Stands centre, opens book, flicks over pages, checking. Puts book on bed, goes off again. Returns carrying pile of books two foot high. Puts them on floor to one side. Woman sings offstage.]

SHE: The Grand old Duke of York
       He had ten thousand men
       He marched them up to the top of the hill
       And he marched them down again.

[He listens to part of this, then returns to book.]

       And when they were up they were up
       And when they were down they were down
       And when they were only halfway up
       They were neither up nor down.

[HE looks up to the door. Long pause. SHE comes in, wearing nightdress, slippers, quilted house-coat. SHE shuts door. Yawns.]

SHE: Oh dear . . .

HE: I'd *already* sung to them.

SHE: They were still talking when I came from the bathroom.

HE: Have they gone down now?

[SHE nods, rubs her hands together.]

SHE: God! This room. Have you written to Mr Tulloch about the radiator?

HE: The fan-heater's been on since six. It seems suffocating to me.

SHE: When the wind's on this side of the house, there's nothing can take the chill off these rooms.

HE: And you've had a scalding bath –

SHE: The dining-room's the same –

HE: I should have thought –

151

SHE: Polystyrene insulation is what's needed. Or mineral wool spread over the attic floor.

HE: Anyway –

SHE: Yes.

> [*They seem to address themselves to the present.* SHE *stands attentively, rubbing her cold hands.* HE *reads the book.*]

HE: Um – well – have you any idea where you'd like to start?

SHE: I haven't looked. Well, only glanced at it with you when it first arrived.

HE: It's been here since yesterday morning.

SHE: But we were out at dinner last night and –

HE: What about today? I purposely left it home.

SHE: I've been with Tony – how could I?

HE: Tony would only have said 'Mummy, why is that man fighting with that lady with no clothes on?'

> [*Pause. They stand together looking at the book.*]

SHE: Wonder how they felt posing for all these?

> [HE *flicks over the pages.*]

HE: A job of work, I suppose.

SHE: They're probably narcissists.

HE: I don't know.

> [*They stop at one.*]

SHE: I don't believe that one, do you?

HE: It does say it will be tiring to all but the most athletic. And if the husband rests his back against a wall, it would –

SHE [*suddenly*]: Ssssh! [*They listen.*] I thought I heard Susan cry.

HE: We'd better start with something simpler.

SHE: I can still see my breath in the air. [*Rubs her arms with her hands.*]

HE [*reads*]: 'This series only recommended for couples roughly the same height.'

> [*Hands her the open book.* SHE *looks at it.* HE *brings half the pile of books, putting it on floor beside her.*]

SHE: We've done this one. Years ago we did this.

HE: Years ago, yes. That's the whole point, love.

SHE: You never liked it. You got cramp.

HE: Shall we try anyway?

> [*Brings rest of books and puts them beside first. Now a double pile*

one foot high. SHE *looks at it.*]

SHE: Susan's encyclopaedias.

HE: The taller you are, the easier it is. As I remember. [*Stands facing her. Smiles and nods.*] One use the salesman didn't mention.

SHE: Mmm.

HE: Are you going to take your clothes off?

SHE: I'm freezing already.

[HE *caresses her face.*]

HE: Oh, love, come on – your house-coat anyway.

SHE: I'm sorry.

[*Fondles her quilted form.*]

HE: Please –

SHE: Well – how about if I unbutton it?

HE: Let me.

[HE *unbuttons the coat.* SHE *sneezes and has to hold his shoulder to steady herself. At last the coat is open, revealing a nightgown like a shroud, opaque and reaching to the floor.* HE *looks at her.* SHE *smiles and hands him the book.* HE *holds it behind her head and reads, while* SHE *unbuttons his dressing-gown.*]

'This position is unusually exciting, because of the close embrace between husband and wife and the ability of each partner to stimulate the other's erogenous areas by gentle but increasingly urgent caress.'

[*With one hand* HE *pulls the braid of his pyjama trousers and they drop to his ankles below the gown. Returns this hand to the book and turns the page.*]

SHE: How are you going to caress me with no hands free?

HE: This one's free. Except for turning the pages.

SHE: Surely we know it?

HE: Yes, but I thought we'd go on in a minute to The Clinging Vine.
[*Shows her next photograph.*]

SHE: What have they done with their legs?

HE: They're standing on one each.
[*Pause.*]

SHE: Yes, but she's not perched on a pile of encyclopaedias.

HE: I wish you wouldn't take that defeatist attitude, love. These positions have been practised by millions of people all over the world for thousands of years. Are we so hopelessly debilitated that we can't follow a few simple instructions?

SHE: Let me have it. [*Takes book and reads.*] I must say, after the mess you made of assembling that kitchen unit –

HE: Oh, for crying out loud.

SHE: Too mean to buy one ready-made. 'I can save all those labour costs.'

HE [*shouting*]: The corner wasn't square.

SHE [*reading*]: 'First the couple embrace each other from the front.'
    [*They do this.*]

HE: It's perfectly adequate. The door sticks a bit.

SHE: 'To insert the penis, the wife lifts one of her legs.' We'd better take that as read, to judge by the look of you.

HE [*stepping back*]: What?

SHE [*pointing*]: Well, it's neither use nor ornament at the moment.

HE [*loud*]: You're not being very provocative! In case you hadn't noticed. That house-coat's like a bell-tent.

SHE: How can I be provocative on this side of the house? [SHE *gets off books.*] *Did* you write to Mr Tulloch about the radiators?

HE: YES!
    [*Pause.*]
    Love, sorry. Let's try again. [*Takes and kisses her hand.*] Please.
    [SHE *relents and steps on to books again.*]

SHE: Are you going to keep your glasses on?

HE: Ah. [*Puts them on floor nearby, returns.*]

SHE: Alright. One: embrace.
    [*They perform to numbers.*]
    Two: lift leg. Three: insert. Take as read. And, provided we get that far, four: husband raises leg.

HE: The opposite one, must be.

SHE: Yes.
    [*But his pyjama trousers prevent this.* HE *kicks them off, then raises leg.*]

SHE [*reads*]: 'Bringing it round to a point high at the back of the wife's thigh. By the careful use of these raised legs, the subsequent movements can be prevented from becoming too vigorous.' Whoops.
    [*They lose balance and* SHE *slips from pile of books. They separate.* HE *impatiently snatches book from her and flips over pages. The*

[*telephone rings;* SHE *answers it, sitting on the bed.* HE *holds the book close to his eyes, realises* HE *has no glasses, goes down on all fours to look for them.*]

Hullo? . . . oh, hullo . . . no, nothing much . . . we're having it later on . . . no, just pottering about . . .

[HE *finds glasses, looks at picture, goes off, leaving book on bed.*]

ah . . . no, of course not . . . yes . . . fine . . . no bother at all . . . I'll keep her till you get back, shall I? . . . I find they're always better with a friend.

[HE *returns dragging a table.* SHE *watches nervously.* HE *stands it centre, shakes it vigorously. Goes off again.*]

Strawberry mousse, I won't give her that . . . anything else, fine . . . .

[HE *returns with an eiderdown, folds it and puts it on edge of table, looks at book again.*]

I'm sorry about your aunt . . . .

[HE *looks at her impatiently, then at his watch.*]

Terribly bad luck at her age . . . um – how long does she expect to be in? . . . oh . . . yes, I suppose I mustn't keep you. Bye. Bye.

[*Puts down phone.*]

Fiona to say she can't meet Susan from school tomorrow afternoon because –

HE [*aggressively*]: 'Three positions where the wife is on a table at her husband's hip-level.'

SHE [*going to him*]: – she's got to visit her aunt who fell down in the snow and broke several ribs.

HE: 'The wife lies on the table, her buttocks resting on the edge. The husband stands facing her –

[*They do all this, still with clothes on.*]

'She raises her legs until the calves are resting on the husband's shoulders as he bends over to caress her breasts. In this position both partners will feel an overpowering desire to penetrate to the limit –'

SHE: Ow. There's something in the small of my back.

HE: I don't care.

SHE: I'm not lying here in misery all twisted up.

HE: I'm taking you, you brazen whore –

[SHE *stands and fumbles in the eiderdown.*]

My balls are aching to squirt their juice –

SHE: We've been looking for that all day. Tony's Chitty-chitty-bang-bang car. [*Holds it up.*]

HE: Please try! Doesn't it seem important?

SHE: Why don't we have some supper and come up later to our nice warm bed?

HE: No.

SHE: We'll have some treats then.

HE: We'll have what some Pacific Islanders call 'The Missionary Position'. With the lights out because they hurt your eyes and your clothes on in case the cold gets in.

SHE: Perhaps in the Pacific it's nice and warm and we could do it in the setting sun. Perhaps we could sneak off into the jungle and the kids wouldn't have to be fetched from school through city traffic.

HE: You'd worry about the insects.

[*Pause. They stand together.*]

HE: You don't seem to be – very concerned – about keeping our marriage –

SHE: Sssh!

[*Pause. They listen.*]

Tony crying. It's his ear again, I expect.

[SHE *goes out.* HE *sits on the table with the book. Pause.*]

HE [*reading*]: '. . . this primal desire to fertilise finds expression in the masterful male urge to penetrate the woman. She, on the other hand – [*turns page*] surrenders to a torrent of sexual imagery, involuntarily arching her back and stabbing with her pelvis, crying out and sometimes passing into unconsciousness . . .' [*Turns page and looks at photographs.*]

SHE [*singing, off*]: And when they were up they were up
    And when they were down they were down.
    And when they were only half-way up
    They were neither up nor down.

CHEZ NOUS

A Domestic Comedy
in Two Acts

Chez Nous

By the early seventies we were living in Blackheath with our three growing children. Of course they needed holidays at the seaside or in the country but my compulsion to write was now so strong that I never wanted to leave off. After a few days away, I began pressing to be back at my desk again. Thelma's solution was to buy a holiday home where they could enjoy and relax and I could get the regular fixes of work that pacified my habit. Such places in Britain were still too dear for us but in Southern France cottages and farms were going for a song. With our youngest child, we flew to Bordeaux and for three days toured the available properties. Most had been made obsolete by modern farming, some were being sold in a hurry before the father died, to avoid Napoleonic laws of inheritance that would divide the small holdings into unworkable fragments. On one occasion, being shown a poor, rundown building by the estate agent and the farmer's wife, we had to pretend not to see the old man dying on a bed in the corner.

We came home with a confused impression of manors, town houses, isolated hamlets and immense barns, and the one we chose we had only visited for fifteen minutes. It was a simple farmhouse on one floor with one room opening into another, a barn the size of a church and more rooms beyond that. It had electricity, well water, no drainage or telephone, but was rich in such appealing features as a bread-oven, a granary, an ox-cart, a cherry orchard and a carp-pond. Together with the dollar premium (a fiscal procedure that was later repealed), the whole place cost less than £4000.

Buying Chez Magnou was one of the luckiest strokes of our life. Some time after we'd had the necessary work done to make it habitable, we discovered a sizeable lake not fifteen minutes' drive away, the only stretch of water for miles around large enough for swimming, boating and pedalo. We were able to tell people that we had a place in the Dordogne, which made them picture the great river running through gorges beneath fairy-tale châteaux or the caves of Lascaux and Cro-Magnon. In fact, we were in the far north of the département, nearly in Charente, a few miles from the undistinguished market-town of Ribérac. The wealthy and successful media people were further south and had gone there earlier. The many English, Dutch, German and Scandinavian families who'd bought properties around Riberac tended to be middle-income people – surveyors, architects, doctors, academics – mostly going there for their long spring and summer holidays, though quite a few were retired people living there all year. Though the French called this invasion a new Hundred Years War, they did well from the spoils, first selling properties the Parisians wouldn't buy and later being paid to do them up and then to supply food, wine and Orangina, Rochefort and Vâche Qui Rit, stoves and washing-machines. We bought power-mowers to cut the neglected grass around our farms, and garden furniture with large umbrellas for shelter while we ate under the midday sun. Most of the invaders were English and kept to themselves, emerging on market day to be spotted at a hundred paces – tall, iron-grey and vague, with shy great children called Tamsin and Xavier.

We had Chez Magnou for ten happy years, spending most Easters and Summers and a few Christmases there. The last years were marred by a nosy and gushing Englishwoman who bought the deserted house across the road. She began speculating with property and, when she arranged for a Dutchman to build a bungalow in the next field, we saw that paradise had been lost again, and sold up. There was never any shortage of visiting friends who came, tense from their journeys, aggressive and demanding, but after a few hours succumbed to the simple charms of the place and to the cheap wine and Thelma's food. This process came slowest to directors. They found it hard to stop directing. In their company I was no better and power struggles soon spoilt the rustic calm. Out of these contests emerged the first draft of a play in August 1971. At first I thought it slick and trivial but a week or two later I'm telling Diary that 'It's the most moral and thoughtful of my plays and actually has A STORY that illustrates its ideas. A middle-aged man makes a thirteen-year-old girl pregnant. This happens in the first act but we don't hear about it till the second, after the child's birth. Nobody talks to the audience and formally the play is absolutely naturalistic.'

The play went through a long and tortuous series of drafts, from 1971 till the end of 1973, when it was finally produced. The boldest change was to cut the first act entirely, moving the action to the following year and confining it to one day and night. Thus it became an Ibsenite construction, and that may have been in conflict with its mood, which was at one time more Chekhovian. Near the end there are lines about cherry-trees and samovars, and they are all that's left of a more reflective and expansive play. The whodunnit nature of the story left no room for lyricism. What emerged, though, was close in essence to what I'd at first outlined, though very much more complex. The past lives of its four principals are now entwined. As with more obviously personal plays, there are numerous 'real' people and events. Some took place at Chez Magnou and were included as soon as they happened. Somehow, though, this time the pain was held at arm's length and the brittle, almost callous style put off audiences who had warmed to my previous plays.

The setting was based precisely on our barn, Michael Annals the designer and Robert Chetwyn the director coming out to stay with us one warm November, taking pictures of the buildings and touring the local farms to buy domestic props that could not be made. An ox-cart that had been rotting in a field was brought to the stage of The Globe and stood in Michael's brilliant set, which often drew applause for itself in the manner of old pantomimes. We had never renovated our barn, only had it cleared of hay and mangers, but in the play Dick and Liz have made it a sophisticated play-space, the first of a number of nursery images that reiterate the essential childishness of these city dudes. Games and holiday pastimes are the only actions of an otherwise conversational play: badminton, home movies, sun-bathing, wine-pouring, swinging on a trapeze, hunting antiques in empty houses, and all this against the bare stone walls and beamed roof of a barn that was so recently part of an earnest, arduous way of life. Only one survivor of this community appears – an itinerant farm labourer who comes to attend to the neighbouring vines and who speaks in a high, unintelligible patois. He was taken straight from life, for the real man wandered into our farm just as his parody did on to the stage of The Globe, going for water in the stream, surprising us in our kitchen, never able to take in the weird fact of our presence.

Albert Finney produced the play (with Michael Medwin) and played Phil. I had always thought he might do the part and the dialogue was written with his cadences in mind. When he read the final draft, he saw at once that it was a less good part than Dick but said never mind, he'd do it anyway, he'd enjoy a straight commercial play after the Beckett and Storey he was in at the Royal Court.

Rehearsals began in December 1973 during Edward Heath's three-day week. At first we were in a Welsh club, later a synagogue. Three working days out of six the actors used torches to read their scripts in the wintry twilight of Soho. I remember one especially murky morning when Geraldine McEwan and Pat Heywood worked on a sun-bathing scene, pretending to anoint their sweaters and trousers with Ambre Solaire by the dim light of candles.

I had a strong foreboding that this play would be my first failure but everyone else spoke of my first real success. During the last days before the opening, I was on Librium to control my growing conviction that the play was too trivial for the spanking production it was getting. Previews were chilling. Audiences seemed to bring the darkness of the streets in with them and, though I knew the evening wasn't working for them, I hadn't a clue how to change things. Perhaps, I felt, this shouldn't have been a West End play at all. On Saturday before the Wednesday opening, Albert and Michael Medwin took Chetwyn and me to lunch. Albert told me to kick the Librium for a few days, as there was still work to do. As it was being played then, Dick ended the play by ending his marriage, going off to his room to write her a farewell note. It was bad stagecraft and untrue to the man.

'Why d'you want him to leave?' Albert insisted. 'You and Thelma are still together, aren't you?'

'He's not me,' I told them, 'and in any case, even if you're right, there's what Henry James called The Dear Little Question of How To Do It.'

I had written a dozen endings already and one of these was now taken up by Michael Medwin. It was his refinement of my thought that showed me what I must do. Next day I wrote what now stands and when Denholm Elliott played this version on Monday night, it was certainly an improvement but not a solution. On Wednesday I couldn't face the first night and walked the West End streets to get into a cinema. But they were all full, so I crept back in through the stage door and sat in an upper box from where I could see a full, attentive, interested house. Princess Margaret sat in the circle, leaning forward, head on hand, with Tony Snowdon beside her, smiling. It was one of those occasions where everything changes for the opening. The morning's press was the best I'd had and Sunday's even better. (Wardle in the *The Times* wrote of 'an extraordinary concluding image, which strikes me as one of the great endings of modern drama'.) Even so, the play never became the commercial success my agent had predicted. It came off after six months to make way for an Alan Ayckbourn that ran for years. It has seldom been produced since.

During its run, the live cockerel that lived with its hen in the wings to be carried on by the French peasant, crowed so early that residents of Soho wrote to complain. Albert apologised for the company adding: 'You'll be glad to hear that the play comes off in a few weeks and then my cock will be withdrawn.'

Chez Nous

First: The Globe Theatre, London, by Memorial Enterprises (Albert Finney and Michael Medwwin), 6th February 1974.

PHIL	Albert Finney
DICK	Denholm Elliott
DIANA	Geraldine McEwan
LIZ	Pat Heywood
GUNGA DIN	Denis Carey
ZOE	Beth Porter
BURT	Glenn Beck

Directed by Robert Chetwyn
Designed by Michael Annals
Lighting by Mick Hughes

Later: at the Manhattan Theatre Club, New York, with a cast that included Sam Waterston and John Tillinger.

The setting represents three walls and part of the roof of an old barn. It has been renovated and turned into a sophisticated 'play-space'. The original rough-stone walls remain and the beams, still unfinished, but now hung with banners painted by children. Modern light fittings, black or chromium, project from the walls or hang from the roof.

On the audience's left, occupying much of the wall, are the main doors, large enough to admit a loaded hay-cart.

Nothing interrupts the facing wall except a staircase of stained but unpainted wood. This leads from right centre to a granary doorway in the right wall. There is a landing before the door itself and a balustrade enclosing it. Hanging on to the balustrade, from the roof-beams, is a steel trapeze with nylon ropes.

Below this attic door is another, on ground level. The floor is fitted with brown terracotta tiles.

Up left corner, an old ox-cart which has been brightly but crudely painted, probably by children. Other relics hang on the walls or stand free: a wooden yoke, ironwork from ploughs and harrows, great broken pots with bullrushes standing in them, a wooden pallet for an oven.

Steel or wooden furniture stands about, all easily movable, very bright and modern. Under the stairs, three up-to-date children's bikes of slightly different sizes.

ACT ONE

SCENE ONE

Main doors are closed at start but light comes from windows in fourth wall to show us the set in detail.

Almost at once the double doors are pulled outwards, staying like that and cutting off any real view of the outside. More light floods in, bright sunlight.

DICK and PHIL come in, carrying suitcases. They are the same age, forty, but PHIL looks younger. They wear casual clothes but DICK manages to make them slightly formal. PHIL speaks with a regional accent.

They look about at the barn, putting the cases down to do so. Or PHIL looks and DICK awaits his reaction.

DICK: Voila!

PHIL: Ah, oui.

DICK: Chic, n'est ce pas?

PHIL: Chouette alors! Vous avez fait une grange de grand-standing.

DICK: C'est ça.

PHIL: Tout cela c'est de nouveau, n'est ce pas?

DICK: Plus ça change, plus c'est la même chose.

PHIL [*like housewife in interview*]: Oh, definitely.

> [LIZ *and* DIANA *follow on, carrying small bags, baskets and odd articles of clothing. They are two years younger than their husbands.* LIZ *looks older and leaves her grey hair undyed. She is more practical than* DIANA *and less elegant. She has a regional accent too but is more inclined to conceal it than* PHIL *is. She often speaks as though addressing a meeting.* DIANA *is languid and a bit actressy, changeable, self-indulgent. She looks around, as* PHIL *did.*]

DIANA: Oh, yes!

LIZ: D'you like it?

DIANA: Oh, yes!

DICK: Oh, good. I'm glad you like it. *We* do.

DIANA: When you think what it was like when we first saw it, Phil!

PHIL: All dust and bird-shit.

DICK: We've breathed on it a bit.

DIANA: Yes, but without spoiling the original rural atmosphere. You've done it beautifully.

DICK: Not actually *us*. Now we're in the money we can afford the local artisans.

DIANA: Oh, I didn't mean you'd actually *done it*.

DICK: They come in their Citroën vans and black berets and shake hands all —

LIZ [*interrupting*]: What we wanted was a place where the kids can do what they like. A kind of – aaah – sophisticated play-space.

DIANA: Yes.

LIZ: An – aah – adventure playground where they can – aah - sleep if they're tired of bedrooms —

DICK: Only in the summer, of course —

LIZ: Oh, yes, it's too cold in winter.

DIANA: Cold? Really? Is it ever cold?

DICK: At Christmas —

LIZ [*almost at same time*]: We had snow at Christmas. And on the same day sat in the orchard having tea with our shirts off.

DICK: It's being so far inland, you see, we —

LIZ: What we've got is a really – ahm – a truly – ahm – continental climate.

> [*Pause.* DICK *stands silenced, looking at the ground. The others look elsewhere.*]

Cold at night and hot by day.

> [PHIL *breaks away, looks about.*]

PHIL: Very good, the children's art-work.

DICK: We let them mess about in here but they're strictly not allowed to bring their junk into the main house.

> [*Pause.* PHIL *looks at cart.*]

PHIL: Great, their decoration of the ox-cart. And what's this?

DICK: That's a pallet for removing bread from an oven.

LIZ: You haven't seen my bread-oven.

PHIL: I haven't had that pleasure, no.

> [*The women laugh.*]

DIANA: We did catch a glimpse of it last summer.

PHIL: *You* may have done.

DIANA [*laughs*]: You remember, it was stuffed up with old kindling and charcoal.

[PHIL *winces. The women laugh again.*]

LIZ: Anyway I cleared it out and got a through-draught going. Lit a faggot in the middle to heat the inside. And now I bake all our bread that way.

[DIANA *and* PHIL *have been steadily chuckling at all this.* DICK *stares at floor. If there is an expression on his face, it is an obviously false smile.* LIZ *is intimidated by his attitude.*]

DIANA: If you've got a bread-oven, keep it in use.

PHIL: That's what she always says.

DIANA: That's what I always say.

PHIL: So this is for pushing in and out.

[DICK *turns his smile towards* PHIL. *Pause.*]

DICK: Exactly. [*Moves to it and shows him.*] I'm afraid it's got the worm rather badly.

[DICK *bursts again.* PHIL *tries not to chuckle.* LIZ *looks nervous.*]

But a few coats of Rentokil.

PHIL: Works wonders.

[DICK *smiles even more falsely.*]

And these stairs are new, of course —

DICK: Yes, and that's my study. It was you suggested making a room of that loft. Don't you remember? We were only renting the place when you came last —

PHIL: Yes —

DICK: But we talked about buying one of these farms if we ever came into money and you said you'd turn the citerne into a bathing pool, get rid of the mosquitoes, put in the stairs and tile the floor . . .

LIZ: Yes, and it was your idea to leave the rough wood of the old stalls over there —

[*They all look towards the Audience.*]

– keep some of the original features, you said, so no one would ever forget what it used to be like.

DICK: We profited from your advice and never paid a fee.

PHIL: Be my guest, I can't remember.

DIANA: Which is why everyone gets rich but us.

DICK: Actually we did discuss asking you to come out and supervise the artisans but —

[*As soon as* DICK *started speaking, a little* FRENCHMAN *came from door, right, carrying a battered tin kettle. He wears a tartan cap, with ear-flaps, a grey shirt, black trousers and plaid-patterned carpet slippers. He is obviously startled to find them there. He begins talking at once in a falsetto gabble, incessant and unintelligible. He comes forward as* DICK *turns to him. They shake hands.* DICK *talks over his gabble, though the man sometimes pauses and might be listening.*]

M'sieur, bonjour . . . ça va? . . . Ça va. M'sieur, vous êtes passé par cette pièce? . . . ah, oui, mais – pendant quelques jours ce monsieur et sa femme —

[*This reminds the* MAN *of his social duty and he goes to the women and shakes hands with them, talking and nodding. They put in their pleasantries.*]

. . . alors . . . ils vont y dormir —

[*The* MAN *goes up to* DICK *and shakes his hand.*]

PHIL: Monsieur.

[*The* MAN *looks at* PHIL *and stops talking. We hear* DICK *clearly at last.*]

DICK: Alors – si vous pourriez passer par l'autre chemin – à l'autre côté de la grange – ou –

[*The* MAN *nods and begins gabbling again, making his good-byes and backing away towards the doors, left. They watch him go in silence.*]

LIZ: D'you think he understood?

DICK: He doesn't listen.

LIZ: He's very deaf.

DICK: I asked him not to come through that room for a few days while you're here.

PHIL: Yes I got that.

DIANA: I didn't.

LIZ: He's an itinerant vine-labourer. When he's in these parts he lives in a hut by the road made of plastic sacks, old fertiliser sacks.

DIANA: I remember him from last year, yes.

DICK: Took one look at your face and backed —

LIZ [*cutting in*]: We call him Gunga Din. Because he seems to have an ancient right-of-way through this property to fetch water from the source in our field. He used to work here when it was a farm.

DICK: If he tries coming through your room again, do tell him he's...

LIZ: Well, he must be told. He keeps popping up in the most embarrassing situations. Like when we're having a cuddle. Or I'm feeding little Sam in the kitchen.

DIANA: Oh, Dick, he's lovely! Don't you love him?

DICK: I don't know that I *love* him. He's certainly a curious little chap. His tartan cap and his battered tin kettle.

DIANA: Not him. Your son. Your new baby.

    [*They laugh.*]

DICK [*smiling falsely again*]: Oh, him. Now you're talking. He's lovely.

DIANA: There was nothing about him in the papers. Everything else about you but not that. So I was amazed when your letter came saying you had a new baby.

LIZ: The whole point – ahm – in coming down here was to keep it a secret.

DICK: We didn't want our family exploited for publicity. You know, they'd make capital out of the baby to run down the book.

DIANA: Well, of course, that occurred to me as soon as I got your news.

DICK: You can see it. 'Teenage-sex-champion's wife has son at thirty-eight.'

PHIL: Oh, I got it all wrong. I thought you said it was a tax dodge.

LIZ: That too, yes. As soon as we got that outraged reaction from all the – ahm – professional moralists, of course the first edition sold out. Ahm—

DICK: They got out a reprint as soon as they could, by which time we could see that, as they say over there, we had a tax problem.

PHIL [*American*]: Every beautiful human being should have such a problem.

DICK: So we decided to—

LIZ [*simultaneously*]: Our accountant said if we wanted—

    [*They break off.* DICK *falsely smiles and indicates that she go on.*]

LIZ: Our accountant said we shouldn't keep any of the money unless we spent a year abroad so – ahm – ahh – straight away we got in touch with the owners and said if the farm was still for sale, we'd like it.

DIANA: How have the children settled in?

LIZ: Oh, terribly well. We're closer to them than ever and, as you know, we've always been a close family.

DICK: We worried about disturbing their education at first but apart from Jane, they're under ten, so I finally decided that – um –

LIZ: You said – ahh – that – ahm – well – acquiring French at their age was – ahm – more useful than yet another school project on the Crystal Palace.

DIANA: I should think so.

LIZ: With the result they all gabble away like mad in froggy lingo.

DICK [*to* PHIL]: Ben and Sarah go to the village school up the road and Jane's at the local lycée.

LIZ: You'll be able to hear. They're coming home the day after tomorrow for Jane's birthday.

PHIL: We may not be staying that long.

LIZ: Whyever not?

PHIL: You know me. Not a country boy. The beaches are beckoning.

DIANA: We'll stay, don't worry. Where are they now?

LIZ: On the coast with friends.

DIANA: Of course I want to see them, but it's nice to have a day or so completely to ourselves.

LIZ: Yes, smashing! It never occurred to me you wouldn't be bringing Emma.

DIANA: She's with Mother.

LIZ: How *is* your mother? [*And to* DICK.] Oh, come on, let's put the cases in their room, then make us a drink and I'll serve the lunch.

[*Picks up luggage and so does* DIANA.]

DIANA: Oh, she's much the same. She says the country's become a second-rate power. You can always tell, she says, when a nation's in decline: it starts producing elaborate postage stamps.

[*They move towards door, right.*]

LIZ: She's right, too, isn't she? All those tiny little Turners and Constables . . .

[*They exit into room.*]

PHIL: I enjoyed the book, by the way. Very much.

DICK: Oh, thank you, very kind.

PHIL: It didn't seem all that shocking.

DICK: No. Nor to me. That was unscrupulous promotion.

PHIL: Yeah, like that dust-jacket. That must have sold a few copies. The naked nymphet with the school satchel over her crotch.

[DICK *turns to back wall and finds a life-size blow-up, with its front to the wall. He turns it and we see that it's the photograph* PHIL *described. No book title, though, to conceal the adolescent girl wearing only a satchel. She's facing the camera and the straps go around her breasts to the bag itself, which she holds in front of her.*]

PHIL: That's the one. That sold a few copies all right. And calling the book *The Nubile Baby*.

DICK: Well, as you know, that was *not* my title.

PHIL: I didn't. What *was* your title?

DICK: *Authoritarian Assumptions in Secondary Education.*

PHIL [*doubtfully*]: Well . . .

DICK [*coming down*]: That *is* what the book's about.

PHIL: You can see the publisher's point.

DICK: Only too well. Shall we get a drink?

[*Takes case to room, right.* PHIL *picks up his and makes to follow.*]

PHIL [*going*]: Still the same pompous prick!

[*Lights to black.*]

SCENE TWO

Lights same as Scene One. LIZ *comes from main doors, left, pushing a white baby-carriage, with its hood raised.* LIZ *wears a skirt and bolero, with slip-on sandals. She has a good, but not a deep, sun-tan.*

LIZ: No, you've had enough sun. It's too hot for you in the afternoon. You have a little snooze in the shade. [*She puts the pram, with hood downstage, somewhere left of centre, out of the patch of bright sunlight falling through the doorway.*]

Yes, yes, you must have forty winks and no arguing.

[DIANA *comes from room, right, wearing a loose shirt over a bikini, with quite elaborate sandals, dark glasses, a scarf enclosing her*

hair, and carrying a basket with other apparatus. Her skin is pale.]
It's no use flashing those great big smiles at me. No, no, I say it's no use at all. No use at all.

[*She does this playfully, tickling the baby, then* DIANA *goes to main doors and stands in the sun for a moment, frowning into it, shielding her eyes, then comes back into cool.*]

DIANA: I wish they'd bring back pale skin. For women with my complexion this is purgatory. I wish we could wear veils like the Edwardians.

LIZ: Wasn't that to hide their syphilis?

DIANA: I don't know. It was very elegant.

LIZ: Put the oil on first, then sit in the open doorway. We can hear people coming before they see us.

DIANA: And retreat into the shade —

LIZ: And we can move back if it gets too hot.

[DIANA *looks into pram and smiles, while* LIZ *gets two folding chairs and opens them near but not in the sun.*]

DIANA: You didn't worry at all about having the baby abroad?

[*She puts down her basket on a chair. During the scene, she anoints her face and limbs with bottled oils.* LIZ *only puts on a little but helps* DIANA *with the difficult places.* DIANA *removes her shirt where necessary.*]

LIZ [*shrugs*]: Dick knows a good deal of obstetrics. And by then we could afford to take on a proper nurse for the other kids. I can't bring myself to call her a nanny. To my class of person, nanny means grandma. Anyway, whatever you call her, she's splendid. She makes it all possible, this lovely life we've got here. And, as you see, I trust her completely to take them away to the seaside for a week without a second thought.

DIANA: You look very well on it.

LIZ: We *should* look well. Everything's turned out so well for us. The book and the baby and this lovely old farm. I always felt – aah – you know, so – ahm – trapped in London. You can't be self-sufficient there. If they dropped the Bomb, for instance. But here – no diesel fumes, no noise, no crowds . . . only fresh well-water, peaches and apples in the orchard . . . cherries and walnuts . . . local wine, wood fires . . . honestly – ahm – sometimes during the last year, with Dick working on his new book up there and the children sauntering home from school with pockets full of pine-cones . . . and I've perhaps been bottling the fallen fruit or scrubbing the flags and honestly I've felt like Tolstoy's wife.

DIANA: And it's such a help that the water's pumped by electricity and having a deep-freeze and a beater . . .

LIZ [*missing the irony*]: And a mixer, yes, and the fridge, oh, yes.

DIANA: Look at that beautiful lizard!

LIZ: Hullo, Percy, what are you after, eh?

[*Pause. They both return to their oiling.*]

And, I mean, it's not even as though we're exploiting the locals or living in a fascist society. The agriculture's gone co-operative and this bit isn't worth cultivating. So there isn't a man under fifty in the whole commune. But I think if enough people buy up the old farms and get the locals to work on them, we might stop the drift to the cities. You remember the village – ahm – not a bistro, not a shop of any kind. The church will be a ruin in ten years.

DIANA: You don't find you miss people?

LIZ: People come to *us*.

DIANA: Really?

LIZ: You're here. And tomorrow two Americans will be interviewing Dick.

DIANA: Amazing they come this far.

LIZ: Oh, there's a steady stream. Journalists, students, television people. We put a a lot of them off but you feel a sort-of – ahm – obligation to help promote the book. Especially now it's coming out in America.

DIANA: You seem to have fallen on your feet.

LIZ: Oh, but, Diana, he's the *greatest* blessing. [*She goes quietly to pram and looks in. Smiles.*] Fast asleep. Are you going to try for another child before it's too late? It's marvellous at our age, really.

DIANA: I can't, dear. My tubes were tied up years ago.

LIZ [*remembering*]: After the Caesarean. After Emma, yes—

DIANA: Doctor Donald said I'd better not risk another, my pelvis simply wasn't made for it. Philip was no help at all.

LIZ: He wanted a child of his own, I suppose—

DIANA: Exactly—

LIZ: Not being Emma's father—

DIANA: Quite—

LIZ: Men worry about all that—

DIANA: But I couldn't go against Doctor Donald, could I? I was left very knocked-about down below. I've never undressed in front of him since. His body's still quite firm and he stands in front of the glass drawing in his stomach and slapping his behind —

LIZ: He's very boyish—

DIANA: But I'm not going to have him lie there criticising my poor crêpey skin. Or asking me to take part in acrobatics.

LIZ: I get that too.

DIANA: And what d'you say?

LIZ: I laugh at him.

DIANA: I said; 'Quite enough bones slip out of place as it is.' Doctor Donald would have a fit if he saw the positions Phil suggests.

LIZ [*laughing*]: He bought a book mail order. It was the best laugh I've had for years.

DIANA: It's not that we don't enjoy ourselves.

LIZ: Oh, so do we.

DIANA: We've got a terrific sex-life—

LIZ: Ours is smashing—

DIANA: – as far as I'm concerned.

LIZ: They always complain, whatever you do. Dick kept on moaning about how seldom we had it, so I started keeping a record. I had this little engagement diary and I started putting M for morning, A for afternoon and N for night, with a cross for when I had the curse. And after three months I collated the figures and I went to him and showed him and I said, 'Now just you look at that!' We were well above the national average published in the *Guardian*.

DIANA: Absolutely. Phil says I get rid of my libido on the cat. It was all because he heard Emma and me talking to each other about the cat one day. And Emma said she thought he was the most mysterious cat she'd ever seen and she was sure he'd been a handsome prince and he'd been turned into a cat by some wicked witch. And one day the right person would come along and kiss the cat and break the spell.

LIZ: How sweet!

DIANA: And Phil said, 'Yes and he'll wake up as a prince and discover his balls have been cut off.'

LIZ: Phil's always had a marvellous sense of humour.

DIANA: He thinks the cat aggravates our asthma. That's another continual cry.

LIZ: He could be right.

DIANA: I think he *is* right. I sometimes watch Emma playing with the animal and I say, 'Now, Emma, just you leave the cat alone because if you go on breathing close to his fur, you'll find yourself gasping for air, you'll be stifling, and the more you try to get your breath, the more you'll panic . . . and then you'll be lying there wheezing away – as we both of us do on a bad day – and I can't do a thing for you except fetch your atomiser . . .'

LIZ: But is it wise to talk to her like that? Don't you excite her more?

DIANA: Wise! There's never been much wisdom in my life, dear.

LIZ: Oh. now, Di —

DIANA: Look at the facts. Look at my love-life. Emma's father was no good to me, himself, our daughter or his wife. And for the sake of that worthless man I sent poor Clive to his death.

LIZ: Who?

DIANA: You remember, he was killed in action soon after I told him he had no chance. People said it was virtually suicide. I don't know. I only know some kind of demon's pursuing me through life. And, like my asthma, seems to have been inherited by poor Emma. [*She undoes her top and begins oiling her pale breasts.*] And what good have I been to Phil? Or he to me, for that matter?

LIZ: Oh, come on, Di, you've given each other —

[*The little* FRENCHMAN *has come from the room, right, and wandered across, obviously taking his usual short-cut to the water. He carries in one hand his battered tin kettle, in the other, by its feet, a live fowl. He almost collides with the pram, looks up and sees them and is startled. They have heard him now and turn, as embarrassed as he is. They cover their bodies. He begins gabbling at once in his falsetto French, looking at the ground.*]

LIZ [*putting a brave front on it*]: Monsieur. Vous êtes passé encore par cette pièce?

[*He nows decides there is no retreat and comes forward to them.* LIZ

177

smiles nervously. He puts down his kettle and shakes hands with
DIANA, *then* LIZ, *talking all the time. He then picks up the kettle
again, then holds out the live fowl to* LIZ. *He seems to expect her
to take it, so she does.*]

For me? Oh, merci, merci bien. God, it's alive! C'est vivant.

DIANA: Is it a gift?

LIZ: He often brings a peace-offering – strawberries, walnuts,
whatever's in season. Mais, m'sieur, merci beaucoup, très gentil.
Mais – ahm, ahh, erm, est-ce que c'est possible à tuer cette
poulet? Monsieur!

[*At her loud tone he stops speaking.*]

Est-ce que possible à tuer? Parce que je suis – ahh – je ne suis
pas une femme de campagne. Je crois que je ne puis pas – vous
comprenez?

[*He makes elaborate signs of understanding, then of breaking the
bird's neck, then gabbles on again, with a little laugh. Takes fowl
from her and goes off through main doorway.*]

Merci bien, monsieur . . . oui, bon à manger . . .

DIANA: Is he a Peeping Tom?

LIZ: Perhaps he didn't understand Dick telling him not to take that
short-cut. All his life he's been coming through here, from the
road through the cattle-sheds. That used to be his room at one
time.

[*They are ready for the sun now and prepare to leave.*]

Just in case he comes back with the dead fowl, let's go into the
orchard.

DIANA: I think so.

[LIZ *tidies the chairs,* DIANA *puts her oils, etc, in the basket and
goes to the pram. She looks at baby.*]

DIANA: Phil wants a son. He was so jealous when we got your letter.
'Another boy,' he said, 'they've got another boy.' For days he
went round talking about adopting one.

LIZ: Why don't you?

DIANA: I said all right, if that's what he wanted, though it seemed
too late in the day. But he never went through with it. He wants
the boy to be his.

LIZ: Well, you're sterilised, it's out of the question. He might as
well face facts.

DIANA: Exactly. I'm no damn use to him at all.

[*She wanders towards the main door, picking up a folding chair, then moving off.* LIZ *watches, then:*]

LIZ: The tragedy queen. I've seen it all before. I saw it first at school. Clytemnestra, was it, or Antigone? One of those. And ever since we've had this carry-on . . . [*Looks into pram.*] You can't win with her. Whatever you say, she goes one worse, Doesn't she, love? Yes, you know, don't you? Yes, you do.

[*She wheels off the pram after* DIANA, *talking to the baby. As she passes through the doors, lights quickly go to black. Few seconds' pause. Long flash of lightning. Two seconds' silence then sudden crack of thunder, very loud. More lightning flashes, almost at once, then more bursts of thunder.*]

SCENE THREE

During one of the lulls, DICK *comes in at main doors, then* PHIL. DICK *switches on lights, artfully disposed spots and strips concealed behind beams. They wear same clothes, but* PHIL *has bottle of wine and a glass. He had obviously drunk some already.*

PHIL *gets badminton racket and hits shuttlecock up and down. Then at* DICK, *who fails to catch it with his hand.* DICK *picks up racket and hits it back to* PHIL *and they play. When they score they say 'sorry'. But* PHIL *makes* DICK *run and in the end* DICK *lets the bird fall. He puts the racket and bird away, climbs stairs to study.*

PHIL: I help?

DICK: Thank you very much.

[PHIL *puts down bottle and follows him. A louder burst of thunder and the lights flicker and go out for a moment.* LIZ *and* DIANA *enter laughing, by main door. They have changed into trouser-suits. They each have a glass.*]

DIANA: Rentacloud!

LIZ: I knew this would happen. We've had sunshine for weeks but the moment you arrive —

DIANA: D'you remember our night at the Post Office Tower?

LIZ: The restaurant turning round and rain beating against the glass. Ahm – London quite invisible.

DIANA: And they were so *proud* of it!

LIZ [*pouring drinks for both*]: The Isle of Wight!

DIANA [*laughing*]: The Isle of Wight! Sou'westers in the sun lounge!

[PHIL *and* DICK *come from study, bringing apparatus.*]

PHIL [*portentously*]: The storm-clouds were gathering over Europe.

DIANA: It's the Isle of Wight all over again!

PHIL: The Isle of Wight! Sou'westers in the sun lounge!

LIZ: And the notice on the glass doors, ahm – d'you remember that? – ahh – 'high winds, danger of breakage, please use other entrance.'

[*The men bring down the apparatus and during this dialogue they fit up a slide projector and a screen on the facing wall. There is a wall-plug by the door, right.*]

DICK: Who was it suggested we hire ourselves out to countries with a water shortage?

DIANA: That was Phil.

DICK: He said, 'If they paid us to meet in the Sahara —'

LIZ: That was me, as a matter of fact, ahm —

DICK: '– it would be much cheaper then planting all those trees.'

LIZ: Or building dams, yes, that was me.

[*The women move chairs into position to watch the screen.*]

PHIL: While you're standing there taking the credit for my jokes, perhaps you could pour me a glass.

[*She does, laughing.*]

LIZ: Lie back and I'll drink it for you.

[PHIL *is upstage arranging the screen, the other three down,* DICK *fitting up projector.*]

It wasn't always rainy when we met. In the early years it was always sunshine.

DICK: That's not how I remember it.

LIZ [*to* DIANA]: He never remembers sunshine.

DICK: D'you mean the years before I went in the army?

LIZ: When we were at school, yes, and you and Di were in love and I used to be gooseberry.

DIANA: Oh, yes, before Phil, yes. The rain didn't start till Phil.

LIZ: Hullo, hullo —

PHIL [*coming down, drinking*]: This is the local wine, you say?

DICK: The Mayor's, yes, the Mayor of the village. He sells us wine and eggs.

LIZ: At one franc a litre, it's less than Coca Cola.

PHIL: Nice and fruity too. I usually drink draught Guinness but when in Rome . . .

DIANA: He's developing a beer-belly too.

> [DICK *has finished the preparations and switches on projector, throwing a white light on the screen. A lightning flash outside and all lights go off for two seconds. Groans from everyone. Thunder. Lights go on again. Cheers.*]

DICK: Right.

> [*Goes to door, right, switches off lights. Only screen and projector lit. Women and* PHIL *have found seats.* DICK *stands at projector.*]

This is a selection, a short-list, a top ten of last year's snaps. If you want more, I've got them, but the quality of the photography will steadily deteriorate the wider we cast our net. Not all of these are of visual interest and the first dozen or so tend to be mainly personal, but all, I think, reach a certain — [*Breaks off.*] – anyway —

> [*Shows first picture – attractive colour print of farmhouse in southern or central France, with sand-rendered walls, white woodwork and decorated eaves. Mutters of approval and recognition continue, as well as the real dialogue.*
>
> *Second picture: a boy of ten, a girl of eight, against a stone wall, wearing only trunks.*]

DIANA: That's nice.

LIZ: Ben and Sarah.

DIANA: Was that when we were here?

DICK: You were here – when? – July?

DIANA: Yes.

DICK: That *was* in July, I think. They're not all July in this batch. They're scattered through the year, but perhaps ninety per cent would be July.

> [*Third picture:* SARAH *and another girl of eight, posing with bicycles.*]

LIZ: Yes, there's Emma. So it must have been while you were here.

DIANA: They got on terribly well together. She's always asking when are we going to Sarah's again?

LIZ: Then why didn't you bring her this time?

DIANA: Phil said he wanted a holiday without her.

PHIL: Don't blame it on me. *I* was happy to bring her. *She* wanted to stay with your mother because she —

DIANA: I didn't think it polite to mention that.

PHIL: – because she gets anything she asks for there.

DIANA: This again?

PHIL: You going to tell me she doesn't get spoilt?

DIANA: She loves her granny, that's all. We're terribly close, all three of us.

PHIL: I'll give you that. Ever since your Mam threw your Dad out —

DIANA: Threw him out? He left —

PHIL: – you've been a right bloody trio.

DIANA: He left her all alone with a growing child —

PHIL: Alone? What about the ever-present Doctor Donald?

DIANA: Ee bai goom.

PHIL: A little touch of Dettol in the night.

DIANA: Ee, thah knows, oor Phil's got a cruel tongue on him.
    [*Pause.*]

LIZ: Tuppence they fight.
    [*Laughter. Fourth picture: same three children together, dressed as princesses and a knight.*]

DIANA: Oh, sweet! Doesn't Ben get all resentful being here with a lot of girls?

DICK [*pouffe voice*]: Thanks very much I'm sure.

LIZ: No, he did at first, you must admit, love. You tended to spend so much time *writing* about children, there wasn't much left when you could actually be *with* them. Aahm. Even before, when you were at the hospital half the time and often on call. But – erhm, ahh – after Ben started going to the village school he settled down.

DICK: He *was* a bit alone at this time, though. So many girls. If *you* could have brought a boy or one of —

LIZ: Poor Ben, the centre of attention at bath-time. The only one with a willie.
    [*Fifth picture: LIZ and a GIRL, posing under a hanging vine or*

fruit-tree, wearing attractive sun-suits. LIZ's *hair is dyed dark brown and she looks years younger.* JANE, *her daughter, is a mature fourteen with a cool demeanour.*]

DIANA: You could be sisters!

LIZ: Oh, come on.

DICK: That may be because Jane looks old for fourteen rather than that you look young for thirty-eight.

LIZ: Thank you.

DICK: I'm sorry, that's awful. No. In fact, you *do* look fantastically young but —

LIZ: Too late now.

PHIL: It's partly your hair, of course. Why have you stopped dyeing it?

LIZ: Imagine the bother here! Awful hairdressers in the local town or doing it myself. One surely only does it at home because everyone else does.

DIANA: Quite.

PHIL: I had a shock when I saw you, though. You realise how old most women would look without cosmetics.

LIZ: But they'd all look the same, it would cancel out.

[*Sixth picture:* PHIL *lying in hammock between two trees, wearing shorts. Laughter.*]

DIANA: Social realism now.

[*Flash of lightning. Picture flickers and goes out briefly but recovers. Thunder.*
Seventh picture: DIANA *in hammock.*]

PHIL: Soon got kicked out of that.

DIANA: You'd been there hours. I asked you to take our picture.

DICK: Ah, that's it. *You* took it, yes. Only it's got a bit of the camera case at the bottom there. See?

PHIL: Oh, yeah. See that, Di? Bit of the camera case?

DICK: The blur at the bottom.

[*Eighth picture: men playing boules in village square.*]

PHIL: That's better. D'you take this, Dick?

DICK: Yes.

PHIL: You can tell.

[*Silence. As no one says anything, he goes on to the ninth; a fortified village church.*]

Très solide, uh?

LIZ: The village church.

PHIL: Très solide, très folklorique, n'est ce pas?

[*Tenth:* DICK *in swimming trunks at lake or sea.*]

Très solide aussi. Formidable.

LIZ: One of the days we persuaded him to come for a swim.

DICK: That was yours, wasn't it, love? Rather nice.

[*Eleventh: similar scene but* PHIL *and* JANE *in swimming clothes, both reaching for a ball. Reactions indistinct and casual.*]

[*Twelfth:* JANE, *same clothes, lying in long grass.*]

DIANA: How could she lie in the grass like that with all those insects and vipers about? I used to look at her bare legs sometimes and think to myself: That girl's asking for it.

DICK: Who took this? I didn't.

LIZ: Not me.

DIANA: No.

PHIL: I might have, I can't remember.

[*Thirteenth:* BEN *at wheel of Citroën, smiling, wearing warmer clothes.*]

DICK: I think this was in the winter, this one. Ben reversing up and down the yard.

[*Fourteenth:* LIZ *with grey hair, wearing bikini.*]

DIANA: Must be later, yes, your hair's grey.

LIZ: This was spring, yes. You see what we were saying about cold nights and warm days, even in January we could wear those clothes.

[*Fifteenth: rather soon, the little* FRENCHMAN, *with a hoe, formally facing camera.* PHIL *and* DICK *at once start imitating his falsetto gabble.*]

Oh, did I tell you, love, he came through their bedroom again today, quite unexpectedly?

DICK: Oh, no —

LIZ: Yes, just as we were oiling our bosoms.

DICK: I'll speak to him again.

DIANA: Dick, let's see that last picture again. I didn't really see.

[*Fourteenth again:* LIZ *in bikini.*]

This can't have been in spring, can't possibly, Liz, you're not pregnant.

DICK: No, this is much earlier, before Christmas, it was pretty chilly in November, then we got these warm afternoons. No, showing it after Ben in the car, I thought it was the same group but obviously —

DIANA: Not November surely, your hair's completely grey. You were in England in October. We met in town, d'you remember? By chance. Your hair was dark-brown then. It couldn't have gone completely grey in a few weeks.

DICK: I expect that was her wig. When you met in town. Must have been.

[*They don't reply.* DICK *puts on picture of little* MAN *again, then next, which is* JANE *on a bike. Lightning flash, thunder crack close by. But* LIZ *has crossed to the wall right and switches on the lights. They all look at her.*]

LIZ: This is stupid. Don't you think so, love?

DICK: Now steady on, don't get excited —

LIZ: I'm not, but Di and Phil are supposed to be our friends, they should share our secrets.

[*Pause. The picture of* JANE *remains on the screen, dimmed by the other lights.*]

I wasn't pregnant in that picture because I'm not Sam's mother. I'm his grandmother.

DICK: Oh, dear.

LIZ: It was Jane who was pregnant, not me. We'd hardly got back to England last year when she told us.

[*They are moving about, she and* DICK. DIANA *and* PHIL *stay seated, listening.*]

Well, of course we thought it must have happened at her comprehensive school. Which I think is a natural assumption.

DICK: And which she initially claimed to be the case.

LIZ: She was frightened and confused, poor love —

[*He turns off the projector.*]

DICK: I'm not blaming her —

LIZ: I know you're not, but we mustn't give the impression she wasn't honest with us. She only lied because she was confused and partly also – ahm —

DICK: Trying to cover up for Monique.

PHIL: Monique?

LIZ: That au-pair girl we had last year, you remember, she was helpful with the language but not much else.

DICK: Well, I could date the beginning of pregnancy and of course she had to admit it had happened in July —

LIZ: While we were staying on the farm.

DICK: Which seemed mysterious —

LIZ: But she at once made a clean breast of the whole business. D'you remember one night she went to town with Monique? I was afraid of her French car-driving.

DICK: The least of our worries.

LIZ: We couldn't know they were going to meet these local boys. They'd picked them up earlier that day while they were supposed to be fetching the family ice-creams. And this night they met in a bar and afterwards went for a country drive and Sam was started in the back of our car.

DIANA: How frightening for you!

DICK: Well, of course, it's easy to look back, now that the worst is over, and pretend to ourselves it wasn't a shock, but if we're honest, we'd have to admit —

LIZ: We had a good cry. But what for me helped to heal the shock and pain was Jane's trust in us. God bless her, as soon as she saw there was no covering up for Monique, she told us everything and said she'd do whatever we thought was best.

PHIL: Did you try to find Monique?

DICK: We knew her address in France —

LIZ: But whatever for? We were dealing here with the promise of a new life.

[LIZ *and* DICK *come together and he puts his arm round her shoulder.*]

And we all agreed that life mustn't start in a cloud of punishment and blame.

DIANA: Didn't you think about an operation?

DICK: Briefly, yes.

LIZ: Oh, Diana, here was I, my children growing up, suddenly presented with a brand-new baby. Ahm, a grandmother at thirty-eight and every chance of living to be a great and even a great-great-grandmother. Ahm. How could we talk about operations?

DICK: Not that it was all that simple. This was in September. *The*

Nubile Baby had just come out.

PHIL: I was thinking, yes —

DICK: You see, Phil?

PHIL: Yes.

DICK: The filth they'd spread across the papers? The way they'd persecute Jane?

LIZ: And the other children. Not to mention Dick himself.

DICK: And, though in some ways the event seemed to be a stunning specific instance of the book's general proposition —

LIZ: We none the less felt – and I mean I think we were unanimous pretty much from the start – ahm – we felt we couldn't submit Jane to all that professional and public hostility.

DICK: So, as soon as it was clear the book was a best-seller, I bought the farm and got a year's leave from the hospital and off we went.

[*Lightning and a great burst of thunder, close. The lights falter, go out and resume.*]

We'd better get back to the house. These lights may go if the storm gets closer. [*He takes down screen, dismantles projector.*]

DIANA [*standing*]: Whose child is he, officially?

LIZ: Oh, Jane's. The local people know, of course. We kept her away from school towards the end but anyone who saw her here would know.

DIANA: The little man?

LIZ: Gunga Din, exactly. But nobody cares and except for the children we live like hermits, don't we, love?

[DICK *nods, busy packing. He goes upstairs with apparatus.*]

But I think the most thrilling aspect of the whole affair is – ahm – the fact that – ahm – Sam's arrival has brought us even closer together as a family. Of course I know that in suffering people find new and deeper relationships, but this was no catastrophe, this was a blessing, yet even so – ahm —

[*Lightning. Lights falter.*]

I think Dick will bear me out here —

[*Thunder overhead. Lights go.*]

PHIL: Jesus, *what a storm!*

[DICK *appears from bedroom shining torch.*]

LIZ [*continuing*]: We all feel as though we've been through the fire together and, though it hasn't always been —

DICK: I'm coming! Hang on.

PHIL: Somebody got the wine? I've found it. Take your glasses.

> [DICK *now leads them off towards the main doors as more flashes are followed by more crashes.*]

LIZ: Certainly hasn't always been a picnic, none the less·– aah – we've found our way through to a deeper family harmony based on absolute trust . . . ahm – in the birth of little Sam we've been, so to speak, regenerated . . .

> [*As she goes off with* DIANA, *led by* DICK, PHIL *follows. He sings above the thunder.*]

PHIL [*singing*]:

> Singing in the rain
> Just singing in the rain —
> [*In a flash of light we see him dancing.*]
> What a wonderful feeling
> I'm happy again . . .

SCENE FOUR

Storm dies away in darkness.

> *Morning light comes up, as in Scene One.*

> *The little* FRENCHMAN *opens the door of* DICK's *study, above right, and comes on to the landing. He is silent and stands uncertainly for a moment, looking back into the room. Then he starts to come downstairs. As usual, he carries the old tin kettle. Reaching the floor, he makes towards the main doors as* DICK *comes from his room.*

DICK: Alors, m'sieur!

> [*The* MAN *stops, turns and waits, while* DICK *follows him down.* DICK *approaches him. Beneath his courtesy he seems distracted, anxious.*]

Vous devez vous tromper, je suis certain . . . mais —

> [*The* MAN *begins denying this, shyly, not looking at* DICK *directly.*]

Oui, oui, je l'ai compris, mais —

[*The* MAN *goes on talking and* DICK *talks over him.*]

Il ne faut pas parler de cette affaire à personne. Merci. Au revoir, m'sieur.

[*Offers his hand and they shake. The little* MAN *holds up his kettle and asks if he may fill it at the spring.*]

Je vous en prie! Mais – rappelez – cette pièce est occupée . . .

[*He points at the bedroom and the little* MAN *nods and says he won't go through there any more. Then he turns and goes by the main doors. As he goes out of sight we hear* LIZ *and* PHIL *greeting him and short, correct replies from him.* DICK *is obviously alarmed by the sound and looks at his watch, glances up at his room as a possible refuge, makes towards the stairs but before he can climb them,* LIZ, DICK *and* DIANA *come in. The women are in skirts and* PHIL *in shorts and a loose shirt.* DIANA *also wears a hat and dark-glasses, which she takes off on entering the semi-darkness of the barn.*]

LIZ: Hullo, love, how are you?

DICK: Hullo.

[*She goes straight to him and embraces him. She kisses him on the mouth and makes relishing sounds.* DIANA *sits in a convenient chair, fanning herself with the hat.*]

LIZ: Did Gunga Din disturb you?

DICK: What?

LIZ: We saw him going, he'd been through here, did you talk to him?

DICK: Yes. Yes. He came through the room again and I heard him and came down and told him not to and then —

LIZ: You shouldn't have broken off from your work.

DICK: My work was going badly anyway.

LIZ: Oh, poor love.

PHIL: I told you, you should have come with us.

DICK: And I explained that my publisher has commissioned a second book and I'm obliged to try and deliver the —

DIANA: He only asked you to come to stop you working. Stop you writing another best-seller.

PHIL: No, but on a day like this Dick surely deserves a walk in the woods.

LIZ: I wish you'd come, love, we never met another soul —

189

DICK: Well, I'm glad you had a nice time. As I said, my morning wasn't nice at all.

LIZ: Poor Dick! I shall make you an extra-special lunch with all your favourite things – ahm – beetroot soup, quiche . . . I got some quiches in the market —

PHIL: Shall we tell him what we really did?

LIZ: Ahm – peaches and brugnons —

PHIL: Shall we, Di?

DIANA: Why ask me?

PHIL: When we got to the pool beyond the clay-pits —

LIZ [*quickly*]: We had a swim.

DICK: Oh, good.

PHIL: Yes, but in the —

LIZ: In the nude. We had no costumes.

DICK: Oh, yes. All of you?

DIANA: Not me.

PHIL: Being a nature-lover, she's afraid of the water-snakes. I told her water-snakes don't bite and there we stood, all hot and dizzy after the walk —

LIZ: It was sweltering, love —

PHIL: Discussing the pros and cons and suddenly it seemed to be getting all too tight-arsed so I dropped my knickers and so did Liz and in we went.

LIZ: It was all very innocent, love.

    [*Pause.*]

DICK: We're not innocent, love. Nothing we do is innocent.

PHIL: This was. A simple spontaneous climax to a —

DICK: You said you stood there discussing it.

DIANA: It was a scream from where I stood.

PHIL: On the bank.

DIANA: D'you remember those awful films with groups of naked people waving at departing Land-Rovers . . . ? [*She laughs.*]

PHIL: Well, of course you've developed a kink about stripping off.

DIANA: Girls in G-strings swabbing the decks of yachts.

LIZ: It was all very middle-aged and middle-class and funny, I suppose, but – ahm – we – ahh – we felt we had to tell you because – ahm – otherwise it would have become something nasty and secretive.

[*Pause.*]

DICK: Why should I ever have found out?

[*Pause.*]

LIZ: Oh, love, I'd have had to tell you sooner or later. [*Then to the others:*] We haven't any secrets from each other. Perhaps that's boring and unsophisticated, but that's the way we are.

DICK: You should have sensed it would be better later. Not this morning, when I've been stuck here, struggling to express some idea that may eventually provide the money to pay for the scenery in which you can go off exposing yourselves in the wood —

PHIL: Oh, come on, Dick, you're building up a fantasy – we were hot, we wanted a swim, we didn't have any trunks – by Christ, Diana sat there watching us!

LIZ: I wished you'd come, darling, there was nothing in it.

DICK: You may not be the best judge of that.

[*She looks at him. He is moving about in an agitated way.*]

I've been told something that I can't possibly ignore, much as I'd like to. If I don't face you with the accusation at the outset, I might get into some kind of paranoid sweat because the implications are —

LIZ: Accusation?

DICK: Well —

LIZ: Who's accusing who?

DICK: No, that's not right, no one's accusing anyone. When I heard Gunga Din coming through that room, startling the baby, making him cry out, I came down and told him not to go through any —

LIZ: Did he wake up? You didn't tell me.

[*She goes towards door but he stops her.*]

DICK: I got him off again. He's all right. Listen to me, please! He said of course he wouldn't and he was sorry he'd woken Sam and wasn't he a fine specimen, which of course we agreed on, then he asked where his father was.

LIZ: Nosey bugger.

DICK: That's what I thought.

LIZ: I hope you told him where to go.

DICK: But after all he's only a funny old peasant —

LIZ: We'll have to stop him coming through altogether —

DICK [*continuing and forcing her to silence*]: And happens to have come to do the vines in March and saw Jane pregnant. So I said, 'We don't know who the father is, some young man in town'.

LIZ: I should have said —

DICK: Which seemed to confuse him. No, he said, the man in that room.

LIZ: What man? Who does he mean?

DIANA: Phil?

PHIL: Me?

DICK: Yesterday, when you arrived, d'you remember he seemed to look a bit funny when he saw your face?

LIZ: Of course!

PHIL: Yes. I was puzzled by that.

DIANA: So he thinks you're the father?

LIZ: No wonder he looked a bit funny. [*She laughs.*]

DIANA: I'd have looked a bit funny. [*She laughs too.*]

PHIL: What gave him the idea?

DICK: Well, according to him —

LIZ: He must be cracked.

DIANA: Wouldn't you be cracked if you lived in a polythene cabin?

LIZ: A misconception of that kind illustrates – ahm – how wide a culture gap can exist even between Europeans.

DICK: According to him, one day last year he was fetching water from his source in the field and wandered on a little further to pick some ceps and —

DIANA: Pick some what?

DICK: Ceps. Fungi.

DIANA: Like chanterelles?

DICK: Not exactly but —

LIZ: Oh, no, chanterelles are small and frilly. Ceps are large and fleshy with brown domes and yellow stalks.

DICK: Anyway —

LIZ: You can feed a family with one good cep.

DICK: He was picking these mushrooms —

LIZ: But you'd need a bowlful of chanterelles.

DICK: – and going deeper into the woods to —

LIZ: The locals call them girolles, of course.

DICK [*shouts*]: For Chrissake! What's it matter?

[*They all look at him, surprised. He does his false smile at* LIZ.]

Sorry. Sorry. But please let me finish. He was going deeper into the woods to find these repulsive bloody mushrooms – and then he says he came across Phil and Jane in a clearing with no clothes on. Now obviously he's mistaken but you asked him what gave him the idea you were Sam's father, so I'm telling you.

[*They look at* PHIL.]

PHIL: That's funny. I didn't notice him. Well, well.

DICK: You were in the woods with Jane?

PHIL: Yes.

DIANA: With no clothes on?

PHIL: Sunbathing, yes. She said she always sunbathed in the nude down here.

LIZ: We all do.

PHIL: Right. I could see that by her tan. I mean, there weren't any white strips. [*He scratches one eye.*]

LIZ: Why didn't you mention it? You wanted to mention our bathe at once. As soon as we met Dick.

PHIL: Didn't Jane mention it?

LIZ: No.

PHIL [*shrugs*]: There you are then. Why should I?

DICK [*false smile*]: Now steady. Let's take it steady, darling —

LIZ: I am steady. I'm not made unsteady by – ahh – people sunbathing, any more than by people taking off their clothes and swimming in a pool. Aaah —

DICK: All right. If that's all. [*To* PHIL.] You were sunbathing?

PHIL: You were all in town or at the lake, I can't remember exactly —

DICK: Yes, all right, yes —

PHIL: And Jane came to me in the hammock. I was playing cassettes and drinking wine. She brought a couple of peaches and asked if I'd seen the cress-bed.

DIANA: The what?

PHIL: The watercress-bed.

DIANA: I've heard some names for it.

DICK: Near the old man's source.

PHIL: Right. Which is why he saw us. Though I didn't see *him*.

DICK: Well, actually, what he says is that you weren't only

sunbathing. He could be mistaken, of course, I'm sure he is, but he says you were lying on her.

[*Pause.*]

LIZ: Lying on Jane?

DICK: Yes.

LIZ: You mean on top of her?

DICK: How else can you lie on someone?

[*They all look at* PHIL. *He looks at floor, then sighs and shrugs*.]

PHIL: I'm sorry.

[DIANA *stands*.]

DIANA: What?

PHIL: I don't know what to say.

DIANA: Are you telling us it's true?

LIZ: You slept with Jane?

PHIL: There wasn't much sleeping. As you know, she's a lively girl and the whole incident —

DICK [*moving threateningly*]: Do I understand you to be making a joke? Do I? Are you? Are you making a joke —

PHIL [*backing away*]: No, I was only —

DICK: — out of raping my fourteen-year-old daughter?

LIZ: Thirteen. She was thirteen then.

DICK: D'you know that's a criminal offence? Do you? Do you know the age of consent is sixteen?

PHIL: This wasn't rape! I never assaulted her. What d'you take me for?

DIANA: A dirty old man.

PHIL: I don't feel old. I'm more at home with kids. As you know, love.

DIANA: Don't call me 'love'.

PHIL: Don't even feel grown-up.

DICK: Time you did.

PHIL: What?

DICK: Grew up.

PHIL: True.

DICK: High time.

DIANA: The greedy spoilt eldest boy who's never been denied anything. Whose mother gave him not only his own butter ration but his sister's too. Who never learnt to resist.

PHIL: Di—

DIANA: You must be three times her age. So Sunday papers! Plastic macs and gym-slips and bicycle saddles, the whole tatty apparatus of—

PHIL: No, no, there was nothing disgusting. I tell you, Di, it was innocent and beautiful.

DIANA: Oh, Jesus Christ.

[*She goes quickly to the bedroom, right, and slams the door behind her.* PHIL *doesn't follow. Hear door bolted.*]

LIZ [*to Audience*]: How could she lie so carefully? For a whole year? A girl of that age? And when she most needed help. What have I done wrong?

DICK [*to Audience*]: I've spent the last nine months down here! Covering up for him! My grandson is his son! [*Then turns and speaks to* LIZ, *pointing at* PHIL.] You're his son's grandmother!

[*She looks at him, moves up a few steps.*]

LIZ: No other response? What matters to me is Jane herself and the way she deceived us so cleverly. It's not natural for a girl of that age. She's suddenly a stranger.

DICK: Don't you feel resentful? Cheated?

LIZ: You never feel anything else.

DICK: I know that but I'm asking about you.

LIZ: I'm going to get some lunch. Is anyone hungry? We'll all think better with a lining to our stomachs. [*She goes out by main doors.*]

DICK [*to Audience*]: They could carve that on her grave.

[*Without looking at* PHIL *again, he follows* LIZ. PHIL *tries to open bedroom door, then knocks. No answer.*]

PHIL: Di! [*Pause.*] Diana! There's a lot more to say. There's a lot I couldn't say to them. Let me in, please. This isn't something you can shout through a door.

[*Pause. No answer.*]

Honestly, I never guessed about the baby. Jane hasn't been in touch. Mind you, I was nervous when you said, 'Let's stop at the farm for a day or so.' But then Liz answered that all the kids would be away. . . . [*Shrugs.*] How could I visualise all this? [*Silence. He makes an angry gesture at the door, nearly moves away, then remembers and says.*] Lunch is nearly up. Why not come and have some lunch?

[*No answer. This time he moves half-way across the barn towards the main doors. The bedroom door is suddenly opened and the white pram is pushed out.* PHIL *turns to catch it as it rolls. The bedroom door is shut again and bolted.* PHIL *looks into pram and we hear sounds of baby preparing to cry.*]

You want some, do you? Want some lunch? [*Makes a face and recoils slightly.*] Need changing too. Shall I change you? Daddy change him? Right. Daddy change. [*Pushes pram towards main door and off.*]

ACT TWO

SCENE ONE

Afternoon. Bright sunlight.
 Door of bedroom, right, at first shut, is soon opened and DICK *and* DIANA *enter pushing an old wooden wheelbarrow containing clogs, books and journals, bottles and a papiermâché corset, which stands erect like a sculptured trunk. They put the barrow centre.*

DIANA: Fantastic a house like that should be allowed to fall apart. Why haven't the English bought it?

DICK: Too far gone, perhaps.

DIANA: At home it would be snapped up. Filled with paper lampshades and stripped pine dressers. . . .

DICK: We found so much interesting stuff in the beginning, I felt sure there was nothing left by now, we've been looting there so often.

   [DIANA *puts down clogs and steps into them. She hobbles about.*]

DIANA: Yes. Well. Perhaps they'll do for decoration. [*Takes them off, picks them up.*] Good soak in Rentokil.

   [DICK *looks at them as she returns them to basket.*]

DICK: I'll put them on the fire.

DIANA: Oh, no. . . .

DICK: The Mayor of our commune told me that the two most vital innovations here were running water and – *what*, d'you think? —

DIANA: Electricity?

DICK: Rubber boots. These sabots accumulated clay till you could hardly walk, they stuck in the ground. Then the poor buggers had to bang them together before they could go on. With boots, the soil slides off.

DIANA: I'll take them home. Home? After this morning?

   [DICK *looks at her, then they turn to the other loot.*]

DICK: This written inscription, look!

DIANA [*looking at prayer-book*]: Isn't that Latin? I can't read Latin.

DICK: No, but the date. Look at the date. 1789.

DIANA: Oh, yes.

DICK: Imagine her, whoever she was, the woman who owned this missal —

DIANA: Gunga Din's great-great-grandma?

DICK: Possibly. And here she was in 1789, with all that fuss going on in Paris, walking to the village church, prayer-book in hand, nodding at the neighbours — as bovine as her animals —

[*Drops book.* DIANA *takes up corset.*]

DIANA: D'you see her wearing this?

[*She puts it around her trunk.* DICK *helps to push it tight. He drums on it noisily.*]

DICK: Très solide.

[*He takes it off, puts it in basket. He seems restless, but she's interested in the objects. Dog barks some way off.* DIANA's *taken up a crumbling journal.*]

DIANA: 1909. Three cows sold . . . one cow bought . . . one bull bought . . . one wagon of earth . . . six calves sold . . . chàr à boeuf. . . .

[*Suddenly the screaming whistle of a jet aircraft, diving low directly overhead.* DIANA *clutches* DICK's *arm. The noise is gone as suddenly as it came but it leaves dogs barking and birds singing.*]

DICK: That happens occasionally. Jet-fighters from Cognac.

DIANA: Where can you escape? Is there anywhere left? When I see a hundred people have died in a jet-crash, I think what a tatty way to go. Smack into a mountain listening to Burt Bacharach.

DICK: I like the planes going over. I like the cars that pass. Anything that moves fast and gets somewhere. Anything for a change. I hate this junk we find in the old house. I hate the old house. [*He kicks the basket of junk. He seems exhilarated by this confession.*] Oh, Christ! This fucking place! A geriatric ward with trees! Everyone under sixty's gone to work in Paris and Bordeaux. Their factory jobs pay them enough to buy Simca saloons in which to drive down here and visit the old folk. Shoot some birds, if they can find any. Then back to town as quick as mustard, thanking God they got away. All very well for English people to buy these dumps, tart them up and carry on about clear well-water drawn up by their electric pumps. Or the fruity local wine that's cheaper than Coke. Or how they feel like Tolstoy's wife. They weren't here in November.

DIANA: I suppose that's not such fun.

DICK: When the rain comes down and the whole place dies? You'd love it.

DIANA: No. You're right. We enjoy it because it's all a change.

DICK: Any place I live in future there won't be anything old. I want everything to be new this week and next week change it all. What's the point of having money otherwise?

DIANA: Now you're going to extremes.

DICK: We're *at* extremes! This situation's extreme! Which is why I welcome it with open arms. We can't pretend we don't know. We can't go on as we did before.

DIANA: Well, all right, yes, but it's not that easy to —

DICK: Even Phil won't let it pass. And he's always had a tiresome attachment to the past. Even he's asking for a change.

DIANA: Is that how you see him? Attached to the past?

DICK: Yes, with his trad jazz and Utopian Socialism and Radiant Cities.

DIANA: He thinks that's modern and all that happened since is tatty profiteering. Where there's muck there's brass.

DICK: In the army in Malaya he and I used to spend hours swatting mosquitoes, planning the new society. It was old hat even then.

DIANA: It always seemed to me like the Co-op, only sexy.

DICK: We thought it could happen. And we of course would be the prime movers. Him with his plate-glass, me with the National Health.

DIANA: You grew up and he didn't.

DICK: Well, I lost that kind of simple faith.

DIANA: He's an innocent. With most men, this Jane business would seem lavatorial but somehow with him —

DICK: And he does see its true importance: that it puts us in a new light. He and Jane are forcing us to change. We should thank them for that.

[DIANA *looks over the junk again, putting it in the barrow.*]

DIANA: I don't care that much for old things. Second-hand things. Just that all our friends at home spend half their lives collecting —

DICK: This situation puts us beyond doing what our friends do.

[*Wheels barrow upstage.*] That's why I'm so glad the old man saw them at it by the spring and —

 [*Breaks off as* LIZ *enters by the main doors carrying a shopping-basket full of corked but empty wine-bottles.*]

LIZ: I thought you might be here. He wants to talk to us.

DICK: What about?

LIZ: I don't know. There's plenty to talk about.

DIANA: I shan't listen. [*Makes towards bedroom.*]

LIZ: Well, love, you'll have to sooner or later. These Yanks are coming some time today and we ought to have sorted out our – ahm – our – erm – intended procedure before they – aaah – before they arrive.

DICK: Intended — ?

LIZ: Aaahm —

DICK: Procedure?

LIZ: Then again, tomorrow afternoon all the children are coming home —

DICK [*persevering*]: What is there to proceed with?

LIZ: And we've got to know where we stand before we talk to Jane.

DICK: Talk to Jane?

LIZ: Well, obviously. We must talk it over surely?

 [PHIL *comes on carrying a large glass bottle in a wickerwork container.*]

PHIL: You sure Sam's all right in the orchard? The sun won't be too hot for him?

LIZ: Through the trees? No.

PHIL: I left the hood up.

 [*And during the following dialogue,* LIZ *and* PHIL *pour red wine from the bonbonne into the bottles. To begin with, it is so heavy that* PHIL *has to support it between his thighs.* LIZ *uses a funnel to get the wine in.* DIANA *sits watching.* DICK *stands.*]

Well. I've been thinking. I dare say we've all been thinking. You don't want my apologies.

LIZ: No, we've had them.

PHIL: Right.

LIZ: Over lunch.

DICK: Diana hasn't. She wasn't there.

DIANA: Hasn't this gone a bit beyond apologies? A thirteen-year-old girl?

PHIL: A very precocious thirteen, nearly fourteen —

DIANA: This isn't like the others, Philip. I mean the secretary, the jazz-band vocalist, the student-nurse —

PHIL: Come on, love, this is —

DIANA: *Don't* call me 'love'.

PHIL: I say this is all beside the point —

DIANA: I suffered those in silence —

PHIL: Not exactly.

DIANA: What?

PHIL: Not exactly silence.

DIANA: Because I was grateful to you. For marrying me when I was pregnant by another man. Well, I think this puts me well in the black.

PHIL: I wasn't going to mention that, but all right, I'm not Emma's father and after she was born you got sterilised.

DIANA: You agreed.

PHIL: Yeah, sure. By Christ the whole birth was touch-and-go, I thought you were going to die. I'd have given anything to keep you. [*Concentrates on pouring wine. Pause.*] So after that you had your tubes tied up.

DIANA: I said we could adopt a boy.

[PHIL *shakes his head.*]

PHIL: The point is now I've got a son. Like you've got a daughter.

DIANA: Emma's father wasn't a thirteen-year-old boy.

PHIL: No. He was a second-hand car salesman. Let's not bicker, Di, that's a dead end. Out there in the orchard is a baby who's given a lot of trouble to his – Liz and Dick. Just as their family's growing up and away and they've every right to expect a bit of time to themselves, spread their wings, see the world, they find themselves with a few more years of stinky-poohs.

LIZ: You needn't think that's any —

PHIL: Droopy-drawers.

LIZ: – hardship because both of —

PHIL: Please, can I finish? I want a son. Di can't have one. You've got three children of your own. And one of mine. The answer's obvious. We'll adopt Sam.

DIANA: We'll what?

PHIL: Is this one full yet?

LIZ: A bit more.

DIANA: Don't you think the very fact that it's happened is bad enough without having a constant reminder in the house all day —

LIZ: Whoa!

[PHIL *stops pouring*.]

PHIL: Emma's been a constant reminder to me since we married. What about some sexual equality?

DIANA: A reminder to me that you seduced a child.

PHIL: She's not a child.

DIANA: Thirteen?

PHIL: You've read his book. They're ready at thirteen, some earlier. Your daughter was a constant reminder to me that you'd slept with half the men in town.

DIANA [*moving towards bedroom*]: Bloody hell!

LIZ: That's what they used to say, love. You slept with half the men in town and I slept with the other half.

DICK: I wonder whether this is strictly to the point.

LIZ: Difficult to see myself as the same girl now.

DICK: You're not.

LIZ: Still, I'm sorry. If I hadn't made myself so available, you might never have plucked up the courage. You never had with anyone else, had you, love? Not even Diana.

DICK: Oh, terrific! Tell everyone, go on! D'you think any man of forty wants the world to know he's only had one girl?

PHIL: We knew already. You told me in our billet in Singapore. I told you about my Chinese bit and asked if you'd care to meet her friend —

DICK: I was scared stiff —

PHIL: – but you said you were saving yourself for Di. And stood her photo on your bedside locker in a bathing suit.

DIANA: We'd sworn undying love before he went away.

LIZ: What's wrong with undying love? It happens.

DIANA: At fifteen? I was fifteen!

PHIL: But you did keep yourself —

LIZ: Just about —

PHIL: – for eighteen months.

DIANA: In those days girls of sixteen didn't jump into bed with every Tom, Dick and —

PHIL: You jumped with me soon enough.

DIANA: I fell for the suntan.

PHIL: And quickly got the taste. Went off me and tried it with the butcher, the baker, the candlestick-maker —

[DIANA *goes off to bedroom.*]

LIZ: You were always there to catch her on the rebound.

DICK [*to* PHIL]: Remember why you went to her in the first place?

PHIL: Yes, to deliver the silk you'd bought her.

DICK: And she wrote thanking me and said she'd fallen for the postman.

PHIL: A mess-pot.

LIZ: I was lucky, wasn't I? If Phil hadn't been demobbed first, you'd have probably gone back to Di. But I'd always fancied you and so when I saw you sad and shy at a party, I took you off to a bedroom and showed you there was nothing to it. I was your first.

DICK: Yes.

PHIL: You're naturally monogamous.

DICK: How can anything be natural that needs such constant attention? Such pruning and watering?

[DIANA *returns with cigarettes and lighter, quickly takes in new situation, smokes during following.*]

LIZ: What about that goose? The – aahm – the greylag goose! Aren't they supposed to be faithful to their mates for fifty years? Surely that's natural?

DICK: Natural to the greylag goose. Not us. We can be anything. Promiscuous, polygamous, polyandrous, carnivorous, homosexual —

LIZ: You're a one-woman man and I'm a one-man woman.

DICK: You can be smug about our monogamy because you've had so much of the other. You're all the same, all three of you!

PHIL: We played the field when we were young. What's the difference now? [*Resumes decanting.*]

DICK [*emphatically*]: I missed my chance and I can never be young again. One of an army of sad middle-aged men forever pining for a youth that passed while we weren't looking.

DIANA: Not only men.

PHIL: You've nothing to complain of.

DIANA: You think not?

LIZ: Diana, really! Half the men in —

DIANA: That! Most of that was a mess. [*To* DICK.] Surely you mean more than *that*.

LIZ: What?

DIANA: Love, surely! Being in *love*.

LIZ [*to* DICK]: Love! You! Romantic love?

DICK [*hurt by her tone*]: Yes, all that! Careless rapture.

LIZ: You were too ambitious. You were going to be a specialist. Even before you'd settled on paediatrics, you – aahm – you —

DICK: I wanted to practise medicine and —

LIZ: You – aahm – you talked of nothing but being a consultant.

DICK: – had to find the field where I could be most effective —

LIZ [*interrupting, to Audience*]: Even as a student walking the wards —

DICK [*giving up*]: Oh, shit —

LIZ: – he had a powerful sense of direction. Aaahm – he – aah —

[*The others, in their different ways, turn their eyes away.* DICK *stares at the ground.*]

I don't mean to say he was mercenary or materialistic, he was in many ways as much an idealist as Phil. Which was arguably their only common factor.

PHIL: That's what brought us together in the —

LIZ: Aaah! However. Aaahm. What he had that Philip, ahm, that Philip lacked was a strong sense of his own importance to the world and the fact that he would one day be an influential and – erm – distinguished figure. Aaah.

[*Pause.* DICK *speaks to Audience more quietly.*]

DICK: And of course in the early years I was always at the hospital or on call in the night, we hardly saw each other. She went on teaching for the first year but only part-time after Jane was born. We treasured all the hours we could snatch to be together. Even someone's flaws can be attractive then. Even their warts. [*To* LIZ.] I was aware of your schoolmistressy manner, of course —

LIZ [*smiling*]: My what, love?

DICK [*louder, silencing her*]: After all, you'd coped with thirty-five teenage roughs and somehow managed to prevent them burning down the school. But this bossiness was never a serious problem till we came down here to look after Philip's son. When at last we were with each other morning, noon and night. [*And again to Audience:*] I'd noticed at home, of course, at dinner-parties, how her voice went ranting on, repeating the same half-formed opinions, and everyone very sorry for her, staring at the tablecloth hoping she'd stop. And when she didn't I'd try to interrupt but no, that's as bad as some yob calling out in class . . . so she aahs and ahms until she's thought what to say next and everyone waits till she's finally talked herself to a standstill. You must have noticed.

[*Pause.*]

PHIL: We're all embarrassing at times. We all get kicked under tables.

LIZ: If we're going to mention each other's shortcomings, you're a far cry from Mister Universe. What about your moccasins? [*To Audience.*] He pads about the place like some filthy old panda. Flip, flop, flip, flop —

DICK: How about that portable litter-bin you call a handbag?

PHIL: Christ, the squalor of handbags! Bus-tickets and toffee-papers stuck to combs . . . and shopping-lists with 'List' written at the top.

DICK: Handbags are a symbol of their bondage.

DIANA: What about you? Your ears? [*To* LIZ.] He puts his finger into his ear and wiggles it about till you can hear the wax move.

[PHIL *gets a bottle and drinks from it during scene.*]

LIZ: Yet we're still expected to be glamorous!

DICK: Glamorous? You don't even bother to dye your hair!

LIZ: I dye my hair in *London*. Ahm. But your wind doesn't stop wherever we are. I'll bet you never fart in front of the nurses.

DICK: You've never objected to my wind before.

LIZ: I shouldn't *need* to. [*To Audience.*] Should I? During meals he does it.

PHIL: She objects to *mine*. She never stops.

DIANA [*to Audience*]: Not so much to the wind as the way he stands there afterwards enjoying it.

DICK: Now steady. These trivial physical differences might – all things being equal – might be part of our affection for each other.

PHIL: Right, I know couples have farting *contests*.

DIANA: I'm sure you do.

DICK: I'm trying to explain what I've learnt down here. For years we were happy – my career, her house, our family —

LIZ: *My* house?

DICK: But it's gradual, like growing old. How could we tell each other we were bored?

LIZ: I wasn't.

DICK: I sent for an illustrated book of sex techniques. You glanced at it, roared with laughter and never opened it again.

LIZ: Well, honestly, picture books! That's not the way to excite a woman.

DICK: What then? Love play? If I try that, she says, 'Stop messing about, get on with it.'

LIZ: No. I mean winning ways, airs and graces.

PHIL: Wining and dining?

LIZ: Absolutely. Dick's hopeless. He parks the car a mile from the restaurant and I have to walk in the rain. Then he wants me to explain the menu —

DICK: I don't care that much for food.

LIZ: I don't care for sexual acrobatics.

DIANA: Food's not the point.

LIZ: Of course not.

DIANA: It's being taken out, looked after, confidently escorted... low lights, ice-cold drinks, flowers, brazen glances from elegant men —

PHIL: *I* take you out.

DIANA: To some noisy basement stinking of beer.

PHIL: She means the jazz-club.

DIANA: Where you eventually join in with the band —

PHIL: *Sit* in —

DIANA: Plonking away on a banjo leaving me to dance with a succession of clumsy Egyptians.

PHIL: I thought you enjoyed the jazz-club.

DIANA: When we were young. It's years since I told you I enjoyed the jazz-club.

PHIL: What *do* you want then?

DIANA: Something better.

PHIL: More expensive. I can't afford it.

LIZ: Dick could.

DIANA: Not more expensive. More suitable. We're middle-aged.

PHIL: So are the other people in the jazz-club.

DIANA: The jazz-club *suits* them. I want something better.

PHIL: It suits me.

LIZ: She's always wanted something better. Even at school.

DIANA: That's all I learnt at school: to long for something better.

LIZ: You had a lovely time at school. We both did.

DIANA: How can you say that?

LIZ: You sat there so cool and smug, surrounded by a bevy of hangers-on, dopey girls, not worthy of you, and I found myself forced to show I was a cut above them. But – aahm – however much one shone, she still preferred Shirley Doncaster and Glenda – aahm —

PHIL: Taylor.

LIZ: Glenda Taylor. How do you know?

PHIL: She still sees them.

DIANA: Glenda never married.

PHIL: Meaning you didn't either till you bloody well had to.

DIANA: At school Glenda and I were always waiting for some fabulous episode.

PHIL: Glenda's still waiting.

DIANA: So am I. For life to begin. Like Emma Bovary or Anna Karenina. I'm as lonely as the women in Jean Rhys. Somewhere the right people in the right place are moving across some hotel lobby. Scott Fitzgerald people —

PHIL: You wouldn't last five minutes. You're more at home in Dulwich.

DIANA: Motorway-protests and parent-teacher meetings.

PHIL: There you are!

DIANA: I could scream sometimes. I sleep so much, that's my escape. Once he's at the office and Emma's at school, I often go back to bed and sleep till it's time to meet her. And when he's away, I go to bed at nine and sleep eleven hours at night as well.

PHIL: Some day her prince will come.

DIANA: That's right. And I mean to be ready.

LIZ: How can you be ready if you're fast asleep?

DICK: Psychiatrists regard excessive sleep as a distress signal.

PHIL: I think while she's been snoring away upstairs, the big thing's happened and you haven't even noticed.

DIANA: What?

PHIL: The birth of Sam.

DIANA: Where's the romantic element in that? It's pure *News of the World*.

PHIL: You haven't even heard my side.

DIANA: I don't want to.

PHIL: You're not being fair —

DIANA: Any more than I want to hear the point of view of the lurkers you sometimes see outside Emma's primary school. With their raincoats and ankle-length trousers.

PHIL: Jane was nearly fourteen! And a precocious fourteen, you must admit. Liz?

LIZ: Precocious enough to deceive us for a whole year.

PHIL: But physically too! She could pass for eighteen.

DIANA: As her parents, I'm surprised you can listen to this. *I* can't.

PHIL: All right. But once these Americans come, we may not have a chance to speak, so let me say again: what could be more reasonable than adoption?

[*They have now moved back into the scene and ignore the Audience.*]

Look, from the outside world's point of view, we want a son, you've had one late, we're friends. No one need ever know.

DIANA: But *I* shall know.

PHIL: I know about Emma. I live with *that*.

[DIANA *moves upstage and nobody speaks for some time.*]

DIANA: Thanks for protecting Emma. I'm sorry we didn't have a boy, that's hard on you, but in a few years' time now she'll be independent. And then, when the whatever-it-is comes that's going to wake me up, I don't want another toddler to cope with. I want to be ready.

PHIL: For the handsome prince cutting through the overgrown garden. That neutered cat of yours perhaps? You'd make a good pair.

DIANA: Thank you.

[PHIL *turns away and drinks from bottle.*]

LIZ: Excuse me interrupting, but aren't you leaving someone out? How's Jane going to feel?

DICK: Judging by her past behaviour —

LIZ: Aahm! I mean, what do any of our feelings matter until we've asked her?

[DICK *hides irritation by going to flask and continuing decanting.*]

PHIL: There are safeguards. No adoption's final for ages. I believe the mother can reclaim the child up to – how much? six months afterwards. That right?

LIZ: Talking away as though she doesn't count. Sam's *her* son, after all. She'd never part with him.

DICK: What makes you say that?

LIZ: Aaahm.

DICK: Don't aahm me. You're not teaching now. What makes you say she wouldn't part with him? She doesn't care, she never has.

LIZ: What d'you know about her? Or any of them, come to that? You're so busy writing about children in general you never notice them in particular.

DICK: Apparently neither of us knows a lot about Jane.

LIZ: Sam's part of our family.

PHIL: And ours.

DIANA: Over my dead body.

DICK: I find his solution quite acceptable, in the circumstances.

LIZ: You would! And I don't! Why did we reorganise our whole way of life, move to a foreign place, go through all this pantomime when we could far more easily have fixed an operation? Well, I'm not parting with him, so get that straight.

[*Turns and goes, by main doors.* DICK *continues decanting wine.* DIANA *goes to help him.*]

PHIL: He's my son.

DIANA: How d'you know? He's certainly *Jane's*.

DICK: We saw him born.

DIANA: But the fact that you and she – how shall I put it? – 'made love' doesn't necessarily mean you're the father. I'm sorry, Dick, but—

DICK: No, no—

DIANA: She did go into town with the French girl. Perhaps her story's true as well. About the back of the car.

PHIL: Come on, what d'you take her for?

DIANA: Well, she made love with you – Uncle Phil. Where d'you expect her to draw the line?

PHIL: I'm the father.

[*They look at him.*]

I know.

DICK: No man ever knows for sure.

PHIL: I know.

[*Drinks again, finds bottle empty, goes to basket and puts in empty bottle, takes out full one, uncorks it and drinks.* DIANA *looks up from holding funnel for* DICK.]

DIANA: Please don't get drunk.

PHIL: That's all right as long as it's Scott Fitzgerald. Yes?

[*She attends to the wine.* PHIL *wanders off, left. She looks after him.* DICK *takes the flask now and* DIANA *the funnel. They continue decanting.*]

DIANA: Whoa.

[*He stops. She corks the bottle and puts it in basket. They begin another.*]

DICK: See what I mean now? What I said about change? Nothing's going to be the same. We're speaking the truth to one another for the first time.

DIANA: I don't know about truth. Whether someone wears slippers or says 'aah'.

DICK: Even that much is a beginning. Perhaps by degrees I may learn to tell her that she's splendid in many ways, wonderfully capable, make some man a marvellous husband, but – she reached her high-point years ago. And I feel mine hasn't come yet.

DIANA: You heard me try to tell *him* that.

DICK: Yes.

DIANA: You heard what he said: I wouldn't last five minutes. He's always laughed at my feeling that life so far's been a kind of sleep.

DICK: So's she.

DIANA: Well, since I married him. Before that, I was awake all right.

DICK: Yes.

DIANA: And if I dare to mention the man who killed himself for me, you should hear the peals of laughter then!

DICK: Killed himself?

DIANA: Oh, we quarrelled. We were always quarrelling. But then I went with another man on the rebound and Clive was so shattered he joined the army. Within a year he was reported killed on active service.

DICK: The Middle East?

DIANA: Catterick. Officially he drove his jeep into a wall. What they couldn't know was he'd been willing his death all along. It's since then life's been a kind of sleep.

DICK: Intensity, that's what they can't understand. You and I feel life's not simply a lot of feeding and sleeping and waking and reproducing the species.

DIANA: That's Phil's dream city – where everyone has enough to eat and there's no war, no conflict. An open-air jazz-club. I say to him, there must be conflict, not this interminable comradeship.

DICK: That's why Liz doesn't really mind that he rogered our daughter. To them that's all the wonder of life. The old, the young, the middle-aged, we're all the same, all happy, as long as we get three square meals a day and regular cuddles. But I've been well behaved and helpful too long. I want to be exceptional! If I told her that, she'd fetch me a bowl of soup to line my stomach.

DIANA: Of course I've always *felt* exceptional. But I've made all the wrong decisions.

DICK: Choosing Phil when he brought my silk. That was the worst.

DIANA: Don't remind me. But if you felt like this, why didn't you go before?

DICK: Cowardice. I buried myself in work. I was afraid of being alone after so much family life.

DIANA: Men are lucky, you can go it alone, but women have to wait till – whoa!

[*He stops pouring. Puts down flask, goes to look out of barn door. She corks bottle and puts it in basket, stands, moves away. He goes to her.*]

DICK: Till what?

DIANA: What?

DICK: Women have to wait till – what?

DIANA: Till they're rescued, I suppose.

DICK: Diana, there are two of us now. The same two as before. You've been waiting for a writer, didn't you say? I've written a best-seller, will that do? I'm well-off. What's to stop us?

[*He touches her arm and she faces him.*]

DIANA: D'you mean leave them?

DICK: We must.

DIANA: How could we?

DICK: My in-tray's full of invitations to international culture-fests, to crack my jaw about modern youth. Ha-ha. We'll take the furthest off.

DIANA: What, go from here, now?

DICK: It'll be like that hotel lobby you mentioned.

DIANA: How about my daughter?

DICK: She's with your mother.

DIANA: Yes.

DICK: You said they get on well.

DIANA: I could let them know. They won't be sorry, they never cared that much for him.

DICK: We'll go first, think later. Further south, for a start, till we've sorted out —

DIANA: The Riviera, yes.

DICK: Or Languedoc or Spain!

DIANA: Is this really happening at last?

DICK [*moves about*]: After so long believing myself to be a husband and father, I suddenly realize I've been untrue to my nature. I'm the kind of man who leaves home!

DIANA: I hate family life. The kind of family *they* want. Suffocation!

DICK: Yes.

DIANA: Boredom!

DICK: Even children bore me.

DIANA: Oh, no, I love Emma.

DICK: I *love* mine, but they're boring! Come on, commit the ultimate modern blasphemy – say it with me. Children are boring.

DIANA: From you it's good. A paediatrician. [*He embraces and kisses her. Then looks at her.*]

DICK: Wakey, wakey, Princess.

DIANA: That's Emma's favourite story. The dogs opened their eyes and·started barking, the kitchen-boy caught the spider —
[*Sounds of car-horn, off.* DICK *goes to see.*]

DICK: The Americans' taxi.

DIANA: Oh, no!

DICK: They're only here this afternoon.

DIANA: I want to go now.

DICK: Tomorrow. I've worked it out. Listen.

DIANA: Worked it out?

DICK: Jane's birthday party. We'll have to take three cars to meet the kids at the station and fetch her guests on the way back —
[*Hear* LIZ, *off, greeting* BURT *and* ZOE.]
You come with me in the slow one, the Deux Chevaux, we'll let them lose us on the way, we'll drive to Bordeaux Airport.

DIANA: We'll have to spend another night with them!

LIZ [*off*]: Dick! Where are you, love?

DICK: Hullo! Coming! [*To* DIANA.] Pack a case in the morning, my love.

DIANA: I can't spend a night with *him*!

DICK: Think of some excuse to keep him out.
[*Squeezes her hand and goes, main doors, taking wine.* DIANA *thinks for a moment. Hears* DICK'S *greeting.*]

DIANA: Asthma! My asthma's coming on. I can feel it. Where did I leave my puffer? [*Turns and goes off to bedroom, shuts and bolts the door.*]
[*Lights to black.*]

SCENE TWO

Lights come up, but cooler. Early evening.

The door in the study, upstairs, is opened and ZOE *comes on to the landing. Early thirties, wears homespun clothes which emphasise her stocky, masculine figure. Her hair is done in a bun but locks are always breaking free to fall over her face, and she makes vain attempts to tuck them away. No shoes, no make-up. Hanging from her neck are cameras and exposure meters. Leaves door open and the voices of* DICK *and* BURT *are heard. She looks at barn, goes to stairs, notices blow-up of the cover-girl. She carries it down the stairs and props it against the stone wall. Uses register, adjusts her camera, takes a couple of pictures.* DICK *comes from study with* BURT, *her likeness in many ways, wearing white shorts, a shirt, sandals and spectacles with library frames, which he often wipes.*

BURT: . . . hopefully sell the movie rights and buy myself a place like this, further south where it's even hotter, sling my hammock . . . plant a field with marijuana . . . Shangri-la! Tahiti before the tourists!

ZOE: Dick, how about coming down on the swing? Make a nifty picture.

DICK [*false smile*]: Wouldn't that look a bit childish?

ZOE: Aren't you a child specialist?

DICK: I'm not a child.

   [DICK *comes downstairs.* BURT *unties trapeze.*]

BURT: Please, teacher, may I do a wee?

ZOE: You may. [*He swings down.*]

BURT: Whee!

   [ZOE *laughs, whoopees and takes picture. He comes to rest but remains sitting on bar.*]

ZOE: All right now, Dick, what have we done so far? The other house, the orchard, down by the pond, outside the barn, your study—

DICK: The bread-oven—

ZOE: Right. A few in here will wrap it up.

BURT: I'm almost through as well.

ZOE: Stay right there, Dick, terrific, between me and that blow-up. Beautiful.

DICK: Blow-up? [*Turns to see picture, moves away.*] Oh, no.

ZOE: But that's your cover picture.

DICK: My publisher's, not mine.

BURT: She's beautiful, though, don't you think? Before I'd even heard of you, I bought the book because of those tits on the bookstall.

ZOE: He almost came in the street.

BURT: I really did. And let me tell you I stood in line with some pretty strange people to get it, too. All the Humbert Humberts in New York City.

DICK: Sorry. I'm not posing with that.

ZOE: All right. On the cart.

[DICK *walks up the shaft on to the cart.*]

Hands on the side, look towards the light. Now to me with your eyes. Oh, nifty. Very nifty. [*She works, sometimes giving instructions quietly to* DICK.]

BURT: Isn't that an ox-cart? On the way from the airport we saw some natives ploughing with an ox-team. Can you imagine such medieval agriculture in the age of the Apollo programme?

ZOE: What d'you want? Poisoned lakes? No birds, no bugs. Only chemical crap?

BURT: Come on, Zoe, you know me.

ZOE: After six years of marriage, believe me.

BURT: I love the country. I was telling Dick, a place —

ZOE: You'd die in the country, Burt, you'd be so bored. Really fantastic, fine.

[*Takes down camera,* DICK *leaves cart.*]

BURT: Bored?

ZOE: Sit on the swing now and I'll do some faces.

[BURT *moves about,* DICK *sits on swing.* ZOE *clicks, moving round.*]

BURT: You once said something that seems to me to encapsulate your entire thinking on the conventionally structured home. You said, 'The Family is like the car. Out of date but we go on using it.' Remember?

DICK: No. I said that?

BURT: I have it amongst your quotes.

DICK: After being stuck in a traffic-jam most likely. One says a good few silly things to journalists, present company excepted. And the silly things you forget to say, they make up for you.

BURT: All right, but you believe the Family is obsolescent as a viable structure? Which in any case won't be too fresh a concept to our level of readership.

DICK: The Family as we've known it. The human pair-bonding that makes possible our artificially extended childhood.

BURT: Right. What zoologists call neoteny.

DICK: Yes.

BURT: Prolonged retention of larval characteristics. And this, you say, is the basis of all our educational systems?

DICK: After all, we've got so much to learn, so many tricks, so many techniques, that we stretch the learning stage to the twenties, sometimes the thirties.

ZOE: I got friends of fifty still living on Guggenheim.

DICK: The Victorians invented childhood. Before that kids were just young people. But the new factories needed semi-literate clerks and skilled workers by the million. And popular education's never looked back.

BURT: But your thinking is not to burn down the schoolhouses. Rather that kids should quit school at puberty and spend their teens in sexual and social experimentation and, if they choose, bearing children.

DICK: I hope you won't exaggerate the sexual aspect. But after all we are physiologically ready at puberty and authoritarian attitudes frustrate the impulse, postpone conception and produce all the effects we know so well: boredom and violence, terrified teachers facing gangs of energetic kids, imprisoned in schools but longing to be out working, living —

BURT: Screwing —

ZOE: Turn this way. Beautiful. Gorgeous.

[DICK *obediently swings to face away from main doors and she takes him from upstage.* PHIL *wanders in, at main doors, carrying a half-empty bottle, stands listening.* BURT *sees him but the other two don't.*]

DICK: And later on another lot of twisted middle-aged men and women, forever wondering what they missed. Knowing they only had one youth and somehow missed it. Time passing like the wind, death coming as sure as night. And a pornographic industry to tickle their chronic itch.

BURT: Hullo.

PHIL: Pretend you can't see me. On my way to the bedroom. Sorry. [*Makes across to door, right.*]

DICK: Diana's asleep.

PHIL: Oh. [*Stops at door, listens, knocks quietly.*] Hullo, love? [*He listens.*]

BURT: All right, as soon as a boy and girl have the equipment, they should get busy fucking. Fine as far —

DICK: Liz is in the house, cooking dinner. We'll join you soon, we've nearly finished here.

[PHIL *turns from door, takes swig at bottle, moves a bit unsteadily towards the left but stops at the blow-up.*]

ZOE: Where've you been all afternoon?

PHIL: Walking.

BURT: Dick, d'you read me?

DICK: What?

PHIL: Taking in the scene.

BURT: All the kids are screwing at twelve, there are contraceptive automats in every school corridor —

DICK: They wouldn't be at school, would they, if my proposals were —

BURT: Right. So they're out in the world, on the pill or having babies and no contract, secular or spiritual, will imply any partnership is permanent.

DICK [*unhappily*]: More or less.

PHIL: You got enough film to take my picture, Zoe?

ZOE: Be my guest.

PHIL: Against this blow-up?

ZOE [*shouting*]: We got another Humbert here.

BURT: Get in line, Mister.

[PHIL *and* ZOE *continue arranging pictures, which she takes during next dialogue.* PHIL *stands in front, behind and at the side of the blow-up.*]

Dick, there's something bothers me: a very marked disparity between your precepts and your practice. What I mean, there you are in the book advocating the immediate demolition of the Family, free fucks for all at twelve, state nurseries, most child-bearing finished by twenty-five and it's a rare man that knows his own father. Then we arrive here to find you have three children at school, you've been married fifteen years and your forty-year-old wife —

DICK: Thirty-eight —

BURT: Pardon me, your thirty-eight-year-old wife is drooling over her newborn baby. In short, about as cosy a domestic set-up as you'd find outside the cereal commercials.

ZOE: How old d'you think she is? That model?

PHIL: I wouldn't know.

BURT: You must admit, that's intriguing, though. An angle that will appeal to our level of readership. Jesus, it appeals to *me*!

ZOE: Sixteen at least.

PHIL: I wouldn't know.

ZOE: She's too nubile for twelve or thirteen.

DICK: Nubile doesn't mean large-breasted.

ZOE: No?

DICK: It means marriageable.

ZOE [*Noël Coward voice*]: Terribly sorry. All finished now thanks.

[PHIL *replaces blow-up at back wall.* ZOE *takes no more pictures but unloads film.* DICK *has left swing and is moving about.*]

BURT: You wouldn't object to that angle for the piece? Here's what he says: The family bla-bla-bla, here's how he lives —

DICK: Phil, why don't you go and help Liz with dinner? She's obviously got a lot to do —

PHIL: I'm interested in this point he's making.

ZOE: Can *I* give her a hand?

PHIL: The gulf between fact and fiction. That right?

BURT: I'm thinking of the ordinary Joe with hairy armpits. Hasn't he a right to expect his gurus to practise what they preach?

DICK: I advocate a new society but I live in the one we've got. Engels was a capitalist.

PHIL: I know this one. The Socialist millionaires, the limousine Liberals.

[LIZ *comes from main doors, wiping hands on teacloth.*]

The middle-class conservationists writing to *The Times* about motor traffic as long as they don't have to give up their own Jags and Volvos —

LIZ: I thought you were interviewing *Dick*.

BURT: I'm trying.

DICK: Phil's coming to help with dinner.

LIZ: Lovely, you can pour some drinks for —

PHIL: No, listen, our friend here from Disneyland —

ZOE: I can help, I'm all through —

PHIL: — has asked Dick why he lives such a quiet life when he's got such sexy ideas.

BURT: Is that what I said?

PHIL: Didn't I get it right? Here's Dick's book saying we should all be free-and-easy where we find our horizontal refreshment and in real life —

LIZ: Now why don't you pour us all a drink, then have —

DICK: You keep going on about sex but in fact the real subject is education —

PHIL: What *I* missed - shall I tell you? —

LIZ: No, love.

PHIL: What I missed was any mention of innocence, first love, romance —

BURT: Right. That kind of subjective phenomena —

PHIL: Which is why only oldies read those books. Written by oldies for oldies. But young people know what they've forgotten.

LIZ: '*They've* forgotten'? Aren't you an oldie too?

DICK: That's not how he sees himself.

PHIL: Well, am I really? I never felt at home in my generation, once they all learnt to be powerful and successful members of various establishments.

LIZ: You mean you still play banjo in a college jazz-band, still march and demonstrate and call on other people to wake up. Pass a joint and abuse the fuzz. Aaahm. You – erm – you can do that only by sheltering behind your business partner. He does all the dirty work, ahm, fixing contracts for you to design a supermarket —

PHIL: He gets all the money too.

LIZ: – or a multi-storey carpark – which incidentally's a very far cry from those ideal cities you built in the old days.

[BURT *and* ZOE *are very embarrassed by this exchange.*]

PHIL: They're still set out in the cellar. Our generation never wanted them built. The powers-that-be.

LIZ: You think the new generation will?

PHIL: No. Our lot have shat on architecture. Handed over to the brutes. Brutalism is the measure of all things. Or tatty glitter. You'd admire me if I'd put up a Hilton. Or one of your new hospitals that *looks* like a Hilton.

LIZ: We'd admire you if you'd taken a few risks. The risk of failing. Or growing up.

DICK: Becoming like the rest of —

LIZ: Aaaahm, yes, exactly, becoming like the rest of us. Boring, grey, responsible, sitting on committees, facing facts.

PHIL: Facts, what facts? The facts in that book of his? A smoke-screen to hide the real facts. Inequality —

LIZ: Why d'you think Diana's got sleeping sickness? She knows you're never going anywhere.

[*Pause.* PHIL *looks at her.*]

DICK: Liz, come on, love, you and Phil go —

LIZ: Yes, right. Sorry. Sorry, Phil. Better out than in.

[*Smiles, moves towards main doors but* PHIL *won't follow.*]

PHIL: Never going anywhere, no, I suppose not. Then again I've got nothing to lose either.

LIZ: Come on.

PHIL [*to* BURT]: You've absolutely put your finger on what's wrong with his book. Like someone said – it was you, Liz – he's so busy looking at children in general he never sees them in particular.

DICK: I see them a good deal as a matter of fact. Mostly illiterate, unsophisticated, underprivileged, often seriously ill —

PHIL: You ought to stay till tomorrow, meet their kids, can't you?

BURT: We'd love to but our schedule's pretty —

PHIL: Their daughter's birthday-party. She's fifteen. You got a family, Burt?

BURT: Up to the present time we don't have any but —

PHIL: You want kids, do you?

ZOE: Actually we have a fertility problem.

BURT: Hopefully we'll adopt.

PHIL: My wife's got a daughter, by a previous marriage. And I want a son. You see. I want a son.

[*He pauses, suddenly overcome. They watch.*]

LIZ: Dinner's burning.

[PHIL *finds his voice to stop her.*]

PHIL: Have you thought about that question, Liz? That question I asked about Sam?

LIZ: I must go. You and I can talk privately, love, it's a private matter.

PHIL: A family matter.

BURT: Time we got the show on the road.

ZOE: Yes. We can eat in a restaurant.

LIZ: Oh, but I've done you a Périgordine speciality —

PHIL: You've seen the baby, have you? Her new baby.

BURT: Honestly, Phil, we've stayed too long already —

PHIL: What d'you think of him? Wouldn't you be proud of a boy like that? Burt?

BURT: Sure.

PHIL: Sure you would. He's a beautiful human being, yes? And according to Dick's book, he should go to whoever wants him, whoever deserves him. But when someone comes along and stakes a claim, he and Liz close ranks.

DICK: Who's closed ranks? You can have him.

LIZ: I'll run you to a village —

ZOE [to PHIL]: Why should you have him?

DICK: He seems to be the father.

BURT: Yeah, well, this is none of our business.

DICK: Not more in line with my preaching?

ZOE: A family matter.

DICK: Family! Our families are breaking up. Our two families. Coalescing. That's in line with the book, surely?

LIZ [ushering them out]: You can eat fairly well in a village the far side of —

DICK: I see what you're thinking. She's Sam's mother? No, it's better than that.

LIZ: Dick, honestly, I —

DICK: D'you know who is? Our teenage daughter. How will that go down with your level of readership?

[LIZ shrugs, giving up. They hesitate near main doors.]

BURT: I'm out of my depth.

PHIL: I'd never have said it.

DICK: You're out of *your* depth? What about me? I've spent my life in the shallow end and now, suddenly, at forty, I can't touch the bottom. Which is a marvellous sensation for a decent law-abiding man.

ZOE [to LIZ, quietly]: D'you mean Phil made love to your daughter?

DICK: Yes. Made love, yes! How's that going to look across a double-page spread?

BURT: You'll never know. Not from us, anyway.

DICK: Mmm?

BURT: What do you take us for? Muckrakers?

DICK: Think of the angle, though.

ZOE: Burt, remind me to tell you I love you. [*To* LIZ:] We shan't breathe a word.

DICK: Why?

ZOE: Why? We respect family life, that's why.

DICK: You too?

BURT: Family life may not be perfect but, like they say about democracy, what else do we have?

PHIL: Right. Most people want to watch their children grow, every day of their lives, through every phase, not just in visiting hours. What's for us in state nurseries?

DICK: D'you know what the permissive society won't permit? A dislike of children. Even being indifferent to children. They are the one class of person we must all love. But what if we don't?

[LIZ *turns and goes.* ZOE *follows but* DICK *catches* BURT *by the arm.*]

I spent my youth paralysed with shyness and my manhood in a mist of drying nappies —

BURT: Start thinking lucky. You're one of the world's overprivileged. I'm blown out of my mind by your whole set-up . . . [*He goes and is off by this time.*]

DICK [*almost simultaneously*]: Decent law-abiding people everywhere I look.

[*They both go.* PHIL *stands near main doors looking off. He holds the bottle up to the light to see how much is left, but does not drink again.*

DIANA *comes from bedroom, right, quietly. Her hair has been let down and she is wearing only a sheet, tied above the bust like a sarong. Sees* PHIL *and advances. Near the swing, she speaks, quietly.*]

DIANA: Bonjour, matelot.

[*He moves across to her, offers the bottle. She swigs. Returns bottle to him, sits on swing, turning round and round, twisting the ropes.*]

Are they going?

PHIL: I don't know.

DIANA: I've been listening. I woke up when you knocked.

PHIL: You heard all that we —

[*She nods. Smiles.*]

What you still haven't heard is *my* side. I had to spare her parents' feelings as much as possible . . . let them believe the best of Jane . . . but ever since it came out, I've been trying to talk to you . . . have you been avoiding me? I'd only thought of Jane as one of the children till that morning when you'd all gone to town. Very athletic. Healthy appetite. Used to sit down to children's tea, then again to grown-ups' supper. Well, you'd all gone and I was in the hammock.

[*She takes her feet off the floor and spins on the swing.*]

She came in shirt and shorts and offered to show me the watercress-bed. Hot morning, like today, with thunder coming and I'd started early on the wine. After the cress, she showed me the chanterelles, then told me she often went down there to take the sun. I took my shirt off and we lay there listening to the grasshoppers . . . squinting at the dragonflies . . .

[DIANA *is still now, not looking at him, but listening.*]

She took some wine and I got the bottle back and she tried to grab it and we wrestled a bit. Then I let her get me down, she rolled over me with her long hair falling on my face. But what I chiefly remember is the smile she had, as though I'd said she could stay up late or have second puddings. She wanted a *treat*. I'm not a womaniser, you know that, but I do respond to – physical situations.

DIANA: Like Southampton.

PHIL: What?

DIANA: It's obvious when you're going to play with the band in Southampton. You always sing in the bath. You may not sing for weeks, then suddenly, like last week, I hear you singing. It's the thought of horizontal refreshment. The prospect of Southampton.

PHIL: Only when you're freezing me out. Such as recently. Think. In the last few weeks, how many cracks have I had at the title? How many turns on Shooter's Hill? [*He pushes her knees so that she swings away and back to him.*] And last July, down here, the same. You were always asleep before I undressed. Lying there, turned away, your skin glistening with insect repellent.

[*She has hands on ropes of swing and is leaning back. He leans over her, his face close to her hair.*]

Not wearing any at the moment, are you?

[*He puts the bottle on the floor. She swings and falls back to him. He takes the sheet where it is knotted and pulls it open. She stands quickly and moved slightly downstage, wrapping the sheet around her again.* PHIL *takes her hands and firmly opens them, so that she is holding out the sheet. They stand at arms' length for a moment,* PHIL *looking at her. Then he moves closer and embraces her behind the sheet. She envelops them both. He goes down on his knees to kiss her body.* DIANA *stands, covering herself with the sheet, but loosely, as with a robe.* PHIL *stands. She goes to bedroom and* PHIL *gets the bottle and follows. Sound of a bolt being pushed into place behind door.*

Go to black.]

SCENE THREE

A dull midday light with no shadows, Cloudy.

LIZ *comes from main doors carrying tray set with crockery, cutlery and cloths. She is wearing an excellent wig and looks years younger, dressed in whatever costume makes the best of her figure. Places tray on chair then goes to bedside door and switches on lights. Thunder, some way off.* PHIL *and* DICK *enter by main doors carrying a long table with folding legs.*

LIZ: About there.

PHIL: D'you hear that thunder?

LIZ: Yes.

PHIL: Hard by.

LIZ: Which is why we must get the food over here before we go for the kids. Then we shan't be running about in the rain with trays of jelly.

PHIL: Shame! I was looking forward to a fête-champêtre in the orchard. Dappled light through the cherry-trees. Straw hats.

DICK: Small cigars.

PHIL: Samovars.

LIZ: Fetch those benches from the cowshed, love. They're in those mangers by the bread-oven. They'll need brushing down. We've got to seat fourteen.

[*Men have set up table down left centre.*]

PHIL: Fourteen?

LIZ [*counting on fingers*]: Us four. Jane, Sarah, Ben. Margaret. That's eight.

PHIL: Margaret?

DICK: Our mother's help.

LIZ: And six French kids from the villages.

PHIL: Fourteen.

[DICK *has gone off and* PHIL *follows.*]

I hope they all turn up—

LIZ: Yes. [*Thinks.*] Why?

[*But he is gone.* LIZ *takes cloth from tray and begins unfolding it.* DIANA *comes from her room, refreshed and dressed.*]

DIANA: Talk about Rentacloud!

LIZ: Hullo, love. Had a nice lie-in?

DIANA: Smashing. Too many drinkie-poohs last night, I'm afraid.

LIZ: Phil *said* they gave you a decent meal. I always enjoy her food. Specially the moules.

DIANA: I had no appetite.

LIZ: Then it's a good job you didn't stay for my Périgordine supper.

DIANA: Ah.

LIZ: I'd laid for you but suddenly we saw your car turning into the road. Dick went to see if you were in your room but came back saying you'd gone with Phil.

DIANA: We wanted to sneak away. We couldn't face the Yanks again.

LIZ: Didn't matter. They ate like horses, I'll say that for them. Peasant soup I gave them, pâté, crudités, melon, écrivisses, guinea-fowl—

[*They are unfolding the cloth together and spreading it on the long table. A white cloth, the only bright thing on a dull stage.*]

DIANA: Nice. We looked for you when we—

LIZ: Aaahm. White and green beans, goat and cow cheese, peach flan – aahm – then, after coffee, and cognac, Dick ran them to their hotel while I cleared away. His face had been like Rentacloud all night. He seemed to be trying to show that he didn't want anything to do with Sam. Trying to keep up the mood of our quarrel.

DIANA: We looked for you when we came back last night but you seemed to have gone to bed.

LIZ: Well, that was it. I thought to myself: the time has come for a few feminine wiles. So I put on a flowing nightgown that's always made him randy – with nothing underneath, and rummaged through the trunk for that book on sex techniques. I had an idea it hadn't been thrown out. Well, I was always afraid of the dustman seeing it.

DIANA: And not quite right for Oxfam.

LIZ: No.

DIANA: You've put your wig on too.

LIZ: Oh, this morning, yes.

DIANA: How many places?

LIZ: Fourteen.

[*They lay places with cutlery and crockery.*]

I shan't embarrass you with the sordid details but let's say one or two of the old tricks came back out of the dim and distant past and – aahm – well, I let him keep the light on and rolled my eyes a bit and made noises – anyway – aahm – the point is, I don't think now he'll be supporting Phil's demand to adopt the baby.

[DIANA *has stopped laying the table.*]

DIANA: I see.

LIZ: Which will surely be a weight off your mind.

DIANA: Yes. But yesterday Dick didn't seem at all prepared —

LIZ: That was yesterday!

DIANA: He didn't seem to care about Sam one way or another.

LIZ: That was bravado. Pique. Men are so concerned about who performed the actual insemination, aren't they? As though it mattered.

DIANA: I'm glad you've made it up. Because Dick yesterday certainly seemed very upset —

LIZ: That was only a tiff, my love. We've been fighting for sixteen years. And what about you and Phil?

DIANA: I wore a sheet.

LIZ: Oh, I've done that before now. Yes.

DIANA: We had a marvellous afternoon.

LIZ: It's best in the afternoon. Before the kids get home from school.

DIANA: And again this morning.

[*Thunder, closer.*]

LIZ: I'm so glad we're all back together again for Jane's party. With no disagreements over Sam. I know you didn't want him, understandably —

DIANA: That part's not so simple, dear.

[*And as* LIZ *stops laying.*]

I pointed out to him the weakness of his case. What claim has he got, after all? The most he can expect is any crumb you like to throw him. He understands that, of course, but that's no consolation. He even talked about paternity pleas but it wasn't serious. However I think we could fob him off with a promise from you.

LIZ: Promise? Of what?

DIANA: Couldn't you offer to let him come and see the baby now and then? Whenever he wants? And you could say that later on, when he's grown a bit, they could go to football or the zoo. In fact, he'll probably go off the whole business after a year or two. Promises don't cost anything. You don't want him making scenes like that with the Americans.

LIZ: I wouldn't mind. And perhaps while he's a baby, you could have him at your place now and then.

[*Pause.* DIANA *looks away.*]

If I'm going to make concessions, you must – aahm – reciprocate. I'm doing it to keep your husband sweet.

DIANA: Not only. It's in your interest too.

LIZ: But you'll have to make an effort.

DIANA: It needn't be too often. You don't want to part with the child and I don't want to have him.

LIZ: Just enough to satisfy his pride.

DIANA: And Dick's contented?

LIZ: Oh, yes. He's quite fond of the children in fact —

DIANA: But generally —?

LIZ: We're going to back to London, of course. He'll be happy there. He misses all those boozy male lunches. We've maybe got a bit *too* close. But you can't keep a quarrel going in a double bed. Here they come. Shall I make Phil the offer?

DIANA: If you like. Only don't give away too much —

[*Breaks off as the men return bringing two wooden benches.* PHIL *puts his down and kisses* DIANA.]

LIZ: Oh, that's super! Now if you can rustle up some chairs, one of you, and the other help me bring the food.

PHIL: Food? That sounds like me.

LIZ [*taking his arm and leading him off*]: Right. You didn't say what madam gave you after the confit d'oie.

PHIL: After the confit d'oie . . . comme dessert – soufflé au grand marnier . . .

[DICK *and* DIANA *alone. She goes on laying places. He arranges benches, goes upstage as if to get a chair, watches* PHIL *and* LIZ *go. Then comes to her. They both start speaking at once.*]

DICK: Whatever made you go out with him last night? I thought he'd gone off alone till I went and knocked on your door and discovered you'd gone too —	DIANA: Oh, Dick, I'm so glad you've decided to stay with Liz, I couldn't think how I was going to face you after saying I'd go away with you –

[*Both stop. Thunder.*]

DICK: Sorry. Never mind. We may only have a minute. Are you ready?

DIANA: Ready?

DICK: Have you packed a case? If not, don't worry. We'll let them go first and say we'll follow in the little car and you can pack one after they've gone. The further we let them get ahead the better.

DIANA: You still want to go? Oh, dear.

DICK: What?

DIANA: Liz seems to think that last night you and she – during the night – you —

DICK: Oh, that! She's hopeless at that, honestly. She's not got the least idea.

DIANA: How d'*you* know?

DICK: What? Well, of course I'm no authority, but – surely it can

228

be better than that! She's more interested in confit d'oie or whatever it is.

DIANA: You shouldn't be *that* disloyal. It's unattractive.

DICK: I'm very fond of her, I love her dearly in many ways. Only I just can't stand her!

[*She goes to get a chair for the table. He follows and gets another.*]

Was he too much of a pest? I was afraid, when I saw you'd gone out together—

DIANA: Listen, Dick.

[*Her tone makes him stop and look at her. She stands behind the chair she's brought.*]

When you asked me yesterday, I was too confused to think. Not to mention excited. At my age, a famous author! As you know, that's been my dream for years, many years. Perhaps too many. And your enthusiasm carried me along, I meant to go, I locked myself in the bedroom and told myself I had asthma. Even began to believe it. Started wheezing and had to use my puffer.

DICK: Are you better now?

DIANA: It stopped.

DICK: Good.

DIANA: Yes, it stopped when I began to think out the implications. Then you and the journalists tramped about upstairs and talked your heads off—

DICK: That's advertising—

DIANA: – and then Phil came and knocked and of course I didn't answer. I was going away with you and couldn't bear the thought of sharing a room with him when I knew next day I'd be leaving.

DICK: Yes. *I* felt very miserable last night deceiving Liz but–

DIANA: Well, as you all talked and Phil interrupted and Liz came in and they had a set-to, everything came clear to me. We need them. We must hang on to them. They're lifegivers and we're in love with death.

DICK: What?

DIANA: You and I.

DICK: Starting in a new direction at our age doesn't sound like death. Slowly decomposing, that's being in love with—

DIANA: You're Cancer, aren't you? Like me.

DICK: Leo, for what that's worth—

229

DIANA: An early Leo. That's nearly Cancer. Liz and Phil are
    Aquarians.

DICK: That's hopeless crap, you know it is —

DIANA: Isn't your favourite season autumn? That's when I come
    alive.

DICK: Because your asthma's calmer then, you can breathe –

DIANA: We're too alike, Dick! We need their vitality! Together
    we'd be in a madhouse in six months.

DICK: You're right, you've been waiting for this too long. And now
    the moment's here, you're backing away out of cowardice. But
    you mustn't be afraid, Diana.

DIANA: I've had to face that too, yes. I am a coward.

DICK: Don't give way to it. You've spent the best years of your life
    regretting what might-have-been. Don't waste the rest.

DIANA: I'm not a free agent. When she's got a child a woman must
    know where she's going, she must be sure of her legal rights —

DICK: Look, here's the note I've written Liz explaining — [*Shows
    her an envelope.*]

DIANA: If I went away with you, I'd give up any claim on Phil. And
    then – if you got tired of me —

DICK: Oh, come on — [*Puts away envelope.*]

DIANA: Or I of you. We easily could. Two Cancers together.

DICK: Tired of you?

    [*Attempts to embrace her but she resists.*]

DIANA: Where would I be? At thirty-eight? With a child?

DICK: All last night in bed with her, d'you know what I kept
    remembering? Your mother's carpet. The carpet in your
    mother's flat where I used to come on the way from school, yes?

DIANA [*struggling*]: You'd get sick of me and my asthma —

DICK: I'm a doctor! I can help!

DIANA: Emma too. When she came to join us. Both of us puffing
    away.

DICK: We used to put cushions on the floor in front of the gas-fire.
    We nearly drove each other mad.

DIANA [*beginning to laugh*]: Wheezing across the hotel lobbies of the
    world!

DICK: Then your mother would come from work at six and
    sometimes we'd go out – you with burning ears and me with an

ache between the legs.

DIANA: Dick, stop it —

DICK: I fainted with frustration once, remember? Actually passed out. In a cinema. Struggling up the aisle —

DIANA: You're making me laugh —

DICK: Till some usherette shone the torch in my face – don't laugh!

DIANA: I can't help it! You keep pointing out the funny side.

DICK: You're laughing out of fear —

DIANA: That when my Famous Writer came along, he turned out to be Dick of the gas-fire, twenty-five years older —

[DICK *attempts to kiss her again. A moment's struggle and the little* FRENCHMAN *comes from the bedroom door and is moving across before he sees them, then starts talking at once.* DICK *turns, leaving* DIANA. *The* MAN *has his kettle and a plastic bag.*]

DICK: M'sieur – ça va? Nous preparons un gouter d'enfants. Oui, l'anniversaire de ma fille . . .

[*The* MAN *shakes hands with both, embarrassed, moving on towards the main doors.*]

DIANA: What an impression he must be forming of English family life!

[LIZ *enters by main doors, carrying loaded trays.*]

LIZ: M'sieur, bonjour! Vous voudrez tirer de l'eau à la source? C'est entendu.

[*Puts tray on table, which* DIANA *goes on laying.* FRENCHMAN *comes to shake hands with* LIZ, *then offers the bag explaining that it's a present for her.*]

Pour moi? Un cadeau? Encore un cadeau? Mais – aahm – vous avez donné un poulet déjà. [*Shows an egg from the bag.*] Très gentil. He's trying to make up for interfering.

DIANA: Take more than a bag of eggs.

LIZ: Merci bien. He didn't know what he was doing. He *was* here first. He was brought up here. [*She is taking eggs from bag and putting them into pudding bowl on table.*] He knew this barn when it was full of beasts. Ça y est. Merci bien, m'sieur.

[*Returns his empty bag. He shows kettle, speaks.*]

Je vous en prie. Il ne fait pas demander.

[*He nods and thanks her, shakes hands with all of them. Wishing them au revoir and a good party, he makes for main doors and*] *almost collides with the white pram, being pushed on by* PHIL. *They look at each other. The* MAN *stops talking and goes past and off.*]

PHIL: Our roving reporter.

[*Puts pram centre. Thunder, closer. The hood is up and on the carriage is a square board and on this a birthday cake with fifteen candles.* LIZ *goes to pram.*]

Thought he'd be best under cover.

LIZ: I'm in the Land of Nod, he says. Let's hope the thunder doesn't wake him.

[PHIL *holds up the cake.*]

PHIL: Aaah!

LIZ: }
DIANA: } Aaah! [*Puts it on table, prominently.*]

LIZ: And see what I've brought! [*Four glasses of opaque Anis, which she gives him.*]

PHIL: We shall need a few Pernods to get through this.

[*Takes a glass to* DICK, *who remains apart.*]

LIZ: We'll finish here, then drive to Mussidan, have another drinkie-pooh, then a leisurely lunch. [*Kisses* DICK, *then moves back to others at table.*]

PHIL [*to* DIANA]: We haven't got her —

LIZ: Aaahm – down to the gare in time for their train, get over the moment of your meeting —

PHIL: We ought to have brought —

LIZ: Then home through the villages picking up their French guests on the way.

PHIL: We should have bought her a present.

LIZ: Time before lunch.

DIANA: Yes. A box of Leggo? A Dutch cap?

[*Pause.*]

PHIL: An Action Man?

[*They smile, slightly embarrassed.*]

Cheers.

LIZ: }
DIANA: } Cheers, le vôtre, etc.

[*They drink. Thunder.*
Lights flicker.]

DICK: We'll have to take all three cars. The Deux Chevaux as well.

LIZ: Shall we?

DICK: Fourteen people. And the baby.

LIZ: We'll all be driving separately. What a shame!

DICK: Diana's a passenger. She can come with me.

LIZ: What for?

DICK: So that I can put my hand on her knee.

PHIL: Be my guest. Very sexy cars, Deux Chevaux. Bobbing up and down. I've had erections just driving behind them.

DIANA: I'll go with Phil.

LIZ: And I'll take Sam.

PHIL: Listen. We were in the kitchen putting the candles on and your wife made a proposition.

DIANA: Hullo, hullo—

PHIL: She's suggested I can take Sam out whenever I like.

LIZ: Whenever you like?

PHIL: And also Diana wouldn't mind him staying with us from time to time. Now that's an advance on the statement we had before – me wanting adoption and Liz saying no. And surely Dick, raising the boy entirely as yours wouldn't be half so easy now you know. You'd see the old genetic rubber stamp clarifying year by year, my features pushing through—

LIZ: Oh, this again? What's it matter who the father is?

PHIL: It matters to him and me.

LIZ: Because you're so competitive. I wish you clever chaps would appreciate another man's work as we do another woman's baby. Just be glad of its existence. But men naturally crave success, the fruits of competition, which is why we're going home, eh, love?

[*She smiles across, holds out her hand as though hoping* DICK *will come and take it, but quickly sees he won't and moves to him, stands with arm round his waist.*]

We'll be back in London, you'll be trotted out at parties, young girls rolling their eyes at you because you're the author of *The Nubile Baby*.

DICK: Is that how you see my aspirations?

LIZ: What?

DICK: Rolling eyes?

LIZ: Well, fame, celebrity. All the fun you've missed down here.

PHIL: But, is it going to work? Sam spending half the time with you and half with us?

DIANA: Half?

PHIL: He's going to be like a shuttlecock.

DIANA: That surely isn't quite what Liz suggested . . .

PHIL: We've somehow got to arrange our lives around him.

LIZ: Now, Phil, I was only making one or two concessions—

PHIL: I know you were. And that's all wrong. We must take an imaginative leap, think of our two families merging, coalescing . . . after all, we're relations now.

LIZ: Can I first of all explain my feelings?

PHIL: Did you sell your house in London?

LIZ: Yes.

PHIL: You'll be looking for another? Right?

DIANA: You'll keep this on as well?

LIZ: Oh, yes, this is our lifeline.

DIANA: Where you can be self-sufficient?

LIZ: Oh, yes.

PHIL: Listen. You know what I'm thinking, Di?

DIANA: What?

PHIL [to LIZ and DICK]: The Camberwell scheme. Our partnership's done this scheme, this group of houses in the garden of an old rectory. Six dwellings. A real community, with the original landscape kept all around, shared by the residents. Now why don't you take two of those and let us have a mortgage on one? With all your royalties, money's no object, surely? Bank of fun, it must be.

LIZ: I don't think Dick's that mad on community living, are you, love?

PHIL: Or simply let us rent one? Good investment . . .

LIZ: Very smashing idea in some ways, but do let's cross that bridge when we get there. All we can say now is we accept some degree of sharing. Our immediate problem is meeting Jane at the station.

DIANA: We'll hang about in the car.

LIZ: We'll warn her on the platform, let her know you're here.

PHIL: It could be a shock if mine was the first face she saw.

LIZ: She needs a shock, that daughter of mine.

DIANA: Phil's very considerate. You don't like hurting people do you?

PHIL: Not if it can be avoided.

DIANA: Or unless it interferes with your own pleasure. A selfish child, aren't you? But he means no harm.

[*Thunder and lights go black.* PHIL *takes matches from tray and lights candles on cake.*]

PHIL: Aaah.

LIZ:
DIANA: } Aaah!

DICK: Alors. If you want to shop before lunch, we'd better be going. I shan't keep up with you in the Deux Chevaux. We'll meet at the restaurant.

LIZ: Can't we manage them in two cars?

DICK: Fourteen people. No point in trying.

LIZ: I'll hang back for you.

DICK: No, you show them the shops.

DIANA: We can find the shops.

[PHIL *has taken an egg from the table and is holding it.*]

PHIL: Have you ever tried to break an egg by squeezing it between forefinger and thumb?

LIZ: Really? Is it a joke?

PHIL: No. Hold it lengthwise and press as hard as you like. Go on.

LIZ: I can feel it giving slightly.

PHIL: Very resilient.

LIZ: Amazing.

DIANA: Press hard, go on.

PHIL: That's the principle of the earthquake-proof hotels. Give but don't crack.

DIANA [*takes egg from* LIZ *and squeezes*]: I've seen a party of strong men tie themselves in knots . . . and in the end there was the egg as safe as houses . . .

[DICK *takes and squeezes the egg and it breaks.*]

DICK: Shit!

DIANA: Christ!

LIZ: Dear oh dear.

[*He catches much of the eggshell and drops it on plate.* LIZ *gives him napkin to wipe hands.*]

DIANA: I've never known that happen.

PHIL: You must have cheated.

DICK: Cheated?

PHIL: Dug your finger-nails into the shell. It couldn't have broken otherwise.

[*He tries it with another egg but it doesn't break.* DIANA *moves to main doors.* LIZ *has finished wiping up mess of egg.*]

DIANA: Seems to be passing.

PHIL: Right, let's get the show on the road. D'you girls want to change your knickers or anything?

[LIZ *is at table covering food with white napkins.* PHIL *crosses to pram.*]

I'll bring the baby. Where's the carricot, Liz?

LIZ: In the big car.

PHIL: We'll be starting all that again. The carricot and the carricot transporter and the rubber sheets and safety pins. And clearing all the lower shelves of books. Remember what Emma did to my political literature? *The British Road to Socialism?* Torn to shreds. Hallo, hallo, had a lickle seep? And is he going to see the choo-choo?

[DIANA *goes into bedroom.* DICK *takes out envelope, looks at letter.*]

LIZ: Dick, you come with me in the big car. We'll squeeze them in, they're mostly children.

DICK: Sorry, I must rewrite this letter.

LIZ: Won't it wait?

DICK: No, it should have gone off long ago.

PHIL: Daddy show him the gee-gees on the way.

LIZ: Three-four-five-six —

PHIL: All the bow-bows.

LIZ: Eleven-twelve-thirteen-fourteen.

PHIL: We'd have to start designing all the fittings and fixtures for children of all ages. [*Takes out baby from pram.*]

LIZ: Shall I take him?

PHIL: I can manage. Di?

[DIANA *comes from bedroom wearing raincoat.*]

DIANA: Getting my puffer.

PHIL: Do you think you're going to need that?

DIANA: You never know.

PHIL: Seepie byes in the car and Daddy wake him for the chuff-chuff?

DIANA: Auntie get his beddy-byes into the brm-brm? [*Takes carry cot.*]

LIZ [*kisses* DICK]: 'Bye, love. Usual place?

PHIL: Bientôt, tout a l'heure, au revoir.

[*All three exit.*]

DICK: Yes. Au revoir. 'Bye 'bye.

[*Returns eagerly to table, takes out letter to* LIZ, *then pen. Turns letter over and writes on the back.*]

Dear Liz? Dearest Liz? 'Liz'.

[*Writes.*]

No.

[*Crosses out. Writes again.*]

My. Dear. Liz. Not 'My'.

[*Crosses out. Throws down pen and paper. Absently picks up an egg from plate.*]

My love – after so many years together how can I — ? How can I begin to— ?

[*Holds egg over plate but it will not break. Squeezes harder. Egg still whole. Again and again he tries, standing, straining at the egg.*]

Oh, no! Break, break, you bastard, break!

[*As he struggles the curtain falls.*]

THE COMMON

A Television Play

The Common

From my diary, May 1st, 1971:

In the afternoon, in cold sunlight and sudden cloud, the Blackheath Fayre with a Y. I suppose The Village, as the middle class residents all call it, only goes back as far as the railway and never was any more than a stop for commuters. Nowadays it's a traffic jam by day and a morgue by night. A sketch in the Fayre's programme of events shows a sort of village green with a bell-tent and a row of quaint shops, though in fact a rat-run for suburban traffic separates green from shops and you're lucky to get across at a swift sprint. This tone of dotty nostalgia is carried through by the Romford Drum and Trumpet Corps ('I need this like an 'ole in the 'ead', said a visiting Cockney), the Paragon Jazz Band ('Rather incongruous', said a local solicitor who usually believes in 'the citizens doing their various THINGS'), the Punch and Judy, the Male Voice Choir in Victorian top hats, and above all by the main attraction, The Sealed Knot. The name apparently comes from a group which plotted for the Restoration of the Monarchy during the Commonwealth. Here, they insist, the similarity ends. Except that you know they'd never use the name of a group which plotted the *overthrow* of the monarchy. Hundreds of them were to be seen in their Royalist and Roundhead gear long before they came to the arena to demonstrate jousting. Dan and I made sure of places by the ropes for the Mock Battle, a re-enactment of a Sham Fight put on during the Civil War itself. A large space had been roped off and some flimsy booths put up at one end to stand for houses. We were near a gap in the fence and an eleven hundred saloon cruised about the ground with a speaker on its roof and inside, on the back seat, a man wearing Cavalier clothes and glasses with a microphone and a lapful of notes.

'Please keep this opening clear,' he kept saying, 'this is for the entry of the cavalry. We don't want anyone hurt in the battle.'

We waited through twenty very cold and miserable minutes with only the Mayor's arrival to watch. Another car joined the first in marshalling the crowds. The driver used his Ford like a modern rancher, driving the public about and muttering through his speaker: 'How many times have I got to tell you?'

Some troops mustered and marched on, a good (or goodly?) sight, making towards the maypole where children from the local dance academy were tripping round. The only other bit of Merrie Englande we could see was the rape of a village maid by two cavaliers. Encouraged by desultory cheers, they did it again but this time people turned away. The Roundheads came on with their six horses and cut off the young man in the car so he had to stay in front of us spoiling the view and fouling the air with petrol fumes, finally getting away by a 14-point turn which threatened more harm to the crowd than any horse could have done. Cannon now went off, the dancers quit their maypole and the roisterers turned to the serious business of defending their plywood houses. A chorus of cheery women began a commentary near us. As the captain of horse roared on his riders to another charge, one said, 'I'll bet he never gets a word in at home'.

'Look, that house is on fire. Bring it up a bit closer, love, we're freezing over here. Hullo, Missus Mayor's had enough, she's getting in the car. No stamina, some of 'em.'

I managed to prise Dan away, after the umpteenth skirmish. We met Michael Frayn, bringing three sheepskin jackets for his family. But it was all in a good cause – or a job lot of good causes, from the South Thames Referees to the Sydenham Guild of Handicapped Scouts.

What with illegal enclosures and various other depredations down the centuries, Blackheath is now only a sizeable open space crossed by the main Dover road with the walled Greenwich Park on one side. In earlier times, it was large enough to accommodate an army, the rallying-point for rebels and a cheeky place from which to threaten and march on London, five miles to the west. Jack Cade camped here with 40,000; so did the Cornish rising against Henry VII and Wat Tyler's Peasants' Revolt not only gathered there but drew the alarmed young King Richard down the Thames for a summit meeting. There's even a Wat Tyler Road, presumably a gesture by a Labour council before the party had to put down its own militants. All this gave me the idea for a television comedy to be filmed entirely on location in the manner of an earlier one called *The Gorge* that Christopher Morahan had done in 1967. He and the BBC encouraged me to write *The Common* but, when they saw the script, said it would go far over the budget of a single drama and wondered if I couldn't re-do it as a domestic play, with the events of the Fayre taking place outside, reported by people looking out of windows. In the event, I was persuaded to write an entirely new play, an adulterous farce across the social classes, with the Peasants' Revolt done as a quasi-Brechtian epic in a secondary modern school. It was a garrulous, argumentative piece, well cast and directed, that got a good review in *The Telegraph* and a generous letter from Terrence Rattigan. As I'd meant it to be a Red-hot exposé of social hypocrisy in contemporary Britain, I had to ask myself where I'd gone wrong.

The BBC had got two plays for the price of one and, of course, the one they produced was much more to their taste. It was ironic, paradoxical, took no sides and was about as far from my original intention as *The Sound of Music*. A comparison of the two plays is an instructive reminder of how gentle the Thought Police can be. *The Common 2* may be a better *play*, so much so that Rattigan urged me to adapt it for the stage. *The Common 1* is a better *film* and sticks to its guns and, as it's never been seen, I am glad of the chance to have it published.

We should remember that this was written under the Heath regime and I was living in a comfortable London suburb and was very conscious of social inequality. We'd joined the middle classes beside the common and it took some getting used to. So the two Blackheath plays give a grudging view of six happy years among kind and interesting neighbours who managed in time to make us feel quite at home among The Common people.

The Common

The version printed here is the first, which was never produced. A second play with the same title but entirely different was shown on BBC TV in 1975, with a cast led by Vivien Merchant, Denis Waterman, Peter Jeffrey and Gwen Taylor. It was directed by Christopher Morahan.

The Common

The version printed here is the first, which was never produced. A second play with the same title but entirely different was shown on BBC TV in 1975, with a cast led by Vivien Merchant, Denis Waterman, Peter Jeffrey and Gwen Taylor. It was directed by Christopher Morahan.

Characters

JANE LAMB, 38
DAVID LAMB, 40
DANIEL LAMB, 14
CHARLOTTE LAMB, 10*
DOREEN CARTER, 42
KEITH CARTER, 45
GARRY CARTER, 16

STEVEN, 17
ROGER, 40+
SEAN, 40+
MARY, 50
JILL, 30*

CROSSING SWEEPER
EDWARDIAN WOMAN
HIGHWAYMAN
TOWN CRIER
NICK, *a driver*
JOHN, *a sound mechanic*
A SHEPHERD*
PICKNICKERS*
YOUNG MAN WITH GLASSES*
FIGURE OF DEATH*

GIRLS FROM A DANCING SCHOOL*
REBELS
STANDARD BEARER*
TOWNSPEOPLE
VISITORS TO THE FAIR*
POLICE*

A MALE VOICE CHOIR

* = *non-speaking*

Opening titles against a background of contemporary sketches of English social life:
In the Middle Ages, peasants ploughing with oxen, nobles hunting;
In the sixteenth century, a royal picnic with lavish pavilions;
In the eighteenth, a military camp;
In the nineteenth, highwaymen, a windmill, an elegant promenade.
All this to a bright tune on pipe and tabor: 'Sumer Is Acumen In.'

The music continues as the prints are replaced by a spacious Georgian living-room on a late afternoon in spring. Sunlight through high windows overlooking a terrace and garden. Not too much furniture and all of it antique. On the plain white walls, some prints or maps; a flamboyant flower arrangement in a Victorian vase; an owl beneath a glass dome; perhaps a grand piano, even a spinet. In the middle ground, JANE LAMB *seated on a chaise-longue stitching the hem of her daughter's dress.* JANE *wears a long skirt and high-necked blouse with puff-sleeves and a cameo pendant at the neck. Her hair is severely drawn into a bun. She could almost have appeared in Bramwell's portrait of the Brontës. Her daughter,* CHARLOTTE, *is standing beside her mother, dressed in a fanciful peasant dress, roughly medieval.*

We have the impression of a period reconstruction of some kind. No movement disturbs the tranquillity and the music continues long enough to settle us to an hour of gracious living. This hope is suddenly foiled by the music being cut off and replaced by the sound-track of an American cartoon film, all distorted voices, violent effects and canned laughter.

A flicker of irritation crosses JANE'S *face and she looks in the direction of the sound. We follow her glance and find* DAN *standing at the television set, having just changed the channel. He wears modern clothes and is our first assurance that the time is the present. He looks at the screen, hidden from us, and backs towards a chair. He collapses into it and sprawls, watching the film.*

JANE *finishes the hem, indicates that* CHARLOTTE *show her that it's alright, snapping off the thread, rolling it on to the reel.* CHARLOTTE *moves away, pirouettes,* JANE *nods, smiles, puts the thread in her workbasket.*

A door slam off and JANE *looks up, crosses the room, puts the basket*

*into a drawer and goes through a doorway into the entrance hall, which
is narrow but bright and elegant, like the room.*

DAVID LAMB *is hanging up a raincoat. He has a worried and
diffident manner, turns to her.*

DAVID: Hullo, darling.

JANE: Hullo, darling.

> [*They kiss.*]

Gorgeous day.

DAVID: Glorious. Even Wigmore Street had a breath of Spring
about it. All the typists in summery dresses. I was telling Mrs
Carter, on days . . . (like this people seem –) . . .

JANE [*breaking in*]: Mrs Carter?

> [*She turns to look up the hall. We now see* DOREEN CARTER *on
> her hands and knees polishing the stained floorboards of the hall.*]

DOREEN: I just said to Mister Lamb, this sort of weather it seems
really wicked to be inside.

JANE: I'd no idea you were still here.

DOREEN: I said it makes you want to be in the country.

JANE: You'll be late for your son getting home from school.

DOREEN: Nice picnic somewhere quiet. Oh, he'll be alright. I
couldn't have sat still the weekend with the thought of this floor
not done.

> [DAVID *has taken an attaché case and is about to go into the room.*
> JANE *puts her hand on his arm, delaying him until* DOREEN *has
> finished speaking.*]

JANE [*quietly*]: Darling, did you go to the bank?

DAVID: What? Oh, yes.

> [*He gives her his wallet and continues into the room.* DOREEN
> *finishes work and stands.*]

DOREEN: Any case, Garry stays late nearly every night down at
school. The film society or the madrigal group . . . Friday nights
I think it's some political effort, run by his history teacher. I said
to him 'Garry, whatever's politics got to do with history?' and
then he gabbles away nineteen to the dozen, you know, about
they're all bound up together.

JANE: He sounds absolutely unstoppable.

> [*Gives her notes.* DOREEN *takes them without looking at them.*]

The living-dining room of a small terraced council-house, about twelve feet square and with a low ceiling. Two doors, one to kitchen, one to front lobby and stairs. A clean, carefully-kept house with cut-price furniture and reproduction of rogue-elephant paintings on the wall. There is little light because the small windows are hung with net curtains.

GARRY CARTER *brings on two plates of ham and puts them on the table, already laid for tea: cups, saucers, bread and butter, a plate of tomatoes. He looks at it, considers it complete, takes and folds a slice of bread and begins to eat it. He sprawls back in a chair, much as* DAN *did, taking a book and finding his place in it.*

JANE *enters her living-room again and passes* DAN, *still staring happily at TV.* DAVID *has taken her place on the chaise and is looking at some typewritten papers from his attaché case.* CHARLOTTE *is lying on the floor near* DAN, *also watching TV.*

JANE: Charlotte, darling, please go and change that costume before it's hopelessly creased.

    [CHARLOTTE *makes an angry face.*]

Now, darling, do as I say, there'll be no time to iron it again in the morning.

    [*Her daughter goes, petulantly, still staring at the screen.* JANE *reaches* DAVID *and gives him his wallet. He glances at the notes. She notices this.*]

JANE: Ten pounds.

DAVID: For cleaning? God.

JANE: And helping with Tuesday's dinner-party. And baby-sitting Sunday.

DAVID: We'll have to cut that down a bit, my love –

JANE: Why? Mrs Carter can do with it.

DAVID: They're not hard up. Her husband's not unemployed, is he?

JANE: She spends it all on her son. He's very brilliant and they want him to stay on at school but all his friends have left and earn enough to buy clothes and pop records and so on and he feels very childish not having –

DAVID: Alright –

JANE: – enough to keep up with them.

DAVID: Fine.

JANE: This is something absolutely direct we can do to help, darling. Rather than all those charities one feels so doubtful about.

DAVID: Alright, fine.

[*Puts away wallet. She sits and kisses him.*]

In the CARTERS' *living-room* GARRY *still reading.* KEITH, *his father, comes into the room from upstairs, wearing trousers and shirt, which he's unbuttoning as he comes in.*

KEITH: No sign of her yet?

GARRY: No.

KEITH: She's late.

GARRY: Yeah.

KEITH: No need for her to work as long as this with the money I give her.

GARRY: Might be the buses.

KEITH: Yeah. The traffic's chronic today. You laid the tea then?

GARRY: Yeah.

KEITH: Suppose we better wait for her.

[*Switches on television. The same noise as in the* LAMBS' *house.* GARRY *glances up and then tries to continue reading. After a while:*]

D'you put the kettle on?

GARRY: I was waiting till Mum's home.

[KEITH *nods, watches screen.*]

DAN *still watching.* DAVID *now standing beside him.*

DAVID: Dan, we want to go through the final arrangements for the Fayre tomorrow so perhaps you wouldn't mind watching on your set in the other room.

DAN: That's only in black-and-white.

DAVID [*after a glance at* JANE]: I'm afraid you'll have to make the best of a bad job. I can't hear myself think with this appalling racket. [*Makes to switch it off, but looks at the picture more closely.*] This *is* the BBC, isn't it?

DAN [*absently*]: No.

DAVID: Then why are you watching it?

DAN: There was only nature on the BBC.

[*Pause.*]

Birds.

[*Pause.*]

There. Over now.

[*Gets up and is about to switch off when* DAVID, *attracted by the picture, stops him.*]

DAVID: Half a mo, Dan. This is one of ours.

DAN: This commercial?

DAVID: Yes.

[*They watch the screen. Sounds of horse whinnying, hooves, clash of swords, then voices.* JANE *joins the men.*]

VOICE: Another busy day, Septimus. And now time to relax.

SECOND VOICE: Try one of these, Cato.

FIRST VOICE: Mmmm.

DAN: Oh, yeah, it's for sweets.

FIRST VOICE: By Jupiter, they're delicious. What are they called?

SECOND VOICE: Their name is Legion.

DAVID: I brought some home when we first took on the account, remember?

JANE: Weren't they rather like Hundreds and Thousands?

DAVID: That's why we called them Legion.

SECOND VOICE: Hey, Cato, go easy with the Legion!

SUNG JINGLE [*to the tune of 'Pop Goes The Weasel'*]: Their name is Legion.

DAVID [*to* DAN]: Off.

[DAN *turns off TV and goes out.*]

Going to be an uphill fight giving the Romans a matey image.

[*They stroll back to the chaise.*]

JANE: What about the *Foreign* Legion?

DAVID: That's coming in the summer.

JANE: Rather fun their name is Legion.

DAVID: Jane –

JANE: Yes, darling?

DAVID: Do the kids often watch the commercial channel?

JANE: Not often, no.

DAVID: I'd rather they didn't.

JANE: Right. Shall I get some tea?
  [*He sits and listens to her question.*]
DAVID: Smashing.

In the CARTERS' *room, as before.*

KEITH: What's the book?
GARRY: *The Condition of the Working Class in England in 1844* by
  Frederick Engels.
  [KEITH *nods.*]
KEITH: Interesting?
GARRY: Not bad.
  [DOREEN *comes in, wearing outdoor clothes, carrying grip.*]
DOREEN: Both home already.
KEITH: Where've you been, love?
DOREEN: Twenty minutes I waited and then four buses came along
  together. One man in the queue he said to the conductor 'Safety
  in numbers, eh?'
KEITH: Even so. You reckon to finish by four, as a rule.
DOREEN: I worked till five for a little extra.
KEITH: I bring you home enough, you don't have to go scrubbing
  floors all hours of the –
DOREEN: Keith, you're not going to start, I hope! One of my
  headaches come on in that queue, I can't stand nagging –
GARRY: D'you want some codeine, Mum?
DOREEN: You've laid the table, there's a good boy. Yes, I'll have
  a couple with my tea.
GARRY: I'll put the kettle on.
  [*He goes to the kitchen. She has taken off outdoor clothes.* KEITH
  sits at table, still watching TV.]
KEITH: Nice turn in the weather. I give a young girl a lift today,
  run out of juice on the Maidstone by-pass. On her way to a
  funeral. Black dress, gloves, feather boa. She was sweltering up
  in the cab. Said it was the first time she'd ever been in a lorry.

In LAMBS' *room,* JANE *and* DAVID *finishing cups of tea, looking at
papers.*

DAVID: These are the leaflets for your prison aftercare stall.

JANE [*looking*]: Super! Terribly good.

DAVID: And these are my anti-lorry petitions.

JANE: What about those nineteenth-century prints?

DAVID: Yes. Trevor in Display is assembling them tonight and bringing them to the site tomorrow morning. Remember how good he was in the campaign against the Urban Motorway?

JANE: Indeed. Rather fun the whole thing.

DAVID [*sips tea*]: I don't know.

JANE: And Dan dressed in his gear in your super play. He looks terrific on a horse.

DAVID: Looking terrific on a horse doesn't seem a lot to show for his expensive education. But apparently it's all we shall get.

JANE: He won't be gaining any Double Firsts, we know that now, he's not equipped, but surely we've agreed that doesn't justify sending him to rot in the C Stream of some educational ghetto. You know you dread a complete meritocracy as much as I do.

DAVID: I was a grammar-school product myself so I can't –

JANE: Clever men in white overalls and high I.Q.'s pushing the rest of us about. There's more in life than intellect and Dan's a generous-natured boy and we can help him to enjoy a good life. Or would you rather he left school this year and started sweeping the streets?

DAVID: Getting on a horse and representing the wrong side in a Pageant was what we were discussing –

JANE: It doesn't make sense, darling, sending him to a bad school, just for some abstract principle.

[DAVID *gets up, drains cup, puts it down and moves to stare out of window at garden.*]

I mean, would it do any good? One less happy person in the world. One less educated person in the world. Darling?

[*He shakes his head.*]

CARTERS' *living room.*
They are eating. TV turned on as before, KEITH *half-turned, watching.*

SECOND VOICE: Hey, Cato, go easy with the Legion.

JINGLE: Their name is Legion.

DOREEN: My head's singing with that noise.

KEITH: Have it off. Load of rubbish. Wonder they get anyone to sit watching it.

[*Turns it off.*]

DOREEN: Just as I was leaving, Mrs Lamb said to me 'We look forward to seeing you again tomorrow'. I said 'No, tomorrow's Saturday' and she said 'Yes at the fair.'

KEITH: Fair?

DOREEN: They're having this fair on The Common up there and she and her husband, they're sort-of the leading lights, you know, and her boy and girl's going to be in some play or dance, I don't know what it's all about.

GARRY: Hands off The Common.

DOREEN: Eh?

GARRY: That's what it's all about. I've seen the adverts. Hands off The Common.

KEITH: The Common's nothing to do with us, though, is it? All people with plenty of money.

DOREEN: Anyone can go. She said that. She's looking forward to meeting you.

KEITH: Me?

DOREEN: Both of you.

KEITH: Saturday afternoon. What about my racing?

DOREEN: I said to her 'Once my husband's sat in front of that sport, you'll need more than gunpowder –'

KEITH: What about my results? It's only one afternoon. I'm sat up there in a cab five days a week breathing a lot of pollution, Saturday afternoon I like to watch a race, some wrestling.

[*Pause. They eat.*]

DOREEN: And Wednesday night.

GARRY: And Saturday night.

KEITH: *You* go. You want to go I'm not stopping you. Do you good a bit of fresh air, by the look of you.

DOREEN: Do you good too. After all that pollution?

GARRY: More tea, Mum.

DOREEN: Please.

GARRY: Please.

KEITH: I got my fresh air today. Stopped at the café on The

Common for a breath, a cup of tea. Very nice too. All the drivers
on the grass enjoying the sunshine.

DOREEN: She said you'd specially enjoy it, Garry. I believe there's
some history in it.

GARRY: Sounds a drag.

KEITH: Drag? What's a drag? It sound like a nice afternoon to me.
You take your mother on the bus. I'll push the boat out.

DOREEN: I've got money, it isn't that. Mrs Lamb's expecting you,
that's all.

KEITH: Too bad. Just because you scrub her floors I'm not in any
way obliged to *her*. Alright?

DOREEN: Oh, my head. [*Swallows another pill with tea.*]

KEITH: A sunny day on The Common, you'll enjoy yourselves, do
you good. [*He eats a cake.*] I'll push the boat out.

Inside the CARTERS' *car, daylight. A two-door saloon, perhaps an
Anglia from a few years ago. Stationary.* KEITH *is resting one elbow
on the wheel,* DOREEN *sits beside him and* GARRY *in the seat behind.
They are silently watching a deluge of water down the windows. A great
noise of water beating down on the roof and windows. Our view at the
beginning is towards the rear.*

KEITH: We've been through this before, Doreen. It's up to Garry.
If he wants to leave school, have a good time, I'm not interfering.
    [*Pause. Again they look out of the windows.*]

DOREEN: Time you did, that's all I can say –

KEITH: And if he wants to stay at school, that's up to him as well.
I never had much of a good time when I was his age, wish I had,
you're only young once.

DOREEN: What's that got to do with it? You never stayed on at
school neither. So what's that got to do with it?
    [*Now take a different view and see water pouring down the side
    windows.* GARRY *listening to his parents, smiling.*]

KEITH: Listen, I didn't start on this, you did. I shan't hear the
results –

DOREEN: My headache's coming on again –

KEITH: I've missed the racing –

DOREEN: I can feel it –

KEITH: I've come with you to see this something fair – ain't that enough?

> [*See the water on the windscreen, from behind* GARRY. *Now the intensity of the deluge relents and only the water that's already fallen dribbles down the glass.*]

DOREEN: You can see the action highlights tonight.

> [KEITH *switches on windscreen wipers.*]

KEITH: I thought I was supposed to be taking you down the pub, see the drag show. [*He starts the motor.*]

DOREEN: I'm not fussy.

Exterior view: the car in automatic car-wash. The weather bright and dry. KEITH *starts the car and moves it forward through the metal frame, while the great nylon brushes settle and shed their water.*

KEITH *waits at the road for a break in the traffic and another car follows in behind and the sprays and brushes go into action again.*

Find KEITH's *car again as he parks on the end of a line of vehicles on a road without buildings, one of the roads crossing The Common. They all get out,* KEITH *checks the doors and then he follows his wife and son, who have begun walking among crowds of people moving in the same direction.*

Pick them up later, still walking, beside the rows of parked cars.

KEITH: Good job I parked where I did. Not another place right across The Common.

> [*They approach a side-road where traffic has been prohibited. People are crossing freely to the site of the fair and a Victorian crossing-sweeper is brushing the road. They try to avoid him but he finds them and rattles a collecting box.*]

SWEEPER: Don't forget the crossing sweeper.

KEITH: What's this in aid of?

SWEEPER: Keep The Common Free. [*Rattles box again.*]

KEITH: I thought it was free already.

SWEEPER: Yes, this is to *keep* it free. Defray the costs of our various legal battles to preserve the character and local amenities.

KEITH: Fair enough. [*Puts coin in box.*]

SWEEPER: Thank you. You'd like a programme, I expect?

DOREEN: Thank you.

SWEEPER: Two pee.

DOREEN: Oh – [*Finds coin in her bag.*]

SWEEPER: Thank you very much.

> [*She follows* KEITH *and* GARRY *across the grass.*]

Don't forget the crossing sweeper.

> [*The* CARTERS *pass under a banner at the entrance to the fair, which reads: Come To The Fayre. Then another: The Common Through The Ages.*]

> [*The first exhibit is a flock of sheep, perhaps half a dozen animals, fenced in a pen, with a keeper beside it dressed as a shepherd in smock and gaiters, holding a crook. He is smoking a white clay pipe and beside him sits a border collie.* GARRY *now has the programme.*]

GARRY [*reading*]: 'Until well into the nineteenth century, sheep and cattle grazed on The Common. The animals on display are provided by the GLC's Mobile Zoo.'

> [*The* KEEPER *nods like a countryman and salutes them with his pipe.* DOREEN *smiles awkwardly.*]

DOREEN: Afternoon.

> [*They pass on.*]

> [*The next stall is a tableau: an Edwardian picnic with a veteran car as background. On the tablecloth are set a number of bottles and jars and a* MAN *and* WOMAN *in turn-of-the-century clothes and offering rings to the crowd.*]

WOMAN: Three rings for five pee. Come along there, try your luck. Money back if your ring goes over. All in a good cause. Hands Off The Common.

GARRY: Hey, Mum, there's Old Steve, he said he might see me up here.

DOREEN: You didn't tell me.

GARRY: He wasn't sure. See you later, okay?

KEITH: You know where the car is. But – here – don't keep us hanging about.

GARRY: If we're not there, don't wait for us. I'll be home on the bus.

> [*They watch him move off and meet* STEVEN, *a boy of about the same age, who has been throwing at coconuts.*]

DOREEN: Blessed Steven. He's all I ever hear about. It's him that's trying to get our Garry to leave school.

KEITH: Blimey, love, he's sixteen. He wants to get out, join the men.

DOREEN: And finish up at forty-five a lorry-driver, yes, I know.

[*She moves to next stall: a young man with long hair wearing velvet breeches and a modern undervest, sitting on a bench with his ankles in the stocks. He wears glasses too. Behind him a canvas screen, above him a bucket of water. Visitors have to overturn the bucket by hurling bean-bags at it. One thrower narrowly misses. Cheers and laughter. Then, some throws later, a direct hit drenches the* YOUNG MAN *who smiles and acknowledges the cheers by raising clasped hands above his head like a boxer. Then removes glasses and wipes them on vest. He is released from the stocks and replaced by* DAN LAMB.]

DOREEN: That's young Dan, Mrs Lamb's boy.

KEITH: Seems a good sport.

[*The next booth is more effectively presented: a number of photostat illustrations of nineteenth-century prisons.* JANE *is on a box in the middle, addressing the passers-by.*]

JANE: And of course they got far worse than water thrown at them. Well, you can see that throughout the centuries this Common has been the scene of many different attempts to enforce law and order.

[DOREEN *smiles at her and* JANE, *mid-course, returns her greeting.*]

There was a pillory here as late as 1830, on the exact site where now you will find another eyesore – the lorry-drivers' café. Then again the preservation society has planted a sapling to mark where the gibbet reared its ugly head over by the GLC Changing Rooms. And highwaymen and footpads weren't the only people hanged there, if you were hungry – and I mean starving! – and stole a joint of meat to feed yourself or your family, you'd either end up hanging there or on a convict ship to Australia. We *are* more humane now, whatever people may say, but not nearly humane enough! Our prisons were mostly built over a hundred years ago and, though you don't have to work a treadmill any more –

[*She points to an engraving which shows this and we move about*

looking at other pictures while she talks.]
– it's still horribly cruel to lock up men and women and give them virtually nothing to do to fill the weeks and months and years. And then to turn them out, just as suddenly, one day . . . to give them a few pounds and shut the door behind them and expect them to build a new life from nothing.

[*A near miss for* DAN, *as someone hits the bucket but fails to overturn it.*]

Which is why we must establish centres to help ex-offenders . . . halfway houses where they can find their feet again . . . not special places miles from anywhere but residential hostels in ordinary streets –

KEITH [*undertone, to* DOREEN]: Long as it's not in *our* street, eh?

DOREEN: Sssh.

KEITH: Come on.

[*He moves on and* DOREEN *has to follow.*]

DOREEN: That's Mrs Lamb. It wouldn't have hurt you to listen.

KEITH: I don't want a lot of convicts next door, if you do.

DOREEN: Who says it's going to be next door?

KEITH: If they're going to put a lot of convicts in a house in an ordinary street, it's got to be next door to *someone*. And I'll lay ten to one they won't be putting them in any of these houses on The Common.

DOREEN: No point putting them next to us. Only get three or four in a house our size.

KEITH: I've heard your views about convicts. Put 'em up against a wall.

DOREEN: There's no need to hurt people's feelings.

[*They arrive at a marquee offering 'Goodlie Fare'. They turn and go in.*]

The marquee is divided into: a cafeteria, with a number of tables and benches for eating and drinking; an organisers' enclosure, with the apparatus of a temporary office. In the public part, there is also a display of prizes on a table. People come and go, eat and drink. The CARTERS *move through and join the queue at the trestle-tables serving as a counter. Middle-class middle-aged women are doing their bit:* MARY *and* JILL.

MARY [*with permanent smile*]: If you'll kindly bear with us for a moment while my friend fetches another pinta, we'll be most grateful.

[*Follow* JILL *into the section marked 'private'. She has to raise and let fall curtain.*

Inside are: DAVID *and two other men of roughly his age,* SEAN *and* ROGER. SEAN, *bearded, long-haired, speaks and moves energetically, a tame bohemian.*

ROGER, *by contrast, seems to be in slow-motion, his manner suggesting everything will come right in the course of time; posh accent, falsely low register.*

JILL *gets a bottle of milk from a crate beside the table, smiles at them.*]

ROGER: There would appear to be an insatiable demand for milk.

[JILL *smiles and nods. The others wait. She goes.*]

DAVID [*at once*]: I'm only saying it's arguable we've not been loyal to the original idea.

SEAN: Which was?

ROGER: Hands Off The Common.

SEAN: Right.

DAVID: In general. And in particular to close down the lorry-drivers' café.

ROGER: Quite.

DAVID: Get the lorries off The Common and make a tiny step towards giving the grass back to the pedestrians, who are the only true commoners left.

SEAN: Well? You've got your soap-box. Most of the other stalls are collecting to support the appeal. There's a bloody great petition getting signed by all the visitors who can make their mark, whether they know what's in it or not.

ROGER: And it was your proposal that the best way to call attention to The Common as part of our national heritage was to recall its history. Indeed, we eagerly accepted your expertise in the field of public persuasion –

DAVID: I never agreed to town-criers ringing bells and shouting Oyez. Nor Pearly Kings doing The Lambeth Walk. Nor the lavatories being called Swains and Wenches. All that suddenly appeared this morning.

SEAN: Well, Christ, it's only a kind of May Day beanfeast and, if you want to be historically pedantic, there's always been a piss-up here in Spring.

ROGER: Correct me if I'm wrong – is it our brief to reaffirm the pleasures of The Common for the delectation of Mr and Mrs Fred Bloggs?

DAVID [*shrugs*]: Yes.

ROGER: In that case, is it fair do's for us in any way to act as censors simply on aesthetic grounds? I *like* to see the citizens doing their several things.

DAVID: Just that I'm not sure they fairly represent the citizens, these Boy Scout Leaders and – Veteran Car Fanatics . . . and WVS Ladies.

SEAN: Oh, these efforts are always run by middle-class cranks. They're the only ones will sacrifice good drinking-time. And we all agreed we had to make an appeal to a load of twits living in little modern boxes full of phoney scrubbed-pine Welsh dressers or plaster ducks, as the case may be –

DAVID: I don't remember agreeing to that.

SEAN: Not in so many words, perhaps.

DAVID: Not in any way at all.

ROGER: You said – and I *am* quoting from memory here – you said we must give The Common a good image. Show people what it is we're asking them to preserve.

DAVID: And what's good about The Common is that it happened to be the scene of several intense displays of popular feeling. Once or twice on this green –

[*And they are standing on grass.*]

our countrymen came very close to bringing off a successful working-class revolution, only to be betrayed when the crunch came by treacherous kings and nobles out to preserve their privileges.

SEAN: That's our Island Story in a nut-shell. Survival of the Fittest.

DAVID: Sean, running an antique shop may be lucrative but it's not the best possible vantage-point for summarising human history.

ROGER: Come, David . . . we're merely providing a harmless jamboree for John Citizen and his wife.

DAVID: Harmless? I'm glad you think so. [*He goes angrily.*]

[*We follow him into the main area where* DOREEN *and* KEITH *are sitting at a table with* JANE, *drinking tea.*]

JANE: David!

    [*He goes to them.*]

DAVID: Mrs Carter, how are you?

DOREEN: This is my husband.

DAVID: David Lamb, how are you?

KEITH: How d'you do?

JANE: D'you want a cup of tea?

MARY [*behind counter*]: D'you want tea, David?

DAVID: Thank you.

MARY: I'll bring it over.

DAVID: The tent seems to have cleared.

JANE: People are gathering to see the pageant.

DOREEN: Is that with Dan and Charlotte in it?

JANE: That's right.

DAVID: It's more a play than a pageant.

DOREEN: We must see that.

DAVID: Strictly speaking.

DAN *is still in the stocks and* GARRY *is throwing a bag, trying to overturn the bucket. He doesn't succeed and he moves off with* STEVEN. DAN *is relieved by the* YOUNG MAN *in glasses.*

In the private sector of the marquee, SEAN *is pouring liquor from an antique hip-flask for himself and* ROGER.

ROGER: Not too much for me.

SEAN: Go on, we'll need if it we're going to caper about on that field like a couple of bloody nanas.

ROGER: Your good health.

    [*They drink,* SEAN *direct from the flask.*]

SEAN: Old David's trouble, he's never faced the fact he may have read history at Oxford but he makes his loot in advertising. Which is why I don't take all that kindly to his half-arsed chats on social justice.

ROGER: Certainly, like many of us, he finds himself uncomfortably, even painfully, perched in a cleft stick. Divided between sympathising with the aspirations of the silent majority and preventing that same silent majority from devastating the environment.

SEAN: And for 'environment', read 'local property values'.

ROGER: Each and every citizen must tend his own particular patch.

SEAN: Keep the buggers down, I say.

ROGER: Yes, I've heard you.

SEAN: It's Them or Us.

[ROGER *finishes drink, looks at watch.*]

ROGER: Hadn't we better get up to the arena?

[*And he leads the way into the cafeteria, passing the* LAMBS *and* CARTERS *still sitting at the table.*]

DOREEN: You'll meet him, yes, he's here somewhere, with this Steven boy, used to be in Garry's class but left school early to get on the building sites and earn a lot of money. I wish he wouldn't go with him, he's always persuading Garry to follow him.

KEITH: He's alright.

[*He winks at* DAVID.]

I tell her, she worries too much, it gives her headaches.

DOREEN [*to* JANE]: Pity he doesn't worry a bit more.

KEITH: What for? Let him enjoy himself, they can today, can't they? More than we ever could. I had to leave school at thirteen to work as a delivery-boy. In the RAF I learnt to drive a lorry. Been driving ever since.

DOREEN: Yes, and he wants Garry to have the same sort of life he had.

KEITH: I only regret I didn't enjoy myself more. I envy the young of today. I'm not one of those who say why should they have it, we never did.

JANE: But, Mr Carter, they enjoy themselves at university, perhaps even more than on the building-sites.

DOREEN: And he'll be qualified for a good job, go and live in a really nice house, overlooking a common perhaps.

DAVID: Don't you think we should try to change the world so that *everyone* could live in a decent house overlooking a common?

DOREEN: Most people don't deserve to, Mr Lamb.

KEITH: Ooops, you've got her going now.

DOREEN: The flats we lived in when we first married, they were lovely, I said to Keith, the glass-tiled partition walls on the stairways, all the tidy lawns between, really nice.

KEITH: And I said, you wait a few months, love, this'll be a slum.

DOREEN: And he was right. I cried one day, he'll tell you, when I saw those yobs had broken the kiddies' swings and torn up the young trees. You don't want that sort of person overlooking The Common.

DAVID: Perhaps they break the swings and trees because they don't feel anyone's listening.

DOREEN: I'd put them up against a wall.

KEITH: They carry on when they're young. All too soon they got to settle down, am I right?

DAVID: I'm only surprised they don't march up to our posh houses and occupy the spare rooms and sit in our huge gardens. Why do they allow us to live so well?

DOREEN: God forbid! I've always had a fear of drunks and tramps and anyone who might turn suddenly nasty. I saw enough of them when I was a kiddie. Getting in with the wrong crowd was my father's weakness. Drank every penny –

KEITH: He went to extremes, we know that.

DOREEN: My poor old Mum worked in the fields to keep our heads above water.

KEITH [to DAVID and JANE]: She's got this feeling life's an uphill struggle. She never rests.

DOREEN: I shall never forget, I had a posh schoolfriend once and we were on our way home and this old woman waved at us from the field and the friend said 'She's waving at you, that old farm-worker' and I made out I didn't know her. I was ashamed of her. But, though my conscience pricks me about it, who can say I wasn't right?

DAN, *still in modern clothes, mounted on a pony, canters about the common, preparing for his part in the pageant. He handles the animal well. A few people watch on a piece of vacant ground apart from the fair and arena.* GARRY *and* STEVEN *are among them and, as* DAN *brings the pony to a halt and dismounts, they turn away and cross the road back to the fair proper.*

264

A male voice choir, wearing Victorian top-hats and frock-coats, is singing traditional songs.

CHOIR: Along with the raggle-taggle gipsies-oh!
SOLO: Oh, what care I for my goosefeather bed
        With the sheet turned down so gradely – Oh?
        Tonight I shall sleep in a cold open field
        Along with the raggle-taggle gipsies oh!
    [GARRY *and* STEVEN *have stopped to listen. They light cigarettes and, when the song ends, join the general applause. The* CHOIRMASTER *bows politely but* GARRY *and* STEVEN *cheer and shout 'bravo'. The* CHOIRMASTER *realises he's being mocked and turns back to the singers.*]
CHOIR: Summer is a-coming in
        Loudly sing cuckoo –

In the marquee, JANE *is showing* DOREEN *a display of goods, set out on a table.*

JANE: These are the raffle prizes.
DOREEN: Aren't they beautiful? That mixer now –
JANE: Oh, yes, and you get the peeler and shredder thrown in.
DOREEN: That heated hair roller set would do me fine. I never seem to get to the hairdressers and sometimes I go out feeling a real sketch. I've said to Keith, when we're watching the local drag-show, I'm afraid they're going to pull me up on the stage.
    [DAVID *and* KEITH *are still at the table finishing their tea, smoking.*]
KEITH: I'm very fond of Garry but I shan't be sorry when he gets off hand.
DAVID: Off hand?
KEITH: You know what I mean, out to work. Bit of money make him independent. I feel very hemmed in sometimes. Forty-five next birthday, I can't believe it. Married nearly twenty years and honestly, where's it gone?
DAVID: Same for me. The years go quicker all the time.
KEITH: So I thought, stir yourself before you're old, take the wife abroad. But till Garry's off hand, it's out of the question.

[DOREEN *and* JANE *return.*]

DOREEN: Lovely prizes, Keith. Give Mrs Lamb fifty pee, will you?
I've bought five tickets each. There's a beautiful Queen Anne
lighter.

KEITH: In aid of charity, is it? [*Gives* JANE *a coin.*]

JANE: Thank you. To raise money to brief counsel at the enquiry
to prevent the lorry-drivers' –

DAVID [*breaking in*]: Hands Off The Common. Preserve the local
amenities. Reminds me, I must get back to my stall.

JANE: Time for the play soon.

DAVID: Yes. [*To* CARTERS.] Nice to see you.

KEITH: Yes. Bye-bye. Cheers.

DAVID: Cheers.

We follow DAVID *as he leaves the marquee and finds his way through
the crowds to his stand, which is between the tent and the arena. But
before reaching it, he passes* GARRY *and* STEVEN *and we stay with
them.*

STEVE: How about a Coke?

GARRY: Yeah.

STEVE: I got the money.

GARRY: *I* got money.

[*They make for the marquee and, at the entrance, nearly collide
with* JANE *coming out.*]

JANE: Sorry.

[*She goes on and they enter.*]

There aren't many people left in the tent and the CARTERS *are preparing
to leave.*

KEITH: Garry. D'you want a drink, son? Here you are.

STEVE: No, I'm getting these.

DOREEN [*coldly*]: Hullo, Steven.

STEVE: Mrs Carter – [*Goes to counter to get drinks.*]

DOREEN: Don't let him pay all the time.

GARRY: I wasn't going to.

KEITH: You got enough?

GARRY: Of course I have.

KEITH: Don't let him think we haven't got two pee to rub together.

DOREEN: I've been looking for you to meet Mrs Lamb, we're going to see her son in the play. Shall we wait for you?

GARRY: Don't bother.

KEITH: Long as we're wanted, that's the main thing.

DOREEN: He didn't mean that, did you?

GARRY: We're having a drink, that's all.

[KEITH *has moved off and now* DOREEN *follows*.]

DOREEN: They don't always want to be with their parents.

[STEVE *returns with cokes and the boys sit to drink*.]

STEVE: That old bag at the counter, Christ, where'd they get her? Can't add up, can't open a bottle –

MARY *[to a* CUSTOMER]: Two nice cups of tea? Right you are. And a piece of home-made cake, yes, I can thoroughly recommend it, I know the kitchen it came from . . . all free-range eggs and butter, no margarine.

GARRY: I've been keeping it fresh between my thighs.

[*They laugh explosively together.*]

Trouble is, my knickers are full of crumbs.

STEVE: Di-i-sgusting!

[*This is like a chant which they repeat at intervals.*]

GARRY: You ever heard so many snotty voices? What my Mum calls beautifully spoken.

MARY: Five, please. Oh, thanks so much, the exact money, that's what we like to see.

STEVE: Because, you see, I'm terribly dim and I can't add up. Actually.

GARRY: I'm only actually doing this for a bit of a giggle.

[*They drink.*]

DOREEN *and* KEITH *are making their way through the fair towards* DAVID's *stall. Suddenly an eighteenth-century* HIGHWAYMAN *leaps out from behind a tent, wearing a black half-mask and brandishing a pistol.*

HIGHWAYMAN: Your money or your life! [*With other hand holds out a collecting box.*] All in a good cause. Hands Off The Common!

[*Smiling and nodding,* KEITH *puts coin in box.*]

Thank you, sir. No lorries on The Common. Close down the café.

Thank you. [*Moves to the next group.*] Your money or your life!

[CARTERS *arrive at* DAVID's *stand. Pictures of lorries on the common, of people waiting at the roadside to cross, etc; maps with urban motorways marked in colour, crossed with a sticker 'defeated'; lists of signatures with pens on strings.*]

DAVID: . . . then there was the proposed urban motorway. Not just a road, a six-lane highway right across The Common. Six rows of heavy traffic day and night, year in, year out. And that would only have been the beginning. Before long, they'd have been saying six lanes weren't enough. Why not eight, ten, twelve? And wouldn't The Common be just the place for a grand clover-leaf crossing? No buildings to knock down. No families to re-house. So while we're about it, how about turning the whole place into a massive car-park? Concrete over the grass. Make a charge. An enormous saving on the rates. Of course, there'd be nothing to do . . .

[*Laughter and vocal support for this.*]

. . . no reason to come. No soccer, no bowls, no tennis, nowhere to walk your dog or fly your kite or sail your boat. No ponds to skate on in winter! No fresh air. But plenty of cars and carbon monoxide.

[*Pause. Lowers his voice.*]

Well, we defeated that. You raised your voice through the Civic Society and said No Motorway and they backed down. They often will if you tell them what you think. Now, as you know, the battle for The Common is never won. The latest threat is the lorry-drivers' tea and coffee stall. It's always been an eyesore but now, with the greater intensity of heavy traffic and the lethal weapons allowed to thunder through our cities, it's become a menace as well.

[*Begin to see the pictures, of container trucks, vans, etc, of the rubbish left, of the drivers lying on the grass.*]

Most days that part of the green is a mess of container trucks. It looks as though some untidy giant had dropped a lot of old boxes there. And the drivers back on and off the grass, belching fumes and littering the grass with disposable cups and crisp-packets. At this moment – but not for long – it is in our power to prevent the stall continuing on its present site and we ask you to support us,

as you did before, by signing our petition.
[*An* ASSISTANT *is helping him with the signatures, urging people to sign. He now asks* DOREEN, *who nods at* DAVID *and takes the pen.*]

In the marquee, the boys as before.

GARRY: These people, they're all living in the past. Making incredible piles of bread out of all this modern technological crap like computers and TV –
STEVE: And rockets and – what d'you call 'em? – defoliants.
GARRY: Yeah. And the great snoring mass of the people, so bored they don't give a shit what happens, long as it's something to look at.
STEVE: Like my old man. Thick.
GARRY: And mine. Stuck up there in a lorry all day, wondering where his life's gone to.

DOREEN *signing the petition, looking for* KEITH *to sign it too.*

DAVID: In the nineteenth century, the railways cast a network of iron roads across London, separating one district from another.
[*But* KEITH *has moved out of earshot and she follows with a nod at* DAVID.]

In the marquee:

GARRY: One thing you can say for him, though, he doesn't make any sense.
STEVE: He hasn't got the brains to, has he?
GARRY: These snotty-voiced people, they think it all makes sense. Old Lawrence, my history teacher, he says they put all these different bits, like, in boxes. How they make their money: one box. Antique furniture and old houses: another box. Central heating and fast cars: another.
STEVEN: What they tell the thicks: another box.
GARRY: But they miss out on the really great news which is it don't none of it make sense.

STEVEN: A looney bin. The whole world's a bin.

The CARTERS *move in the crowd between the various stalls. A* TOWN-CRIER *with a handbell and scroll is addressing the public.*

CRIER: Oyez, oyez. Hear ye, hear ye. In the arena, starting shortly, a Grand Historical Reconstruction of a Very Famous and Notable Encounter between the King and the Commons. Together with Dancing, Equestrian Displays, and a Show of Arms. Hurry, hurry, starting soon. Punch and Judy will be beside the refreshment tent again at . . .
  [*Fades away and the* CARTERS *arrive at a large grass area, roped off and already surrounded by a line of waiting spectators. This is to be known as the arena.*
  The male voice choir are busy.]
CHOIR: What shall we do with the drunken sailor?
          What shall we do with the drunken sailor?
  [*The* CARTERS *move along the line, seeking a good vantage point.*]

In the marquee: the last people are leaving their table. GARRY *and* STEVEN *are left with* MARY *and* JILL.

STEVEN: What's his name again?
GARRY: Who?
STEVEN: That history teacher?
GARRY: Lawrence.
STEVEN: Yeah. You told him you're leaving school?
GARRY: Not yet. I'm saving it up. He ties himself in knots finding reasons why I ought to go on and be a teacher. And I keep saying: 'Teach what? History? History says there's no progress, order, reason anywhere. We came from nowhere, we ain't going anywhere.' I say: 'It was *you* showed me what a binny lot we all are.' He don't know which way to turn, honest.
STEVEN: I used to play him up pretty bad. Used to get hard touching up a girl in the back row, then I'd go up and show him and ask him what to do with it.
  [*They laugh.*]
GARRY: Di-i-sgusting!
STEVEN: Di-i-sgusting!

[MARY *has come to their table.*]

MARY: Have you finished with these bottles now? We rather want to get cleared up during this hiatus.

GARRY: Oh, gosh!

STEVEN: Well, actually we'd rather like another couple of Cokes.

GARRY: I'll get these.

[*And he goes with* MARY *to the counter.*]

DOREEN *and* KEITH *arrive at a gap in the rope-fence, where no-one is standing.*

CHOIR [*a long way off*]:
> Oh, ay, and up she rises
> Earl-ie in the morning.

[*Scattered applause. They bow and leave the arena.*

ROGER, *dressed as a fourteenth-century mayor of London, walks across the open space. We follow his stately progress and see the crowd's interest in him. He reaches an 1100 saloon and climbs into the back seat.* NICK, *a young man in modern clothes, drives the car across the arena to the place where the* CARTERS *have set themselves.*

ROGER, *in the car, holds a mike near his mouth and addresses them through a speaker on the roof.*]

ROGER: Ladies and gentlemen, we must ask you to keep these openings clear. Wherever the enclosure is not roped awf, please don't stand acrawse.

[*A few people have joined the* CARTERS *and they all stare at the car as though the order didn't refer to them.*]

These gaps in the paling are for the horses to come on and awf. So will you please help us here? In case one of the horses takes fright, he must have a clear exit. We don't want anyone getting hurt during the battle.

[*Nobody moves. The car is driven aggressively close by* NICK, *who then slows down and pushes the people gently with his fender. They break away a little and join the crowd at other points.*]

We're very grateful for your co-operation. And please make sure your children don't get lawst and wander awf acrawse this break in the palisade.

[*Car is driven off at hectic speed to another corner of the filled where the people need talking to.*

We now see the background setting of the pageant: flimsy mock-up of fourteenth-century London, with one grand house standing out as three-dimensional. Beside this is a platform, with a lectern and table. On the table a tape-deck and on the grass nearby two loudspeakers. DAVID *walks across the grass, clothed as lay preacher of the time, carrying a folio of notes. His arrival is greeted by derisory applause from the impatient crowd. He climbs to the platform where* JOHN, *a young mechanic, is fiddling with the sound equipment. There is a mike on the lectern.* DAVID *has arranged his notes and now nods at* JOHN, *who sets off a fanfare. This is at once followed by music on pipe and tabor: 'Sumer Is Acumen In', which is the cue for the entry of a class of dancing* GIRLS *from the local academy, dressed as* CHARLOTTE *was at the start. We now concentrate on* CHARLOTTE, *as each girl grabs a strand on the maypole. They weave around it in elaborate patterns.*]

In the fair itself, a few latecomers are passing between the stalls, throwing rings, etc. One or two pause to listen to JANE.

JANE: My aim today is to convince you that this isn't a scheme to fill the district with criminals. These will be ex-offenders who have taken their punishment and want, very earnestly, to get back on the straight and narrow. Homeless, vulnerable victims of their own weak wills and society's indifference. *Our* indifference.

In the marquee: GARRY *and* STEVEN *with more cokes, nearly half gone.* MARY *and* JILL *washing up.*

STEVEN: Seen those raffle prizes?
GARRY [*looking across at the display*]: Yeah. What old Lawrence would call the detritus of an acquisitive system.
STEVEN: What's that mean, Sir? A load of old rubbish?
GARRY: Precisely, Steven, and take your hand off Sandra's knee.
STEVE: Ooo, sir, di-i-sgusting!
[JILL *looks at them. They laugh.*]

That hair dryer's worth a bit. Least a ten pound note.

GARRY: What about the transistor?

STEVE: Decent model. Ten. Twelve.

GARRY: What else we got? Champagne, couple of maps –

STEVEN: Ship in a bottle, electric blanket . . .

Arena: the GIRLS *are dancing still but* DAVID, *on his platform, nods to* JOHN, *who turns down the music.*

DAVID: But life in fourteenth-century England wasn't all maypoles and merriment.

> [*From behind one of the 'houses' comes a Figure of* DEATH, *black cloak, skull-face and scythe. The* GIRLS *fall back in alarm and the Figure makes sweeping motions in the air.*]

In about thirteen-fifty, The Black Death swept Europe and at last reached this island, killing at least one out of every three English men, women and children.

> [*The* DEATH *Figure sweeps them with his scythe and almost half the* DANCERS *fall down. The others turn from them in horror and* DEATH *makes off triumphantly.*]

Of course, as usual, the rich survived rather better than the poor because they could hide away more easily. Then as now. In some places, half the people died; in some, no-one was left at all.

> [*The* DANCERS *now make circling, sweeping movements, gathering up the ones who have fallen, and leave the scene. Applause from crowd.* DOREEN *and* KEITH *are in a bad position, straining to see over other heads.*]

DOREEN: Didn't they look pretty in those frocks?

KEITH: I can't see a thing.

DOREEN: Mrs Lamb was finishing Charlotte's right up to yesterday.

KEITH: Let's move over here.

> [*They change their position.*]

DAVID: The survivors, of course, weren't free men but serfs. They owned nothing, not even themselves. Their souls belonged to the Lord above, their bodies to their lord down here and both bled them for every shilling. They were slaves in all but name. And, when a new shilling poll-tax was levied to pay for the wars abroad, the working-class of England suddenly decided they'd had enough.

[*The 1100 saloon, leaving a clear space, is driven to the far end of the enclosure, as aggressively as ever, by the lolling* NICK.]
NICK.]

ROGER [*through speaker*]: Ladies and gentlemen, would you please help by not closing these openings as soon as we've gawn awff?

[*The people in the opening,* KEITH *and* DOREEN *among them, look at each other.* NICK, *lolling with one arm on the wheel, now grabs the mike from* ROGER.]

NICK: Look, how many times have you got to be told, you people? We're doing this for your own good, so do as we say and find somewhere else.

[*Still driving with one hand, he edges the car forward, revving loudly but controlling it with the clutch. The people move away but* KEITH *bangs on the bonnet with his fist.*]

KEITH: Who d'you think you're shoving?

NICK [*through speaker*]: You lay hands on my car again, I'll give you something to shout about.

KEITH: You'll what.

ROGER: Just a second, that's no way –

NICK: So why not be a sensible chap and do as I say?

[ROGER *grabs the mike.*]

ROGER: Thank you indeed for being so co-operative, we're most grateful.

[KEITH *is soothed by* ROGER'*s tone and glad to avoid a serious and embarrassing encounter with the driver.*]

In the marquee: MARY *and* JILL *still clearing tables, washing up, etc.* JILL *looks at* STEVEN *and* GARRY *pointedly but they ignore her and she moves off.*

STEVEN [*quietly*]: What's the point of it, though?

GARRY: The point is there isn't any point. That's the beauty.

[*Pause. See the prizes again.*]

STEVEN: Could do with that transistor.

GARRY: We'll leave that then. It's got to be something useless, something really stupid.

[*Pause. They smoke.*]
What's in that box?
STEVEN: The flat box? Electric blanket.
GARRY: No, next to it.
STEVEN: Hair rollers. For women to curl their hair at home.
[*They look at each other.*]

The arena: as before.

DAVID: The men of Essex and Kent refused to pay this outrageous tax. They rose and killed the collectors, they burnt the homes of government officials and began at last to murder their oppressors.
[*Through the opening just cleared by* NICK *and* ROGER, *a mob of ragged people comes. The 1100 saloon, trapped in the apex of the triangle, waits, revving its engine.* NICK *lights a cigarette, using his cigar lighter. Close-up: the exhaust pipe discharging fumes over the spectators.*
The mob moves angrily down the field, shouting polite abuse and waving sticks, some smiling with embarrassment. Two MEN *drag a farm cart. We go with them down the field.*]
DAVID: But feeling and a right cause weren't enough. They had to find leaders – men who'd turn them from an angry mob into a disciplined army. And all over the Eastern counties village champions appeared – Litster, Jack Straw, Farringdon. And, in Kent, the boldest and most brilliant of all, – Wat Tyler!
[*The cart has come to a halt and the rebels surround it. On to it now leaps a swashbuckling Tyler, played by* SEAN *in the Robert Newton manner. He wears a sword and scraps of armour remaining from the French Wars. He is greeted by a roar from the crowd, which he acknowledges. He raises one hand to demand silence, the other to put a loud-hailer to his mouth.*]
SEAN: My fellows –
[*Great cheer.*]
So far, so good. We have paid a few tax-gatherers more than they asked –
[*Gestures hanging. Crowd cheers.*]
We have taken Canterbury and Rochester Castles, freed the prisoners and burnt the rolls, which show you and me to be not

men but property!

[*Angry cry from* REBELS.]

The property of tyrannous nobles! And now we are marching on the capital to remonstrate with the King. He is young and will understand. If not, we shall amend our own conditions.

[*Cheers.*]

And – though there be more kings than one in the land – we shall admit no allegiance, save to King Richard and The True Commons!

[*Cheers.* SEAN *puts down his hailer. A* WOMAN *climbs on to the cart and gives him a flagon. He takes it, kisses the* WOMAN *boisterously and raises his jar to his* FOLLOWERS *before drinking. On his platform,* DAVID *seems upset.*]

DAVID [*through speakers*]: Strictly in the interests of historical accuracy, I must point out that Wat Tyler wasn't known to be a drunken lecher and, in fact, the whole rebellion was very disciplined, especially in its early stages.

[SEAN *grins at him, wipes his mouth. Belches. Then jumps down from cart.*]

The men of Kent and Essex were so patriotic that they wouldn't allow anyone living within twelve miles of the sea to join them. They wouldn't leave the English coast undefended against the French.

[*Several people have begun to fill the other gaps in the far corner of the field.* KEITH *and* DOREEN *join them.*

At the apex of the field, the 1100 saloon is still being revved by NICK. ROGER *is getting out. He shuts the car door and leaves the enclosure through the clear gap. Now the car tears down the field, reaching the other gap.*]

NICK [*through speaker*]: Alright, alright, I can see you. Get back, come on, out of it!

In the marquee: MARY *and* JILL *now have their counter in order.*

MARY: No, really, Jill, go on. Everything's done. You don't want to miss your husband in the play.

[JILL *smiles and goes from the tent.* MARY *pours the last of a bottle of milk into a large jug. She looks about for more.*]

Outside: JILL *makes towards the arena.* JANE *sees her go from her stall. As there are now few passers-by and those making mostly in the same direction, she climbs down and looks quickly at the signatures on her petition.*

In the marquee: MARY *goes with the empty bottle into the organisers' enclosure.* STEVEN *nods to* GARRY *and* GARRY *goes up to the trestle-tables and stands there, apparently waiting to be served, but also very attentively watching, for* MARY's *return and the arrival of any new customers by the entrance.* STEVEN *goes to the display of prizes and is about to help himself when* GARRY *whistles quietly and the* TOWN CRIER *wanders in at the entrance, ringing his bell.*

TOWN CRIER: Hear ye, hear ye –
> [*He looks about and goes again.* STEVEN *grabs the roller-set, closes the box and signals to* GARRY: *okay. Makes towards entrance.* MARY, *returning with a full milk bottle, sees* GARRY *at the counter.*]

MARY: Oh – is there something else you want? Surprising how much milk's consumed simply in cups of tea.
> [*Sees* STEVEN *making for the exit.*]

Now just a minute – what have you got there?
> [*But* STEVEN *gets away.*]

Outside: JANE *is approaching the marquee as* STEVEN *runs past her. Surprised and mystified, she quickens her pace and now hears* MARY.

MARY: No, no, no, that boy's stolen something, hasn't he? Stop that boy!
> [GARRY *runs from the marquee as* JANE *arrives. He stares at her, then dodges round her and away.* JANE *looks into the tent.*]

In marquee: MARY *hurrying to the exit.*

JANE: Are you alright, Mary?
MARY: They've stolen one of the raffle prizes. Those two boys. I'm alright.
> [JANE *turns and goes after* GARRY.]

Arena: DAVID *on his platform. The* REBELS *are marching about towing the cart.*

DAVID: That night the men of Kent, tired and hungry, but burning with enthusiasm, camped on this very Common. Thousands of them. And across the river the Essex rebels waited too at Whitechapel, outside the city walls. Each army could see the other's bonfires.

SEAN [*in cart again*]: My fellows – I commend you to a man of God who was first a priest, till he saw the sinfulness of the Church, then began to speak the true word of Our Lord on the highways of the land. For this they excommunicated him and threw him into jail. And thence we have freed him. The Commons' true priest: John Ball. Give him a big hand.

    [DAVID *looks at him quickly as the* REBELS *move to the platform.*]

REBELS: Havoc, havoc, smite fast, give good knock!

JANE *is chasing* GARRY *along the more or less deserted aisles of the fair. He is adroit but she can run like a schoolgirl athlete.*

DAVID *holds up hand for silence.*

DAVID: When Adam delved and Eve span
          Who was then the gentleman?
From the beginning all men were created equal by nature but servitude has been introduced by wicked men against God's will. For if it had pleased Him to create serfs, surely in the beginning of the world He would have decreed who should be a serf and who a lord.

STEVEN, *holding the stolen prize, is waiting at the back of a canvas stall and, when* GARRY *runs into sight, calls him.*

STEVEN: Garry! Here!
    [GARRY *follows as he runs along behind the fair.* JANE *appears, chasing* GARRY, *and looks about, finally deciding she's lost him. She returns down central aisle. She then spots* STEVEN *through a gap in the stalls.* STEVEN *rushes off and* JANE *goes along to intercept him beyond the next stall.*]

DAVID [*as before*]: My good friends, matters cannot go well in England until all things be held in Common. When there shall be neither slaves nor lords. How ill they behave to us! Are we not all descended from the same parents, Adam and Eve?

GARRY *has gone the opposite way and now adjusts his coat so that we see the prize. He arrives at the edge of the fair and looks about before making off across the road towards the arena. He wanders along the three-deep crowd watching the pageant.*

DAVID: First we must kill the great lords of England. Then the lawyers, judges and jurors – all those who speak the truth for a price or do justice for reward, because they sell God, who is Himself both truth and justice –
REBELS: Yes! Kill the judges, string them up, long overdue, etc.
DAVID: And root out all those who could at any future time mean harm to the Commons or the Commonweal. Because, brothers, fellowship is heaven and lack of fellowship is hell. Fellowship is life and lack of fellowship is death. And the deeds that you do upon the earth it is for fellowship's sake that you do them.
[REBELS *cheer and shout slogans.*]

STEVEN *emerges from beside a stall into the central aisle, still holding his jacket as though hiding something there. He looks behind him briefly, then turns to move along the main way. He at once comes upon the* HIGHWAYMAN, *who levels pistol at him.*

HIGHWAYMAN: Your money or your life!
    All in a good cause.
    [*Holds out collecting box.* STEVEN *moves past as* JANE *follows from behind stall. She sees him and runs again but* STEVEN *is away.*]
JANE [*passing* HIGHWAYMAN]: Call the police, quick!
    [HIGHWAYMAN *tries to collect his wits. At some distance from* JANE, STEVEN *shows he isn't carrying anything.* JANE *stops.* STEVEN *shrugs and goes to move off at an easy pace.* JANE *follows.*]
    You won't get away with this, you know. Where's that friend of yours?

GARRY *is moving along the crowd still. The people are now more interested in the pageant. Their interest is mainly due to the cut-out buildings having been set alight.* TYLER'S REBELS *are milling about, taking prisoners, swigging from upturned flagons, plundering, raping and generally enjoying themselves.* SEAN *enters with a head on a pole and meets another of his mob with another such head. They cause the heads to 'kiss' in the air. Cheers from crowd. But* DAVID *on the platform is upset and signals to* JOHN *to reduce his sound effects. The crowd noises thin out.*

DAVID: Enjoyable as it may be to watch all this raping and looting and so on, I must point out that in fact no women or children were molested at all, not even noblewomen. And, though the Palace of Savoy, belonging to the King's hated uncle, John of Gaunt, was burnt to the ground, the rebels didn't waste time with looting. They spent far more time releasing all the poor wretches rotting in jails –

SEAN [*through hailer*]: They killed the archbishop, didn't they? And the Lord Chief Justice?

DAVID: Only after some time – and anyway these men were their natural enemies.

SEAN: And they carried their heads about on pikes, making them talk and kiss each other –

DAVID: Which was done to any common criminal or poor person beheaded for stealing food –

SEAN: Havoc, havoc, smite fast!

REBELS: Smite fast, give good knock!

SEAN: With King Richard and the true Commons.

    [GARRY, *moving along the crowd, arrives at the gap near the apex. He stands near the front, hoping to be concealed from any pursuers. But the 1100 comes tearing up the field with* NICK *shouting into the speaker.*]

NICK: You horrible little man, what are you? Stand there you'll be trampled to death.

    [GARRY, *frightened to be picked on, backs out of the way as* DAN *rides through the gap on horseback, dressed as Richard II, a splendid figure. Beside him is* ROGER *as Walworth, the mayor. A* STANDARD-BEARER *rides with them.*]

[JOHN *switches on a fanfare.* DAN's *trio rides down the field and the rebels turn at the trumpets' sound.*]

[DOREEN *and* KEITH *are at the other gap.*]

DOREEN: *That's* young Dan, look, on the horse.

[*Great shout, augmented by the loudspeakers.*]

REBELS: King Richard and the true Commons.

[DAN *raises hand to silence them. Most people kneel silently. There is a moment's reverent hush, then the angry cry breaks from the speakers: 'Kill him, kill the murderer!'*]

[DAVID *turns anxiously to* JOHN, *who consults his clip-board and switches off the tapes.*]

JOHN: Sorry.

[*The* STANDARD-BEARER *passes* DAN *a loud-hailer.*]

DAN: Sirs! What is it that you want? Here I am to talk to you. I and the Lord Mayor of London. Who will speak for *you*?

[*As* DOREEN *and* KEITH *sidle into the gap for a better view,* SEAN *comes trotting through it on a little horse, narrowly avoiding them.*]

SEAN: That's a bloody stupid place to stand. [*Rides on and up to* DAN.]

[NICK, *in the 1100, sees the incident and turns his car.*]

I speak for my – oh, hang on! [*Raises his hailer.*] I speak for my – Jesus! [*Switches it on. Blows into it twice.*] That's better. I speak for my fellows, brother. We mean no harm to you. In fact, we come to deliver you from traitors. Stand up, brothers, and present our petition.

[REBELS *stand.* ONE MAN *presents petition to* DAN, *who signals* ROGER *to take it.*]

[NICK *has arrived at the lower gap.*]

NICK: Oh, no, it's not you again? What have you got between the ears, you two?

KEITH: Saucy little bugger –

NICK: I must have told you –

[SEAN *turns his hailer towards them.*]

SEAN: Could we have a little bit of hush there? Thank you.

[*The spectators titter, but* KEITH *is opening the car door and* NICK *is trying to hold it shut.* KEITH *wins and pulls* NICK *on to the grass.*]

KEITH: What was that you said to me?

[NICK *is seen to be a very small man.* GARRY *misses this because he's left the arena and is making along behind the burning scenery and towards the surrounding streets. But now, at some distance, he sees the* HIGHWAYMAN *talking to a* POLICE SERGEANT *beside a car in which another* POLICEMAN *is sitting.* GARRY *turns and makes for the fair itself, looking for* STEVEN.

ROGER *has taken* DAN's *hailer and now says, reading from the petition:*]

ROGER: Your majesty, they ask for the heads of your uncle, the Duke of Lancaster, and every leading member of your government.

SEAN: In other words, all the traitors who govern us instead of you, my brother.

DAN [*taking hailer*]: All shall be punished who are proved to be traitors by due process of law.

SEAN: Law! There shall be no law except the law of Winchester. No lords and lordships. The goods of the church shall not be kept for the clergy but shared, as Christ would have had it. Shared among the Commons.

[KEITH *and* NICK *still wrangling beside the 1100.*]

NICK: With an operation of this size, people have got to do as they're told or someone's –

KEITH: There's a way to speak to a lady, sonny. Your education should have taught you that.

[GARRY *has reached the tents and stalls and is hoping to make for the houses this way.*]

DAN: I promise the abolition of serfdom and grant you all free pardons and an amnesty if you will now return quietly to your villages. I – and all of you, I think – must be sorry for this violence you've done. But most of you are good men, I am sure, sincerely believing you are saving me and my realm from treachery.

REBELS: Ay, we do, dead right, etc.

GARRY, *moving to houses, sees* MARY *talking to another* POLICEMAN *and pointing towards fair. Again he turns and heads this time into the thick of the tents.*

SEAN [*turning to the 1100*]: Would you please belt up over there?
　　[KEITH *and* NICK *still arguing.*]
DOREEN: Come on, Keith, everyone's looking.
KEITH: He's going to apologise, love.
DOREEN: It doesn't matter.
NICK: Alright, if it makes you any happier . . .
SEAN: Give me some ale there!
　　[*Someone hands him a flagon and he quaffs and then rinses his
　　mouth and squirts it on to the ground.*]
DAVID [*upset*]: I should like to point out that, though this might
　　seem arrogant behaviour, it *was* five o'clock of a baking summer
　　afternoon, so Tyler probably needed to rinse his mouth –
SEAN [*breaking in, to* DAN]: Brother, be of good cheer, for you shall
　　have within the next fortnight, forty thousand more of the
　　Commons and we shall be good companions.
DAVID [*back to script*]: And he was right. The country was up in
　　arms from Devon to Yorkshire. For perhaps the first and last
　　time in the history of England, there was nothing to stop the
　　people taking control.

JANE *is leaving the fair and making for the arena, but suddenly she sees*
GARRY *moving back towards the tents. She changes direction and sprints
to hide from him and track him along the lanes between the stalls.*

ROGER [*taking* DAN's *hailer*]: You should have more respect, in the
　　presence of your king.
SEAN: The king's my fellow too.
ROGER: Fellow?
SEAN: Ay. And haven't you heard the saying that fellowship is
　　heaven and lack of fellowship is hell?
ROGER: Whose saying is that?
SEAN: Our priest John Ball.
ROGER: A hedgerow preacher.
SEAN: That's where many of us live, in the hedgerows. That's why
　　he speaks there.
ROGER: He's a Common agitator.
SEAN: Common, is he? Well. He shall be next archbishop.

ROGER: And you're the greatest thief and robber in all Kent.

SEAN: Which may be one better than a whoremonger. We've already burnt down your bawdy house at Southwark, Mister Walworth, and now we shall deal with you.

ROGER: I arrest you for contempt and –

SEAN [*riding forward*]: Arrest me, do you?

[*And he stabs* ROGER *in the stomach.*]

DAVID: But the Mayor was wearing armour beneath his cloak.

[ROGER *is unharmed and draws his sword. He strikes* SEAN *a couple of times and the* STANDARD-BEARER *also closes and runs him through.*]

GARRY *is stealthily and swiftly moving through the fair towards the parked cars. Now he sees more* POLICE PATROLMEN *crossing the road.* THE SWEEPER *watches them with interest. They have a dog with them.* GARRY *turns back and glimpses* JANE.

SEAN *breaks free and rides a few steps before falling off. He lies on the grass and calls to the crowd.*

SEAN: Avenge me, fellows!

REBELS: Kill him! Kill the murderer!

[JOHN *now brings in his crowd cries on the right cue to back up the real voices. He smiles at* DAVID.]

GARRY *is running for it and* JANE *is after him. He throws down the box but* MARY, *coming after the* POLICE, *picks it up.* JANE *brings* GARRY *down in a flying tackle. Then the* POLICE *arrive and take control.* GARRY *looks at* JANE *intently as though trying to understand her.*

MARY [*arriving*]: Jane, darling, are you alright? What a simply marvellous tackle!

STEVEN *is moving along by the shops and passes a crowd of* MEN *staring into a window in which there's a horse-race on TV.* KEITH *is one of the watching men.*

STEVEN: Hullo, Mr Carter.

KEITH: Eh? Oh, Steven.

STEVEN: Seen Garry?

KEITH: Thought he was with you.

[*Returns to watching.* STEVEN *moves on and is lost among the people in the streets.*]

ROGER, *as Walworth, is threatened by the* REBELS *with their pikes. One or two* ARCHERS *draw their bows.* ROGER *turns his horse away.* DAN *rides forward.*

DAN [*through hailer*]: Sirs! Will you shoot your King? I am your captain. I will be your leader. Let him who loves me follow me.

[*A bewildered pause. One or two* REBELS *kneel.* DAN *waits. Silence.*]

GARRY, *standing between* POLICE, *still watching* JANE. MARY *examining the damaged box of hair rollers.* JANE *avoiding* GARRY'*s stare, also looking at rollers.*

MARY: What do you think, Jane? Shall we prosecute? I mean, he *did* steal it and it *is* a prize for charity. I simply don't know.

DAN *waits until all the* REBELS *are kneeling.*

JANE: It's not for me to decide. I want to see my son in the –

MARY: Who d'you think we should ask?

JANE: I don't know. Wouldn't it be a committee matter?

MARY: I'm not sure all the members are here –

[*But* JANE *has moved off.*]

DAN *turns his horse and is now making towards the exit at the apex, followed by an obedient troop of* REBELS. *Triumphant music from speakers. Two* REBELS *drag* TYLER *into a cart and begin wheeling it after the others. Boos from spectators.* SEAN *wakes and shakes his fist at them. More boos and some laughter. He gets to his knees and drinks from the flagon. A Robert Newton exit which the crowd loves.* DAVID *fumes on his platform.* JANE *arrives at the arena and moves along for a good view.* DOREEN *has found a good place and waves to* JANE.

JANE: Have I missed it all?

DOREEN: Danny's just gone off. He looked wonderful.

DAVID [*through speakers*]: Wat Tyler was mortally wounded and died in hospital. Then began the hanging, drawing and quartering of the rebel leaders. Young Richard the Second had saved the nobility, he'd kept the power from the people once again and now he sat beside the judges as they sentenced the rebels to death.

[ROGER *and* DAN *ride on again.*]

DOREEN: Here he comes again.

JANE: Ah!

DAVID: The Lord Mayor received a knighthood for murdering Tyler. He had a distinguished career ahead of him, became very rich and acquired a fine collection of books.

[*Small groups of* REBELS *enters on foot.*]

DAN: Who are these, Sir William?

ROGER: A deputation of the Commons, sire, to ask that you carry out your promises.

[*The* MEN *approach and kneel on the grass before* DAN.]

DAN: Promises? You call them promises? Forced upon me by an armed rabble? I call them nothing.

GARRY *is taken across the field by two* POLICEMEN *to one of their patrol cars.*

DAN: Serfs you are still and serfs you shall remain.

[*Spurs his horse and it rears up.* REBELS *cower.* DAN *wheels and canters up the field and off, followed by* ROGER.]

DOREEN: Takes his part very well.

JANE: I'm glad to find there's something he can do.

DAVID [*through speakers*]: Well, as we know, the young king wasn't entirely right there. Those serfs very gradually, some would say too gradually, became the free men we are today. And The Common that was free land then is free land still.

[*People start moving away, to the shops or cars or the fair.*]

In law, if not in fact. But it's always threatened and the oppressors today aren't boy kings or greedy priests, they're container trucks and motorway planners. The modern mania for mobility. We must protect –

[*The 1100 saloon turns on the disintegrating audience.*]

NICK: Now just a minute. Nobody said 'go'. There's still something important to listen to after this is over.

[SEAN *has come up on to the platform and leans over the mike.*]

SEAN [*quietly*]: Shan't be half a mo. [*Then loudly.*] While you're all here together, ladies and gentlemen, we'd like to announce the winning raffle-ticket numbers. The Mayor of the Borough has kindly made the draw, so get out those grubby bits of paper and Eyes Down, Looking.

[DAVID *withdraws wearily and leaves the platform. Making his way through the crowd, he meets* JANE.]

JANE: Hullo, darling.

DAVID: Hullo, darling. Did you see it?

JANE: The last bit. Seemed very good. Dan was terribly distinguished.

DAVID: Dan was excellent but, Christ, that idiot Sean. We nearly had a public set-to earlier on.

JANE: I missed that. I've had rather an adventure of my own actually.

GARRY *peers from window of patrol car as he is driven off across the common.*

CHARLOTTE *runs up to* DAVID *and* JANE *as they move through the crowd.*

JANE: Darling! You were terribly good, really.

SEAN [*through speakers*]: The prizes will be presented in the marquee, so lucky winners hurry along, please. Thank you.

[DAN *is looking after his horse.* ROGER *is nearby taking off his costume.*]

ROGER: Shan't be sorry to get all this awf.

DAN: Think it went well, though, don't you, sir?

ROGER: From all appearances, yes. The various assembled Joe Soaps highly enjoyed ones humble efforts.

KEITH, *returning to the arena, meets* DOREEN, *making for the fair.*

KEITH: You'd never believe those results.

DOREEN: There you are. Listen –

KEITH: Good day for the bookies. Mine included.

DOREEN: Never mind that. One of our numbers came up on the raffle.

KEITH: Go on.

DOREEN: Must be the first time ever.

KEITH: What d'you get?

DOREEN: I'm on my way to find out.

> [*And, as they move with the crowd into the central aisle, see from their point of view:* DAVID, *back on his stand.*]

DAVID: . . . you've had a good chance to see some of its exciting history. And how powerful groups of people can ride roughshod over the common good. [*Waves at* CARTERS, *who pass by.*] And one of the most powerful pressure-groups at the moment are the robber barons of road transport. Destroying our cities for their own profit . . .

> [DOREEN *and* KEITH *go into the marquee.*]

The YOUNG MAN *in glasses is back at the Aunt Sally where people throw bean-bags at the bucket.* JANE *is at her stall next to him.*

JANE: . . . and even if we haven't so far found a better way of protecting society than sending them to prison – when often their only crime was not being clever enough to escape –

> [CHARLOTTE *is giving out leaflets to passers-by.* DOREEN *and* KEITH *come along, carrying a wrapped package.*]

DOREEN: Charlotte, you danced very nice in the play.

> [*She goes to* JANE, *who pauses.*]

We've won a prize in the raffle.

JANE: Marvellous!

KEITH: An old map of The Common.

JANE: Oh, yes, it's splendid.

> [*They move on.*]

We must surely see to it that these more vulnerable and helpless victims of society's callousness are given a decent chance to make a clean start after they've taken their medicine.

The SHEPHERD *and his collie are driving the sheep into a GLC van.*
Hear their bleating.

A row of visitors standing by their cars, fiddling with the locks, then
opening the doors, then getting in.

The sheep are in the van. The doors are shut on them.

The car doors shut in unison.

In the arena, the male voice CHOIR *is in full cry.*

CHOIR: He promised to buy me a beautiful faring
       A gay bit of lace that the lassies are wearing
       He promised to buy me a bunch of blue ribbons
       To tie up my bonny brown hair.
       And it's oh, dear what can the matter be?
       Oh, dear what can the matter be?
       Oh, dear, what can the matter be?
       Johnny's so long at the fair.

PRIVATES ON PARADE

A Play with Songs
in Two Acts

Privates on Parade

Ches Nous, neither a hit nor a flop, had been followed closely by the outright failure of *The Freeway* in a production by the National Theatre at the Old Vic later in the same year. During the writing of this play, I never doubted that it was my best to date, so that its hostile reception made me wonder (not for the first or last time) whether I was in the wrong business. Hard upon it came *Harding's Luck*, my adaptation of two time fantasies by E. Nesbit, put on at Greenwich for Christmas of 1974. On the first night, the mechanical scenery exploded and nervous parents hustled their children to the exits, believing it was the latest of a spate of I.R.A. bombings. Few plays recover from disastrous openings and this was no exception. So in one year I'd tried the West End, the National Theatre and my local rep, and all had been partial or total failures. I decided the time had come to go abroad and clear my mind but this took time to arrange, and meanwhile I began reworking an old play about my airforce days to stop myself brooding. There'd been a good few false starts over the years, including one attempt at co-authorship with Charles Wood, but none had got beyond the opening scenes. All that survived from these were the opening chorus and the name of the entertainments company – Song and Dance Unit South East Asia or SADUSEA. Looking up the precise meaning of a Sadducee, I found that he was a sceptical materialist, member of a sect that denied the resurrection of the dead. Its first titles were 'Malayan Moonshine', 'Tropic Scandals' and 'Jungle Jamboree', which I've always preferred, with its echoes of Baden-Powell and Duke Ellington. Strictly speaking, there were no privates in Combined Services Entertainments. We were all made honorary sergeants for reasons explained by Corporal Bonny in the first scene.

Any reader interested enough to compare the truth with the dramatic fiction can find the real story in Chapter 6 of my autobiography, *Feeling You're Behind*. My first cracks at it were out of Büchner, Brecht, *Schweik* and *Oh What a Lovely War*. I never meant it to be a musical or even (as I still prefer to call it) a play with songs, but soon realised that a show about a gang of singers and dancers which had no songs would be a flightless bird. There were quite a few bad omens to frighten me off trying it at all – a television series about a similar unit in India was on even as I wrote the first scenes. Charles Wood had a new play set in Singapore. When I rang to ask him about it, he told me yes, it was about a concert party during the Malayan Emergency.

'Bastard!' I shouted into the phone and he laughed and said no, it took place in Raffles Hotel at the time of Singapore's surrender to the Japs. It was good to know his sense of humour hadn't changed. Kenneth Williams and other survivors helped a great deal with their memories and mementoes of the real events, but the only members of CSE to appear in the final play are the sergeant-major and the civilian drag-artiste and dancer. The other men and the Eurasian girl were gleaned from the rest of my two-and-a-half years' National Service. I researched the period in the Imperial War Museum and came upon the model for Giles Flack in the author of a book about the Green Howards' operations round about Kuala Lumpur. My diary for April 1975 says:

> I want to set the dutiful, decent attitudes of such a man against the hedonism of the dancer. I also dipped into a couple of Montgomery's books, *Forward From Victory* and *The Path to Leadership*, full of exhortations to the soldiers and, when there were none of them left to listen, to youth-leaders and Mothers' Unions. Sad and frightening and funny all at once.

The rule that all songs in musicals must advance the story is one of those say-so's that have led, in the latest shows, to the elimination of dialogue altogether. There is more than one reason to sing or dance. The lyrics I wrote for *Privates* were from a wide variety of originals – an imperial hymn, a march, a choral 'Greensleeves' but mostly popular songs from well-known performers: Vera Lynn, Noël Coward, Marlene Dietrich, Gene Kelly and Frank Sinatra, Astaire and Rogers, Carmen Miranda and Flanagan and Allen. They don't advance the story but colour it with period detail and remind us of current attitudes. Coward, for instance, is the voice of the post-war English middle-class wondering who really won in 1945 when Britain seemed to be losing everything. Miranda did her bit for tourism in Batista's Cuba; Dietrich of *The Blue Angel* was caught on the wrong side of the Berlin Wall. And, mostly sung by or for sex-starved adolescent squaddies, the songs were almost all saturated with double-entendres. The title-song itself is a sustained metaphor on the phallic symbolism of weaponry. On the page all this is pretty clear but, once the words had been set so accurately and tunefully by Denis King and sung with such verve by Denis Quilley and the others, the point was often lost. The sabbatical I had arranged during darker days now came through. The Royal Shakespeare Company were doing the play and got Michael Blakemore to direct it. We cast it together, agreed on Michael Annals's designs and finished off the songs. I flew to Minneapolis for much of the year, leaving Michael in charge. He had his chance to begin rehearsals without me and, when I came back, the thing had taken on a life of its own. The 'play' suffered, the show won. The Chinese prompters, representing the entire native population, had become mere supers and the balance between East and West was lost. The young lovers and their story moved upstage into the bedroom; the singing and dancing kept close to us and shone in brilliant light. There's usually one performance from a production that stays in the memory and mine is of the last run-through in the dingy rehearsal-room in Covent Garden when Trevor Nunn and other brasshats came to see what the lads had put together. It was also the last time the balance was right. After that, the costumes, the orchestra, the lights, the settings, all allowed the song-and-dance to dominate. I always enjoyed watching *Privates* but never knew how to give the play back what the show had taken.

The version here is my latest attempt to restore the balance. It includes various changes from the first Aldwych production and later ones from the revival at the Piccadilly, the only American showing at New Haven and my screenplay for the feature film. An Andrews Sisters song, added for the film, is also retained. The 'new' ending of Sylvia's story is a return to the first version I ever wrote, which turns out to be the strongest and most true and was used in the film.

The critics gave the production full marks and the play five out of ten. I was told to try harder – or not so hard. Or something. One reviewer, having quoted twenty of my jokes to enliven his column, ticked me off for putting in too many jokes. Most weren't sure whether the songs were new or who had written them. A splinter-group of Gay Liberation denounced it and another flounced to its defence. Awards went to Denis Quilley and Nigel Hawthorne, the play was voted Best Comedy twice and got an Ivor Novello bronze for Best British Musical. Queen's Rhapsody?

Privates on Parade

First: at the Aldwych Theatre, London, by the Royal Shakespeare Company in February 1977.

CORPORAL LEN BONNY	Joe Melia
PRIVATE STEPHEN FLOWERS	Ian Gelder
CAPTAIN TERRI DENNIS	Denis Quilley
MAJOR GILES FLACK	Nigel Hawthorne
F/SERGEANT KEVIN CARTWRIGHT	Ben Cross
LEADING AIRCRAFTMAN ERIC YOUNG-LOVE	Simon Jones
SYLVIA MORGAN	Emma Williams
LANCE CORPORAL CHARLES BISHOP	Tim Wylton
SERGEANT MAJOR REG DRUMMOND	David Daker
CHENG	John Venning
LEE	Richard Rees

Directed by Michael Blakemore
Designed by Michael Annals
Choreography by Eleanor Fazan and Malcolm Goddard
Music by Denis King

In February 1978, the same production was presented at the Piccadilly Theatre by Eddie Kulukundis and Memorial Enterprises, with these changes of cast:

F/SERGEANT KEVIN CARTWRIGHT	Neril McCaul
SERGEANT MAJOR RED DRUMMOND	Shaun Curry
CHENG	Eiji Kusuhara
LEE	Cecil Cheng

On June 6th, 1979, it opened at Long Wharf Theatre, New Haven, directed by Arvin Brown and with Jim Dale as Terri Dennis and Robert Joy as Stephen Flowers. It won the Standard Drama Award and Society of West End Theatres' Award as Best Comedy and the Ivor Novello Best Musical Award.

In 1983, Handmade Films released a version in which John Cleese played Major Flack. Denis Quilley repeated his part, as did Joe Melia and Simon Jones. Michael Blakemore again directed.

The sets more or less alternate front-cloth and full stage, in the manner of the variety theatre. Lee and Cheng sometimes move furniture and props, to the accompaniment of percussion, thus suggesting the popular Chinese opera.

Over the proscenium, downstage, is a signwriting screen on which are flashed the names of the various scenes, given in the script.

Steps provide easy access from stalls to stage and musicians are unseen in a pit.

A front-cloth is down as audience arrives.

ACT ONE

SCENE ONE

The Quartermaster's Stores.

The front-cloth shows a jungle design with the play's title.

Lights go down and out and cloth flies. Bare stage, and no lights for some time. At last someone strikes a match upstage and comes down by its light.

We see STEVEN FLOWERS, *in khaki drill and beret, shouldering kit-bag with bush-hat strung to it. Match burns low and he blows it out. He drops kit bag on floor, waits again, wipes face with handkerchief.*

STEVE: Anyone home?
> [*Pause. No answer.*]
> Hullo?
> [*Waits again. Shrugs, takes piece of paper from tunic pocket, looks at it. Picks up kit-bag again and makes to go. As he disappears an overhead light is switched on, showing a narrow circle of stage floor.* LEN BONNY *comes from side, pushing a skip. Dressed as* STEVE *but with three stripes. On skip is clipboard with papers.* LEN *is by turns aggressive and morose, with a Midlands accent.* STEVE *comes back into the light.* LEN *jumps.*]

LEN: Where d'you fucking come from?

STEVE: Bukit Timah, Sarge. Up the Bukit Timah Road.

LEN: I don't mean where d'you fucking come from in Singapore? I mean what you doing creeping in here like a fucking mouse?

STEVE: Come to get my arrival chitty cleared.
> [LEN *takes* STEVE's *chit, looks at it with some suspicion, forms words with his lips.*]

LEN: Private Flowers.
> [*Looks at him as if to verify this. He seems a twenty year old, untouched, suntanned conscript who speaks with a West Country accent.*]

> Clerk special duties. In . . . tell . . .

STEVE: Intelligence.

[LEN *looks at him again.*]

LEN: I can fucking read! Intelligence, eh? You'll be alright here. It's all fucking long words here. A shower of fucking Einsteins here. Where d'you come from?

STEVE: Bukit Timah, Sarge. In a gharrie up the Bukit Timah Road.

LEN: Not in Singapore! In Blighty.

STEVE: Swindon.

LEN: Railway junction.

STEVE: That's it.

LEN: Railway town. D'you work on the railway?

STEVE: I came in straight from school. I'm going to be a teacher.

LEN: *You'll be alright here. All la-di-dah round here. And fucking elocution. [Looks at chit again.]* Demob Group Seventy- Three.

STEVE: Roll on the boat!

LEN: Not for you, not yet, sonny boy. You won't be getting no cunting boat for a good while yet.

STEVE: What's your demob group, Sarge?

LEN: You don't catch me with no group number. No fucking fear. Regular me. Five year tour. Three up, two to go.
   [*Pulls down a small shelf at side of stage, stands behind it. Puts chit on shelf and issues kit.*]
   Stripes, sergeant's, khaki drill, pairs two. Everyone here gets three stripes up.

STEVE: You mean we're all sergeants? Just like that?

LEN: Temporary, acting, unpaid. Just so we can use the messes when we go away. And all the civvies got some pips up. So don't call me fucking sergeant. Only two of my stripes is substantive.

STEVE: Right you are, corporal.

LEN: No, it's all fucking first names here. So you better call me Len and I'll call you fucking Einstein, alright?
   [STEVE *has taken the stripes and is trying them against his sleeve.*]
   Or I could call you Swindon. See how things turn out.
   [LEN *ticks list on board, goes off.* STEVE *pins the stripes on, looks at them, smiles with pleasure.*]

STEVE [*quietly*]: Dear Everyone at 56, as you see by the top of this letter form, from now on your errant son and heir is to be addressed as *Sergeant* Flowers. Which I take to be a long-overdue recognition of my innate genius.

LEN [*reappearing*]: Badges, cap, pairs, one. Incorporating faces, pairs one, face to the left smiling, face to the right browned off.

    [STEVE *looks at badges.*]

STEVE: They're the tragic and comic masks.

LEN: The what?

STEVE: The masks of tragedy and comedy.

LEN: Get out! Typical, that is. No cunt never tells me nothing. Stores-basher me, always have been, that's my trade, right? I know stocktaking, requisitioning, I know the regulation issue backwards. [*Fast.*] Boots, mosquito, jungle-green, soldier's.

STEVE: See what you mean, Len.

LEN: Comforters, cap, khaki, other ranks. Alright, then all of a sudden I'm posted here and put to handling these cunts: shoes, black-patent, dancing, tap. Type Astaire, Fred. Pairs, one.

    [*Gives shoes to* STEVE, *ticks list.* STEVE *stows in kitbag.* LEN *produces cardboard box.*]

Sticks, greasepaint, assorted, six. Putty, nose, portions one. Shadow, eye, jars one. Puffs, powder, other ranks, one. *And* I wasn't put on no course, I had to pick it all up. [*Points to side.*] But what about that lot over there? How'm I supposed to inventory all this? Tights, fishnet, black, sergeant's. Male oblique female. Brassière sequinned, inflatable, sergeant's. Wigs, auburn, wavy, officers.

    [*He has shown* STEVE *some of these.*]

STEVE: The lady officers?

LEN: The fucking men. Ain't enough tarts to go round so the men get up in frocks.

STEVE: Do I get a frock?

LEN: Only against a proper requisition.

STEVE: I don't fancy wearing frocks.

LEN: Nil desperandum. It may never happen. You can come here as a concert fucking pianist and end up shovelling shit. Look at me – sparks, chippy, Jack-of-fucking-all-Trades. And I came in as an *accordionist*! You'll be attached to Captain Dennis. I'll take you along there now.

STEVE [*shouldering bag*]: What's he like?

LEN: Terri? Easy-going. San Fairy Fucking Ann. You know, typical civvie.

TERRI [*from back of theatre*]: There you are, Leonora! At long last!

SCENE TWO

On with the Show.

LEN: Hullo, Terri. We been waiting for you.

TERRI: Who's your friend?

LEN: Sergeant Flowers. He's going to be attached to your section.

TERRI [*arriving on stage from stalls*]: It sounds heaven.

[*He is suntanned, has dyed blonde hair, plucked and pencilled eyebrows, matt tan base, wearing pastel-coloured slacks and shirt, smoking cigarette in holder. His voice is Shaftesbury Avenue pasted over Lancashire.*]

Sweetie, I can hardly wait to attach you to my section but we're supposed to be rehearsing and let's face it, we've wasted enough time –

LEN: We been waiting for *you*.

TERRI: You dare speak to an officer like that I'll scream the place down. Go to your post this instant! And you, duckie, I should drop that expensive looking handbag and find yourself somewhere to sit.

[STEVE *drops kit bag on stage.*]

Not here, duckie, this is the stage. Those are the wings, that is the front-of-house, up there are the flies and the whole bag of tricks is known as The Theatre.

[LEN *leads the bewildered* STEVE *into the wings.*]

And now perhaps young Tom Edison will give us our opening lights. And is everyone ready backstage?

CHORUS [*off*]: Yes, all ready, is everyone ready backstage? etc.

[*House lights up.*]

TERRI: It's fabulous!

[*Goes off, immediately comes back acting. He's a stilted performer, always playing out front, even when speaking to someone on stage.*]

Great Heavens, look at this! Rehearsals due and no one here. I've never seen such amateurs. Dear oh Lord! Are *you* there, Sparks?

LEN: Yes, I'm here, Terri.

TERRI: Then give me your working lights.

    [*Overhead light comes on.*]

  And take out your house lights.

    [*Blackout.*]

LEN [*off*]: Fucking thing!

    [*Working lights on again. In the blackout* KEVIN *has come on: twenty odd, good-looking, wearing sun-glasses and white shirt, khaki shorts, etc. London accent, awkward actor.*]

KEVIN: Hullo, Terri –

TERRI: Ah! Someone's condescended to join me. [*To audience.*] Flight Sergeant Kevin Cartwright, R.A.F.

KEVIN: Sorry I wasn't here on time. I couldn't find my glasses. And one of them had a drink left in it.

TERRI: One of them had a drink – I find that totally outrageous.

    [CHARLES *comes on, twenty but putting on weight and losing hair, camp but matronly, Yorkshire accent.*]

CHARLES: Sorry I wasn't here on time.

TERRI: Well, Sergeant Charles Bishop, Royal Army Medical Corps, what's your excuse?

CHARLES: You know how fond I am of music.

TERRI: Well?

CHARLES: I've been listening to a three-piece orchestra.

TERRI: Yes?

CHARLES: And the third piece was rather long.

TERRI: This is too much honestly! Take your places without another word.

    [LEN *has come on. He cannot act at all.*]

LEN: Sorry I was not here on time.

TERRI: Never mind, Sergeant Len Bonny, Royal Electrical and Mechanical Engineers, tell me, where've you been?

LEN: I've been buying my wife a dress.

TERRI: A dress? That's nice. What kind of a dress?

LEN: A Biblical dress.

TERRI: A Biblical dress? What's that when it's at home?

LEN: You know – Low and Behold!

TERRI [*with gestures to explain*]: Low – and behold?

LEN: I shall find it hard to look her in the face.

TERRI: You'll find it hard to look – I refuse to listen to another solitary word.

[ERIC *has come on, twenty, plain, ungainly, hair shaved well above ears, wearing issue glasses and sweating profusely into KD. Has plummy voice and hearty demotic manner.*]

Who's this? Sergeant Eric Young-Love, R.A.F. You're late for rehearsal.

ERIC: I've been eating at my girl-friend's.

TERRI: Is your girl-friend a good cook?

ERIC: Oh Lord no! Even the mouse ite eat. Mice eat out!

TERRI: Oh, Jesus!

ERIC: I can do it, honestly, Terri –

TERRI: Even Leonora got her lines right.

LEN: And I didn't come here as an actor. I came as a fucking accordionist.

TERRI: Alright! Carry on. [*Claps hand for attention.*] Well, everyone's here but Sylvia. Where is Sylvia, where is she?

[*They all pretend to search the stage.* SYLVIA *appears centre: twenty-eight, Eurasian, beautiful, speaks with Indian intonation, wears dress and high heeled shoes.*]

SYLVIA [*joins them looking*]: Who are we looking for?

TERRI: You! Temporary Lieutenant Sylvia Morgan of no fixed abode. Where have you been?

SYLVIA: I'd rather you didn't say that, Terri.

TERRI: What – where've you been?

SYLVIA: Of no fixed abode. It doesn't sound very nice.

TERRI: It only means you're not in any of the services, duckie.

SYLVIA: I'm sorry but it makes me sound not entirely respectable.

TERRI: My dears, the temperament. You'd think it was Drury Lane. Get on!

SYLVIA: I've been answering an advert for a girl to help in the officers' mess.

TERRI: Did you get the job?

SYLVIA: No, they said they wanted a girl who'd been in a mess before.

TERRI: I will not countenance another word! Are you all ready?

CHORUS: Yes.

TERRI: Are you all steady?

CHORUS: Yes.
TERRI: Then lights, action, music!
 [*Stage lighting, they line up and band strikes up. They sing their opener.*]
CHORUS: What shall we do for an opening number?
    Waltzes are schmaltz and we're sick of the rumba,
FRONT ROW: Crests of the wave are too hackneyed by far.
CHORUS: Hey, what about letting them know who we are?
    We're SADUSEA
    And on the other hand we're glad to see
    You've come along tonight to join our laughter,
    To see our dance,
    To feel a touch of magic and a breath of romance.
    We've taken pains
    To see our show's the sort that entertains
    And now there's nothing very much remaining
    Except for naming
    The company:
    We're SADUSEA,
    We're S.A.D.U.S.E.A.,
    Song and Dance Unit South East Asia.
 [*They move about in planned confusion and take individual lines in the next verse.*]
LEN: What . . . ?
TERRI: Not yet.
CHORUS: What can we do for the rest of the chorus?
    They know who we are so they know what to call us,
    We're ready and steady and rarin' to go.
    Hey, what about saying the name of the show?
 [*Form line and sing in unison.*]
    It's Jamboree,
    We're bringing you a Jungle Jamboree.
LEN: We've got together in this equatorial latitude,
CHORUS: To chase your blues away and change your attitude.
    So now you'll see
    We've got the kind of personality
    To make you come with us upon a spree
    Or a pot-pourri
    Or a jubilee

LEN: So one-two-three for
CHORUS: S.A.D.U.S.E.A.
And their Jingle-Jangle-Jungle Jamboree!
[*They dance off.*]

SCENE THREE

Single Men in Barracks.

Cloth flown to reveal a bar-counter with shelves of bottles behind, stools in front, LEE *and* CHENG *wearing black, place other chairs and table downstairs while Chinese percussion is played. After setting stage, they bow.* LEE *goes behind the bar,* CHENG *stands to one side.*

Enter REG DRUMMOND, *tough, good-looking, wearing CSM's insignia. He is followed by* STEVE, *still shouldering kit-bag.*

REG: This is the mess.
STEVE: Very nice.
REG: And I'm the mess steward. Any complaints, any problems let me know. Any cheek from Lee. This is Lee. He number one boy. Sarnt Flowers, he belongee mess now.
[LEE, *polishing glasses, nods.*]
And this is Cheng, Cheng take Sergeant's kit to bearer, tell him fix velly good bed chop-chop, or Tuan ask plenty questions. Savvy?
[CHENG *nods, takes bag from* STEVE, *goes.*]
Sit down, have a drink.
STEVE: Well, thanks, sergeant-major, I'll have a ginger-beer shandy.
REG: Two large gins, Lee. Plenty big like-so.
[*They sit at a table while* LEE *prepares drinks.*]
You'd better get used to calling me Reg. Who else have you met so far?
STEVE: Sarnt Bonny gave me my kit, then –
REG: Poor old Len. Puggled.
STEVE: Is he?

REG: Wouldn't *you* be round the bend if they'd posted you direct from Iceland to India? Straight from jackets fleece-lined to nets mosquito?

[*He laughs. Drinks served.*]

Cheers.

STEVE: Cheers.

[*They drink.* STEVE *coughs on his.*]

Could I have some orange in it? Then I saw Captain Dennis.

REG: What d'you make of Captain Dennis?

STEVE: He struck me as a bit of a pseudo-intellectual.

REG: *Did* he?

STEVE: A bit of an eccentric Bohemian, I thought.

REG: Not to mention a bum-boy.

STEVE: Is he?

REG: A raver.

STEVE: Is he a homo then? I'm not sure I've ever met any homos before, not to speak to.

REG: You will here. Queen's Own, this is. The Middlesex Regiment. And if you want my advice you'll give the bum-boys a wide berth. That is, if you don't want to be R.T.U.'d.

STEVE: R.T.U.'d?

REG: Returned to Unit. Major Flack doesn't like the bum-boys either. He doesn't want his brother-officers saying 'Hullo there, Giles, how are those bum-boys of yours coming along?' Have another?

STEVE: I'd like to buy *you* one but till next pay-day I'm a bit –

REG: You can start running up a bill now you're a member. Two more, Lee, bookee to Sarnt Flowers. And if you get any trouble with any of them, funny business in the ablutions, admiring your John Thomas, any of that, have a word with me. Deal with them between us, eh?

STEVE: Right-oh, Sarnt-Major.

REG: Reg.

STEVE: Reg.

REG: Deal with them the same way we used to in the Force.

STEVE: The force?

REG: The Metropolitan Police. Cheers. Same with the Chinese boys. Or your Indian bearer.

STEVE: Are they bum-boys as well then?

REG: Stealing I mean. Insubordination. Being late with the dhobi. I got a room on the perimeter, what I call my interrogation room. Haven't I, Lee? You've been there once, haven't you? They don't often go twice, do they, Lee? Tell him what it's like, go on. No windows, no furniture, an old guard-house. White-washed walls. I have them white-washed periodically. I won't have uppity wogs on my patch. Will I, Lee?

STEVE: Cheers. [*Drinks as* LEE *returns to bar. Presenting his arrival chit.*] If you'll sign my arrival chitty, I'll be getting on.

[REG *drinks.* STEVE *lays the chit on the table before him.* STEVE *finishes his gin, coughs, while* REG *slowly looks at his form. Then he sits up and studies* STEVE.]

REG: Intelligence.

STEVE: Attached to the service corps, yes.

REG: Criminal Investigation, by any chance?

STEVE: No, just routine security stuff. Trying to stop the stores being nicked.

REG: No stores being nicked round here. No loose-wallahs in my bailiwick.

[LEN *and* CHARLES *come on.* LEN *sits at table.*]

LEN: Fucking foot-rash. Itches to buggery. Shall I take me shoes off now, Charlie?

CHARLES: Yes, you'd better. Two Tigers, Lee, there's a sweetheart. Cheng, run and get that lotion on our bedside table.

[CHENG *goes, as* KEVIN *comes on.*]

LEN: D'you reckon it's tinea this or athlete's foot?

KEVIN: Tinea's what you get on your knackers.

LEN: I got it on my knackers and all. I'm fucking covered in gentian violet.

KEVIN [*sings*]: There's a blue ring round my balls
                It's Tinea –

LEN: I thought what you got on your knackers was dhobi itch.

CHARLES: Never mind what it's called. Just remember to change the dressing regularly and let the air get to it.

[CHENG *returns with bottle of lotion and* CHARLES *kneels and applies it to* LEN's *feet.*]

Wear chapplies whenever you can. What's the use me doing a

Florence Nightingale if you don't follow instructions?

REG: I'm going. I can't watch this.

[*Goes off. Unsteadily, lurching into* CHENG *who holds him up.* REG *wrenches away.* CHARLES *continues kneeling before* LEN, *who drinks beer.*]

KEVIN: The wogs and Chinks all see the day approaching when the British go for good. Don't you, Sidney? [*This is to* CHENG *at the bar.*] You'll be sorry then, I'll tell you.

LEN: Ta, Charlie. Just have a lie-down before khana. Don't be long. [*Goes.*]

CHARLES: I'm coming.

[LEN *goes same way as* REG. ERIC *arrives other way, carrying a large tin cylinder which he dumps noisily on the floor.* CHARLES *finishes beer.*]

ERIC: Strewth! Pour me a glass of iced water, Johnny. Had to remain under cover till I saw Reg go to the basha. You know what he's like about anything under the counter.

CHARLES: Erica, what are you up to now?

ERIC [*pointing finger*]: None of that, Bishop. Nothing queer about me. Anyone says there is gets a bunch of fives.

[*Takes out handkerchief and mops face, neck, arms, legs. His shirt shows great sweaty patches.*]

CHARLES [*to others*]: What have I said?

ERIC: My name's Eric. Or Young. Or Love. Or Young-Love hyphenated. But don't give me any of that Erica stuff, alright?

CHARLES: The lady doth protest too much, methinks.

ERIC: I'm warning you, Bishop.

KEVIN: What's in the tin?

ERIC: Lemonade powder.

KEVIN: Roll on!

ERIC: Wizard scrounge. Made a couple of mates in the other ranks' cookhouse. Bang-on skive. All this cost me was a tin of issue cigarettes.

KEVIN: You flogging it to the wogs or what?

ERIC: No fear, matey. I'm drinking it. Well, not all of it. You can have some too.

CHARLES: A tinful? That's enough to keep the whole unit in lemonade for a good twelvemonth.

KEVIN: We'll all be home by then.

ERIC: Oh, dash it, look at that, broken my penknife now. Cheap Chinese rubbish. Borrow your screwdriver, Kevin?

KEVIN: You touch my stuff you get a boot in your marbles.

ERIC: Steady the buffs. Charles, I know *you've* got a knife.

CHARLES: Wrong again.

ERIC [*to* STEVE]: You, what's-your-name, Steve?

STEVE: Sorry, not a thing.

ERIC [*sudden outburst*]: Right, I've got your numbers. You've had your ruddy chips. Just come whining to me for lemonade, see what you get. A bunch of fives.

[*Picks up tin, with difficulty, and carries it off to billet.*]

CHARLES [*following*]: Now don't get in a paddy, Love, you know how it aggravates your prickly heat.

[KEVIN *and* STEVE *watch them go.*]

KEVIN: Old Charles takes care of all of us. Male nurse he was.

STEVE: He looks a bit of a homo.

KEVIN: Oh, he's raving. But faithful to poor old Len.

STEVE: Is Len a homo too? As well as puggled?

KEVIN: He's easy. He's got a wife in Blighty. But he likes to be looked after. Don't we all?

STEVE: Not by a bloke.

KEVIN: You got a bint at home?

STEVE: Girl I write to.

KEVIN: Me too. Mine's at school. All love and kisses and current affairs but I have the odd wank over her photo. Funny thing, I've never had a white bint. You?

STEVE: No.

KEVIN: Plenty of chicks, one or two Malays, the odd wog and a few Anglos. But when it comes to white bints, I tuck in my mosquito net and think about Rita Hayworth.

STEVE: Don't we all!

SCENE FOUR

Les Girls.

Musical intro behind this and he sings a verse, Gene Kelly style. During this song, curtains close behind them.

KEVIN: When things are getting kinda tough
    And maybe I feel I've had enough,
    I shut my ears and close my eyes
    And turn on my technicolour paradise.

STEVE: When the mercury starts to soar
    And I can't keep control any more,
    I study the cinema magazines
    Imagining all those glamour queens.

BOTH [*chorus*]: In my mind there's a movie show
    Of the kind I can always go
    To find my favourite Hollywood star
    From Esther Williams to Hedy Lamarr.

    Night and day on that silver screen
    Alice Faye can be heard and seen
    And Lena Horne's waiting patiently
    Till Lauren Bacall's had enough of me.

KEVIN: Some of them are wrapped in sable,
STEVE: Some can hardly move for pearls:
KEVIN: Paulette Goddard
STEVE: Betty Grable
BOTH: All the world's most glamorous girls!

    Left alone I would stay for good
    In my own private Hollywood
    And I'd never let the curtain fall
    On this million-dollar carnival,
    The movie to end them all!

[*They are now joined by* ERIC *and* CHARLES *and sing:*]

QUARTET: Shady joint, streets of sin,
    Silken stockings, old Berlin,
    Ich lieber dich, auf wiedersehen,
    Damen und herren, it's Marlene!

[*Tabs open on art deco outlines, drifting smoke,* TERRI *as Dietrich in 'Blue Angel', straddling a Bentwood chair.*]

TERRI: In a sleazy cabaret
    Where the clients were so pally

Once I sang the night away
That's become the Karl Marx Alley
Danke schon, comrades, danke schon..

Once I sat across a chair
Drinking schnapps in dirty glasses
Now it's Friedrich Engels Square
Strictly for the working classes
Danke schon for nothing, cameraden, danke schon.

I can't run in heels like this,
So come on, boys, one last kiss.
Danke schon for nicht, cameraden, danke schon.
Auf wiedersehen.

[*Men shoulder* TERRI *and carry him upstage. Tableau. Curtains.*
STEVE *remains downstage. Speaks to audience.*]

STEVE: Dad will, I am convinced, insist on knowing the whys and
wherefores. SADUSEA is a small part of a large transit camp.
Each pair of men shares a room with a balcony, from which one
can look down on the small marquee which is our dining-room,
with its adjacent ping-pong table and piano. As for the personnel
of this outré establishment, it has its usual quota of illiterate
morons but also quite a few pseudo-intellectuals. One of these is
Captain Dennis, who may be a genius but it's too early to judge.
I will write more tomorrow after seeing him tonight in the dress-
rehearsal of his show at the Garrison Theatre. I wanted to dash
down these first and no doubt erroneous impressions. Love to
you, all. Yours, Steve.

[*He goes off as* REG *comes on other side, furtively. He watches*
STEVE *go, then turns to us.*]

REG: They must think I'm a bloody zombie, a moon man. Royal
Army Service Corps? A likely story. Special Investigation Branch
if I know anything. Well, Private Flowers, you'll need to get your
knees very brown to catch me. And I hope wherever they train
you spies they pay attention to your weapon training. You're
going to need it.

[*Turns and goes, unsteadily.*]

SCENE FIVE

Beginners, Please.

Tabs part on TERRI's *dressing-room. A table to one side with electric bulbs round a mirror.* TERRI *as Dietrich is sitting at table with glass of spirit, lighting a cigarette. Percussion ends. Knock on door.*

TERRI: Come in, if you're pretty.

    [STEVE *enters uncertainly, dressed KD.* TERRI *looks him over.*]

    Quite right. Pretty as a picture.

STEVE: You told me to come round half-time and you'd clear my chitty.

TERRI: Sometimes I go too far.

STEVE: So you could accept me on your strength.

TERRI: D'you think we've time before 'beginners'?

STEVE: Then you said you were going to think how to use me in the show.

TERRI: Well, now, let me see.

    [*Takes off top hat and puts it on table, leaves on wig. During this scene he changes from this into the uniform of a Royal Naval Rating. It is done in a way to frighten or excite* STEVE. *He pours a glass of gin, gives it to* STEVE.]

    Drinkie?

STEVE: Thanks.

TERRI: You see, we're a bit short on the technical side.

STEVE: I thought Len Bonny did the stage managing?

TERRI: Leonora can't really cope. She's like my mother in the old folks' home, forever losing her teeth or catching fire to her knickers or wet-dreaming of Charlotte. We need someone to arrange things, fix the meals, the sleeping quarters, see we've got a practical piano. Could you cope?

STEVE: You mean: could I handle the business end?

TERRI [*ogling*]: You come right out with it, don't you?

STEVE: I think I could, yes.

TERRI: Then, dear heart, you're engaged.

STEVE: And what should I do in the show?

TERRI: Well, a bit here, a bit there.

STEVE: That's alright. I don't expect to hold down any big parts right away.

TERRI: Few of us are that lucky.

STEVE: That's part of the job, isn't it? My father's always telling me that.

TERRI: She knows her onions, then. You'll play as cast, with or without drag. That means wearing frocks.

STEVE: Mister Dennis, I think it's only fair to warn you I'm not a homosexual.

TERRI: Don't worry, love, it won't show from the front.

STEVE: Obviously there are quite a few homosexuals here, which is perfectly alright as far as I'm concerned –

TERRI: Bona for you –

STEVE: But I'm not at all that way inclined myself.

TERRI: Oh, I can see. You positively shriek butch from every pore. But then you can't always judge a sausage by its foreskin. Half the rough trade walking about you'd never tell were queens.

STEVE: Sorry?

TERRI: Why d'you think they call it the *Royal* Navy? It's all part of life's rich tapestry, ducks, the gay panoply of the passing years.

[*He has removed the stockings, suspenders, etc., and the female face but retains wig. He now stands and takes off the dress, revealing a tanned body naked but for bikini briefs. He moves across, passing close to* STEVE, *who recoils.* TERRI *stares at him.*]

You flatter yourself. No one's that irresistible.

STEVE: I was only getting out of your way.

TERRI: We know what you were doing, Ada. You thought I was after your nuts.

[*Hangs dress on rail and takes sailor costume, begins putting it on.*]

What was your name? Stephanie, didn't you say? Pour me another gin, dear, and have one yourself.

[STEVE *goes to table and obeys.* TERRI *watches.*]

I bet the future Mrs Flowers can't wait for the day she sees you standing there with your discharge in your hand? Eh? That's better. You've got a *nice* smile, you should use it more often.

STEVE: There isn't any future Mrs Flowers. Just a pen friend. A schoolgirl.

TERRI: So you're not keeping yourself? In that case, I suppose

you're down Racecourse Road every night touching up the Taxi
Girls—

STEVE: Quite a few of the bods do but I find that such a squalid
transaction. Putting love on a commercial basis. Have you read
Mrs Warren's Profession?

TERRI: Oh that Bernadette Shaw! What a chatterbox! Nags away
from asshole to breakfast-time but never sees what's staring her
in the face.

STEVE: Oh, I couldn't agree with that.

TERRI: But she never even lost her maidenhead till she was fifty-
eight or something. Are *you* a virgin, sweetie?

STEVE: Me? No! Not really.

TERRI: You can talk to your auntie, dear. I know what it's like when
you're young. The pressure to be a big strong man. I went
through all that. My father thought the ultimate in masculinity
was to stick your chopper into anything that wore a skirt.

STEVE: Mine isn't at all like that. In fact, I've never thought of him
having sex at all.

TERRI: I tried not to disappoint my father, much as I disliked her.
God knows I tried. I remember as though it was yesterday the
first time I got my hand on a girl's tit. In a cinema, it was, in
Walthamstow.

[*He's now got on the bell-bottoms and takes off the wig and puts
on the sweater.* STEVE *sits at table, facing away, gulping gin and
pouring another glass.*]

I'd got my arm round the other side but I found I couldn't do
much with that so I started on the near side with the free hand.
The first discovery was that it was all soft.

STEVE: Didn't you know *that?*

TERRI: I was never quite sure till then that tits didn't have bones.
Anyway. Next I twiddled with the nipple for a bit.

STEVE: Through her dress?

TERRI: Under her jumper. I'd pulled her bra down on my side.

STEVE: Did you like it? Twiddling her nipple?

TERRI: It was a lot like tuning a wireless.

STEVE: Did *she* like it?

TERRI: God knows. I looked at her face from time to time but she
was staring at the screen as though she was hypnotised. I began

to wonder if touching their tits sent them into a coma.

STEVE: Not as a general rule, no.

TERRI: Anyway I sat there holding this great thing in my hand, in agony with pins and needles, but it seemed rude to put it back so I kept on squeezing and tweaking till suddenly the lights went up and I dropped it like a hot brick.

STEVE: Didn't she react at all?

TERRI: She looked at me and said 'That was smashing, I liked the ending, how about getting me a choc-ice?' And while I was queueing up, I thought to myself; Ada, that's strictly not for you.

[*Now dressed as a sailor, he moves towards* STEVE.]

STEVE: Well, it is for me. If only I knew *how*.

TERRI: Don't you then?

STEVE: Well . . . several times at home I got a woman in my upstairs room . . . used to get in a hell of a state with ears all red and hair messed up . . . I could undo their bras alright . . . got my hand up their skirts once or twice but – what d'you do after *that*?

TERRI: Are you asking *me*, duckie? I gather you're supposed to titillate the clitoris.

STEVE: Yes, but where *is* it?

TERRI: Search me.

STEVE: When sergeant-majors say 'You'd know it if it had hairs round it,' the fact is most of us wouldn't.

LEN [*off*]: Second half beginners, please.

TERRI [*calling*]: Merci blow-through.

STEVE: I better get back to my seat.

[*While they talk,* TERRI *signs his form. With eyebrow pencil.*]

TERRI: Enjoying the Dress Rehearsal?

STEVE: I think it'll go down very well.

TERRI: I get a bit puffed these days. Too many Churchmans, too many choppers. Here. And if I were you, some day soon I'd pick up a Chinese girl in the Happy World. They're professionals, dear, they've even got a union.

STEVE: Yes, but I feel that physical love must grow from personal affection, there must be –

TERRI: Leave your name and number, ducks, we'll be in touch.

[STEVE *smiles, makes for door, staggers slightly.*]

Ooops.

STEVE: Not used to all this gin.

[*Goes,* TERRI *checks appearance in glass, then turns to audience.*]

TERRI: I was like her once upon a time, believe it or not. Romantic, idealistic. Nothing sordid or unforgivable could happen. Nobody could break your heart, nobody could use you or degrade you or steal from you or chuck you off like an old pair of drawers when they'd finished with you. But after one or two had trampled over me on their way up the ladder, I thought to myself, 'Ada, you're becoming a soft touch' and from that time I played it for pleasure, never fell in love and rarely got hurt. A short life and a gay one. I had a fabulous time, and let's face it I gave good value. Pretty as paint and witty with it. Then just before the war I fell in love again, this time for keeps. And what did he have to be? A matelot, of course. And what was he on as soon as it started? Atlantic convoys, naturally. And how long was it before the U-boats got him? Just over a year. The next-of-kin were informed, his wife and his mother, but I had to hear it a long time after from someone off the same ship in a gay bar.

[*Cloth has come down behind him, lights have gone, but for spot on him.* TERRI *claps his hands.*]

So. Boys and girls. What you're going to see now is my own dance fantasia dedicated to the memory of all the boys in navy blue who laid down their lives for a better, freer, gayer world. And also to the women and children and the poor old queens who waited for them at home. Thank you.

SCENE SIX

Western Approaches.

A piano, concerto begins, pastiche-Grieg, Rachmaninov and Gershwin. Cloth goes.

Spot on SYLVIA *in belted raincoat, headscarf and ballet-shoes. Lights on backcloth representing a stormy sky.* SYLVIA *mimes and dances, signifying by looks at her watch, etc. that she is keeping a rendezvous.*

Change in the music brings on KEVIN *in polo-neck sweater, cap, dark trousers.* SYLVIA *backs away but* KEVIN *pursues, rips off her headscarf and her long hair falls free. Exit barred other side by* CHARLES, *dressed like* KEVIN. *Flashes on skycloth as she runs from the rapists and they throw her about, Apache-style.*

TERRI *leaps on as matelot and saves her. Attackers produce knives but he disarms them and sends them away, one injured.*

The violence gives way to a lush melodic theme as they dance their love in full stage lighting but this is soon interrupted.

REG [*from audience*]: Take your coat off!
    [*Dance continues uneasily.* REG *claps hands, standing in an aisle.*]
  Take your coat off! What's she wearing a raincoat for?
TERRI: What's the matter?
    [*Music stops.*]
REG: During the rape Miss Morgan's coat ought to be torn off.
TERRI: This isn't a strip-tease.
REG: Steady on, Terri. I only said the coat. I want to see the dress underneath. This number's gloomy, you need a splash of colour.
TERRI: But Reggie dear, this isn't a colourful number. It's meant to be in muted tones.
REG: The boys up-country want a splash of colour.
SYLVIA: This is symbolic, don't you see that? I'm not only meant to be a girl being raped. On an altogether deeper level I represent a fleet of merchant ships.
TERRI: I shouldn't bother, duckie –
SYLVIA: Charles and Kevin are U-boats and Terri is the Naval convoy that beats off their attack. After which he and I continue our vital journey across the Atlantic. My Lord I should have thought *anyone* could see that!
TERRI: Regina, dear, I hope you aren't trying to teach your auntie to suck eggs because I've been in this business all my life –
REG: And look where you've finished up –
    [*For once* TERRI *is silenced. Out of it* SYLVIA *speaks.*]
SYLVIA: You will kindly apologise for that remark.
REG: What did you say? I'll what-did-you-say?
TERRI [*to* REG]: You dare shake your handbag at me! An officer and a lady!
REG: Are you giving me bum-boy lip? Are you?

[REG *climbs onto stage unsteadily.*]

SYLVIA: He's been drinking. He can't see straight.

[CHARLES *and* KEVIN *are onstage now, watching.*]

REG: Can't I? I can see you, black as you are. And remember this, I don't take cheek from the Bombay Welsh.

[SYLVIA *slaps his face.*]

REG [*raising hand*]: By Christ!

STEVE [*from audience*]: Don't you touch her!

REG: Who's that?

STEVE [*arriving onstage*]: You better not.

REG: As you were, sonny. I've already warned you –

STEVE: And I'm warning you.

[*He staggers too.*]

TERRI: She's pissed as well.

REG: One step out of line, you'll be R.T.U.'d.

STEVE: You people think you can tell the world what to do.

REG: I'll throw the book at you, make no error.

SYLVIA: Whoever you are, please don't risk trouble.

STEVE: I don't care. They can't be allowed to tell creative people what to do –

REG: Alright, soldier, I've cautioned you. Don't imagine being a spy can frighten me. You're Returned to Unit.

CHARLES: He's only just arrived.

TERRI: Sergeant-Major, I'll say whether Private Flowers is going to stay or not. Don't forget I'm an honorary captain and if there's any more sauce I'll have you on the carpet, though quite honestly I don't fancy it.

REG: You better lock me up. You better put me under close arrest because if you don't I may do something I'll regret. I may strike an honorary captain and that could mean a court-martial.

TERRI: Oh, come on, give us a kiss and make friends –

REG: I mean it! Put me under close arrest.

TERRI: Jessica Christ. Well, how do I do it?

REG: Get two sergeants to escort me to the guardroom.

TERRI: Kevin and Charles, arrest the sergeant-major and take him to his quarters –

REG: Not them! They can't, they're improperly dressed!

TERRI: Really! [*Calling.*] Eric, Len come on here!

[ERIC *enters in Scottish costume, kilt, sporran, etc.,* LEN *follows in drag – crinoline, powdered wig, etc., carrying usual clip-board.*]

ERIC: I don't think I can make that change in time –

REG: D'you call that properly dressed?

CHARLES: Steve's the only one who is.

ERIC: What's going on?

REG: He's a Private. He's not a substantive sergeant.

TERRI: Have a heart, Reg, where can I find a substantive sergeant at this time of night?

KEVIN: I'm a substantive flight-sergeant.

LEN: You're dressed as a fucking U-boat.

REG: There's an enormous transit camp out there, with a sergeants' mess not fifty yards off.

TERRI: Steven, would you be a dear. Run out and fetch me two properly dressed substantive sergeants –

REG: Warrant officers.

TERRI: Warrant officers then.

STEVE: What shall I tell them?

TERRI: Say we want to arrest our sergeant-major but the only officer's dressed as a sailor and one of the sergeants is in a crinoline and in any case we haven't the faintest idea . . .

GILES [*from auditorium*]: Thank you, Mister Dennis.

TERRI [*peering out*]: Who's *that*?

GILES: Major Flack.

REG: Company, Commanding Officer on Parade, Company 'shun.
[*The service personnel obey as best they can.*]
[GILES *wears Major's insignia on KD, carries a walking stick; a spare ascetic man, authoritative, quiet, with the air of an earnest scoutmaster.*]

GILES [*coming down aisle on to stage*]: Stand easy. I'm afraid you've had an uninvited audience for this particular turn –

TERRI: You're always welcome, Major, I've told you –

GILES: Not me. There's been a huddle of transit camp personnel at every window of the hall.

REG: Sarnt Bonny, detail some men to close the shutters.

LEN: Sir!

GILES: I've already packed them off. But I'm afraid they've seen this sketch or whatever it is you're practising. And most of them found it amusing so I suppose you know what you're doing . . .

TERRI: This isn't a sketch, Major, only a difference of opinion.

SYLVIA: Sergeant Major Drummond wants to see a rape. He says all the boys want to see me being raped and in a rape my raincoat would be torn off.

TERRI: But this is not a rape, Major, it's a choreographic fantasia.

SYLVIA [*takes it off*]: Alright. There. And in case you're wondering about the bruises on my thigh here and my shoulder there, I dare say Sarnt-Major Drummond –

REG: I only want the coat removed in order to countercheck the wardrobe requisition.

GILES [*mystified*]: Miss Morgan, you were about to say – ?

[*But* SYLVIA *runs from the stage crying. Drops coat by* STEVE *who picks it up.*]

TERRI: Satisfied?

REG: No. Where's the dress?

TERRI: I never asked for a frock for this number, lovie, only a mac and headscarf.

REG: Sarnt, you got that requisition?

LEN: Sir!

[LEN *provides the clip-board, which* REG *shows* GILES.]

REG: Here we are, sir. Dress satin scarlet one, comprising skirts full one, bodices low-cut one, Western Approaches Ballet for the use of.

GILES: Is that your signature, Mister Dennis?

TERRI [*glancing*]: Let's face it, if you're going to take us back over every bleeding form we've ever signed! I'm an artiste, not a haberdasher!

GILES: Surely it must be clear even to an *artiste* that equipment supplied out of public money must be accounted for and having been provided must be deployed to maximum advantage. Whether it's a battleship or a ball-gown. Extravagance is always bad thinking. Signifies luxury. And we know what luxury leads to: The Russian Revolution. The Fall of France.

TERRI: But Jesus Christ, I didn't ask for the silly frock!

[*Pause.* GILES *draws himself up, glances at the men.*]

GILES: Neither does being an *artiste* justify casual blasphemy. Especially from someone who might be expected to set his men

GILES: Neither does being an *artiste* justify casual blasphemy. Especially from someone who might be expected to set his men an example of respect for his God and King. [*He is now addressing everyone onstage.*] We defend a righteous flag and we bring the news of Christ's mercy to peoples who have never known it. Otherwise what are we? At best unwelcome guests, at worst unscrupulous invaders. Sarnt Major, dismiss the company and parade again tomorrow morning for further practice.

REG: Sah!

[*He salutes and* GILES *returns it.*]

Company, dismiss!

[GILES *goes first with* REG, *then others shuffle off, leaving* TERRI *alone.* LEN *lets in front-cloth behind him while* TERRI *speaks to us.*]

TERRI: And she swept off with Regina and left me feeling about this small. Well, it didn't say anything in my contract about setting an example. There was no work in England, the panto season was over and life under Clementina Attlee wasn't exactly the Roman Empire. So I signed on for sun and fun. With never a mention of God or Georgina the Sixth. And I certainly got what I came for. Singapore, 1948, and they'd booked me in at Raffles. Antiquated even then but terribly Somerset Maugham. Only snag, it was out of bounds to other ranks. Luckily my room had a balcony with an easy climb from the garden. And most naval ratings are very nimble nipping up the rigging after weeks afloat doing the Captain Bligh stint. Then, to a mature woman, how romantic, standing in the moonlight saying 'Matelot, matelot, wherefore art thou, matelot?'

SCENE SEVEN

Get up them Stairs.

Cloth rises revealing TERRI's *dressing-room re-dressed to serve as* SYLVIA's. *She's sitting at table, turned from us, wearing kimono, nervously smoking.*

TERRI: Backstage I pulled rank and detailed Steve to return Sylvia's mac, knowing one thing may very well lead to another. Which may cause a few of you to shriek 'Get Ada doing her martyred bit' but I'm like that – generous to a fault. Anyway the Fleet Club awaited me –

[STEVE *has come on and knocks at door.* SYLVIA *stands.*]

SYLVIA: Who is it?

STEVE: Private Flowers.

TERRI: So now she's helped young love to have its fling.
       'Tis time your Fairy Queen was on the wing.

[*Entrechats off as* SYLVIA *opens door.*]

SYLVIA: Come in.

STEVE: I've brought your coat, that's all.

[*She pulls him in, steps out and looks about. He is mystified. She comes in again, turns key in lock.*]

SYLVIA: I wanted to thank you for coming to the rescue of a damsel in distress.

STEVE: The Philistines must be resisted.

SYLVIA [*taking coat, hanging it, going to table*]: I only hope you don't get into hot water.

[*She starts to do her face and hair.*]

STEVE: Didn't do much good. He still managed to stop the dress rehearsal.

SYLVIA: What did you think of the show so far? Isn't Terri terrific?

STEVE: He gets about very well for his age. But what an outrageous bum-boy!

SYLVIA: I'd rather you didn't use expressions like that, thank you all the same.

STEVE [*embarrassed*]: Sorry.

SYLVIA: Shall I tell you something? Terri is probably the only man in my whole life to be kind to me without wanting to – use me in some way. I was on my beam-ends when he auditioned me. I don't know how I'd have managed if he hadn't taken me on as his partner.

STEVE: You're such a brilliant dancer and so graceful and everything I can't believe you're not making a fortune. You would in England. Why don't you go?

SYLVIA: Just like that? Eight thousand miles? Have you the slightest idea how much that costs? All my life I've wanted to go. Good grief, Mummy and I used to talk by the hour of how we'd

go for tea at Lyons' Corner House before taking in a show at
Covent Garden.

STEVE: *I've* been to the Corner House. They've got a gipsy
orchestra.

SYLVIA: Who doesn't know *that*?

STEVE: How d'you know if you've never been?

SYLVIA: Daddy told me. He was in the Welsh Fusiliers.

STEVE: Why didn't he take you then?

[SYLVIA *stands, looks on rack for dress, takes it down.*]

SYLVIA: A chapter of accidents. We were in Calcutta, the regiment
had been posted home, everything was packed, Mummy's trunk
was marked 'Not Wanted On Voyage'. Then the war broke out.
Daddy was killed soon afterwards in Burma, we lost our married
quarters and had to manage on a sergeant's pension.

STEVE: I was in Calcutta more than a year.

SYLVIA: I hated it. But nonetheless Mummy's worst day was when
we left to come down here. 'It's the wrong direction' she kept
saying, 'it's further East.'

[*She suddenly takes off her wrap and is in briefs.* STEVE *nervously
looks away.*]

STEVE: I better go.

SYLVIA: Oh, no, please, don't –

STEVE: I was only detailed to bring your coat –

SYLVIA: I'll play you some music to remind you of England.

[*She winds portable gramophone and puts on record of 'An English
Country Garden'. She dances to it.* STEVE *watches fascinated.*
REG *approaches outside the door.* SYLVIA *makes* STEVE *sit at her
table and is about to dress when* REG *tries door, then bangs on it.
She puts her hand over* STEVE's *mouth, waits.* REG *knocks again.*]

REG: Sylvia! You coming?

SYLVIA: Who's that?

REG: What d'you mean 'Who's that?' What's this locked for? Open
it up, come on. [*He rattles the door again.*]

SYLVIA: Terri's taking me home tonight.

REG: *Is* he?

SYLVIA: Thanks all the same.

[*She has moved towards the door.* REG *waits.*]

REG: Right. Just checking.

SYLVIA: Thanks. Goodnight.

[REG *moves off.* SYLVIA *hears, returns to* STEVE, *puts on dress.*]

STEVE: I must be getting along now –

SYLVIA: See me home, please –

STEVE: But you said –

SYLVIA: I've got a whole collection of English records at my flat in town. Do me up at the back.

[*He does, fumbling. She stops music.*]

Percy Grainger, Ralph Vaughan Williams, Eric Coates. I'll make you a really nice cup of tea. And I'm pretty sure I've got some biscuits. D'you like Lincoln Creams?

[*She takes his hand, kisses it.*]

A little treat, mm? You pack the portable while I finish dressing.

[*He packs gramophone. She puts on shoes.*]

STEVE: Why didn't you stay in India?

SYLVIA: After the British quit? With all those Hindu and Moslem savages killing each other by the millions? Mummy and I were Chapel!

STEVE: Does she share the flat with you?

SYLVIA: She passed on a year ago. And now it's the same for me all over again – after they kick the British out of *here*, where shall I go then? Hong Kong?

STEVE: Who's going to kick us out?

SYLVIA: The Communists. Or if not them, someone else. Nobody believes in you any more since you surrendered to the Japs.

STEVE: Don't blame me. I was only twelve at the time.

[*Now ready, she switches out the dressing lights, listens at the door, unlocks it, goes out and looks about.* STEVE *follows with gramophone. She locks door after her, then takes* STEVE'*s hand to lead away but* REG *appears, stopping their way.*]

REG: Miss Morgan. Lucky I caught you.

SYLVIA: Why are you always following me? I feel I've got no privacy.

REG: Privacy? That's American, that is. You'd better say 'privacy' if you want to pass muster in the Burlington Arcade.

SYLVIA: Please, Reg –

REG: 'Privacy'! You been talking to the Yanks again?

SYLVIA: Don't!

REG: Can't leave them alone, can you?

[*Moves unsteadily towards her, she flinches, but* REG *passes her for* STEVE.]

I'll take that, soldier –

STEVE: Captain Dennis –

REG: Captain Dennis went off long ago. Good job I checked. Full steam ahead to our boys in blue, I expect.

STEVE: He detailed me to escort Miss Morgan –

SYLVIA: No, it's alright. You must come some other time.

[STEVE *relinquishes portable to* REG. SYLVIA *kisses* STEVE. REG *waits and she goes with him.* STEVE *turns to audience.*]

STEVE: Dearest Heather, it is bewildering to your peripatetic but otherwise constant devotee to discover how many different sorts of people there are and how many different ways they have. It's going to be an enormous task educating them all, even if the teaching profession is bursting with brilliant geniuses like yours truly. If only you could be here for a day so I could show you how little there is in common between Singapore and Fernleaze Crescent! But do keep writing with the news. We all long for the mail to come and you can imagine that the unfortunate wretch who receives no letter is a prey to morbid imaginings and nervous breakdowns. Love and all that, your itinerant but ever-faithful Steve.

[*Music. Curtains part.* STEVE *goes.*]

SCENE EIGHT

Forces' Sweetheart.

TERRI *appears, wearing long white dress and wig, seated writing letter. On the desk a lighted candle. On the refrain the men hum to his singing.*

TERRI: My dearest I'm writing once again
From the still of my lonely room
And dreaming of the moment when
We'll stand as bride and groom.

For though today you're oh-so-far-away,
I imagine all we'll do and say.

When the shadows creep
Over fields of sheep
With a love that's deep
You and I will go to sleep
Doing all those little things we used to do.

When the chapel bell
Says 'Good night, sleep well'
To the wishing-well
And the children's carousel,
We'll do all those little things we used to do.

Remember September,
The country weekends,
The yearning we felt inside?
And Autumn recalls
Such wonderful balls,
The organ at eventide.

We'll be true until
In a church that's still
I shall know the thrill
Of whispering 'I will',
Then we'll do those little things we used to do before
But with roses around the door.

[*Accompaniment and male chanting goes on through next speech.*]

Darling, do you remember V.E. Night and V.J. Night, how we danced and sang in the streets? The bonfires and the crowds? Everyone felt so glad peace was here again and we could all get on with the job of building a-new? But in three short years the world is once more torn by strife and that's why boys like you have got to be over there keeping the peace till everyone's come to their senses again. And then, dearest, there'll be so many wonderful things to do together and all the time in the world to do them in.

Remember December,
Those Christmases past,

The mistletoe where we kissed?
The carols, the tree,
Your presents to me,
The stuffing we couldn't resist?

ALL: On a day new born
In a field of corn
There's an April morn
When we'll welcome in the dawn
Doing all those little things that we used to do before
But we'll do them forever more.

[TERRI *goes and music ends. Lights now reveal a row of cubicles upstage.*]

[STEVE, KEVIN, CHARLES *and* ERIC *are preparing to take showers. They have been singing with* TERRI *on the last refrain. They are wearing only towels round their waists.* LEN *enters, also in towel, with mail for them. Others have drinks.*]

LEN: Letter for you, Charlie, from Yorkshire. Fucker for me and all from the fucking wife.

CHARLES: Gawd help us. My mother. The voice of doom.

[LEN *gives out letters as he names them.*]

LEN: Wimbledon, cop hold of that. One from your young tart.

ERIC: Bang on, Squire.

LEN: Einstein, fucker for you. Lambeth, there's even a cunt for you.

KEVIN: I wish there was. A nice white one.

[*All look at their mail, settle to read and give extracts aloud.*]

ERIC: This is from Susan alright. Wizard!

KEVIN: My young lady pen-friend. 'Dear Kevin, thank you for the snap you sent. How brown you look! Am I right in saying you are something like Gene Kelly only younger?'

LEN: 'My dear hubby, not much to write about as per usual. Aldershot is much the same and most things rationed still even bread now, it makes you wish old Winnie was back and all parcels very welcome as per usual . . . .'

ERIC: 'You will see from the background of the enclosed snap that New Malden is as beautiful as ever.' [*Looks at snap.*] Not only the background, but Susan in the front. [*Kisses photo, goes on with letter.*] 'The cherry blossom makes you wonder what they mean by a Cold War but Dad says it's all due to the miners not being able to dig enough coal to warm it up, however much they get paid. He keeps us in fits with his jokes.'

LEN: 'Do you remember Corporal Pratt that we knew in Iceland?' I remember him, the randy cunt. 'He has turned up here, what a small world . . .'

KEVIN: 'When you go swimming do watch out for those man-eating sharks you wrote about in your . . .'

[*Men jeer.*]

Belt up!

ERIC: 'Mum says she can't make out why our boys in the R.A.F. are dropping food on Berlin when it seems only yesterday they were dropping bombs . . . .'

LEN: 'Working in the NAAFI is very hard on nylons and I see where you are getting an increment in your overseas allowance. Do let me have a pound or two to buy some clothing coupons on the black market and oblige your loving wife Valerie . . . .'

CHARLES: So she can oblige Corporal Pratt, I imagine.

LEN: You wouldn't fucking knob it. What's your mother got to say?

CHARLES: Auntie May's had a prolapse. Dad's having a stone removed, her feet are playing up. It's more like *The Lancet* than a letter.

LEN: Johnny! Couple of Tigers. Chop-chop!

KEVIN: Make that three!

ERIC: I'll have one, Squire.

STEVE: That's five, Cheng.

ERIC: Dad says the way to cure your prickly heat is to stand in the pouring rain with no clothes on.

CHARLES: My dear!

ERIC: Watch it, Bishop!

KEVIN: 'We are doing Malaya in Geography and I asked Miss why you're out there and she said it was to do with letting Stalin have some rubber.' [*Looks up.*] That's not right, is it?

STEVE: Listen to what my mate says: 'You needn't think you are going to impress people with your uniforms. They couldn't care less. They don't even know there *is* an army in Malaya.'

ERIC: 'Your friend Corporal Lawrence hasn't come here yet to deliver the silk for my wedding dress. Princess Elizabeth's marriage set me looking forward to ours all over again . . . .'

KEVIN: Not even sent a photo this time.

ERIC: Susan has.

KEVIN [*taking snap*]: That her?

ERIC: That's my bit of kaifa, matey, waiting for me in New Malden.

KEVIN: You'll be alright there. Bit like Deborah Kerr, is she?

ERIC: Alright? Is that all? I'll be laughing, mate. In the lifeboat. Asbestos.

    [KEVIN *returns snap, goes into cubicle.* ERIC *reads on.*]

KEVIN: You going to know what to do, though? You don't want to disappoint her first time. You come down Racecourse Road one night, let some Chinky tart show you what to do.

ERIC: No fear. I'm staying clean for Susan.

KEVIN: Here's a better idea! How d'you fancy a touch of Black Velvet? Old Sylvia now? She's a good sort. Clever too. They reckon she can smoke a cheroot in her minge.

LEN: Blow smoke rings and all, can't she?

KEVIN: Used to do it in Calcutta, didn't she, for the Yanks? In the cabaret?

LEN: Takes some fucking muscle control, mind.

CHARLES: You're pathetic, both of you, with your tatty fantasies.

KEVIN: You want to teach your Susan that.

ERIC [*threatening*]: Now watch it, Lambeth.

KEVIN: Go down well in New Malden.

ERIC: I've warned you –

KEVIN: The Young Conservatives' Garden Party.

ERIC [*out of shower*]: Talk as dirty as you like about half-caste tarts but start on Susan and see what you get –

KEVIN [*coming out*]: What then? What? Come on! What?

ERIC [*showing fist*]: A bunch of fives! That's what.

CHARLES: Not again! If Love came to visit you in *hospital*, he'd bring you a bunch of fives.

ERIC [*turning on him*]: I'll deal with you in a minute, Bishop.

    [KEVIN *has grabbed his towel and flicks it at* ERIC's *buttocks.*]

Ow! Right, that's it. I've ruddy well warned you, Cartwright, now you're for it – You've had your chips, chiefy, mark my words – hey, steady on, that hurt –

[*The others are all out by now and have towelled and put on their towels.*]

[REG *enters, properly dressed, with cap.*]

REG: Company, attention. Officer Commanding!

[GILES *enters, as men come to attention.* KEVIN *quickly wraps on his towel.* ERIC *is left without and has to find his in the cubicles. Then he tries to wring it out while* GILES *waits in silence.*]

Hurry it up, there.

ERIC: Sah!

[*Finds and wraps towel around him, comes to attention.*]

GILES: Carry on, Sarnt-Major.

REG: Last night's guard detail, one pace forward – march!

[ERIC *smartly steps forward, stamps with bare feet.*]

Name, rank and number.

ERIC: 2231747, Acting-Sergeant Young-Love, sah!

GILES: Were you on guard duty last night!

ERIC: Sah!

GILES: And do you remember my staff car leaving my quarters some time after midnight?

ERIC: About two hundred hours, sir, yessir. I saw you coming, lifted the barrier and presented arms. You acknowledged the salute, sir, in the back seat.

GILES: No.

ERIC: Thought you did, sah.

GILES: I wasn't in the back seat. I wasn't in the car at all.

ERIC: Your driver certainly did, sir.

GILES: That wasn't my driver, that was a Chinese communist.

ERIC: Sah?

GILES: He was stealing my car, Sarnt. We cannot say for what reason. It was later found burnt out on the Bukit Timah Road.

ERIC: I recognised your car, sir, I naturally thought –

REG: Can I offer you a drink, sir?

GILES: A lemonade, thank you.

REG: Cheng. Two lemonade, chop-chop. Makee from big tin of powder you've got backside of bar. Savvy?

[CHENG *goes with tray.*]

GILES: Now I understand the guard for our compound is drawn from transit personnel. So why were you, an acting NCO,

331

patrolling our lines?

ERIC: Volunteer, sah. I've volunteered for permanent Friday night guard duty.

GILES: What for?

ERIC [*shrugs, attempts pleasantry*]: Keeps me out of trouble, sah.

GILES: Not on this occasion.

ERIC: I mean it stops me spending money in the mess, sir, or Singapore. I'm saving all my pay towards my marriage.

GILES: I wish you every happiness.

ERIC: Keep myself very busy, sir, all through my service. Volunteer for everything: fire-fighter, assistant in the early treatment room, clerk to the Catholic padre, dog-shooter, magician, anti-malarial officer –

GILES: Magician?

ERIC: In the show, sir.

GILES: Ah.

CHARLES: He makes cars disappear.

[*Men laugh.* GILES *stiffens.*]

GILES: You wouldn't find it quite so funny if the Communists had burnt your billet with you inside. Or lined you and your family up against a wall and sprayed you with machine-gun fire. That's already happening, d'you know that? Not only to British planters but Indian managers, Chinese businessmen, Malayan farmers. Anyone's fair game! As you were. Anyone prepared to save Malaya from a new dark age of atheism. That is what we're here for. And that is why we'll stay.

[CHENG *returns with two glasses of lemonade.*]

Thanks, boy. Now – though I myself am a life-abstainer, I never object to moderate drinking in others. So finish your beers by joining me in a toast.

[*The men get their glasses,* REG *and* GILES *the lemonade.* CHENG *stands waiting.*]

To the defeat of Communism in South East Asia Command Malaya and Singapore and the victory of Christian enlightenment!

MEN [*mumbling*]: To the defeat of Communism in South East Asia Command Malaya and Singapore and the victory of Christian enlightenment.

[*They all drink.*]

GILES: Excellent lemonade. Now some of you may be saying 'Yes, that's all very well, but law luv a duck, we're only peace-time conscripts waiting for the boat back to dear old Blighty.' And others may say 'But cor stone the crows, this is a non combatant unit after all.' But, as we see from last night's episode, we *are* a military target. And if we don't defend ourselves, no one else will. From now on we're not relying on transit personnel to patrol our perimeter. Mister Drummond's drawn up a roster for the coming months.

[CHENG *has moved about collecting glasses.* GILES *finishes his drink, returns glass to him.*]

Singing and dancing's all very well but it won't stop Communistic Chinamen. That's all, men.

REG: Company, attention!

[*The men come to attention.* GILES *makes to exit but pauses, sniffing the air.*]

GILES: Do I smell women's perfume?

REG: There's a distinct suggestion of it, sir.

GILES: I hope you're none of you allowing women in these quarters. Strictly out of bounds.

REG: I don't think it's women, sir.

CHARLES: It's mine. I wear it.

GILES: Bless my soul! What for?

CHARLES: My part in the show, sir. Female impersonation.

STEVE: We all do, sir.

GILES: You're the new man, aren't you?

STEVE: Sarnt Flowers, sir.

GILES: Settling in?

STEVE: Yes, thanks very much.

GILES: Alright. No perfume on guard duty, eh? No mufti either. Properly dressed, fixed bayonets. But – [*To* CHARLES.] Well done, Sergeant. That's the kind of keenness we like to see, isn't it, Mister Drummond?

REG: Company, fall out!

[*He goes and* REG *comes straight to audience. Cloth down behind him.*]

REG: Talk about the three monkeys! He's the lot rolled into one.

Bum-boys crawling out the woodwork and he doesn't even see. Still, I got rather more pressing problems. Such as what to do about our pet spy from the Special Investigation Branch.

SCENE NINE

Harmony Time.

Cloth flown, black out. Single torchlight from beneath. KEVIN *sings to the tune of 'Greensleeves', lyrically arranged so that only the words are coarse.*

KEVIN: There was a dusky Eurasian maid,
          In old Bombay she plied her trade
          And in Calcutta and in Madras
          And by special request up the Khyber Pass.

[*Other torches now light the faces of* TERRI, CHARLES, LEN, ERIC. *They form a male voice choir.*]

CHOIR: Black velvet was full of joy
          For every British soldier boy.
          She guaranteed to please
          And the most that it cost you was five rupees.

LEN: There came a soldier-boy fully grown
          Who till that moment had held his own.
          And though he'd served on several fronts
          He'd never seen action on ladies once.

ALL: Black velvet had great allure
          For such a private, so young and pure.
          She took him well in hand
          And showed him the way to the promised land.

ERIC: She took off all her seven veils
          And then she told him she came from Wales
          And how she'd seen the Forth Bridge one day
          While gazing out across Tiger Bay.

ALL: Meanwhile she softly read
          The Khamasutra from A to Z
          And after that was done
          They started again at chapter one.

CHOIR: She demonstrated the clinging vine
            And quickly taught him the sixty-nine
            She showed him some of the ways there are
            That a lady can draw on a man's cigar

[*Lights have come up on* SYLVIA's *room in Singapore. Window with city view, two doorways, one bead-curtained, other with closed door.* STEVE *and* SYLVIA *are naked in bed, making love. At the end of the song the* CHOIR *goes off.*]

STEVE: These bruises. I want to kiss them better.

SYLVIA: They don't hurt any more.

STEVE: How did you get them?

SYLVIA: Don't you know?

[*He doesn't answer, shakes head.*]

For answering back at the dress-rehearsal.

[*He stares. Pause.*]

From Reg.

STEVE: Reg *hit* you?

SYLVIA [*laughing*]: It wasn't the first time.

STEVE: Just for arguing about a dress?

SYLVIA: He was afraid I was going to say why so many costumes were signed for and paid for by the Army but never seemed to appear on stage.

STEVE [*after another pause*]: Well?

SYLVIA: Well. They were used in Reg's sideline.

STEVE: Sideline?

SYLVIA: One of his sidelines. Boy prostitutes. There's a brisk demand for them from the British, the Americans, the Aussies.

STEVE: Boys wear frocks when they – ?

SYLVIA: Mine are probably too large for the smaller boys. But they'd fit young teen-agers.

STEVE: What are his other sidelines?

SYLVIA [*shrugs*]: Import-export. Thai silk, jade, works of art looted from Buddhist temples, gun-running, opium –

STEVE: Gun-running? Come on, Sylvia –

SYLVIA: I thought you knew all this.

STEVE: Me? Why should *I* know?

SYLVIA: *Reg* thinks you know. Aren't you in Intelligence?

STEVE: I was. But I don't know anything about gun-running.

SYLVIA: Only to protect his various interests at first and to help him with his extortion and so on but then he saw there was a steady demand from the Communists. So he formed a partnership with a captain in the ordinance corps. They supply the Commies from the armoury in the transit camp.

STEVE: How d'you know this?

SYLVIA: He uses this place to meet his clients and associates and I have to entertain them. I get sent out when they talk business but I hear from the kitchen when he shouts. They use different transport all the time. Last week they took the Major's staff-car to make a delivery on the mainland. On the way back the driver went into a –

STEVE [*joining in*]: Tree on the Bukit Timah Road. Yes. We must tell somebody. We must stop him.

SYLVIA: He'd get you first if you breathed a word. He'd kill us both.

STEVE: We can't let him go on selling guns to the enemy. And I won't stand for him knocking you about.

SYLVIA: That's been going on for two years now. I'm used to it.

STEVE: Well, I'm not. And I won't have him bullying the girl I love.

SYLVIA: Love? Oh, come on, Steve, pull the other.

STEVE: I've told you a dozen times in the last hour how much I love you.

SYLVIA: But every boy says that when he's doing jig-jig.

STEVE: Does he?

SYLVIA: Don't you? Don't you usually?

STEVE: This was my first time.

SYLVIA: Good grief. My young virgin.

    [*She kisses him.*]

    [*Westminster Chimes sound the hour.*]

    Hey, listen, that's six o'clock.

STEVE: The lorry leaves at half-past. We better get dressed.

SYLVIA: Where are we playing tonight?

STEVE: Royal Airforce Base at Changi.

    [*They begin dressing in clothes that are strewn on the bed and chairs.*]

SYLVIA: Whenever I hear the Westminster Chime from St

Andrew's Cathedral I imagine I'm in England.

STEVE: How badly d'you want to go?

SYLVIA: Mummy and I talked of nothing else. Just think, she never even saw the Oxford-Cambridge Boat Race except on newsreels.

STEVE: But I mean not just visit. Do you want to stay forever?

SYLVIA: Of course I do.

STEVE: Then – the answer's easy.

SYLVIA: Easy?

STEVE: Easy as falling off a log.

    [*Partly dressed, he now sings like Fred Astaire.*]

        I've just had an inspiration,

        The solution's clear to me.

        Take it as an invitation

        And it's marked R.S.V.P.

SYLVIA: Nothing is so fine or so divine as being able to say yes

        But until she's heard the question how can any lady acquiesce?

STEVE: Come, I want you to lead me a dance!

        Why don't you give our rhythm a chance?

        Our partnership could be something big,

        You've already taught me to do the jig-jig,

        And now that I know how lovely it feels,

        Let's show the world a clean pair of heels.

        Please answer, darling, don't leave me in doubt.

        It's better far than sitting this life out.

    [*The music continues, repeating the chorus while they talk and finish dressing.*]

SYLVIA: You talk in riddles. Tell me what you mean.

STEVE: It's crystal clear. Be my partner. For life. Marry me.

SYLVIA: You'd do that for my sake?

STEVE: Hell, no. For mine. And when the time's up you'll come home with me to Fernleaze Crescent. And Reg will never hurt you again.

SYLVIA: He mustn't find out. He'll kill you if he knows. You must apply to Major Flack for an interview on personal grounds. That's in King's Regulations.

STEVE: I'll say, 'Permission to make Miss Morgan my partner, sah, so we can dance the jig-jig morning, noon and night, sah!'

SYLVIA: Don't you dare.

STEVE: 'Like Fred and Ginger, sah! We may never want to change partners again.'

SYLVIA: Already we're an elegant pair,
    In time we'll both be floating on air.
    Here's some tuition that never fails,
    Put on your top hat, your white tie, and tails,
    And dance, as long as the orchestra plays
    Quick-stepping to the end of our days,
    We'll show the others what love's all about.
    It's better far than sitting this life out.

[*During the reprise of the music she teaches him some new steps, using sticks and top hats from the tin trunk. At the end they go off as they sing.*]

BOTH: It's better far than sitting this life –

STEVE: I'm your partner –

SYLVIA: I'll be your wife –

BOTH: Better far than sitting this life out.

[SYLVIA *and* STEVE *go, as* REG *appears watching them. The tabs close.*]

SCENE TEN

Our Sergeant-Major.

REG *speaks to himself.*

REG: I should have known! Our Bonnie Black Madrassi's always been one to mix business and pleasure. She not only contacts their intelligence agent but lets him slip her a length into the bargain. Excuse my French but I'm under pressure. [*Suddenly shouts.*] Lee! I bet they think they've got me over a barrel. Well, you watch it, Sergeant Flowers, don't go up any dark alleys. [*Shouts.*] Cheng!

[LEE *has appeared other way.* REG *is startled to find him.*]

Ah, Lee! Harkee. Missee Morgan shop me to police. Me no can

go my flat, no can go Missee's room. Police search my billet too but you got my revolver, yes?

[LEE *nods.*]

Okay. You blingee me chop-chop.

[CHENG *has come on.* LEE *now goes.*]

Cheng, Special Investigation Branch think they got me by short and curlee. But me ex-copper. Missee Morgan have to get her knees velly brown to catch me.

[*Then, taking out handerkerchief to wipe palms, he speaks again to himself.*]

As you were, her knees *are* brown! She's brown all over. Except for where she's black and blue. That was an error, I see that now, but I was provoked. I won't have pushy tarts on my patch.

[*Becomes aware of* CHENG *watching and waiting.*]

Listen! You tell your Commie boss: if police catch me, me spillee beans. Savvy? Your boss catch plenty trouble.

[LEE *reappears with revolver, gives it to* REG.]

Good boy, Lee. You my friend. You both my friends. We together. [*He loads the gun while talking.*] Your people in jungle need me keep quiet. Me know plenty, can tell plenty. But you all help me hold tongue. Number One Job: Sergeant spy go on guard tonight but maybe he not come off, okay? Softee softee catchee monkey. Number Two, we deal with Missee.

[*Begins to talk to himself again.*]

What made you shop me, Sylvia? Just the bruises? That's only my way. I'd have taken you home to see your grannie in Swansea . . . I would! But now –

[*Recovers, speaks to Chinese.*]

So tell your boss I need your help and see me bimeby.

[*Shakes hands with each and smiles. Then goes.*
Chinese percussion: LEE *and* CHENG *look at each other. Then* LEE *quickly gestures to* CHENG *to follow* REG. LEE *goes other way.*
Darkness.
Sound of heavy rain, nocturnal animals. Long lightning flash reveals figure in bush-hat and monsoon cape on guard duty. Leans rifle against tree and brings out torch to read from a letter.]

STEVE: Dear Heather, in your last missive you remarked how much you envied me here in the lovely tropical sunshine. As I seem to remember you being top of our class in geography –

[*A nearby whistle makes him look to far side of stage.*]

Hullo? Anyone there? I mean, who goes there?

[*No answer. He returns to letter.*]

Perhaps you will recall that Singapore's climate is characterised by far heavier rainfall than you ever get in Fernleaze Crescent. Tonight, for example –

[*Whistle again.* STEVE *moves a few paces towards it and behind him* LEE *comes on and takes his rifle and goes.* STEVE *returns to letter and place.*]

Tonight, for example, I am on guard duty in a virtual deluge, which means standing under a tree with a rifle and fixed bayonet for two hours at a time –

[REG *has appeared upstage and approaches* STEVE, *holds revolver towards him. Another whistle makes* REG *hesitate and turn as* LEE *runs from behind* STEVE *and as* REG *turns back he is run through by the bayonet. He falls with a groan.*]

Halt, who goes there?

[STEVE *looks for gun, finds it missing, shines torch in* LEE'S *face.*]

Friend or foe?

[CHENG *comes other side and calls to* LEE. *They go off into jungle.*]

Halt or I – . . . blow my whistle! [*Moves after them but falls over* REG'S *body.*] Who's that? Reg! What's up?

REG: Bastard!

STEVE: You hurt? [*Touches him, finds wound, looks at bloody hand.*] Christ! . . . get you what? . . . who won't get you? Don't talk any more, I'll call for help. [*Goes to side, shouts.*] Love! Sergeant Love! Anyone, come here, quick!

[*He blows piercing whistle, returns to* REG, *who's still muttering.*]

What you doing creeping about in the dark? Who knifed you? The SIB? . . . What's the SIB got to do with it?

[ERIC *comes on, naked but for boots but with gun.*]

ERIC: What's the palaver? Swindon, is that you?

STEVE: Love, over here! What you doing bollock-naked?

ERIC: I've been standing in the monsoon rain trying to cure my prickly heat.

STEVE: Look, the Sergeant-Major's hurt. Help me carry him to the guard-room.

340

ERIC: What? Hullo, Chiefy . . . he's talking . . . what's he saying?
. . . what's the S.I.B.?

STEVE: Take his feet.

ERIC: He's bleeding. Lord, he's covered in blood.

STEVE: Stop nattering, for Christ's sake!

ERIC: I can hardly see with all this rain on my glasses. Alright,
Chiefy, nil desperandum . . . you'll be alright.

[*They carry him off into the darkness.*]

SCENE ELEVEN

Lest We Forget.

Rain stops. March beat on drum. Bright light. LEN *marches on, KD,
carrying clipboard, wearing black armband.*

LEN: Right, guard of honour, form up, stand easy, but pay
attention. Major Flack has detailed me as senior NCO to be i/c
the cortège. I only want to say one thing before we fetch him from
the mortuary. Remember, this is a military funeral and will be
tantamount to a church parade. So best behaviour, mind. No
acting like cunts in the House of The Lord. Squad, attention,
right turn, quick march, hef, right, hef, right . . .

[*Bare stage.* LEE *and* CHENG *come on upstage with shovels and
prepare a grave-trap.* TERRI *comes on as* LEN *goes off. He wears
Officer's KD with arm-band.*]

TERRI: We were all ordered on that parade. I thought of wearing
the little black number from our Latin-American Medley but no,
it had to be the full captain's drag with only a discreet arm-band.
I chose the fairly butch day-slap, no rouge or lipstick and the
merest suspicion of eye-shadow. Well, funerals and weddings
play havoc with mascara.

[*The drum starts again, now muffled. Slow-marching with a rifle.
The coffin is draped with the Union Jack.*]

And as soon as the Tiller Girls carried her in there wasn't a dry
eye in the cemetery.

[GILES *follows KD, with sword at present. Bearers turn upstage and place the coffin over the trap.* SYLVIA *is last, also in black. All arrive at trap as the bearers lower the coffin on ropes.*]

When the padre said 'In the midst of life we are in death', I thought well, many a true word spoken in jest.

GILES: In sure and certain hope of the resurrection to eternal life, through our Lord Jesus Christ . . .

[LEN *fires a round into the air.* TERRI *puts hands on ears.*]

TERRI: They always do that, apparently, when some queen's given her all on active service. I said, well I've done that many a time and never got more than a port-and-lemon.

[*He goes upstage to join the funeral group. Mourners throw earth on coffin. Muffled drum resumes and the bearers slow-march away.* LEN *brings flag and men bring poles. Chinese shovel earth into the trap.* GILES *comes down to address audience as lights go and cloth comes down.*]

GILES: We mourn the loss of our comrade-in-arms. Both as a man and a Company Sergeant-Major, Mr Drummond deserved the admiration of us all. Not least in his attention to detail. Nothing was too trivial, be it in the prevention of rabies, the insubordination of a native bearer or the detection of women's perfume in the men's ablutions. He was not, by his own admission, a God-fearing man. Indeed, fear was not in his nature. But in his care for you young men, his concern that none of you be corrupted by waste or idleness, he retained many qualities from his previous service as a London bobby: dependability, discipline, devotion to duty. This devotion it was that led to his savage murder, for it was he who went out in heavy rain to inspect the guard and came instead upon the gang of Communistic Chinamen who knifed him.

[*He pauses, clears his throat, moves and resumes.*]

It should not have needed this atrocity to awaken us to our danger but it has. Like the British here in Forty-One, Forty-Two; drowsily playing cricket on a lawn beside a Gothic Cathedral. And if you'd said 'But look here, you should be arming yourselves, the yellow men are on the way', they'd have answered, 'My dear chap, Britannia rules the waves, remember. If their tinpot ships try to sail into Singapore, our great guns will pick them off like pigeons'. Well, as you know, our friends from Tokyo came the other way. Down through the mainland riding bikes. Across the causeway, ting-a-ling, 'velly solly, no more clicket now'. It's not funny, sergeant! Let us give thanks to God for this ghastly warning. Heaven be praised we've heard the bicycle bells in time. And look here, it makes no odds that this is a song-and-dance unit. Never send to know for whom the bells toll. They toll for *thee*. Me. All of us.

GILES: Behold the army of the Prince of Peace
               Conquering that his kingdom may increase
               Taking to some distant Asian shore
               His cleansing and redemption evermore.

ALL: Many a laughing savage lives and dies
               In ignorance of Jesus' sacrifice
               And sun-kissed children swing beneath the palms
               Hid from the mercy-mercy-mercy of his loving arms.

STEVE [*while the company goes on humming hymn-tune*]: Dear Everyone at Fifty-Six, I'm sorry to hear from Dad that the spirit of post-war idealism hasn't lasted. I still believe education is the only hope for the world though, of course, in the light of experience, it won't be nearly as easy as I once imagined. If one genius may paraphrase another, there are more things in Heaven and earth than are dreamt of in Fernleaze Crescent.

ALL: Fight! until men and women are all freed
               From every primitive, enslaving creed,
               Then shall each soldier sheath his holy sword
               And all mankind surrender to the Lord.
               Amen.

ACT TWO

SCENE ONE

Noël, Noël.

TERRI *comes before tabs wearing DJ, carrying cigarette holder, and sings the following.*

TERRI: Dear whomever it may concern at the BBC,
   Pass this letter to the brains trust very urgently.

   Throughout the war we soldiered on
   When almost every hope had gone
   And pinned our flagging faith to Vera Lynn.
   We turned our railings into tanks
   And smiled politely at the Yanks
   When all they sent across was Errol Flynn.
   But when the lights went on we saw the vict'ry was a sham,
   The lion's share turned out to be a smaller slice of Spam.
   The bluebirds came one dreary day,
   Looked at Dover and flew away
   And grim spectators murmured 'Why can't I?'
   They might go down to the sea in ships
   But that's forbidden by Stafford Cripps
   And the nightingale in Berkeley Square can only sit and cry:

CHORUS: Could you please inform us who it was that won the war?
   The outcome isn't certain, heaven knows.
   Now everyone's so keen to put the Germans on their feet,
   For apparently
   The majority
   Are really rather sweet.
   Meanwhile back in Britain we're still lining up in rows
   To buy enough to keep ourselves alive.

So could you please inform us how we came to lose the
    war
That we won in nineteen-forty-five?

Land of Clement Attlee
Where the teeth are free!

2ND VERSE: Our former wealth is going to
    Augment the Inland Revenue
    And though our situation might seem hard
    At least you needn't work these days,
    The Ministry of Labour pays
    You well, provided someone's stamped your card.
    The National Health is failing fast and no one gives a
      fig,
    The corpse will look delightful in a newly-issued wig.
    Our image for posterity
    Is one of grim austerity,
    The socialist nirvana's on the way:
    New ministries proliferate
    Whose function is to allocate
    To everyone his fair and proper share of sweet F.A.

    So – could you please inform us how we came to lose
      the peace?
    Perhaps it's best to be the losing side,
    Now that the Americans are sponsoring the Japs,
    Taking the view
    That but for a few
    They're awfully decent chaps.
    Such a strange development is wounding to our pride
    The countrymen of Wellington and Clive.
    So Bevin only knows how Britain came to lose the
      peace
    When she won in nineteen-forty-five
    Four, three, two, one,
    Yes *won* in nineteen-forty-five?

[TERRI *goes. Tabs rise or part.*]

SCENE TWO

Kernel of the Knuts.

Tabs go up on a backcloth of office wall, featuring large map of Malaya and photo of George the Sixth. Plain desk and two chairs. CHENG *is onstage pouring tea into cup.* GILES *comes from side, addresses us:*

GILES: Why did we lose the peace? I can answer that question. There was never a peace to lose. There was only a temporary truce and a slight change of enemy. No sooner had the Yanks exploded that contraption than bands of agitators turned from killing Japs to killing us. Well, now at last it's official – 'an emergency' they're calling it but everyone knows it's the start of The Third World War. Soon as –

[LEE *comes on with* STEVE, *who salutes.*]

STEVE: Sergeant Flowers, sir.

GILES: Ah, yes. Stand easy. I'd offer you tea but it's China.

STEVE: I like China tea, sir.

GILES: Ming! Another cup.

[CHENG *goes.*]

Sit down.

[STEVE *does.*]

I understand the tour of Singapore Island is being well-received.

STEVE: They seem to like it, yessir.

GILES: No accounting for taste. But then I'm no judge. Last time I saw a show was – what? – 1935. Puerile drivel. Once saw half a film and walked out. Can't conceive why anyone wastes their time with it when they might be reading Bunyan or the Bard.

[CHENG *returns with cup and pours for both.*]

Or learning to tell one constellation from another. One bird from another. Most of them don't know a wren from a tit.

STEVE: Sir.

[GILES *sits, looks at papers on desk.*]

GILES: Thank you, Ming. Glowing reports on you as company manager. Miss Morgan, for instance, says you grow more capable every day. Captain Dennis particularly praises the way you've handled the business end. Even Sergeant Bonny, as far as I can make out from his semi-literate scrawl, confirms your qualities of leadership. Now. As you know there's a war on.

STEVE: You mean the state of emergency?

GILES: That's softly-softly officialese. The Communists used to call themselves the Malayan People's Anti-Japanese Army; now it's the Anti-British army. What's that if not a declaration of war? I immediately applied for posting to an active command. I want to serve my God, my King and my country. Are you a Christian?

STEVE: I was in the choir for a time, sir.

GILES: Churchgoing family?

STEVE: My father manages the local co-op. He believes more in fair shares, moderation.

GILES: What do you believe in?

STEVE: Well, Education, first, sir, then –

GILES: Not good enough. Why don't you sign on with Christ? Oh, I know what you're going to say, you're going to say 'Yes, but look here, I didn't ask him to go and die for me on the cross like that.'

STEVE: Well, sir, I didn't. I wasn't even born.

GILES: Be your age, sergeant, look beyond your nose. You'd better start believing in something. We'd *all* better. Because *they* do. The Russians, the Chinese, the Malayan People's Anti-British Army. *What* d'you think?

STEVE: Sir?

GILES: *What* do they believe in?

STEVE: Equality, sir? Fair shares? Social justice?

GILES: Exactly. Pie in the sky. Jam tomorrow. Take equality. Think of Sergeant Bonny. Look at Bonny's handwriting. Visualise Bonny's brain. Out of the sewers of Birmingham into the jungles of Malaya. Backbone of the army, of course, loyal to a fault, obedient, dependable. But is Stalin going to give him command of a division out of a belief in equality. Is he? Yes or no?

STEVE: Well, sir, what Marx actually said was from each according to his ability . . .

GILES: No's the answer. Because Uncle Joe is a wily old bounder and Bonny's as dim as a nun's night-light. He might just let him command a latrine. And indeed so would I. No more. So much for equality, a notion by which millions of child-like people are led into prison-camps. Millions of Bonnys. And make no mistake, they must be led one way or another. Either into Siberia or the Kingdom of Heaven.

STEVE: I think, sir, that if education begins early enough –

GILES: You can't educate what isn't there. The Bonnys of this world must be *told*. They *want* to be. Form fours. Present Arms. Stand easy. And someone has to tell them. Me, of course. Or Mister Drummond. Or since his murder perhaps you.

STEVE: Me, sir?

GILES: Our unit's strength is short of one sergeant-major. I can apply for a new sergeant-major or I can make you up to that rank. How d'you feel about sharing the burden of command?

STEVE: Sorry, sir. Are you –

GILES: I'm offering you a crown. D'you want time to think it over?

STEVE: No, sir. I'd like to help – like to share the burden, sir –

GILES: Well done, well done! I shan't pretend this isn't going to be a tough assignment. We may well get into a spot of bother up-country.

STEVE: You mean because of HQ saying we've got to charge admission?

GILES: What?

STEVE: The shows have always been free before, sir, the men may not take to it kindly. I know it's only a few cents but –

GILES: I said *trouble*, son. Bandits . . . Communistic Terrorists . . .

STEVE: But since The Emergency started –

GILES: Since the war broke out –

STEVE: Yessir – isn't our tour confined to the coastal area? [*Points to map.*] Kuala Lumpur, Ipoh, Penang, Butterworth, not many bandits there, sir.

GILES: Look here, sergeant, it may have been someone's idea of a joke to give me command of a concert-party but command it I do and our itinerary is no business of the desk-wallahs at GHQ – I'm reverting to the one worked out by Sarnt-Major Drummond.

STEVE: Sarnt-Major – ?

GILES: Precisely. Good thinking. What you and the SIB have told me since his death makes it clear he was using the concert-party as a decoy for illegal arms-trafficking. Well, what if the show's *still* a decoy?

STEVE: You mean set a trap?

GILES: Precisely. With the troupe as bait.

STEVE: But we're not an armed unit, sir.

GILES: We will be – armed and ready. How's that for a Jungle Jamboree, eh? Somewhere here – [*Pointing to map.*] after the Cameron Highlands. That's where we'll flush them out of cover. So we'll play to everyone – not only British but Malays, Gurkhas, Indians –

[CHENG *has been watching and listening to all this.*]

STEVE: Will they understand the show, d'you think?

GILES: Give them a splash of colour, plenty of movement. You've got a conjurer, haven't you?

[CHENG's *gone off with tea.* GILES *locks paper in drawer.*]

STEVE: Yessir.

GILES: Dancing girls?

STEVE: One, sir. Miss Morgan. Matter of fact, that's why I applied for this personal interview. To ask your permission to marry her.

GILES: The Anglo girl?

STEVE: Yes.

GILES: Handsome.

STEVE: I think so, sir.

GILES: Women of mixed blood often are. Early on. Snag is, they tend to put on weight rather soon. How old is she?

STEVE: Twenty-eight.

GILES [*whistles amazement*]: That almost certainly means thirty. When you're thirty she'll be forty. Middle aged. And, of course, they find it difficult settling down in the UK. Climate's not what they're used to. They don't like the food.

STEVE: Oh, she's very British, sir. Her Dad was in the Welsh Fusiliers.

GILES: Welsh and Indian? Combustible mixture. Don't say anything to her till you're perfectly sure in your own mind.

STEVE: I've already asked her, sir. And been accepted.

GILES [*sighs*]: She's after a free trip home, you see. Quite a consideration. On the other hand, they don't take an engagement as seriously as English girls. Remember you're going to have your

work cut out upcountry. You'll need mens sana in corpore sano.
If you understand me?

STEVE [*after a pause*]: A sound mind in a healthy body.

GILES: Yes but do you catch my drift?

STEVE: I'm not sure, sir.

GILES: Difficult. I have no son. Daughters, yes, but my wife
handled all that, of course. How's your French?

STEVE: Alright up to School Certificate.

GILES: Alors . . . vous savez . . . physiquement les femmes
orientales sont très belles, très mignonnes, n'est ce pas?

STEVE: Biensure, mon commandant.

GILES: Mais il y a toujours la possibilité d'attraper les maladies . . .

STEVE: Maladies?

GILES: Les maladies d'amour.

STEVE: Illnesses of love? Ah, oui, love-sickness.

GILES: No, that's mal d'amour. I was using amour in its other
sense, of Eros or Venus.

STEVE: The illnesses of . . . I'm sorry, sir . . .

GILES: Look, all I mean to say is: mull it over while we're out on
tour. See a bit less of her for a few weeks. Meanwhile I'll get the
wheels in motion for your crown. Wong!

[LEE *comes forward and opens door for* STEVE.]

I needn't tell you this is all top secret. Strictly between the two
of us.

STEVE: Entre nous, sir.

GILES: Good thinking.

STEVE: Sir! And thank you.

GILES: Thank you, Sergeant. Command can be lonely.

[STEVE *goes.* LEE *remains, hands* GILES *his cap and he comes
downstage.*]

Dear Margaret, there's a young soldier here I'd like to invite
down to the mill-house when I get home. Decent, intelligent boy,
very much the kind I'd have liked as a son, had God so willed.
He's in a spot of bother at the moment but I mean to help him
out of that. As I would my own. [*Moving off, putting on cap.*] How
splendid your roses winning first prize again this year . . .

[*He goes.*]

SCENE THREE

A Tricycle Made For Three.

Cloth flown, furniture removed by CHENG *in black. On to clear stage with night lighting* LEE *drives a trishaw in which* TERRI *and* SYLVIA *are sitting. Pulls up centre and waits. They get out. Piano plays ballad accompaniment to this scene.*

SYLVIA: Terri!

TERRI: Good night, lovie.

SYLVIA: Thank you. Thank you so much!

[*She kisses him and hugs him.*]

TERRI: My dear, what have I done? Given you a lift home in a trishaw? You mustn't sell your favours so cheap.

SYLVIA: Oh good heavens, it isn't that! I'm thanking you for bringing Steve and me together and for making me so happy.

TERRI: Oh, there again I was only being the good fairy. I rather fancied her first of all but baby-snatching's not my line and she had so much to learn . . .

SYLVIA: Oh, didn't he? Even now I keep on finding how little he knows. When I told him I was going to have his baby, for instance, he asked me how I could tell. D'you know, he thought babies came out of the woman's stomach? Out of her navel!

TERRI: Feminine hygiene's still no part of an English education.

SYLVIA: Imagine at twenty years of age not knowing that.

TERRI: But anyway she understands now?

SYLVIA: I think so, yes. I did some drawings.

TERRI: And everything's alright?

SYLVIA: He's going to see the Major soon. And, listen, d'you think it's a good idea, I suggested Steve should ask him to be Best Man?

TERRI: Major Flack? Why not indeed?

SYLVIA: And how would you feel about giving the bride away? I've no living relatives here.

TERRI: If I must, but I shan't enjoy it.

SYLVIA: Why ever not?

TERRI: I've only just found you, a partner in a million. And next we know you'll be standing there with a swollen belly saying 'I will' to a hushed congregation.

351

SYLVIA: Will you do it or no?

TERRI: I certainly won't let anyone else.

SYLVIA: Thank you again. [*Kisses him.*] For everything.

TERRI: Good night, duckie.

[SYLVIA *goes.*]

Now what shall I wear? The white suit from the Jolson Medley would be discreet. Or perhaps the dark dress with the half-veil. Tremendously dignified with everyone whispering 'Who *is* she?' And 'It's Greer Garson!'

[LEE *waiting with trishaw rings bell.* TERRI *turns to him.*]

Thank you, Ada. [*He climbs aboard.*]

Your Fairy Queen's done all the good she may
So Fleet Club, sweetie, by the shortest way!

[LEE *rings bell and drives off*, TERRI *waving and blowing kisses to us.*]

SCENE FOUR

Privates on Parade.

STEVE *marches on with S-M insignia, leading squad all in KD:* LEN, KEVIN, CHARLES *and* ERIC. *Drumbeat as they march.*

STEVE: By the front – quick march. Eff, right, eff, right, eff, right. Squad – halt. Left – turn. Order – hype!

GILES: Stand the men easy, Sarnt-Major.

STEVE: Squad, stand at – ease. Stand easy.

GILES: The tour of Singapore is now over and the time has come for us to go up-country. Bring a bit of song-and-dance to those chaps who suddenly find themselves chasing bandits in the ulu. Ulu. That's the jungle. But one or two of you might be saying: 'Yes, that's all very well but half a mo, here's the old man telling us to go up-country, likely to get in a spot of bother with the bandits, while he's here in a cushy billet. Seems a rum kind-of a go.' And you'd be right. But I'm not staying here. I'm coming *with* you. I dare say one or two of you are thinking, 'Just a tick, what use is he gonna be in a show? Reckon by the looks of him he's got a tin ear and two left feet.' And that again would be good thinking. You must be able to look after yourselves if there's any trouble. And that's where I can help. During the next few days I'll be putting you through a refresher course in basic training: small arms drill, grenade throwing, unarmed combat, plus as much of a notion of conditions in the ulu as I can give you before the off. So carry on sarnt-major.

STEVE: Sir. Right. Get fell in. Squad! Squad – 'shun. Right – dress. From the right number!

LINE-UP: One – two – three – four.

STEVE: Slope – hype. By the right, quick – march. Eff, right, eff, right, eff, right. About turn. About turn. About turn. Eff, right, eff, right, eff, right. Squad – halt. Left turn.

[GILES *salutes and everyone sings a rousing march, with martial choreography.*]

ALL: Come, see the privates on parade,
         You'll say: how proudly they're displayed.
         And when we hear the music of a milit'ry band
         You'll be amazed how smartly we can take our stand.
         For when the bugle sounds attack
         Up goes the good old Union Jack.
         You may as well surrender when you hear our battle-cry
         There'll be no more escaping when we raise our weapons high
         And in the vict'ry cavalcade
         You'll see the privates on parade.

[*Much countermarching to music and they exit leaving* GILES *who detains* LEN.]

GILES: Sarnt Bonny, a word with you. As you know, you're in line for another stripe. I've been watching you on the square. Well done. But leadership also calls for qualities of tact, diplomacy, understanding.

LEN: I ain't never gone after promotion –

GILES: So let's suppose we're faced with a tricky situation here and now, shall we? See how we'd cope. Here's a platoon of squaddies lined up and you've got to announce some tragic news to just one man. Here he is in Singapore and home in England his mother has suddenly, unexpectedly died. How d'you break it to him?

LEN [*after a pause*]: What's his name, sir?

GILES [*impatiently*]: Not important. Charlie Farnes-Barnes. Come on, Bonny, thinking on your feet, another of the qualities of leadership.

LEN: Private Farnes-Barnes, one step forward march. Right, son, pay attention, your mother's dead.

GILES: Hell's bells, man, you'll have him in sick bay suffering from shock. Think of something more subtle, a roundabout approach. Indirect.

LEN [*after thinking*]: Right, squad, pay attention. All those men going to see their mothers next time they're on leave, one pace forward march – where the fuck are you going, Farnes-Barnes?

[*The men march on, now with* TERRI *and* SYLVIA.]

STEVE: Ready, aim, fire!

[*Gun goes off.*]

ALL: We are the C of E Brigade.

STEVE: Fire! [*Bang!*]

ALL: We're marching on a new crusade.

STEVE: Fire! [*Bang!*]

[*No lyrics to next couplet but dialogue over marching.*]

TERRI [*to* STEVE]: Vada the little tiaras, duckie.

STEVE: What?

TERRI: The crowns on your sleeve.

STEVE: Oh.

TERRI: Bona. Suits you.

ALL: You'll need a piece of four-by-two
          To get a really good pull-through.
          The enemy's resisting and the trumpet sounds advance
          They'd best lay down their arms because they haven't
            got a chance
          Faced with the cocksure cannonade
          Of the Privates on Parade.

[STEVE *puts them through paces as S-Major. Then they exit but* GILES *and* KEVIN *remain this time.*]

GILES: Cartwright!

KEVIN: Sir.

GILES: More to your liking, Cartwright?

KEVIN: What, sir?

GILES: More like being a soldier?

KEVIN: Oh. Do with a bit more jungle training, not so much bull.

GILES: All in good time.

KEVIN: We don't hold with bull in the R.A.F.

GILES: You were air crew, weren't you?

KEVIN: Navigator bomb-aimer. I joined under-age to get a crack at Jerry. Soon as I passed out flight-sergeant, ready to go on ops, old Adolf packs it in. Right, I thought to myself, see if we can't chalk up a few Nips. No sooner reach Ceylon than Tojo says *he* don't want to play no more. I put in for my release. I said, 'You want a navigator bomb-aimer to drive a lorry for three years?' Jesus Christ Almighty! A few weeks sooner I could have bombed Dresden.

GILES: A word to the wise, Flight Sergeant.

[*Sings.*]

> Wise soldiers generally refrain
> From taking Jesus' name in vain.
> One day you'll need to call him in the clamour of a war
> Then he could say 'Look here. You've often called on me before.
> I'm an extremely busy bloke.
> You shouldn't use my name in joke.'

ALL:
> And when we're standing on parade
> Each with his rifle and grenade
> You'll hear the sergeant cry:

STEVE:
> Presenting arms to the right!

SYLVIA:
> And all the girls declare 'They've never seen such a sight.'

ALL:
> To know that God is on our side
> Makes every private swell with pride.
> We'll press upon our enemy until he's in a funk

GILES:
> And show him it's no easy thing
> Resisting British spunk.

ALL:
> He'll feel the forceful fusillade
> Of the privates on parade.

[*Others come on, while music continues.* GILES *watches as they practise unarmed combat, assault course, swinging across on ropes, etc. At end* GILES *orders:*]

GILES: Right, well done, fall out, gather round.

> [*They obey, crouching downstage facing up, while the Malayan map cloth comes down and* GILES *briefs, using the map and his stick.*]

GILES: The Malayan peninsula is slightly smaller than England and Wales and four-fifths impenetrable jungle. Rich in game but also crawling with every kind of hazard – soldier ants, centipedes, scorpions, typhus ticks, leeches – and if *they* don't worry you the plants tear your clothes and the grass cuts like a saw. By day it's deathly quiet but at nightfall pandemonium breaks out as all these chaps get weaving on their various chores. Yet the odds are all you'll see will be a few fireflies or the eyes of a panther. Which might or might not be the signals of a Chinese terrorist.

TERRI: Major, I'm sure my contract stipulates we'll be doing the Number One Tour and keeping to the main roads. There's nothing about the jungle.

GILES: No need for alarm, Mr Dennis. We'll be following the route taken by the previous parties, the route planned by Mr Drummond. But: this country is a powder keg. Even the main roads are a death trap. Once we're on the mainland, we'll be in the front line. A theatre of war.

ALL: You may as well surrender when you hear our battle
            cry.
        There'll be no more escaping when we raise our
            weapons high.
        And in the vict'ry cavalcade
        You'll see the privates on parade

        We're SADUSEA
        And on the other hand we're glad to see
        You've come along tonight to . . .

        We've taken pains
        To see our show's the sort that entertains

        What can we do for the rest of the chorus?
        They know who we are, so they know . . .
        Entertains
        To see our show's the sort that entertains
        To see our show's the sort that entertains

Entertains
Entertains
S.A.D.U.S.E.A.
Song and Dance Unit, South East A . . . sia.

SCENE FIVE

The Midnight Choo-Choo.

Sounds of steam train heard and clouds of vapour blown about in flashing lights. Music represents labouring engine and whistle suggests departing train. All but REG, CHENG *and* LEE *enter in a row, working arms together like pistons. Gradually they accelerate, singing whistle sounds together and working way across the stage.*

They haul a truck representing a railway compartment: bench each side, table between, windows and corridor upstage.

LEE *and* CHENG *come on with large cards naming places on the journey: Jahore Bahru and Kluang. Others continue with Tampin, Kotan, etc. Perhaps the Malayan map has dropped in behind and their journey is traced by a moving spot.*

LEN, KEVIN, CHARLES *and* ERIC *occupy the benches, smoking, playing cards, etc.* LEE *in corridor wearing railway cap.*

LEN: Kiswasti you come, Johnny? You want dekko railway warrants? You go ekdum sergeant-major sahib juldi juldi. Doosrah compartment. Burra sahib keep warrants sub-cheese fucking sahibs and mem-sahib. You get pukka shifti, malam? Tikh-hai.
  [LEE *nods, goes. Noise of travelling train continues.*]
CHARLES: He was Malayan.
LEN: I know that.
CHARLES: They don't speak Hindustani.
KEVIN: *That* what it was?
LEN: Fucking understood anyroad.
KEVIN: You can't even speak the King's English.
LEN: I can speak the King's fucking English better than any Cockney fucker, now then!

KEVIN: Not without effing and blinding every other word.

CHARLES: Right. Time for another five minutes with the swear-box. [*Puts a small tin moneybox on table.*] You've got your small change out for cards. And remember I'm the referee, if I say it's swearing it is.

LEN: Already had this once today. I'm nearly fucking skint.

CHARLES: One.

LEN: Oh, fuck it.

CHARLES: Two.

[LEN *puts two coins in box.*]

LEN: Deal the cards so we don't have to talk.

[KEVIN *collects the pack.* ERIC *performs a strange movement: he shoots out one arm, displays wrist-watch, reaches into pocket and brings out cigarette-case and lighter. He takes out an imaginary lighter and lights it. Others watch.*]

CHARLES: What's that meant to be?

ERIC: What d'you *think*?

CHARLES: Some curious tropical variant of St Vitus' Dance?

ERIC: I'm working out a movement for when I'm back in Blighty, to display my Swiss watch, silver cigarette case and Ronson lighter all in one. I haven't yet included my Parker pen but all in good time . . .

CHARLES: I'd advise against adding any other movement. It already looks like an epileptic seizure.

ERIC: Practice makes perfect, Squire. And when you imagine me in rimless specs and a Harris Tweed jacket –

CHARLES: I've seen the jacket. I've seen you trying it on in the basha.

KEVIN: We've all seen you. Sitting there in your Chinese Harris Tweed jacket drinking lemonade.

CHARLES: That's what aggravates your prickly heat.

ERIC: I happen to think a little discomfort is easily borne for the sake of cutting a dash.

LEN: You look like something the cat's dragged in.

[*They laugh.*]

ERIC: Laugh away. The day I walk up Susan's garden path we'll see who's laughing –

KEVIN: How much this lighter cost you?

ERIC: Ten chips. Which you'll agree is rock-bottom for a genuine English Ronson.

KEVIN [*looking at it carefully*]: You read what it says on this genuine English Ronson? 'Made in British.' [*He laughs.*]

CHARLES: Oh, no. Love, you've done it again. It's Hong Kong imitation.

ERIC [*looking at lighter*]: Ruddy cheek! Well, anyway, they won't know the difference back home. I'll give it to Susan's Dad. Token of my esteem.

LEN: Here, look at that. All that fucking panic getting off I forgot this letter come for you this morning. That's your financée's hand-writing, ain't it?

CHARLES: Swearword.

[*LEN gives letter to ERIC, feeds coin into box.*]

ERIC: A New Malden postmark but it's not Susan's writing, no. Not her Dad's either.

[*During the following he opens and reads the letter.*]

LEN: What about dealing them sodding cards, Lambeth?

[*CHARLES rattles box.*]

LEN: Sodding?

[*CHARLES nods and LEN pays. And so on throughout scene.*]

KEVIN [*shuffling*]: Eh, Brum, how d'you get in this skive in the first place?

LEN: What? Entertainments? Ain't I never told you?

KEVIN: Elocution, wasn't it? Shakespeare? Or was it to clean out the crapper? I forget.

LEN: I come in as an accordionist. Piano-fucking-accordionist. I used to be with Al Fresco and his Piano-accordion Hooligans.

KEVIN: Go on.

LEN: Straight up.

KEVIN: You ain't really played with them, have you?

LEN: Ain't I never showed you the picture?

KEVIN: Picture?

LEN: Photograph.

[*He has been taking out wallet and now shows KEVIN.*]

There you are. Didn't believe me, did you?

KEVIN: This is just you on your own in the back-yard playing the accordion.

LEN: What d'you think it was going to be?

KEVIN: I thought it was going to be with Fresco's Accordion Hooligans.

LEN: I had to fucking practise, didn't I?

KEVIN: You aren't half a dopey sod. How d'you stand him, Charlotte?

CHARLES: I love him – so it's easy –

[*Becomes aware of* ERIC *staring at the letter.*]

What's the matter, is Susan alright? Who's the letter from?

ERIC: My mucker Roy Lawrence.

CHARLES: I remember. Billed himself as the Airman with the Flying Feet.

ERIC: I asked him to deliver the silk and lace for Susan's wedding dress.

CHARLES: Oh, yes. Did he manage it?

ERIC [*nods*]: She's going to marry *him* instead. 'Neither of us meant this to happen but we couldn't help ourselves. It is hard to put into words but when you come home I will explain everything.'

[*Puts down letter. Others silent.*]

I'll say he'll ruddy well explain everything. At the double, before he gets a bunch of fives where it hurts him most.

CHARLES: Now, come on, Eric, take it easy –

ERIC: I'll soon have this lot sorted out, never fear. Who do they think they are, what? Damned cheek! Couldn't help themselves? Why not, would you mind telling me?

[*He looks at the others as though expecting an answer. Train sounds continue.*]

KEVIN: Looks to me as though he's helped himself to quite a tidy slice.

[ERIC *takes off glasses and polishes with handkerchief.*]

ERIC: Here have I been keeping myself for her and all of a sudden, out of the blue, I get a mess-pot. And she doesn't even send it, she gets *him* to send it. She and I used to do our prep together . . . we were tennis partners . . . she assisted with the magic . . . and now she can turn me down for – . . . he never even went to a decent grammar school, just some wretched elementary . . .

[*Stops, bites lip, stands and makes to go.*]

CHARLES: Shall I make you some lemonade? You brought a tin of crystals?

[LEN *gives them to him.* ERIC *goes, taking letter. Silence for a moment, but for the train wheels.*]

LEN: Women? A load of cunts. [*Puts coins in tin.*]

[CHARLES *puts his hand on* LEN'S, *raises it to his lips and kisses it.*]

[*Train music and the line pistons across again, drawing off the compartment with steam and whistles. The music slows down to a halt.*]

[GILES *enters.*]

GILES: From Kuala Lumpur we went by road – a couple of jeeps, a fifteen hundredweight and a three-ton gharry. At the rear armed sentries, tail-boards down for a quick getaway in case of ambush. Bren guns loaded with actions cocked, mounted on the driver's cabin, raking the road ahead. Next stop, the Cameron Highlands. And then, the Ulu! I felt a familiar but almost forgotten tightening of the stomach. Years of boredom fell away like an old skin. Now that our lives were in danger, they suddenly became infinitely precious. I prayed for our safety and thanked Almighty God that at last the real show was beginning.

[*Chinese prompters bring on place-name cards: Kuala Kangar, Sungei Siput, Kampong Malang . . .*]

SCENE SIX

GILES *and* LEN *in frilly shirts plays guitars, etc,* TERRI *as Carmen Miranda sings:*

TERRI: Have you ever been – a
Down in Argentina?
Have you ever known zat special thrill?
How d'you like to mail a
Card from Venezuela?
You could find romance in old Brazil.
And in Valparaiso
Girls would roll their eyes so
That you could not tear yourself away.

Come and have a gala
Down in Guatamala,
The Latin-American way.

Come and spend a weeka
Down in Costa Rica,
Come and lose your heart in Vera Cruz.
Easy to catch a barracuda
Right by your hotel in Bermuda,
That's the way we chase away the blues.
Think how you could brag you are
Weekending in Nicaragua
Or wearing funny hats in Uruguay.
Kill a nice vicuna
Underneath the moon-a,
The Latin American way.

Every señorita
Welcome in the fleet-a
And she pray her favourite saint to bless.
Guys who rock the boat-a,
They won't get my vota,
I prefer American Express.
Down in old Havana,
Life is all mañana,
No-one work and everybody play.
How could you resist a
Weekend with Batista?
The Latin American way.

SCENE SEVEN

The North of Gongapooch.

*Hangings or screens represent an improvised dressing-room. A fold-up
table and chairs either side with make-up etc, single overhead light bulb,
clothes on rack. Hear the concert-party performing offstage.* CHARLES
is finishing his face in a hand-mirror. TERRI *enters as Miranda, tearing
off head-dress.*

362

TERRI: Well, I've played some number three touring-dates in my time but never anything to touch Kampong Uvula.

CHARLES: I don't remember coming here with Tropic Scandals.

TERRI: Terri Dennis thanks Gillian Flack for a most enjoyable engagement at His Majesty's, Tampon Kotex, with many happy memories of the star dressing-room.

CHARLES: And the lovely audience.

TERRI: Oh don't! Not a single white face, just row upon row of brave little Gurkhas. It's like staring at a pound of prunes.

CHARLES: They say they never take out their kukris without drawing blood.

TERRI: I've always wanted to put that to the test.

CHARLES: Oh, dear. Another double-entendre.

TERRI: Hello.

CHARLES: Well, there's nothing very funny about Gurkhas, is there? A race of mercenary savages who'll fight for the British against their fellow-Asians.

TERRI: My dear, is it your time of the month?

CHARLES: Don't you ever tire of changing he to she or calling men by women's names? There's nothing funny about being like this, either.

TERRI: Like what? Gay, you mean?

CHARLES: *Queer.* What's gay about it? Most men like women and most women like men. We're queer, Terri, queer as coots. And I don't think we should flaunt this cruel trick of nature. I think we should behave ourselves *more* than normal people. Your kind of promiscuity goes too far. At your age you should be settling down. There.

[*Pause.* TERRI *lights a cigarette, sits facing* CHARLES.]

TERRI: And of course you're safe in the arms of Jessica.

CHARLES: Sorry. Did it sound like that? My Salvationist background.

TERRI: You're safe for the time being but sooner or later you'll be on the boat, leaving hubby on the Equator. England, 1948, is a far cry from the Fleet Club, duckie. One lonely night you'll say a few flattering words to some nice chap in a cottage and next you know a cow of a magistrate's giving you three months.

CHARLES: I'm not going home. I'm signing on to stay with Len.

We've sworn to stay with each other, whatever happens.

TERRI: Not going on the stage then?

CHARLES: Well, tell me honestly, d'you think I've got a chance?

TERRI: One must have talent or looks or preferably both. I was never Nijinsky, but I was a pretty face.

CHARLES: And I'm not?

TERRI: The head in the middle's not bad.

CHARLES: Thank you. So I suspected. And as I'm no ornament I might as well be useful. I'm going back to male nursing.

TERRI: What about Len's wife?

CHARLES: She's not bothered, there's plenty of what she wants at Aldershot.

TERRI: Len's a lucky man.

CHARLES: I'm lucky too.

[STEVE *enters in the drag of a U.S. servicewoman.*]

STEVE: Where's Kevin? We're on.

TERRI: Thank your lucky stars you didn't fall for our new sergeant-major. He'd have put you in the family way and left you for some suck-off-antics with the Major.

CHARLES: Any British turned up yet?

STEVE: Still out on patrol. Where's Cartwright?

[STEVE *makes to go.*]

TERRI: Wouldn't you? Duckie?

STEVE: What you on about?

TERRI: Oh, come on, Ada. Ever since you got the tiaras on the sleeve she never sees you.

STEVE: Who?

TERRI: Who? My partner, the girl you wanted to marry, the one with the bun in the oven. All the time you should be with her she spends crying on auntie's shoulder.

STEVE: Since my crown, I hardly get a moment –

TERRI: Tell the truth, I've never thought dead man's shoes were at all *you*. What do you and the Major get up to together? People are beginning to *talk*.

STEVE: We're reading *Pilgrim's Progress*, alright?

TERRI: I'll tell Sylvia. Be a great comfort to her.

STEVE [*almost pleading*]: I'm only trying to do my best by everyone. Kevin!

[*Goes off.* CHARLES *remains. Looks at his face in glass, puts on a battered boater.* TERRI *goes on dressing.*]

SCENE EIGHT

Les Girls Encore.

SYLVIA, KEVIN *and* STEVE *sing an Andrews Sisters song in US Army uniforms.*

SYLVIA, KEVIN, STEVE:

    He was born in Oklahoma where the cowboys are,
    Traded in his saddle for an armoured car,
    He's got a new corral today,
    He rides a range that's far away
    And the whole Pacific knows,
    Out of all the GI Joes,
    He's the pistol-packing deputy of Okinawa.

    Ever since he handed in his sheriff's star,
    Drumming out a war-cry on his old guitar,
    He's still the fastest on the draw
    And in the jungle he's The Law.
    The Yellow folk all understand
    That he's sure to get his man.
    They call him pistol-packing deputy of Okinawa.

    O-k-i-n-a-w-a – Okinawa!

SCENE NINE

Even Their Relations Think They're Funny.

TERRI *enters in light suit as compere.*

TERRI: Thank you so much. Thank you for that nice little warm brown hand on our opening. So now you've seen a little of Costa

Rica, we've brought you the heart-aches and joys of an Atlantic convoy and we've heard from one of the girls who's waiting for you at home. Well, not *you*, perhaps – anyway now Deception with a Difference brought to you by Love the Magician. Or for those of you who speak Spanish. El Amor Brujo. Not a titter. As a matter of interest, how many of you even speak English?

GILES [*from audience*]: *I* speak English.

TERRI: Well, screw *you* for a start.

GILES: Please watch your language, Mister Dennis –

TERRI: Oh, you! Then you're the only one who's got the faintest idea what we're on about. No wonder it's so quiet.

GILES: They're enjoying it in their own way. They'll understand the conjuring. Carry on!

TERRI: Sir! Here she is then – Mean, Moody, Magnificent – Young-Love!

[ERIC *comes on wearing flowing gown, smoking cigarette. Stares at* TERRI *angrily but* TERRI *goes.* ERIC *does some passes, makes cigarette vanish, reappear, etc.*]

ERIC: The last time I did this trick was at Raffles Hotel, Singapore. I think. [*Takes silver spoon from pocket, looks at it.*] Yes, Raffles Hotel. As a matter of fact, this isn't my usual line at all. I'm an operatic tenor. I was trained abroad. All the neighbours made a collection. My favourite song is the Milkmaid's Song: We must all pull together.

GILES: Too much talk. Get on with it, man.

ERIC: Sir! This is known as the Russian Shuffle. Because, as you see, the cards are Russian from one end to the other. And now my assistant, Miss Morgan, will show you that there is nothing in the cylinder. [SYLVIA *re-enters in dress, bringing table and props, offers cylinder. He takes it from her and waves with magic wand.*] Completely empty. It's rather like a girl on a windy day. Now you see it, now you don't.

ERIC: No, sir. I give it two taps with the magic wand. Two taps – one hot, one cold – and hey presto –

[*The lights go out.*]

Ah, now there appears to be a slight technical hitch.

GILES: Oh dear! I'll go and have a look at the generator. I'll soon have it mended. Carry on conjuring.

ERIC: Hey presto, voilà! I should perhaps explain that at this moment I am producing a variety of coloured handkerchiefs from the apparently empty cylinder. Hm. Er.

[*Pause.*]

SYLVIA: The last time he did this trick . . .

ERIC: The last time I did this trick I had the audience in the palm of my hand. Which will give you some idea of the size of the audience.

[*Shriek of an animal in the jungle.*]

Observe also that during this trick my hand never leaves the end of my arm. And there they are, all tied together. Thank you. And now my assistant is going to come down amongst you for a volunteer –

SYLVIA: Don't be absurd, Eric! I wouldn't go near those fellows in the dark.

TERRI: Pack it in, love. I'll get the pianist to play something –

[*Lights on.* ERIC *is falling with the table. Props everywhere.* SYLVIA *and others help him clear them up.* TERRI *comes down.*]

And now may I have your attention for something a shade more serious?

[*The animal shrieks again.*]

Thank you, Ada. A dramatic recitation.

> By the old Moulmein Pagoda looking eastward to sea
> There's a Burma girl a-waiting and I know she thinks of me;
> For the wind is in the palm-trees and the temple-bells –

KEVIN [*entering*]: Excuse me.

TERRI: What? I'm trying to recite.

KEVIN: I've got an urgent police message.

TERRI: An urgent police message? Then read it this instant.

KEVIN [*reading note*]: Will the person known as Pharaoh last heard of two thousand years ago in Egypt, please go to the British Museum where his mummy's lying dangerously ill.

TERRI: Will you please get off the stage and permit me to continue. 'For the wind is in the palm-trees –'

[STEVE *comes on with a bucket.*]

Where are you off to?

STEVE: To see my brother.

TERRI: Where is he?

STEVE: He's in jail.

TERRI: What's the bucket for?

STEVE: To bail him out.

TERRI: I'm trying to give these little brown gentlemen a recitation. 'Come you back, you British soldier, come you back to Mandalay –'

[LEN *returns with bucket, wearing crinoline and wig.*]

Where are you going?

LEN: To milk a cow.

TERRI: In that wig?

LEN: No, in this bucket. [*Goes off, spilling water from bucket.*]

TERRI: Kindly leave the upturned tea-chests. 'For the wind is in the palm-trees and the temple bells they say –'

KEVIN: Bottle of truth, bottle of truth!

TERRI: What's that?

KEVIN: One drink of this and you must tell the truth!

TERRI: Let me try that . . . it's paraffin.

KEVIN: That's the truth!

[CHARLES *comes on as* KEVIN *goes off.*]

TERRI: 'And the temple bells they say –'

CHARLES: Excuse me –

TERRI: Excuse me, British soldier – no! D'you mind? I'm trying to recite poetry.

CHARLES: Poetry? Ah, poetry! 'The dog stood on the burning deck, The flames were leaping round his neck' – Hot dog!

TERRI [*desperate*]: Come you back, you British soldier –

KEVIN [*entering*]: Where's the Major?

TERRI: Where's the Major? I don't know, where *is* –

KEVIN: They're attacking the camp –

TERRI: I'm attempting to recite Kipling –

KEVIN: They're inside, I've seen them –

TERRI: I don't remember this, duckie, what's the –

[LEN *runs on, wearing crinoline.*]

LEN: They've knifed the fucking guard, the fucking Commies.

[*He turns to shout at audience as* LEE *and* CHENG *come on upstage with stens.*]

Bandit shoot Gurkha chowkidar –

[*Lights go out and in the darkness* LEE *and* CHENG *fire rapid bursts towards audience. Cries of alarm and pain from everyone onstage.*]

STEVE: Sylvia!

[STEVE *and* SYLVIA *find each other through the carnage and embrace, looking at their friends, groaning on the floor.*

GILES *enters downstage and speaks to Front of House.*]

GILES: Right. Thank you . . .

[*Lights go off the scene as* STEVE *and* SYLVIA *attend to wounded. Spot on* GILES.]

GILES: So? Was I right? Had it been good thinking? Yes is the answer – and sucks to the desk-wallahs at GHQ! I sensed as soon as the lights went out that my little plan was beginning to bear fruit. I made for the generator and sure enough found that the juice had been switched off. So that when I turned the lights on, imagine the terrorists' consternation at being faced by row upon row of unsmiling Mongol faces watching a British comedy show. Moreover a show performed by highly trained jungle fighters. This was indeed a Jungle Jamboree they had not anticipated. At any rate they panicked and let off bursts of rapid fire into the midst of them. Now that was very bad thinking because Johnny Gurkha doesn't stand arguing the toss, it's out with his kukri and off with their heads. The terrorist got a total bag of four: three Gurkhas and one BOR. Making a final score of six-four to us.

[*Lights behind show various casualties lying about in tableau, attended or mourned by the others.* LEN *is particularly clear, lying on his own while* SYLVIA *bandages* TERRI's *leg.* SYLVIA *and* STEVE *nurse* KEVIN *and* ERIC *moves about with buckets.* GILES *does not acknowledge this.*]

I was sorry to lose poor Bonny. He was one of the best. Not perhaps bursting with imagination but steady, loyal, dependable. After being brought up in the sewers of Birmingham, the darkness and filth of the jungle held no terrors for him. And if you'd praised him for playing his part in the defence of freedom, he might well have protested 'Lor' bless my soul, sir, that's a load of 'umbug and no error . . . .'

[CHARLES *comes down to* LEN *and kneels beside him.*]

A particularly tragic aspect of his death is that I'd recently arranged – without his knowledge – to have his wife posted out to join him. This was to have been a pleasant surprise on our return to Singapore.

[CHARLES *kisses* LEN's *face*.]

Alas, this happy reunion was not to be. And as he went he said 'Death, where is thy sting?' And as he went down deeper he said 'Grave where is thy victory?' So he passed over and all the trumpets sounded for him on the other side.

SCENE TEN

Not Wanted on Voyage.

The last trumpet from scene nine plays through the fade to darkness as CHARLES *stays with* LEN's *body.*

Lights up on SYLVIA's *room. Chinese street sounds as before.* SYLVIA's *in her kimono, bent over on the bed, rocking silently like an unhappy child.* STEVE's *watching, standing some way off, one arm in sling.*

STEVE: I mean – better now than later. Eh, Sylvia?

[*She goes on rocking.*]

I was going to write you a letter but – that would have been easier but not fair to you. You know today was pay day? Look – [*Takes out wad of banknotes.*] Here's my back pay for the extra stripes from the day Reg got killed. I've talked to one or two people who've been around a bit and they say that should be more than enough for a decent operation. Nothing risky or sordid but a real nursing-home – well, you'd know more about that than –

[*She looks up at him. A flash of pride and anger.*]

Not you especially, I don't mean that, of course, but being a woman. *Any* woman would be bound to know more than me. More than *I*.

[*She turns and stares away from him.*]

You must have half-expected from the last few times we've met that I couldn't –

SYLVIA: This is what *you* want, is it?

STEVE: Christ, no. They're just not ready for it in Fernleaze Crescent.

SYLVIA: Not even if we're married and it's all pukka?

STEVE: Dad's quite broad-minded but Mum still thinks I'm a kid. She last saw me when I was just eighteen. If I came home with a foreign wife – [*He shakes his head hopelessly.*]

SYLVIA: Half-caste, you mean.

STEVE: It's not what *I* want. Only that society's such a mess. And until we can change society how can we change ourselves? And that means changing every single person in society so that there'll be no more wars or colonies or race prejudice . . .

SYLVIA: Come and sit by me here. Come and hold my hand.

STEVE [*looks at watch*]: I can't. The old man's expecting me. We're *winding up the unit. Fixing our embarkation* – [*Puts the banknotes on the bed.*] Let me know if that's *not* enough.

[*She knocks the money off the bed on to the floor.* STEVE *leaves and makes to go. Opens door to find* TERRI *about to knock.* STEVE *pushes past him and out.*]

TERRI: Don't run off on my account, duckie. I'm only doing my District Nurse stint.

SYLVIA: Let him go. Shut the door.

[TERRI *does, comes in, walking on crutches, looks at money on floor.*]

TERRI: Why is she flouncing off?

[SYLVIA *stands, showing her pregnancy now, comes to pick up the money.*]

What's this for?

SYLVIA: Three guesses.

[TERRI *takes it in, turns back to the door, opens it, hobbles out and calls:*]

TERRI: Steven! Come back this minute –

[*But he gives up, returns, shuts door.*]

I won't have it. D'you hear me, girl?

SYLVIA: It's me that won't have it.

TERRI: It's no laughing matter. It's a baby.

SYLVIA: With all that shooting in the jungle it's a miracle I didn't miscarry anyway.

TERRI: A miracle. Exactly. Your child's been saved to be born.

SYLVIA: As a love-baby to a black-velvet girl with no husband?

TERRI: I'll make him marry you. I'll speak to Gillian.

SYLVIA [*shakes head*]: You think he doesn't know? This is the way they deal with it. Always.

[*SYLVIA looks in the glass at her face, wipes eyes dry, starts making up, taking cosmetics from the top of her tin trunk, which is all ready for despatch.*]

Not Wanted on Voyage. It's the official policy. At least he's paying for the abortion.

TERRI: How can you be so tolerant? I'd want him dead. He doesn't *deserve* to be the father of your child.

SYLVIA: He's not.

TERRI: Not what?

SYLVIA: The father's dead.

TERRI [*after a pause*]: Not Regina?

[*SYLVIA nods her head. TERRI embraces her and they stand rocking, comforting each other.*]

SYLVIA: What else could I do?

TERRI: It's going to be alright. Don't you worry, sweetheart. Trust your auntie. Your auntie knows.

[*Music of 'Sunnyside Lane' while all this goes.*]

SCENE ELEVEN

Bless 'em All.

As music fades, the jocular voice of the newsreel commentary is heard over the front of house speakers.

COMMENTARY: Happy scenes at Singapore's dockside as another troopship of time-expired men embarks for old Blighty's shores. And amongst them a very special party, homeward bound before their numbers are up. For, as tension mounts in strife-torn Malaya, the singers and dancers of SADUSEA have rung down their final curtain.

[*At the back a huge painted cloth represents the dock: godown, piles of cargo, the white ocean-going liner. Some luggage and kit awaits loading. STEVE marches on at the head of his party: ERIC with a patch over one eye, CHARLES pushing KEVIN in an invalid chair. STEVE still has arm in sling.*]

STEVE: Epp, ite, epp ite epp. Squad – halt!

[ERIC *does it all properly*, CHARLES *takes no notice. But* ERIC *can't see very well and bumps into* STEVE *as he halts.*]

COMMENTARY: The valiant survivors of a brutal terrorist ambush can go home knowing they've kept the Reds off Asia's stage – and told them in no uncertain terms not to try an encore.

STEVE: Watch it, Love.

ERIC: Sorry, Chief.

[*They go aside to look at the boat.*]

KEVIN: There she is, Charlie. The boat. We made it.

CHARLES: Some of us.

KEVIN: After a fashion.

CHARLES: There is some corner of a foreign field that is forever fucking England.

KEVIN: I'm glad to see it all the same. Glad to be going home and all, even though I'll never know what it's like to have a white bint. I mean, it was all in a good cause. We kept the old flag flying, eh? Helped save a bit of the empire from the Chinese, eh?

CHARLES: Having brought them here in the first place to work our tin-mines.

KEVIN: We may be a tiny little island, Charlie, but no-one pushes us about.

CHARLES: My dear, keeping rubber for democracy won't give you back your balls. Or Len his wife. What odds would it make to Len whether England was Communist, fascist or Anabaptist? He'd still be working in a stores somewhere, making lists, getting the best he could out of life.

KEVIN: I reckon if Len could speak to us now –

CHARLES: He can't though, can he? He never could. Born in a dump in Smethwick that's not one of the things you learn.

COMMENTARY [*as* ERIC *turns to join them*]: Aircraftsman Young-Love lost one eye but says the other will be quite enough for him to see the White Cliffs of Dover – and to recognise his fiancée Susan who'll be waiting for him in Wimbledon.

STEVE: What d'you want to tell them that for?

ERIC: What's that, Chiefy?

STEVE: Well, she isn't, is she? Waiting for you. She's engaged to old Lawrence with the flying feet.

ERIC: And they can ruddy well get *dis*engaged, my old mate, at the double! If I know my Susan, when she sees me in Movietone News, she'll show Lawrence the door, juldi juldi. We're going home as heroes, don't forget that. [*He's trying to make his lighter work but it doesn't.*] I hope this is the last I see of damned cheapjack Chinese rubbish!

[KEVIN *offers him a light as* STEVE *comes forward.*]

STEVE: Dear everyone at Fifty-Six. Five weeks at sea and I'll be with you all, by which time my arm should be well on the mend. Give Heather my love and tell her, yes, the army has made a man of me at last. Dad, I'm sorry you feel the spirit of post-war idealism hasn't lasted. Here too the moral issues are by no means clear and education seems to be the only hope –

COMMENTARY [*interrupting*]: Partners in dance onstage and newly-wed partners in real life are Terri and Sylvia Dennis.

[*As* TERRI *and* SYLVIA *are driven on in a trishaw by* LEE. TERRI *gets out. Using one stick, helps out an evidently pregnant* SYLVIA.] Proud mother-to-be Mrs Dennis was born in India but is looking forward to meeting her Welsh grannie and taking tea in Lyons' Corner House. It's a happy ending for Terri too, who says he came to the East only to give his all for the boys.

[TERRI *and* SYLVIA *pose for camera (us) and the others throw confetti.*]

Here's wishing you a safe passage not only now but through all the years to come.

[LEE *unloads their cases.*]

TERRI: Well, what are we waiting for?

STEVE: The old man. We've all got to assemble here. He wants to say a few words.

TERRI: Tell me when she doesn't. Jessica, what a chatterbox!

TANNOY ANNOUNCEMENT [*very posh English*]: All visitors ashore, please. All visitors ashore. Sub-cheese coolies ashore karao. Juldi-juldi.

STEVE: You better get on board, I'll wait for the Major. [*But as they move, he sees* GILES *coming from the side and shouts.*] Commanding Officer on parade, company atten-shun!

[CHENG *comes behind carrying* GILES's *personal kit, carries it aboard.* LEE *takes* TERRI's *and* SYLVIA's. *They form up to listen to* GILES.]

GILES [*saluting*]: Stand easy. Well, everyone, we shall certainly meet again during the five weeks at sea but as fellow-passengers, not comrades-in-arms. So I want to take this last opportunity of inviting you to drop in for tea if you find yourself in Berkshire. Nothing remarkable, of course, only a simple seventeenth-century mill-house, typical of hundreds throughout the length and breadth of England. No very brilliant company either – only my wife and the Labradors.

[*He addresses much of this to* STEVE.]

Perhaps a spot of hunting, freshwater fishing. If any of you is a rubber there's a fine Jacobean brass in the Norman church. In other words, the ordinary everyday England we've been striving to save. Worth fighting for. Worth dying for. For whether he chooses a humble cottage, a great house or only a bamboo hovel in a jungle clearing, every soldier dreams of the day when he can say – as we say now –

[*He leads them into a reprise of the Home-Sweet-Home song.*]

ALL: We're going back
           To that homely little shack
           On the sunny side of any street.
           We've been too long
           From the laughter and the song
           That we'll share with all the folks we're going to meet.

           I know a lady living there
           With shining eyes and silver hair
           And when she offers me a chair
           I'm going to feel a millionaire.

           So though we've travelled around
           Now's the time to settle down
           And when we're there we'll never more roam
           From the heart of home-sweet-home.

[LEE *and* CHENG *return from ship,* GILES *and* TERRI *give them tips.*]

[*The chorus-line of casualties forms again to follow* GILES *up the gangplank, singing a reprise of the last lines:* KEVIN *on wheels pushed by* CHARLES, ERIC *with hand on* STEVE's *shoulder,*

STEVE *with arm in sling*, SYLVIA *pregnant*, TERRI *on stick*.]

ALL: So though we've travelled around
      Now's the time to settle down
      And when we're there we'll never more stray
      From the paradise that's sunny all day,
      Which is why we're sailing over the foam
      To the heart of home-sweet-home.

[*By means of a gauze, the boat seems to recede as* LEE *and* CHENG
*remain on the dockside waving goodbye. When it's gone, they sit
on* LEE's *trishaw and light cigarettes.*
Curtain.]

Further titles in the
World Dramatists series
of paperback play collections
are described on the following pages

John Arden
Plays : One
Serjeant Musgrave's Dance, The Workhouse Donkey,
Armstrong's Last Goodnight
INTRODUCTION BY John Arden

Brendan Behan
The Complete Plays
The Quare Fellow, The Hostage, Richard's Cork Leg,
Moving Out, A Garden Party, The Big House
INTRODUCTION BY Alan Simpson

Edward Bond
INTRODUCTIONS BY Edward Bond

Plays : One
Saved, Early Morning, The Pope's Wedding

Plays : Two
Lear, The Sea, Narrow Road to the Deep North,
Black Mass, Passion

Howard Brenton
Plays : One
Christie in Love, Magnificence, The Churchill Play,
Weapons of Happiness, Epsom Downs, Sore Throats
INTRODUCTION BY Howard Brenton

Caryl Churchill
Plays : One
Owners, Traps, Vinegar Tom,
Light Shining in Buckinghamshire, Cloud Nine
INTRODUCTION BY Caryl Churchill

Noël Coward

Plays : One

Hay Fever, The Vortex, Fallen Angels, Easy Virtue

INTRODUCTION BY Mander and Mitchenson

Plays : Two

Privates Lives, Bitter-Sweet, The Marquise,
Post-Mortem

INTRODUCTION BY Sheridan Morley

Plays : Three

Design for Living, Cavalcade, Conversation Piece,
To-night at 8.30 (Hands Across the Sea, Still Life,
Fumed Oak)

INTRODUCTION BY Sheridan Morley

Plays : Four

Blithe Spirit, Present Laughter, This Happy Breed,
To-night at 8.30 (Ways and Means, The Astonished Heart,
'Red Peppers')

INTRODUCTION BY Mander and Mitchenson

Plays : Five

Relative Values, Look After Lulu!, Waiting in the Wings,
Suite in Three Keys

INTRODUCTION BY Mander and Mitchenson

Georg Büchner
The Complete Plays

Danton's Death, Leonce and Lena,
Woyzeck with The Hessian Courier, Leaz,
On Cranial Nerves and Selected Letters

INTRODUCTION BY Michael Patterson

David Edgar
Plays : One

Destiny, Mary Barnes, The Jail Diary of Albie Sachs,
Saigon Rose, O Fair Jerusalem

INTRODUCTION BY David Edgar

Michael Frayn
Plays : One

Alphabetical Order, Donkey's Years, Clouds, Make and Break,
Noises Off

INTRODUCTION BY Michael Frayn

John Galsworthy
Five Plays

Strife, Justice, The Eldest Son, The Skin Game, Loyalties

INTRODUCTION BY Benedict Nightingale

Simon Gray
Plays : One

Butley, Otherwise Engaged, The Rear Column,
Quartermaine's Terms, The Common Pursuit

INTRODUCTION BY Simon Gray

Joe Orton
The Complete Plays

Entertaining Mr Sloane, Loot, What the Butler Saw,
The Ruffian on the Stair, The Erpingham Camp,
Funeral Games, The Good and Faithful Servant

INTRODUCTION BY John Lahr

Harold Pinter

INTRODUCTIONS BY Harold Pinter

Plays : One

The Birthday Party, The Room, The Dumb Waiter,
A Slight Ache, The Hothouse, A Night Out

Plays : Two

The Caretaker, The Dwarfs, The Collection, The Lover,
Night School, Trouble in the Works, The Black and White,
Request Stop, Last to Go, Special Offer

Plays : Three

The Homecoming, Tea Party, The Basement, Landscape,
Silence, That's Your Trouble, That's All, Applicant, Interview,
Dialogue for Three, Night

Plays : Four

Old Times, No Man's Land, Betrayal, Monologue,
Family Voices

August Strindberg

TRANSLATED AND INTRODUCED BY Michael Meyer

Plays : One

The Father, Miss Julie and The Ghost Sonata

Plays : Two

A Dream Play, The Dance of Death, The Stronger

Synge

The Complete Plays

The Playboy of the Western World, The Tinker's Wedding,
In the Shadow of the Glen, Riders to the Sea,
The Well of the Saints, Deirdre of the Sorrows

INTRODUCTION BY T. R. Henn

Wilde

Three Plays

The Importance of Being Earnest, Lady Windermere's Fan,
An Ideal Husband

INTRODUCTION BY H. Montgomery Hyde